'A marvellously practical handbook which takes you from pregnancy to your child's early years at school.' *Annabel*

'No mother should ever contemplate going back to work without this book by her side. It is, quite simply, excellent!' *Universe Magazine*

'To call it a sensible buy for anyone contemplating becoming a working mum is a vast understatement.' *Bolton Evening News*

'A wealth of useful ideas and experiences to help working mothers cope day-to-day and in an emergency.' *Yorkshire Evening Press*

About the authors

Sarah Litvinoff was on the National Committee of the Working Mothers Association for seven years – two as Chair. She is a writer specialising in family and relationship issues. She has a grown-up daughter and lives in Islington.

Marianne Velmans is the mother of two children, and works as a Publishing Director at a general trade book publishing company. She lives with her husband and two children in West London.

WORKING MOTHER

A Practical Handbook
for the Nineties

by

Sarah Litvinoff and Marianne Velmans

POCKET
BOOKS

New York   London   Toronto   Sydney   Tokyo   Singapore

First published in Great Britain by Corgi Books
First published in Pocket Books,
an imprint of Simon & Schuster Ltd, in 1993

Simon & Schuster Ltd
West Garden Place
Kendal Street
London W2 2AQ

Simon & Schuster of Australia Pty Ltd
Sydney

A CIP catalogue record for this book is
available from the British Library
ISBN 0–671–71540–2

Photoset in North Wales by
Derek Doyle & Associates, Mold, Clwyd
Printed and bound in Great Britain by
Harper*Collins* Manufacturing, Glasgow

To Paul *(the working father)*,
Jack and Saskia

To Cherry *(an example to all working mothers)*
and Jemilah

Contents

Contents

Contents

Contents

Contents

Contents

Acknowledgements

The authors would like to thank the women who were interviewed or who filled in questionnaires: Anne Babb; Kristine Band; M Bartley; Susan Bate; Maeve Beattie; Angela Bishop; Elizabeth Blacklaw; Margaret Bluman; Janet Boulding; Judith Briggs; Daphne Brinklow; Lizy Buchan; Marie Burke; Ellen Carmichael; Evelyn Carter; Linda Caughley; Jenny Clarke; Hazel Coates; Maureen Collie; Alyson Curry; Glynis Day; Alison Downer; Phyl Driffield; Jean Ellwood; Sheila Evans; Sharon Foor; Margaret Gledhill; Eleo Gordon; Gladys Gregg; Lynne Hainsworth; S Halfyard; Susan Harnott; Mary Heaton; Barbara Herbert; S L Hoey; Julie Howell; Irene Johnston; Judith Jupe; Sue Key; Rosemary Kirk; Jane R Lee; Sue Lewis; Gita Liven; Heather Lockett; Susan Lumb; Mrs Mayes; Sandra McDonald; Rosemary McGhee; Jo Musham; Anne-Lucie Norton; Jane Parkin; Sheila Paul; Sandra Paxman; Sue Peskett; Joan Phillips; Maggie Piggott; C S Quinn; Susan Ridley; Anne Rigby; Sheila Robertson; Lesley Schatzberger; Betty Shepherd; L Shields; Jackie Smith; Margarette Smith; Elizabeth Squires; Pauline Taylor; May Thah-Lee; Sarah Thomson; Jill Thornton; Bernadette Tubridy; Laura Walker; Marianne Walsh; Wendy Wass; Jayne Woodman; Judith Wright; Anneliese Young; and all the women who filled in the questionnaires anonymously.

We would also like to thank the following: Bernice

Cahill of the Equal Opportunities Commission; Hester Cherneff; Janet Cohen of the Swiss Cottage Citizens Advice Bureau; Lynn Durward of the Maternity Alliance; Victoria Huxley; Pam Jones of the Wandsworth Childminding Association; Dr Justin Livingstone; Mrs Long of Knightsbridge Nannies; The National Council for One Parent Families; Sue Owen of The National Childminding Association; Joan Springall of the National Advisory Centre on Careers for Women; Fanny Rowe; Sophie Smith; Wendy Tury; Greg Wales FCA; and the members of the Chiswick Working Mothers Group.

For the revised edition, we would like to thank Irene Pilia of the Working Mothers Association, for her help and advice; and Vida Adamoli, who researched the changes.

Finally, our grateful thanks to all the working mothers we have not named but with whom we have talked over the years, and who have contributed, consciously or not, to the ideas, experiences and tips that constitute this book.

Preface:
Why We Wrote This Book

We wrote this book to help other mothers like ourselves with the most demanding period of their lives: bringing up young children while continuing to work; women who wanted to do their best in all areas of their lives. We wrote it at a time when there was almost no help for women like us.

But why have we revised the book, when since that time many other books have emerged, and organisations such as the Working Mothers Association have raised the profile of working mothers and offer excellent, practical help?

Well, we blush to say it, but it is the response of women who have read the book over the years that has spurred us to produce a new edition. We've lost count of the number of women who have told us that it has been their inspiration and support ('bible' is the word used most often). Many tell us that they keep one battered copy by the bed, while another copy does the round of friends. As it became increasingly out of date, they told us that it didn't matter − most important was the emotional support they felt was given to them by the women who contributed to the book: the first-person experiences of good times, bad times, pride, doubt, love and commitment. Nevertheless, *we* minded that the practical aspects were out of date, even though the emotional content was timeless. Se we embarked on the revision.

Things *have* changed since 1987. Now 42 per cent of mothers with children under five work, full- or part-time, as against 35 per cent then (from General Household Survey figures collected between April 1991 and March 1992). There has been a shift in attitude towards working mothers: they are considered normal, acceptable, even admirable. So much so that there is now another backlash: a new organisation, The Full-Time Mothers Association, says that what we are doing is bad for our children, and an increasing number of celebrities are standing up and saying that they think it is wrong to work while their children are young. Perhaps the most disturbing was Carol Thatcher, who said that she would never be a working mother because her experience of being the child of one was horrendous.

It hurts. It is worrying. The working mother is always vulnerable to suggestions that what she is doing might be harmful for her children. We have never suggested that all mothers should have work outside the home as well as the full-time work they do within it. We admire the women who want to stay at home, and who are lucky enough to have the choice.

The true facts of the situation are that yes, some working mothers are bad mothers – but most of us aren't: our children are happy, well balanced and well cared for. They benefit from having mothers whose work gives them increased self-esteem, interest and *money*. And yes, many full-time mothers are excellent mothers, but some feel depressed, under-valued, trapped – and their children suffer as a consequence.

This backlash is another reason why we wanted to revise this book: to give a new generation of first-time working mothers the support they need to do their best by their children, their jobs and their partners – as all the women who contributed have done.

Marianne Velmans (personal note 1987)

I have been a working mother since I had my son, Jack, two years ago. People are always asking me, 'How do you do it – a full-time job, with a small child at home and a household to run?' This question always strikes me as rather unfair, because the alternative – giving up my job and staying at home – appears to me to be by far the harder and more admirable choice, yet I know it would not elicit the same sympathetic concern. I know I am privileged: I have a husband who shares the housework and childcare equally with me, we can afford a nanny and a cleaner, and I have a job I enjoy.

Yet when I was pregnant, I found I needed special help and advice. When should I tell my employer? What were my rights? How long could I go on working? What were my childcare options, and how much would they cost? How did you set about finding them? How would my baby feel about it? Was it possible to breastfeed if you intended to return to work? I looked for a book on the subject, but could not find one. I saw books on pregnancy and childbirth; childcare; working women (with a few pages on working mothers); single parents; even theoretical, serious books about whether women should go out to work or stay at home with their children. But there was nothing that answered all my own basic, practical questions.

I was fortunate to have a number of friends who had recently become mothers and who had carried on working. It was they who gave me all the practical advice I needed. But then I started to wonder about the problems that still loomed ahead. How did other working mums cope when their children were ill? What did they do if they had several children of different ages? Did they manage to get home by the time their children came home from school, or if not, what happened? What did they do during the school holidays, or when the teachers were on strike? What if they had to travel for their job (as I had to)? What shortcuts did they use at home? How did they manage to be good, caring mothers and continue to be good at their jobs as well? And how did mothers who had taken time off work to look after their small children recover their self-confidence when they tried to return to work once their kids were older? (My own mother, who was trained as a psychologist, never really got her self-confidence back after breaking her career to have children: I have always had a slight sense of regret and guilt about this.)

The industry I am in, publishing, happens to be one that is tolerant of working mothers, (perhaps because it relies so heavily on a female workforce), so I knew a lot of women in the same position – a kind of informal support group. But I started to wonder about those women in other occupations who might not be surrounded by this kind of support, who might not be so aware of their maternity rights and what kind of help some of the more progressive employers offer their working mothers. It seemed to me that there was a need for a practical, supportive book, full of all the information needed by women who had decided, for whatever reason, to be working mothers. Something that would attempt to give the answers to all these questions and more – not from the point of view of the 'experts' (all those doctors, psychologists, sociologists, campaigners) but drawing on the experience of other working mothers: the *real* experts.

Update 1992

The first edition of this book came out when my son, Jack, was two years old, and I was full of the wonders and pressures of my new life as a working mum. Jack is now eight, and I have meanwhile also acquired a daughter, Saskia, aged two and a half. The five-and-a-half-year gap is a repeat of a pattern established in both my husband's and my own families. It worked out very well: Jack was at school by the time the new baby came, so we avoided jealousy and rivalry: he genuinely loved his sister from the very first and there has never been any friction between them at all.

As with my first pregnancy, I worked right up to the Friday before the Monday Saskia was born, and had just under four months off work. I had planned to keep on my nanny during my maternity leave, but researching and writing this book has not meant I have been immune to making mistakes myself in choosing nannies. Only days after returning home from hospital, I realised that I had the wrong person for looking after a young baby. But after a month or so, I found the best nanny we have ever had, a loving, lovable and sensible young woman from Ireland who, touch wood, is still with us today. Sometimes I think that having a second child was just an excuse to be able to justify employing a full-time nanny for another five years!

The biggest difference now is that my job has changed – from running a very small office rather independently, to a more senior, creative and high-pressure job in a large company. I would certainly not have had the time to write this book if I had had this job then! My closest colleague now is also a working mother, and she went off to have *her* second child two weeks after I returned from maternity leave – and we have always denied that we planned it that way . . .

Other things have changed. Five years ago, when I first joined my new company, I was almost the only working mother. Now I am one of a crowd – and many of us have embarked on the second round. It seems to have become the norm, rather than the exception, to return to work quickly after having a baby – something which is reflected in recent statistics about the pattern in the country as a whole. But tellingly, perhaps, when a group of working mothers in my firm met recently to discuss whether we should ask our company to consider offering childcare vouchers to all working parents, we realised that we could not name a single male employee who would be entitled to such a payment – they all have wives who stay at home to look after their children. Ironically, the idea came from my own husband, who is entitled to a childcare allowance from his firm.

Working with other women with children is a great support. After having been up all night with a sick child, it is great to be able to come in to the office and just have a good laugh about the unspeakable messes one is subject to clearing up when one has children, with someone who knows what one is talking about. Not to mention the fact that my colleague and I can sometimes call on each other to help out in a crisis – at home as well as at work.

I don't want to make it sound easy. There are times when I am overwhelmed by worries about failing as a mother, and failing at my job. There is never enough time in a day, in a week, in a weekend, for all the tasks I set myself. Having a better-paid job takes away some of the worry – but I now have to be away from home for work between three and six nights, four times a year. Yet I have never seriously considered the alternative options of not going out to work at all, or of simply moving into a less demanding, less full-time job. Not only because we rely on the two incomes; not only because I feel who I am is tied up with what I do; not only because my children seem to be happy and well-adjusted; but perhaps because, on a good day, I have the sneaking suspicion that I do have the best of both worlds, that I am having my cake and eating it too.

Sarah Litvinoff (personal note 1987)

I am the daughter of a working mother, and it never crossed my mind not to be one myself. My mother was self-employed and ran a thriving business. She was always on the go, but she always had time for us: sensitive, sympathetic, involved in what we were doing – usually tired but almost never irritable, and always ready for fun and cuddles; among my friends, she was definitely the most popular mother. I followed family tradition and had my baby early: I was only nineteen when Jemilah was born, and pretty soon I was a 'single parent' – although I have never thought of myself as bringing her up alone. My mother is always there, of course, and every member of my family has been involved. We are not a little two-person unit – Jemilah, at fourteen, is simply the youngest (almost) of the extended clan.

When Marianne asked me to collaborate on this book with her, it immediately struck me that we were a good combination because our experiences have been so different. I was desperately hard-up in Jemilah's early years of life, and she has been suspicious of brown window envelopes ever since. I muddled through – it never even occurred to me to *look* for a book such as this, though I needed it more than anyone. I didn't even claim child benefit until Jemilah was four, when my horrified father found out that I hadn't done so, and sent off for the necessary forms (it is *not* backdated to birth). However, I did devour childcare and child development books and was always left with a bleak gut feeling that I was doing something bad by Jemilah because I was working: the nagging guilt every working mother knows. Guilt can make commonsense desert you: I would look at Jemilah and see that she was happy, well-adjusted, doing well all round, yet still feel fearful. That was one of the main reasons I wanted to write this book.

A nanny was out of the question for me. Jemilah went to a childminder – a forty-minute journey on public transport (and another forty minutes to get to work), the same in the evening. After that she went to a local authority day nursery (an even longer journey), and later I tore my hair over what to do with her at the end of a school day and in the holidays, all only partially resolved when I went freelance. But the fact that my family are close by and willing to help always made things easier. Marianne had Jack at a sensible age, in her thirties when her career and marriage were well-established. They are a two-income family and can afford a nanny. But her family live in America and her husband's family live outside London. They have problems that simply never occurred to me, such as the regular one of babysitters – and sophisticated worries such as how to work out the tax for their nanny (solved in this book).

Update 1992

The new version of this book coincides with my daughter being fully grown-up, a working woman herself. Her first job is in a television company – another industry hit by the recession, and where dozens of people compete for each vacancy. She got it in the face of stiff competition from older and more qualified people because she just stood out. At nineteen she shows all the positive qualities of a child brought up by a mother who worked. She's independent, responsible, with masses of initiative. We protect our children, but foster any small spark of independence at the right time, because the more they can take responsibility for themselves, the more we can cut from our own list of duties.

Looking back, I can say that she gained something from all her childcare experiences – childminder, nursery, out-of-school care. Perhaps it was lucky that she was a bright, robust child who loved company and a variety of experiences. Or perhaps the situation created these qualities. Who can say?

I'm not saying that it was all wonderful and I never worried. There have been bad times and difficulties. There were any number of times while she was growing up when she was unhappy. I can say, hand on heart, that none of these had to do with me working, and that we coped with them together. There were times when my work clashed with the need to look after her because she was ill. That was no fun, but it passes. There was a period during adolescence when she couldn't stand me. All my sins were remembered – and believe me, every mother, working or not, commits them – that's the nature of the job. It was very upsetting. I knew that it was a normal part of adolescence – indeed an essential, healthy part – but it still hurt. When this highly intelligent girl told me that she had decided that further education wasn't for her and she needed hands-on work experience, I wondered whether I had gone too far in making her independent-minded. But I didn't want to undo it all by imposing my will. I trusted her good sense and crossed my fingers. It was the right decision, and my trust has added to her feelings of self-worth.

Jemilah is certainly not a perfect human being, free from problems and anxieties or faults. But then, neither were Dr Spock's children, and nor are her friends whose mothers didn't work. I have also failed, as so many mothers do, in getting her to help in the house. It was always quicker to do it myself than spend time bringing her up to an acceptable level of competence. She can cook a limited repertoire fairly well. But washing up? Cleaning? Tidying? I'm lucky if it happens once in a blue moon. Poor thing, when she sets up on her own or with someone else, she has it all to learn.

Jemilah says she perceives me as a successful woman, doing well a job that gives her satisfaction. It's what she automatically expects from herself. She believes, as an unquestionable fact, that women can achieve whatever they want – she finds any other idea quaint, like old theories of the earth being flat. I'm proud of that. I'm proud of her altogether. What more can a mother say?

Introduction

The Short Introduction for Very Busy Readers

We hope you will read the entire introduction. But as one working mother said, 'When does a working mum ever have time to read a book from cover to cover?' If you are too busy and want to dive straight in, this is what the book sets out to do:

* Give you practical information about all aspects of combining motherhood with other work.

* Tell you what the solution to your particular problem is, if there is one (How do I find a childminder?)

* Provide suggestions where there is no single obvious solution (What do I do with my child during school holidays?)

* Give you information from the real experts: other working mothers, who provide advice, tips and personal experiences.

The book is divided into two parts. The first is chronological, taking you from pre-parenthood, through pregnancy, maternity leave, finding pre-school childcare, working while your child is under five, and coping with school-age children and teenagers.

The second section deals with general topics: your house and your partner, lone parenthood, crises, why you shouldn't feel guilty, how to find work and your career.

It is a reference book, designed to help you at whatever stage you find yourself now – you don't have to read it straight through.

To help you look up the topic that particularly interests or concerns you at this moment, there is a detailed contents list on p. vii and there is also a full index at the back of the book.

Setting the Record Straight

All mothers work extremely hard. What distinguishes the so-called working mother is that she combines being a mother and running a home with some other job. Forty-two per cent of mothers now return to work or enter employment by the time their first child is two, and this percentage rises steadily to 78 per cent of women whose youngest is eleven or older.

Many mothers work because they have to: because they head lone-parent families, because their husbands or partners are unemployed, or because they prefer to be financially independent. Many other mothers work because they want to: so that they can continue in the profession for which they have been trained, or because they find their job interesting or rewarding and they would be bored or frustrated at home.

Psychological research has shown that the children of working mothers do not suffer any disadvantage, in fact they positively thrive – as long as quality substitute care is available. Yet many working mothers feel guilty and apologetic, and fear that they are depriving or harming their children by going out to work. The popular childcare advice books don't do much to allay their fears; they are mainly addressed to mothers who stay at home while their children are small. Public opinion is still prejudiced against working mothers, even five years after first writing this book, although the climate is slowly changing. This prejudice is reinforced by the press, which uses emotive phrases such as 'latch-key kids' to give working mothers a bad name. This is despite the fact that there is no evidence to show that the well-cared-for children of working mothers become juvenile delinquents, or suffer in any other way.

When we first wrote the book we anticipated certain critical reactions to it – flak from at least three areas. Although the response we received was overwhelmingly positive, it did come from working mothers like ourselves. It is still relevant to put the record straight as far as our critics might be concerned.

Working mothers versus housewife mothers

First of all we don't want anyone to think that by calling our book *Working Mother* we intend any slight to mothers who do stay at home with their children when they are small. We do not mean to belittle those women; on the contrary, we believe they have chosen the most difficult and demanding career: all the hard work without the perks of money or someone to say 'Thank you', or 'Well done!' at the end of the day. A true labour of love. Neither do we believe that all women *should* combine motherhood with a job if they don't want to or don't need to.

Working mothers versus working fathers

Then there are those who will say we are sexist because we address this book to mothers only, instead of working parents. After all, men and women are meant to share the responsibility for children and home equally now. Nevertheless we recognise the fact that in the overwhelming majority of families in Britain today – even where both partners have full-time jobs – it is the woman who still carries the major burden of responsibility for the children and the home. There are signs of change, and we hope that in future there will only be 'working parents'. In the meantime, we apologise to those working fathers who are interested enough to read this book, and ask them to substitute 'working parent' for 'working mother': except for the sections dealing with pregnancy, maternity leave, breastfeeding, and so on – which will probably always be exclusively female concerns!

The need for change

Finally people may accuse us of being complacent. We are telling working mothers how to make the best of a bad job: to work within the limitations of the system that conspires against the working woman with children. We do not dwell at length on the injustice or the difficulties of the situation, or use much space to urge you to fight against it. However we do feel angry about the difficulties working mothers face, especially the lower paid; particularly at the fact that there is little provision for decent, accessible, reasonably priced pre-school childcare, particularly that some mothers have to let little children come home alone from school to an empty house because there is simply no alternative. We find it incomprehensible that we lag far behind other European countries in every aspect of protective legislation for mothers and children. We welcome the fact that this last fact should change, however, as EC rulings bring Britain into line with the other European countries.

We became even angrier while writing this book because we wanted to be able to offer real working solutions to every aspect of the problem of combining a job with motherhood, and these solutions often don't exist. Even five years down the line there has been little practical improvement in the scope and availability of childcare. We want things to change, and put ourselves fully behind campaigns to reform this unsatisfactory situation.

But that is for the future, and we are concerned with what is happening *now*.

We are writing this book for women like ourselves: often tired, sometimes over-stretched, *loving* mothers who adore our children and also believe our work to be important. It is for women who need solutions now (however cobbled together) so that they can do the very best by their children; indeed who want to ensure that nothing they care about suffers: children, partner or work.

These are some of the difficulties that face working mothers: many employers are wary of us because they think we are unreliable; many of us are forced to stay in low-paid and part-time, dead-end jobs, because the better jobs are not flexible enough to accommodate our responsibilities to our children; our partners may help, but most of the childcare problems and the day-to-day running of the home fall to us even when we have a full-time job; it is very hard to find good childcare, and when we do it is expensive (most women pay between a quarter and a half of their take-home pay, whatever that might be, on care for under-fives); what we pay for childcare is not tax deductible; there is precious little provision for looking after children out of school; maternity legislation is ungenerous and hard to understand; there are no statutory rights allowing mothers time to look after sick children. On top of this we all suffer from guilt – is what we are doing bad for our children? Can we do our jobs adequately? Will we be able to maintain good relationships with our partners? What about our homes and everything that has to be done there?

There are no easy solutions to these problems.

But having finished moaning, we want to make one thing quite clear: neither of us feels defeated or depressed about being a working mother. We have moments of guilt (when can you *really* be sure that you have done the right thing by your children?); we have times of rebellion and utter exhaustion, or panic when things seem to be going wrong. But on the whole we are happy and fulfilled: it is a choice we have made and with which we are content.

And we are not unique. Many thousands of working mothers bring up their children excellently, while also fulfilling their work commitments very well. They do it because women are resourceful, hard-working, inventive. Women under pressure cope. They ask other mothers what *they* do, they enlist support where and when they can. They cut corners. If necessary they will get up at 5.30 in the morning and go to bed after midnight, so that no one else suffers for their decision to work and have children. They show that it is possible to be a successful working mother without being a superwoman: like us; like you.

The Women Who Helped on the Book

The real experts on working mothers are other working mothers. When you want to know what to do you don't necessarily ask the health visitor, Citizens Advice Bureau, or even consult a book. You ask the woman down the road or the other mothers you know at work: what do you do? How do you cope? What am I going to do if . . . ?

For this book we have gathered whatever existing help and information there is from public sources. But for the real help – which is, as often as not, ideas, advice, hints – we have drawn on our own experiences as working mothers and above all the suggestions and ideas of others in the same situation.

The questionnaire

One way we did this was to send out a questionnaire. We

hoped in this way to get over our main drawback as authors: we are both London-based, and the London experience can be very different from the rest of the country.

The questionnaire was an amateur effort, and with hindsight could have been much improved, but it served its purpose. We asked general questions about the woman, her family and her job, and specific questions about pregnancy, maternity leave, pre-school childcare, school-age children, and coping with the house. In the belief that the questions to some extent determine the mood of the response, we didn't only ask about problems. We wanted to know what she felt were the positive aspects of working, and if her children had benefited in any way from the fact that she was working. (In the majority of cases there was an emphatic 'yes', and a heart-warming variety of positive answers. The almost universal message was 'It's good for me, and good for my kids'.)

The women who replied

We wrote to local newspapers around Britain asking any working mothers who felt like helping to send off for our questionnaire. We reasoned that anyone who bothered to write to ask for a questionnaire was likely to be motivated to fill one in – and you had to be motivated, because it was long. About three-quarters of the women who received a questionnaire did indeed fill it in carefully and at length.

The replies came from much of Britain: Bangor; Bedfordshire; Belfast; Buckinghamshire; Cleveland; Cornwall; County Down; Devon; Dundee; Elgin; Glasgow; Huddersfield; Hull; Humberside; Lancashire; Lincolnshire; Liverpool; Londonderry; Manchester; Merseyside; Newtonabbey; Paisley; Sheffield; Stockport; West Midlands; West Yorkshire; York.

We heard from women in a wide variety of jobs, from doctors to sales assistants, musicians to school dinner ladies. We were not surprised that about 30 per cent worked as teachers or in other jobs in the education sector that follow school terms, and that another 30 per cent worked in the health sector.

But the response surprised us in other ways. One was the size of it – we had expected just a useful handful of replies. We were also surprised at how *positive* the response was. We had expected that many of the women who wrote would want to share their troubles and complaints, but the overwhelming majority were reporting with pride on the success of their arrangements. By no means all of them were in highly paid professional jobs. Many of the women were in fairly lowly or part-time work, yet almost all were proud to be working, said it was important to them, and felt that they were able to perform the working mother's juggling act with positive benefits to themselves, their children and their partners. In answer to the question 'Would you work if you didn't have to?' only two women said 'no'.

We asked for any extra comments that were not covered by the questions, or asked them to continue their replies on the other side of the paper if there wasn't enough space. We were touched by how much extra many of the women wrote. They were generously anxious to share their experiences and advice with other women, and clearly pleased to have the chance to talk about the way they managed their own lives. As one of them wrote: 'It is pleasant to be able to respond to someone with an interest in working mothers and their experiences, rather than having to apologise for being a working mother.' They also confirmed the need for a book such as this. As one woman pointed out, 'I feel very strongly that so much advice is available for every other stage of life except this one, which can last twenty years for some working mums. We all learn to cope as we go along but it would ease the problems to read other mums' experiences and advice before we made the same mistakes.'

Some of the women who answered the questionnaire were tired, some were over-worked, they were occasionally harassed, or remembered times when everything had seemed too much – but on the whole they were in good spirits: women whose busy lives gave them confidence and self-respect.

Obviously this response can have no statistical usefulness, but it convinced us that working mothers can and do cope well, and the picture is not gloomy because the women themselves won't let it be.

The interviews

We also interviewed a smaller number of mothers face-to-face. Because we live in London, the majority of these women lived in and around London and came from our own circle of aquaintances or from contacts made, for example, through the Chiswick Working Mothers group. They were a less representative sample of the working mothers in Britain, the majority being in professional or executive jobs. We asked similar questions to those on the questionnaire, but as we used a tape-recorder for a detailed transcript of the interview, which lasted several hours, we were able to get more expansive thoughts on topics of particular interest.

Updating the questionnaires and interviews

Looking at what these women said, five years later, we recognised that it is still as relevant today as it was then. The daily experiences of working mothers, and their emotional responses don't change. We have left their quotes as they were, with the ages of their children at the time. It was only necessary, occasionally, to take out references to precise sums of money – as now these can look ridiculously cheap!

Use of names

On the questionnaire we asked the women to say whether they minded their names being used or not. Some said we could use their names; some didn't say either way (perhaps they wouldn't have minded, but we decided not to take the risk); the rest either returned the questionnaire anonymously (so we couldn't even write and thank them!) or said they didn't want their names used.

Most of the spoken interviews were given under the impression that the women would not be named, so we have not identified them: their answers to certain questions might have been less frank if they had chosen to have their names used.

That is why, where we have used names, the same women seem to crop up quite often. We have not standardised the way in which we have presented the quotes. Sometimes it seems right to have a name attached; sometimes it is the area the woman lives in that seems most relevant, at other times it is the ages of her children, or her marital status, or the nature of her job. On some occasions all this information seems pertinent to the issue on which we quote her, and sometimes none of it does, so a quote goes unattributed. Sometimes one of us is the anonymous woman quoted: that is when what we have to say is more relevant as an 'experience' than as an author's statement.

Facts, figures, names, addresses and telephone numbers

Information about benefits, rights and taxation has changed substantially since the first edition of the book, and we have brought it up to date. But because of the time-lag between a book being written and revised and its publication, the new information will date as well. All information is correct as at the end of 1992. You would be wise to check any of the information if it is important and relevant to your situation. We have checked all names, addresses and telephone numbers, but people do move, and errors occasionally creep in. We apologise in advance if anything proves to be wrong, and would welcome any letters telling us so, or commenting on any other aspect of the book.

Part One

CHAPTER 1
Work and Pre-Motherhood

Most women who read this book will be mothers already, or pregnant – but we also wanted to say a little to the working woman who wants to have a child at some time and has to make a decision about when to do so.

As contraception is now so efficient, for the first time ever women can plan their children: how many to have, when to have them, what kind of gap to leave between each child. This is marvellously liberating in one way, but it causes its own problems. Women are now faced with what looks like the chance to choose the mythical 'best' time to have their babies.

So: does best mean when you are young, healthy and vigorous – or mature and settled in your relationship with your partner? Should you have one now, when you are hard-up but flexible and open to change, or when you have more money and a large house – when a baby could be disruptive to your settled, affluent, sociable life-style? Should you have them close together and get all the nappies and sleepless nights out of the way, or spaced out so that you can completely recover each time from the hurly burly of infancy? Would it be harmful to have an only child? Is this man *really* the right man: do you want to be bound together by the strongest of all ties?

When you add to this bewildering set of questions the

extra one of the effect motherhood is going to have on your career, it is no wonder that the issue completely paralyses some women. Nowadays you can only feel the decision is truly out of your hands when biologically your time is running out and it is now or never, or if you are infertile.

The short answer to most of the questions about the best time to have your baby – and all the others – is: it depends. We can point to women who brilliantly exemplify any of the solutions: big family, small family, young motherhood, late start, lone parent, only child, and so on. You, your circumstances, your partner, your children – and luck – all contribute in a way that no outsider can judge or foresee. Which is no great help if what you want is practical advice. But what we can offer are some career considerations that you may want to take into account when coming to your decision.

Choosing a Career You Can Pursue as a Mother

Your choice of job

In an ideal world the fact that a woman has children should be no impediment to her career if she wants to pursue one. The Equal Opportunities Commission and others are doing their best to make this so. In practice your progress in some careers is impeded or halted by the fact of having children, either because even a short career break makes you hopelessly out of date, or because restrictions on your time and mobility caused by day-to-day care of children and the need to preserve the continuity of their daily lives means that your male colleagues forge ahead and grab the promotions. Again, there are the outstanding exceptions: a determined woman who earns enough money to buy flexible extended, good-quality care for her children will always make it – particularly if doing so is very high on her list of priorities. It probably goes against the spirit of the Equal Opportunity laws to say this: but some professions are more suited to the working mother in that they offer a degree of flexibility on a daily and a long-term basis, and because the personal qualities a mother brings to her work are particularly valued and sought after.

Girl school leavers and their advisers are often criticised for not making sensible career decisions (choosing degree courses that do not lead to the male-oriented better-paid jobs, for instance): they do not think through the long-term implications of what they choose to do, often assuming that they will give up on marriage.

But high-flying career girls can be equally short-sighted, plunging into careers that they suddenly find are short-circuited when they have children. A girl who is fairly sure that she wants to have children some day, yet wants to keep pace with (or overtake) her male colleagues, needs to give thought to the effect children will have on her career. This does not mean avoiding male-oriented jobs. Take an example from the excellent *Equal Opportunities: a Careers Guide* by Ruth Miller and Anna Alston (Penguin): operational research, a male-dominated field. On the position of women Ruth Miller says, 'Women who try to get in do very well', on the subject of a career break to have children she observes, 'Should be no problem for those who keep in touch; updating courses available to all operational research workers can be adapted as refresher courses.' Contrast this with a career-break in marketing: 'It is not likely that in this competitive field it will be easy for any but the best and most determined women to return to what is essentially still a young – and a men's – career.'

It makes sense for any woman starting out – and any schoolgirl making exam choices – to think about these things. *Equal Opportunities* should be required reading at an early stage. You can decide to be the exception to the general rules, but it is as well to be forewarned of the possible pitfalls.

In more general terms, these are the points that we believe make a job good or bad in terms of the working mother:

Good jobs

These are a combination of the following things:

Career break no disadvantage

If you want to take more than the statutory maternity leave break when you have children then you need a career that won't suffer too much from a gap:

* Jobs where you don't constantly need to update your skills and knowledge in order to remain competitive.

* Jobs in which you will learn and perfect a skill, or gain expertise and experience which you can then exploit on a freelance basis from home when you have children if you want to.

* Jobs where the employers actively welcome returners – for instance with schemes that keep you in touch with the work on an occasional basis so that you can return years later.

* Fields where there is always temporary work available.

Flexibility

Even if you don't take a long break after childbirth, the fact of having children in your life means that you need flexibility:

* Jobs that allow you most flexibility with time.

* Jobs that allow you to organise your own working hours: so that if necessary you can catch up on work in your own time.

* Jobs that take you out of the workplace so that you are not so rigidly held to set hours.

* Jobs that lend themselves to job-sharing.

* Jobs that can be carried out part-time without loss of prestige or promotion prospects.

* Jobs with school hours and terms.

Good employers

If you find yourself in the position to shop around for jobs, and choose who *you* want to work for, you should bear some of these points in mind when checking out employers:

* Middle-to-large employers if you want to take maternity leave and return quickly. In an organisation below a certain size you have no right to your job back until the law changes in 1994.

* Employers with generous maternity agreements, over and above the statutory minimum. Discreet enquiries in the right place (e.g. the union) will tell you about the employer's maternity policies before you accept the job.

* Employers offering flexitime.

* Employers who use job-sharers.

* Employers who are sympathetic to parents, offering compassionate leave for children's sickness, etc.

* Employers who consider maturity and experience valuable commodities.

* Employers who are corporate members of the Working Mothers Association or Opportunity 2000 – thereby showing a commitment in principle to family-friendly policies.

Location

This may change as you switch companies in an upward climb, but it helps if by the time you have your children your place of employment is close to home. (For a more detailed discussion of all these considerations see *Finding Work* p.448)

Bad jobs

* Jobs where 18-hour days are normal, which require evenings out, working at weekends, ostentatious overtime to prove that you are committed and worthy of promotion.

* Jobs that require long business trips, or where you need to relocate regularly.

* Jobs that require you to live on your nerves.

* Jobs in highly competitive fields, always on the look out for new, young talent.

* Jobs in which skills date.

* Jobs that allow no flexibility in hours.

* Jobs in which you are only as valuable as your contacts – if they will change while you're temporarily away on maternity leave or child-gapping.

Whatever career you have started in, by the time your thoughts turn to motherhood you may decide that a tactical switch is necessary. A sideways move, adapting your skills and experiences to another field, can be a good idea if you recognise that having babies will be an impediment to your future prospects. This should be planned carefully: until 1994 your rights to return to your existing job are dependent on length of service (see *Your Rights* p.517), so you could be in trouble if you switch jobs while pregnant, or become pregnant shortly afterwards. (If you are planning a change see *Finding Work* p.461.)

The Best Time to Have Children for Your Career

These are some general points to bear in mind when you are deciding when to have your children:

* You should make sure you are fully aware of your re-entry prospects in your chosen career, particularly if you plan to take a break.

* Plan to take a break when you have proved yourself (been promoted, for instance). This can happen early in a career, as well as later. It helps when you try to return.

* Use the opportunity to assess your career: you may want to use a break to make a career change if you are finding that it doesn't suit you. Can you study for new qualifications while you are at home? (See *Finding Work* p.465.)

Having children early

The main career advantage of having your children in your early to mid-twenties is that by your thirties you will find yourself with greater freedom and more time to devote to your career. Because you got your children 'out of the way' first, you have plenty of time to build up a career or business of your own, with a major part of your working life stretching out in front of you uninterrupted. You are also relatively young when it comes to retraining for a second career – particularly useful if your first choice of job was dead-end or unstimulating.

The disadvantage is that you may not have had enough time to establish yourself in your career before you give up work. If you take a long career break you may find yourself coming in at a junior level with less chance of promotion, overtaken by others much younger than yourself.

Related considerations:

* You have the youth and energy to cope with the demands of pregnancy and infants if you want to continue working with as short a break as possible.

* You are not too set in your ways to find the arrival of children disruptive.

Having children later

An increasing number of dedicated career women have their children when they are already established on a career ladder, between their late twenties and early forties.

The main advantage of this depends on the degree to which you have established yourself. If you have made yourself indispensable at work you may find that you are so highly valued that you can more or less dictate the terms on which you are prepared to go on working. Then you have the greatest chance of keeping your job status and high pay, even if you opt to work shorter hours.

Here is one woman's experience. She is a highly paid market-researcher, and her employers bent over backwards to make sure she would come back to work after maternity leave:

Because I was a fairly senior person when it happened they paid me my full salary for the five months I was away, and I was able to keep my company car as well. My boss wouldn't hear of it being any other way, and insisted that I wasn't to lose my holiday entitlement for that year either. And I was made a director in my absence, as well. The only other person who has gone on maternity leave is our receptionist, but I'm sure they weren't so generous with her. I do think it is because of the level I was at in the company.

Alternatively you may be able to keep your career going from home, if you have skills that are in demand.

The main disadvantage is that having a break from work to raise a baby, or even switching to a less than full-time commitment at a crucial stage in your career, can spoil your chances of ever getting beyond a certain level in your chosen profession. By the time you are ready to start functioning on all cylinders again, you may appear to have missed the boat: bluntly, to be too old.

Related considerations:

* You may be better off financially, so that you can choose the childcare you want without counting the cost.

* You are more likely to have the security of owning your own house, and perhaps have a partner who is equally successful, which will make being a working mother easier in money terms.

* A good job carries pressures that may make working through pregnancy harder.

* You may have less energy to cope with the exhausting months of looking after a young infant.

The X ingredient in all this is you: from your career choice to when to have your baby. Ideal or not, you'll make it work whatever you decide, if you really want to. Unfortunately no job on close examination turns out to be ideal: even teaching, which keeps school terms and hours and therefore removes one major headache, has a big drawback: its hours are completely inflexible, and if you can't come in to work you can't catch up on another day – someone has to be found to take over.

It may be repetitious to insist that there is no 'right' time to have your children. But it is worth stressing that the best time is the time that suits you, when you are ready to cope with the responsibilities, stresses and joys that they bring.

CHAPTER 2
Pregnancy and Work

Working Through Your Pregnancy

If you enjoy your work and are reasonably healthy there is no reason to stop working when you are pregnant. Make sure that you read Chapter 18, *Your Rights*, for a detailed explanation of your maternity rights at work.

Reasons to continue working

Most women who plan to go back to work after they have children are concerned to cause as little disruption as possible to their employers, colleagues and themselves, so they usually want to continue working as long as they legally have to, if not longer. But there may be other positive reasons for continuing to work while pregnant. Even the most conservative, patronising doctors admit that if you have a fairly sedentary job, you will probably be just as well off at work as at home – or in some cases even better.

* You will be less bored.

* You will probably be happier continuing the daily

social interaction with your fellow workers. A pregnancy can seem endless, and with little to do at home you could find yourself moping around willing the weeks to speed by.

* You will be better off financially – not only will you be earning your own money, and perhaps saving some for the drain the baby is going to be on your resources, but also you may have less time to drift around the shops being tempted into spending too much money on your baby's layette and equipment!

* You may be less tired if you have a desk job, especially if you are one of those women who feel their time at home should be spent papering the baby's room or similar.

* You may be less tempted to lie around overeating for two.

* Keeping busy at work may allow you to forget about some of the more unpleasant aspects of pregnancy, for instance nausea or heartburn.

Possible reasons to stop working

There are very few occupations that cannot be continued while pregnant: even if your job falls into one of the categories below, do explore with your employer or union representative the possibility of temporarily transferring to another job which does not expose you to hazards during your pregnancy, or which is less demanding. Under the government maternity provisions, you can complain of unfair dismissal if you are dismissed because of your condition without being offered a suitable alternative vacancy. For instance British Airways won't let air hostesses fly after the third month of pregnancy, but offer ground jobs instead.

If there is no suitable alternative vacancy and you have

to leave work early in your pregnancy for this reason, you still retain your right to maternity pay and your job back after maternity leave if you want it. But if you do, you will have to make this clear to your employer at the time of leaving by putting it in writing. If it looks as if you have resigned voluntarily, you will have no legal rights. See p.517 for a fuller discussion of unfair and fair dismissal during pregnancy.

Work-related health hazards

You may be advised to stop working by your doctor or employer, or may want to seek an alternative occupation within your organisation for some of the following reasons:

* Your job is unusually strenuous or dangerous, involving heavy manual work or lifting heavy weights, exposure to excessive levels of noise, heat or stress, or is in any other way dangerous. For example if you are a nurse in a ward where you have to lift heavy patients, a show jumper, a stuntwoman, a trapeze artist, or if you work in certain factories. This kind of work can be most dangerous to your pregnancy in the first three months, before it is firmly established, and in the last stage.

* You come into contact with potentially toxic chemicals or materials at work, including lead, mercury, anaesthetic gases, vinyl chloride, certain solvents etc. For example, dentists or dental assistants, nurses or doctors, people working in the pharmaceutical industry, workers in occupations that involve soldering or glueing and so on.
   N.B. The exposure of women to lead is regulated by law and pregnant women are prohibited from working with lead.

27

* You come into contact with potentially high levels of radiation, for example health workers working with X-rays, workers in the nuclear power industry, airport baggage scanner attendants.

  N.B. The exposure of pregnant women to ionizing radiation is regulated by law. Maximum exposure during pregnancy is laid down as 0.01 Sv (1 rem). If you work with this kind of radiation, make sure your radiation level is regularly monitored.

* You come into contact with potentially harmful infections, for example workers in hospitals or laboratories.

* Your job demands excessively long shifts, long periods standing up without a chance to sit down, or constant travel (for example air hostess or pilot, shop assistant, news reporter, waitress).

* You have a previous history of miscarriage, bleeding or cramping, and your doctor advises complete bed rest.

* Many women express concern about working with photocopying machines or VDUs (visual display units on computers and word processors) during the early stages of pregnancy. The evidence so far has been inconclusive: no danger has been proved to exist to the foetus from the very low levels of radiation emitted from these sources. However the fact that nothing has been proved as yet is not necessarily reassuring. To be extra safe, we suggest that if you are pregnant (or think you may be), you do not expose yourself to the light from the copying machine (by keeping the lid firmly closed and standing well back). Ask your employer to check that the flyback transformer (the high voltage source) of any VDU or TV set is well shielded, or ask to be switched to a machine with a liquid crystal display (as used, for

example, in digital watches) which carries no risk of radiation. Or you can try requesting to be moved to work which does not involve sitting in front of a VDU. In America, some pregnant women have been demanding that their employers supply lead-lined aprons to shield the foetus when working in front of VDUs.

This is only a very rough guide to the possible hazards at work during pregnancy, and it is not comprehensive. If you are concerned that what you do might be dangerous during your pregnancy you should consult your doctor and employer or union safety representative.

It should also be pointed out that a number of the chemicals and other hazards outlined above are suspected not only of being dangerous during your pregnancy (for example in causing miscarriage or damage to the foetus) but may be equally hazardous to men's reproductive health. For example, they may be the cause of infertility in both men and women. So if you are planning a pregnancy, it is as well to make sure that neither you nor your partner is exposed to anything hazardous.

When to tell your employer and fellow workers you are pregnant

If you can resist blurting out the news at work the minute you have had the result of your test from the doctor, there is a lot to be said for deferring saying anything about being pregnant for a while.

Obviously you will have to explain you are pregnant if you are feeling very sick and it is affecting your time-keeping or your work, or if you have to change what you do because your normal duties are too dangerous. And you will wish to give your employer plenty of time to organise your replacement while you are on maternity leave.

But your pregnancy will come to seem interminable and exceedingly tedious to your fellow-workers if they have had to listen to a blow-by-blow account of it from the first day you missed your period. In fact, several of the women we talked to were reluctant to reveal that they were pregnant until the first three months were over, because they did not want anyone to know if they miscarried:

> I didn't tell anyone until I was five months gone. I didn't want anyone to feel sorry for me if I lost the baby.

Other women just felt it would be disruptive of their work, and the way they were treated at work. As one woman wrote,

> Because of the changes being made to my job, I didn't, in fact, tell my bosses until I was five months pregnant (I wasn't very big), and although everyone was shocked when I did break the news, it had at least meant peace from people asking me whether I wanted a boy or a girl, what I was going to call it, ad nauseam (I know people mean well, but it does get boring).

Jennie Flamank, a singer and entertainer, had other reasons for hiding her pregnancy:

> My manager (a woman) said it would be better for it not to be known in the business that I was pregnant (because she felt people might not make advance bookings for the time ahead when I would be the mother of a young baby). She thought people would worry that I would become unreliable as a working mother. I hid my pregnancy very well for six months. I dropped out of the mainstream of work after that and only did a bit of private recording (not cabaret functions). With hindsight, my manager was right, as some agents have said they wouldn't have booked me if they had known I was going to work as well a being a mother. However now they can see that it has caused no problems.

When to stop work

You will not qualify for maternity pay unless you work up to three months before your baby is due, and if you want the right to return to your job after you have had the baby, you must work up to the eleventh week before your due date (unless you have special reasons for quitting earlier). To help you remember to take all the proper steps at the right time in your pregnancy and qualify for all your maternity rights, turn to the Pregnancy and Maternity Leave Calendar on p.536.

Many employers expect you to stop working eleven weeks before the baby is due simply because that is when maternity pay and leave start to become available. You may come across the kind of attitude that this social worker encountered:

> I found the personnel officer who deals with maternity leave unhelpful. She seemed to find sorting out any maternity leave an unnecessary chore and was reluctant to consider any deviations from the standard practice of leaving at the twenty-ninth week of pregnancy and returning twenty-nine weeks after birth. At one point she commented that she had noticed that women working beyond the twenty-ninth week of pregnancy often developed complications like high blood pressure!

Several women complained that their doctors put pressure upon them to stop work before they were ready to do so. Kristine Band, a PR consultant from Bedfordshire, writes,

> The consultant insisted at first that I should stop working ten weeks before the birth. He was not very reasonable so I stopped trying to discuss it. He assumed I had stopped, I guess, as he never mentioned it again after the ten-week deadline.

In fact, she worked up to the very day she gave birth, and if her labour pains had not started during the night, she would have been at a meeting with clients scheduled for the next day. Another woman, from London, reports,

> By the time the relaxation classes started at the hospital at twenty-six weeks, I was the only one in my class still at work. The rest of them seemed to be spending their time worrying about what pram to buy and what would happen during labour. My doctor didn't approve either but when I explained that my job was quite relaxed and that I sat at my desk all day with my feet up on a stool, she agreed that I was probably exerting myself less at work than I would be at home!

Often doctors have set ideas about these things, but the best ones are prepared to listen if you put the facts clearly and explain in what ways you are prepared to take things easier. But if there are real medical reasons for you to stop work, don't be stubborn, like this woman who suffered from pre-eclampsia (high blood pressure, swelling of the hands and feet, protein in urine) but could not make herself slow down as her doctors advised: she had to have an emergency Caesarean in her seventh month, at great risk to her baby and herself:

> I had rushed around too much. I didn't want to behave like an invalid, so I brought it on myself. The doctor did try to persuade me to stop work in my sixth month, and gave in to me too easily. They should have been tougher on me and made me stop.

However there is no reason to give up work at this stage if you are fit and well and don't wish to stop, and an Employment Appeal Tribunal has confirmed the right of women to go on working after the eleventh week before their expected date of confinement. Indeed, the new Statutory Maternity Pay regulations uphold this. You can now choose to stay at work up to the sixth week before your due date and still qualify for your full SMP entitlement. Of course you have every right to go on working after this, right up to the moment your contractions start, if you want to (even though it does mean losing some of your maternity pay entitlement). However, if you work in a factory it is illegal for your employer to allow you to continue at work after the fourth week before your due date.

Many women do indeed work up to a week or two before their due date, or even right up to the moment before labour starts. Unfortunately you cannot use the weeks you have 'saved' from your total maternity leave entitlement and add them on to your maternity leave after the baby is born. Several women made the point that they would rather have more time off after the birth than before, for example this psychologist from County Down, Northern Ireland:

> Full maternity pay is only granted if you take at least six weeks before birth. This is stupid as it is the time after the birth that is particularly necessary. New regulations now allow you to take the paid time as you wish – i.e. longer after the birth, less before. But if you do work beyond the sixth week, you lose a certain amount of maternity benefit. The only way around this is for the doctor to pretend your estimated delivery date is much later than it actually is.

Few mothers-to-be, however, were as brazen as one woman working in a publishing company, who was at the office conducting a telephone auction for the serial rights in a hotly contested new book when her contractions started for her second child. She managed to hang on until the auction had been won, then coolly took a taxi straight to the hospital, having arranged to meet her husband there, and having organised for her mother to pick up her daughter from the minder's. Not that this approach is to be endorsed: most employers would feel very nervous about having a woman employee about to 'pop' hanging around the office, and she could have endangered her baby and herself if she had delayed too long.

Your changing body and feelings

Do not be tempted to ignore the physiological changes that take place in your body when you are pregnant. The changes start before you are even sure you are pregnant. As a woman from Glasgow wrote to us:

> I was working in a chemist, and had done for four years. One day (before I actually knew I was pregnant) I had a particularly difficult customer who wanted to try all the sun care products and who ended up buying nothing. Normally that wouldn't have bothered me, but to my own and everyone else's surprise I started shouting at her and ended up in tears. My boss had to calm things down and apologise for me. But a couple of weeks later when I told him I was pregnant he laughed and said he now realised why I had acted so out of character. It proves your hormones can affect you, even before you know.

Another woman had a similar experience,

> I was very lucky and had a very easy pregnancy. My only problem was that I was a bit emotional in the first three months – I just felt tears welling up inside in the middle of meetings!

The first three months

The overwhelming tiredness you will probably experience in the first three months must be one of nature's ways of telling you to take it easy. Most women find that their bodies clamour for extra rest and sleep. As one mother wrote to us, 'It's a shame you can't take your maternity leave in the first three months of pregnancy when you often feel most in need of it.'

If your early pregnancy is trouble-free, you may well like to keep it to yourself. Some colleagues prefer this attitude too. A doctor from Belfast wrote:

> I didn't like being pregnant. I didn't talk about it and tended to ignore it at work. This suited my colleagues who all (to a man) detest very domestic women and seemed to be terrified I'd be knitting bootees at coffee and lunch times!

During this period you may be experiencing morning sickness, which won't help, especially if you are not yet ready to tell your employer and fellow workers that you are pregnant.

For most women, morning sickness is a feeling of nausea confined to one period of the day (it can even be the evening). It usually disappears around week twelve, though if you are unfortunate it can go on much longer. It can be particularly difficult coping with the nausea at work, and if you want to continue as normal it is worth following the suggested rules:

* Eat little and often, starting in the morning with dry toast, a biscuit or crisps in bed. Never let your stomach become completely empty.

* Follow your cravings *in moderation*. If potatoes, pasta and other starchy food are what you fancy during the period that you feel nauseous, then don't feel you have to avoid them for the so-called 'healthier' salad foods: in fact, they are equally healthy! Watch your weight by cutting down on fats.

* B-vitamin foods sometimes help: wheatgerm, brewer's yeast and wholemeal bread are good sources.

These are some of the morning sickness tips we received from other working mothers:

* **Regular doses of ginger beer used to work.**

* **A lot of people thought I was mad but I found that chocolate helped a lot with morning sickness.**

* Much to the disgust of my fellow nurses, four Mars bars during the morning helped me survive morning sickness.

* I think I only had to go home early once because of pregnancy nausea, but I felt terrible for about four months and kept to my office drinking Bovril and Lucozade (but not both at once).

* Eat little and often to help with tiredness and sickness while at work. Apples are good to ease sickness.

On the other hand, some pregnant women who only suffer from mild nausea find that being busy at work helps them to forget about it – another good reason for continuing to work. As one woman said, 'I always seemed to feel much sicker at the weekend, when I could laze about the house and think about it.'

The middle three months

Except for the few for whom the entire pregnancy is difficult, most women find that this is the best period of their pregnancy. It is a good time to do anything you can towards preparing for the coming baby. Don't assume you are going to continue feeling healthy and energetic, and so leave everything to the last few weeks, when you may be off on maternity leave. You may find that you appreciate having organised well in advance so that you can use the later weeks to rest.

The last three months

Some women are lucky and find that they feel well enough to work efficiently until quite late in their pregnancies, though being pregnant can cause unusual problems. One educational psychologist had this to contend with:

> In late pregnancy I went out to see one child in the home
> of an immigrant family. They had no furniture and I
> was offered the only place to sit – a deckchair. When it
> came to be time to go, I couldn't get out of it. A couple
> of them had to heave me out!

Another woman, who works in publishing, wrote to us
about her problem:

> I had a tendency to get nose bleeds towards the end. It
> was most embarrassing, sitting in a meeting in an ad
> agency, all very Conran, trying to ignore the bump and
> look cool, then be politely informed there was blood
> running down my face . . .

A teacher who was able to work until she was due to take
maternity leave found that her problems tended to occur in
the evenings, when she went out for a meal with her
husband. Once, she was feeling faint and went to the ladies
to recover, while her husband hovered outside:

> Another lady customer approached the door, and my
> husband said to her: 'Please could you see if my wife's
> all right, she's having a baby!' 'What! Now!??' she said
> horrified, rushing in immediately. She was relieved to
> find me looking reasonably well by that time and
> refreshing my make-up.

On another occasion she managed to hold out till the meal
was over, and walked with her husband to the reception
desk to receive the bill. But the moment they were
presented with it, she writes:

> I slumped forward over the desk in a faint. I was guided
> backwards into an easy chair by my husband and the
> very perplexed manager. I must be one of the few who
> can *honestly* say they have fainted at the sight of the bill!

Don't be surprised, however, if you can't manage to work
right up to the end of your third trimester: if you have had
a fairly energetic, problem-free pregnancy you may not be

37

prepared for the overwhelming lassitude and heaviness that can overtake you in your last month – possibly aggravated by sleeplessness, backache, heartburn and other common problems:

> When I was two weeks off my due date, I woke up one morning and thought: I simply can't drag myself to work another day. I spent the rest of the time lying on my bed, or on the couch, like a great, beached, dreamy whale.

Another woman found that she felt the same way:

> I always thought that when I took time off, for the last two weeks before my date, I'd go off to art galleries and films, but I did absolutely nothing, just sort of slumped at home in a pregnant stupor.

Another symptom that might make working difficult in the last three months is 'maternal amnesia'. Some women find that towards the end of pregnancy their brains cease to function in the usual way. Many women find it persists for a few months after the birth too. One woman said that she was pleased that this only started to happen to her a week or so before she began her maternity leave:

> I would read a page of a book, and have no idea of what it meant, or clear recollection of what it said. I would sit and listen to people talking around me and find it difficult to follow the thread of the argument. I had never heard of this happening to anyone else, and wondered for a while if somehow or other I was suffering from brain damage! Then my mother told me that it had happened to her, and it goes away of its own accord!

Staying Well During Pregnancy

Saving your strength

Although you should be able to carry on working except in exceptional circumstances, you shouldn't expect too much of yourself. Slow down where you can, be easy on yourself, avoid getting excessively tired.

Here are some tips for saving your strength:

* Get enough sleep, even if it means doing less in the evenings for a while (and make sure your partner understands this). Go to bed earlier than usual, and if necessary use the weekends to lie in and catch up on extra sleep.

* Rest as much as possible during the day: instead of going out to lunch, or rushing round the shops during your lunch break, have your break at your desk with your feet propped up or try lying on the floor for ten minutes, and practise your relaxation technique (or pelvic floor exercises).

* Phyl Driffield, a full-time deputy ward sister from York, counsels, 'It is essential that you make use of tea and meal breaks by always resting. Put your feet up. Force yourself to take breaks even if you have a heavy work load.'

* Watch out if you are in a solitary job, as Alison Downer writes, 'While pregnant I worked on an RAF switchboard and once dozed off in an armchair in my lunchbreak and slept and slept until the supervisor woke me up to go home at the end of my shift.'

* When you arrive home in the evening, stretch out on your bed or on the sofa for half an hour before preparing the evening meal or better still, let your partner cook dinner.

* Several working mothers strongly recommend a bath when you come in from work. Heather Lockett, a full-time teacher from Merseyside, said, 'A bath when you arrive home is a must – it really does make you feel refreshed and so much better. I managed it during my second pregnancy by getting in with my two-year-old who loved being close to mum and the growing baby.'

* If you sit at a desk at work, find or improvise a footstool that you keep under your desk to prop up your legs throughout the working day. Get up to stretch your legs from time to time. Bring in a cushion for the small of your back, and make sure you sit up properly – slouching will lead to back problems.

* If your job involves a lot of standing or walking, make sure you sit down (or even lie down) as much as you can: discuss how you can achieve this with your boss or union representative. Wear maternity support tights and comfortable low-heeled shoes.

* Organise as much help as you can in the home. Don't hesitate to ask for it, especially if you have other children. Your partner, children, friends, mother or other relatives can help with the shopping, cooking and cleaning. If you can afford it, hire a cleaner, if only once a week to do the heavy domestic work (if you do, you're bound to want to keep the cleaner on once the baby is born!).

* Cut back on your social life. Don't commit to cooking fancy dinner parties (especially in the first three or four months, when the very thought of food may turn your stomach) even if you used to take this in your stride.

Travelling to work

One of the most tiring things during a working pregnancy

can be your journey to work: it is amazing how exhausting that forty-minute commute can become once you're pregnant. Julie Howell says,

> **Travelling was very difficult. I suffered badly from sickness throughout the whole of the nine months. I travelled to and from work by bus. Most days I was sure I was either going to be ill on the bus or have to get off to walk the four miles into work.**

Consider other ways of getting to work, to find what suits you best. For example, you may want to switch to going by bus instead of tube – it may take longer, but it could be closer door-to-door and involve less changing; perhaps you can drive to work, and persuade your employer to pay for parking. Or a colleague or acquaintance may offer you a lift on a regular basis. If you can afford it, treat yourself to the occasional taxi.

One woman, who lives in York, wrote,

> **I was surprised to find that cycling was a good way to get around right up to the birth. I found it less tiring than walking in summer and okay if I was careful to keep balanced! But of course York is very flat and I don't think it would be a good idea in hilly areas!**

Neither would cycling be a good idea if you are not used to it – or in heavy traffic, and in later months, when your centre of gravity changes, you may find it too wobbly!

One woman learnt from her first pregnancy:

> **I remembered that travel on public transport contributed to a lot of the strain of the first pregnancy. I got incredibly tired as a result. With the second one I was a bit more sensible and I drove into work when I got big, and that did make an enormous difference. I also persuaded my employers to give me a parking space.**

Yet another woman found that this was not the solution

for her: 'I drove myself to work but found that in later pregnancy I could not cope with heavy traffic.'

* If you can arrange it with your employer, try scheduling your hours so that you don't have to travel during the rush-hour. For example, come in to work later, leave later, or come in and leave early before the rush begins.

An additional problem of regular travelling to work when pregnant is that people don't automatically offer their seat to a pregnant woman clinging to a strap in the bus or train, at least not in London. One woman told us,

> Not one person has offered me their seat on the bus during my whole pregnancy. Standing is ghastly, when you get those ligament pains – when your pelvis opens up, or whatever it is. *I* would always leap up for someone who was pregnant. I've been quite shocked about it.

And a London barrister says,

> I was actually beaten to a seat on the tube, literally, by a bloke squeezing in front of me. I was seven months pregnant. I just glared at him and stuck my bump out. But I never had the nerve to ask someone to give up their seat. I'd just stand there with the adrenaline pumping, thinking 'the bloody so-and-sos . . . '

This woman complained to London Transport, and had a long correspondence with them.

> In reply to my suggestion that they should add pregnant women on to the stickers asking you to give up your seat for the disabled and elderly, they said that if they started

opening up the categories everyone would want to be added to it – and anyway they had already added 'women with heavy shopping' on buses. I wrote back that carrying heavy shopping during rush hour is a choice you make – but you cannot put down an extra stone and a half that you are carrying inside you.

The best way to make people behave chivalrously is politely to ask someone near you outright whether they'd mind if you sat down, explaining you're pregnant (let them pretend they hadn't noticed!). A friendly, polite request without any aggression or complaint is almost impossible to ignore – though it may be hard for you to bring yourself to ask. To be fair, sometimes they might *not* have noticed you were pregnant. One woman wrote,

> Whilst pregnant with my first child I was 'goosed' from the rear by a football supporter in the London Underground. I was so angry I turned round and gave him a black eye – the look of shock when he saw my bulge was so funny it was almost worth the fright.

Changing your hours

If it all proves too much for you, your employer may agree to let you work a shorter week, shorter hours or to take some work home, on a temporary basis. But be very careful if this change is put on a formal footing. It can affect your statutory right to maternity pay, especially if you do not earn enough to pay National Insurance contributions in the period immediately before your maternity leave. And if you are working part-time or are doing a less demanding job in the period immediately before you leave, it can mean that your employer need only offer you that part-time or less demanding job when you return to work after the baby, instead of your old job.

Exercise and posture

Exercise in moderation can be of great benefit during pregnancy to keep you fit and in shape for the strain of labour and the first few months of caring for the baby. If you enjoy exercise, and it is a regular part of your life, you can probably continue with any form of it that you are already used to – such as swimming, cycling, dancing, tennis, yoga – provided you don't push yourself and it doesn't make you even more tired – and that you check with your doctor first.

Doctors on the whole recommend not taking up any new sport or form of exercise while pregnant, and they give good reasons for not participating at all in certain sports, such as horseback riding and marathon running, while pregnant. If you are lucky enough to find an antenatal keep-fit class near your home or work, you may be well advised to join it, after checking with your doctor. If you have a responsible keep-fit teacher you may be able to attend a 'normal' keep-fit class so long as your teacher is aware that you are pregnant and will make sure you don't do anything dangerous or strenuous.

However, if you already find it hard to fit everything you want and need to do into the working day, don't feel that any of this is absolutely essential. Many generations of mothers coped with labour and motherhood without an Olympic training programme during pregnancy!

Whether you actually exercise or not, you should be careful about your posture at this time. The extra weight of your bump encourages the typical pregnant swayback. Not only will you *look* more pregnant if you allow yourself to stand like this, you will also be putting a lot of strain on your lower back. Remembering to stand tall and tuck your tummy in and your bottom under as much as possible will strengthen your back.

Dental treatment and prescriptions

Take advantage of the fact that dental treatment while you are pregnant – and for a year after your baby is born – is free. So are all your prescriptions (you need form FW8 from your doctor or midwife).

> My dentist (who I've had since I was a child) was very gleeful when I told him I was pregnant. He embarked on some lengthy, but non-essential, work in my mouth, tickled pink that I wouldn't have to pay. I'm sure that's not quite right, but I'm not complaining.

Diet

You will be given plenty of advice during your pregnancy about diet, and this advice is as relevant to the working mother as to the woman who gives up work: you must not gain too much weight and you should eat a good balanced diet, with plenty of fresh fruit and vegetables and lots of liquids.

It can however be a little harder for the working woman to ensure that her lunch is healthy than a woman who is at home all day, and requires some forethought.

* If your lunch at work usually consists of a sandwich, try making your own or finding somewhere that will do you a wholemeal sandwich with fresh salad to add to the fillings. Eat a piece of fruit or yogurt afterwards.

* Steer clear of the office or canteen coffee or tea. Bring in some natural fruit juice or low-calorie drinks, which you can drink diluted with water, or drink milk.

* If you often have a business, restaurant or pub lunch, avoid alcohol. The excuse of pregnancy should shut up even the 'come on have a little one, don't be a spoil

sport' brigade, as it has now been proved that alcohol can be a danger to the unborn baby. As research has not yet established a 'safe' daily level of alcohol intake it is probably better not to drink at all during pregnancy (or as little as possible).

* In a restaurant order a big bottle of mineral water, and try to drink as much of it as possible. Choose plain grilled lean meats or fish, and fresh vegetables, or salads.

* Whatever any nice, kind, misguided person says, don't 'eat for two'. As one mother sadly reports:

> The one bit of advice I ignored was not to put on too much weight. I thought for once in my life I had an excuse to overeat! I'd go out to lunch and allow myself all the things I would normally ignore: rolls and butter, potatoes, puddings. A year and a half later, I still have a couple of stone to lose.

Antenatal Care and Childbirth Classes

Regular antenatal check-ups are essential when you are pregnant, and the law allows you to take paid time off work for them. Your employer is entitled to ask you to show your certificate of pregnancy, which you get from your doctor or community midwife, and your clinic appointment card (obtained from your clinic) as proof that you have attended the appointment.

In the average, normal pregnancy, you'll be asked to come for a check-up once a month for about the first seven months, then once a fortnight, until in the last month you'll probably be going once a week. Visits to antenatal clinics are often extremely time consuming, and even though the law allows you to take time off, you may feel very frustrated and annoyed at having taken so much precious time off just to hang around.

> After the first, detailed booking clinic, my antenatal check-ups consisted of the standard weight, blood pressure and urine checks by a midwife, and a quick prod of my tummy by a junior doctor (I never saw 'my' consultant after the first visit) – the whole lot took ten minutes maximum. But I was never at the clinic for less than two hours, and a couple of times considerably longer. The waiting was endless: first you'd have to queue up at reception, then you'd wait in a waiting room, then your name would finally get called and you'd get to wait in a corridor, then you'd finally get into an examination room and wait for the midwife to materialise from another door, then you'd be left to wait for the same door to open to reveal the doctor.

It is a good idea, as an expectant mother who intends to carry on working, to consider very carefully the different antenatal care arrangements available in your area from the point of view of your convenience, and accessibility both from your home and your workplace. Many National Health antenatal clinics seem to be scheduled for late mornings or early afternoons, and if your clinic is a long way from your workplace, you may find you have to take half or even a whole day off work to attend, or else exhaust yourself with extra travelling.

You may find it most convenient to opt for one of the schemes which leave the major part of your antenatal checks in the hands of your own GP (see below), who may agree to see you at early morning or evening surgery even if the practice has a special antenatal clinic at a less convenient time.

Another option is to book yourself into a hospital which is easy to get to from your place of work rather than from your home (also weighing up how easy it will be for your partner to visit you in hospital). If combining antenatal appointments with your work proves difficult, don't be tempted to skip them: they are the only way your doctor and midwife can make sure you and your baby stay healthy, and you certainly won't want to do anything to endanger your baby or yourself.

Do discuss your practical problems with your doctor or clinic staff: they may be prepared to make special arrangements for you, or there may be evening antenatal clinics you could attend.

Antenatal care options under the National Health

Find out from your doctor which of these schemes are available in your area:

Hospital care

Your GP refers you to a hospital, where you attend antenatal clinics and where your baby will ultimately be born.

Advantages: you will get to know the hospital and the hospital staff before you go into hospital to have your baby. You will have the full choice of pain relief, highly qualified medical staff and the range of facilities for childbirth. If you take your childbirth classes at the same hospital you may be able to schedule your appointment and classes for the same morning or afternoon.

Disadvantages: long waiting periods in antenatal clinics; possibly lack of continuity in the doctors and midwives you see; certainly more impersonal care.

Shared care

Your antenatal check-ups are shared between your GP and the hospital (you will see your doctor more frequently early in the pregnancy, the hospital more often at the end). You will be given a card with your records on it to carry with you (ask them to explain it to you).

Advantages: the more personal relationship with your GP; at the same time you get an opportunity to familiarise yourself with the hospital where you will have your baby.

Disadvantages: a certain lack of continuity in your care, as your GP will not deliver your baby.

Home care

Your antenatal check-ups are handled by your GP and a community midwife, and they deliver your baby in your own home. It is a struggle to arrange to have your baby at home, and you need to find a supportive GP (most doctors are reluctant to take the risk of being responsible for home deliveries). Only the most persistent natural childbirth devotees prepared to fight the system, who have probably already had one baby and an impeccable obstetric record, are likely to succeed to get their doctors' agreement.

Advantages: antenatal check-ups at your doctor's surgery or midwife's clinic; personal relationship; baby born in the comfort of your own home without drugs or the trappings of a high-tech birth.

Disadvantages: the reason doctors are so reluctant to support home births is that if anything goes wrong, the time to get you or your baby to hospital may be the difference between life and death.

Domino scheme

This means your antenatal care is in the hands of your GP and community midwife, and when it comes to having the baby, your own community midwife accompanies you to hospital, helps to deliver your baby and takes you and your baby home some hours after delivery.

Advantages: this has all the advantages of home care without the risks of having a baby at home.

Disadvantages: if you are exhausted after the birth, or

have small children at home, you may find a few days in hospital more relaxing than going straight home.

General practitioner maternity unit

This involves antenatal care by your GP and community midwife and delivery in a small local maternity unit by your own GP and midwife.

Advantages: personal care; low-tech delivery (more intimate surroundings than a big hospital).

Disadvantages: they won't offer the same pain-killing facilities as a big hospital (for example, epidural).

Whichever sort of care you opt for, remember to come well-prepared to the clinic. You can use the waiting time to make a list of any worries or queries. In a survey run by *Parents* magazine, half the pregnant mothers questioned didn't feel they could ask the questions they wanted to during the appointment. A list will ensure that you don't forget anything, and may prompt you to ask, however small or silly your questions might seem.

Childbirth classes

If this is your first pregnancy, it is worthwhile finding the time to attend childbirth classes. They teach you how to stay fit during pregnancy, what actually happens in labour, how to cope with the pain – and how to deal with a newborn baby. They will also give you the opportunity to meet other pregnant women in your area, some of whom may be working mothers too, with whom you can share your experiences.

This is a great opportunity to start building a working mother network: you may be able to form an informal support group with these mothers when the baby is born, to share information on local childminders, nurseries and other local facilities for mothers and children, or even find someone to share a nanny with. The Working Mothers Association started in just this way: women who had become friends during their National Childbirth Trust classes kept in touch afterwards so that they could help each other, and then recognised that there was a national need for such support.

Childbirth classes usually start around the sixth month of your pregnancy. You should, however, find out about classes as soon as you know you are pregnant, and book yourself into the class of your choice in advance. In some areas childbirth classes are often heavily oversubscribed and can't meet the demand (particularly the NCT or other private ones). If you leave it too late, you may find you are told the class is fully booked and that you'll have to postpone your baby's birth to get in!

Hospital/NHS childbirth classes

These are held at your hospital, clinic or doctor's surgery and are free. They usually cover relaxation, labour, pain relief, and parentcraft (practical advice on bathing, feeding your baby and so on). As they are run by professional midwives and physiotherapists you may find that most of the classes are held during the day (except for a few extra evening classes designed for partners to accompany you), which means more time off work if you are still working. However, you may be able to schedule them so that you go to some before or after an antenatal appointment at the same hospital. One advantage of attending hospital classes is that they usually show you around the labour ward and postnatal ward so that you are familiar with them before you enter hospital.

National Childbirth Trust classes

I regret not having found out about NCT classes until it was too late. I thought it stood for *natural* childbirth, which didn't particularly interest me, whereas they're not all extreme, and they provide such good support and such an easy way to meet other women in the same boat.

You have to pay for these and they are often held in the instructor's own home. You are more likely to be offered the choice of an evening class. They offer the usual relaxation lessons, pain-relief techniques in labour, and parentcraft. Many NCT branches also organise various pre- and postnatal support groups. These deal with special problems like morning sickness, twins and postnatal depression – and, of course, working mothers too. Some branches also offer maternity keep-fit classes, and/or postnatal exercise classes. The NCT also provides a nationwide network of breastfeeding counsellors and has an electric breastpump hiring service. (See *Further Help*, p.569.)

Other private classes

Apart from the NCT, there are a number of other private organisations which offer instruction and support in various types of natural childbirth. See *Further Help* for addresses.

Maternity Wardrobe for the Working Woman

Looking Smart

If you don't have to worry about looking smart for your job you should consider yourself lucky. You can appear in the ubiquitous maternity dungarees, jogging suit or jumpsuit and you will be blissfully comfortable. Hazel Coates, a Belfast physiotherapist, reports that 'Baggy dungarees were very comfortable – especially for my active job.' She, and other women working for the Health

Service, noted that larger uniforms were supplied as they grew bigger. A teacher from Manchester found it convenient to live in flowered smocks. She had three – one on, one in the wash and one waiting to be ironed. She grew to loathe them, but they served their purpose.

However, for many women it is important to look smart and business-like at work even when pregnant. For some this is because they want to maintain the professional image essential to their work, others want to for their own pride and dignity, or because they don't think they should have to compromise their sense of style just because they are pregnant.

As one doctor wrote to us, 'If you are professional get as many decent clothes as you can manage (about 50 per cent of mine were borrowed!): it's good for the morale.'

This is perhaps especially important if you work in a masculine environment, where the pastel frills of the virgin-madonna look traditionally promoted by maternity-wear designers could start bringing out all those patronising protective instincts you have spent years suppressing in your male colleagues. Or, on the other hand, where your swelling breasts and growing bump may be an uncomfortable reminder of your sexuality to men who have hitherto regarded you as one of the boys.

The clothes you wear can contribute substantially to the way you are treated at work when pregnant: they can help to disguise your pregnancy and they can also help you say 'Yes, I'm pregnant, but I haven't changed', especially if you manage to keep your own sense of style and sense of fun. Certainly you owe it to yourself not to let yourself go or dress in clothes you loathe just because you're pregnant.

It is gratifying to see that many manufacturers of pregnancy wear have recognised the need for professional clothes for pregnant women, which was not the case when we were first writing this book. As well as the usual outlets, there are some specialist firms mentioned in *Further Help*.

Here are some tips to keep in mind when planning your working maternity wardrobe:

Basic ground rules

* Before you buy anything have a good look through your wardrobe and pull out anything that may be suitable to your expanding girth: big shirts; wide sweaters and tops; big, boxy or long jackets or cardigans, skirts and trousers with elasticated or drawstring waists, wide dresses with self-tie belts, or drop-waist dresses. You may be surprised how many of your normal clothes will see you through your pregnancy – or at least the first five or six months.

* When you buy, stick to your normal style and colours: don't feel obliged to wear floral prints now that you're pregnant if you otherwise wouldn't be seen dead in them: don't wear coy pussy cat bows if you usually leave the top buttons of your shirt undone (for many women, this is the one time in their lives they can actually show a bit of cleavage!).

* Don't buy your whole maternity wardrobe at once. You are going to get very sick of your maternity clothes, so it may be psychologically helpful to save some money to buy something to make you feel nice when you are feeling fatter and drabber than you do now. And don't invest in once-in-a-lifetime maternity clothes either – buying something new for your subsequent pregnancy will be equally good for morale.

* Don't limit your shopping to maternity wear shops: normal fashion outlets often have plenty of useful things, such as wide tops and dresses and oversized jackets in more fashionable fabrics and colours. Sometimes you can get away with buying clothes you like in your favourite store, but in a much bigger size,

or even in a man's size. This is particularly true with knitwear.

* Don't listen when the lady in the shop tells you that you will wear that expensive maternity dress with a belt for years after the baby is born: most mothers confess that they loathe their maternity clothes by the end of their pregnancy, and long to get rid of them.

* Buy easy-care fabrics. You may find you get very clumsy, as this woman did:

> As my pregnancy wore on, I became more and more messy, and could never eat anything without spilling something down my front. I thought I was regressing to babyhood, but it probably had something to do with the fact that I hadn't caught up with my new body image, and kept forgetting how far I had to sit from the table to fit my tummy in.

In any case, once your baby is born you'll never want to wear anything that is 'Dry Clean Only' unless you own a dry cleaner's.

* You may not get your figure back sufficiently to fit into your old clothes by the time you return to work. Have one or two maternity dresses that you can continue to wear until you do. Try to buy clothes that are front-opening if you plan to breastfeed (surprisingly few maternity dresses are designed for this).

* Choose clothes that are comfortable and unrestricting. Avoid wearing anything that is tight anywhere, but most especially round your so-called waist.

* Jewellery: many women find their hands swell during pregnancy, and one mother counsels: 'Start taking off rings as soon as they begin to get a little tighter. Don't wait until it's too late and you have to have them cut off!'

> My maternity trousers wouldn't stay up – at first because *they* were too big, now because *I'm* too big – so I borrowed my husband's braces to hold them up.

So comfortable! I wear them under my top or sweater, so they don't show. You can do it with a skirt you can't do up at the waist anymore too, as long as you wear something loose over the top.

Warm/cold weather wear

* Work out in what season you are going to be at your biggest. If you are going to invest in special maternity clothes you must buy with that season in mind. For instance, it may be winter now, but if your baby is due in June, you may not grow out of your usual winter coat before March, when it may just start getting warm enough not to need one at all.

* If you do need a warm outer garment, consider alternatives like a cape, poncho or shawl.

* When it is hot you'll want to wear the lightest, airiest cottons you can find.

* When it is cold, wear a number of thin layers which you can strip off.

Tights and shoes

* If your feet and ankles swell up and you are threatened with varicose veins, you will want to wear comfortable, flat shoes and possibly support tights.

* 'One problem is how to keep tights from falling down when there is no waistline to anchor them. You can buy special maternity tights with a wide front panel, but even these can roll down. To keep them up, wear a maternity panty girdle (not too tight!) over the top of your tights.'

* You may have to buy a pair of shoes in as much as a half or whole size bigger than normal. Buy them in a neutral colour, with low heels – if you wear high heels

you're in danger of putting your back out because your centre of gravity changes and you might end up falling flat on face! Don't squeeze your feet into tight shoes: your comfort is too important during this time, and as your ligaments become soft you could do permanent damage to your feet.

* Wear popsocks instead of tights.

Shapes to look out for

* Long jackets and cardigans worn open are great for disguising the line of that bump.

* Emphasising the head/neck line to draw attention away from the bump is an established rule in pregnancy dressing. Exaggerating your shoulders with shoulder pads will also help balance your shape. Tuck loose pads under your bra straps or use safety pins or strips of velcro to attach them to the garment.

* Boxy or long jackets worn with skirts and trousers with expandable waistbands. Waistbands that you can adjust as you grow larger with buttons or hooks are best, especially if they have cleverly positioned pleating that manages to stay looking tailored.

* Wide, long tunics with slim-looking skirt or trousers (the kind with a special elasticated front panel which will be hidden by the tunic) are good camouflage. But one mother told us that straight skirts with elastic pregnancy panels can be uncomfortable when you sit down.

* Drop waist dresses, big T-shirt dresses, especially in the shape of an inverted triangle, pinafore dresses. Remember that the bigger you get, the more uncomfortable waistbands will become, so dresses are a lot more comfortable near the end than skirts, and

can look as smart as a suit, especially if worn with a jacket.

Keeping the cost down

*   Most women are reluctant to spend much money on a maternity wardrobe, but crave choice in what to wear to work nevertheless. See if you can borrow maternity clothes from relatives or friends or even swap outfits with other pregnant women you meet at the clinic.

*   'I am still wearing non-maternity trousers and skirts in knit fabric, with elastic waistbands. They may get stretched hopelessly out of shape, but they do stay up – unlike 'maternity' elastic panels, etc. I replaced the elastic in the waist of a jersey pair of trousers with a looser piece – I can then tighten it again post partum.'

*   Put a notice up in the clinic aimed at mothers who are further on in their pregnancy than you are, saying that you would be interested in buying larger size clothes from them once their babies are born.

*   'At the beginning of my pregnancy when my trousers were just a bit tight I tied a piece of elastic to the buttonhole and used it as an expanding buttonhole for a good few weeks. Nobody can see it with a sweater on top.'

*   You could try hiring an outfit for a special occasion, or if your job requires you to dress with greater variety than you can afford (see *Further Help*).

Labour

Labour is no different for working women than for any others: but we feel that one aspect should be covered: natural versus high-tech delivery. It is clear that a good number of working women – particularly those used to being efficient and in control – convince themselves that they can sail through labour, so long as they are fully prepared – and are disappointed and sometimes badly depressed when they find that they can't.

There is a classic cry from newly delivered, first-time mothers: 'Why didn't anyone *tell* me how much it hurt?' The answer usually is, 'They did, but you didn't listen.'

One of the reasons why they didn't listen is because a new myth has arisen: if you do it right giving birth shouldn't hurt too much. The first doctors to write about natural childbirth and birth without fear recognised that fear of pain increased pain, and very laudably started to re-educate women to be in touch with what was happening in their bodies during labour. It is true that this helps, as does practising the psychoprophylactic techniques, such as breathing and relaxation, which make you feel in control of your body during labour. But it is self-deceptive and damaging to read into childbirth books the idea that pain in labour is all in the mind. If you read the experts carefully, none of them says that (although some say that there are women who do not experience pain in childbirth: if this is true, there must be very few of them!). You'll have an awful shock if you expect the pain to disappear just because you are not afraid and are breathing properly.

For most women, labour hurts. Although you may be able to keep the pain under control for many hours with breathing and relaxation techniques, there might come a time when you feel you can't cope without the intervention of medical pain relief. But the recent emphasis on natural childbirth methods has led some women (and their partners!) to believe that it's the only 'good' way of giving birth, and that you have failed if you accept medical intervention or pain relief.

This is silly: pain-controlling drugs and methods to ease delivery were developed because in the primitive societies the natural childbirth radicals hark back to, women suffered terribly in childbirth, and there was an extremely high maternal and infant mortality rate. Nobody wants things to be *that* natural.

Although natural childbirth can be a wonderful and satisfying experience for those who manage it, it is psychologically damaging (and occasionally dangerous) to set your heart on it. One mother told us that she had resisted all pain relief and intervention during a very hard, tiring and slow labour. In the end the baby, in distress, had to be delivered with forceps, lights blazing, and twenty people anxiously rushing around. Although her baby boy was no worse for the experience, her overwhelming emotion was guilt because she had been so obsessed with having a natural labour that she felt she had subjected him to unnecessary stress and pain.

You should keep an open mind in labour. Your most important objective is to produce a healthy baby – don't attach all importance to the way in which the baby is born. Decide to try for a natural birth if that is what you want, but accept the help and advice of doctors if your labour doesn't go the way you imagined.

This may be your first lesson in the plain truth that foresight, planning, preparation, good intentions and being thoroughly clued-up are all important in your career, but that everything to do with your children is essentially unpredictable:

> I remember the look of horror when I told a pregnant friend of mine that my baby was born under the old system, before the new theories had emerged. My labour was induced for the doctor's convenience; at birth she was slapped sharply on the bottom and taken away immediately and washed and dressed before she was presented to me; I was not encouraged to put her to the breast. All this seems like unimaginable cruelty now. But it did no harm – bonding wasn't disrupted or anything like that. This same friend was a lucky woman who had a near-perfect natural birth: but then she went

on to have a horrific first year – she loathed her baby and said so! I think this shows that there is no 'right' way to go about things when we are dealing with human beings. Believing that you can guarantee a perfect birth and become a perfect mother by following the books leaves you defenceless when things are different from what you expect.

CHAPTER 3
Maternity Leave Blues

The birth of a baby is an enormous upheaval – and that is an understatement. Some first-time mothers are totally unprepared for the exhaustion and emotional strain that often affect those first weeks at home:

> I thought I was so well prepared, but the books and antenatal classes concentrated on the birth. Then, it was supposed to be happy ever after. I wish somebody had told me babies don't sleep through the night. That came as such a shock that I really resented the baby for my broken nights.

Even the second or third time round it can come as a shock to be forced to remember just how physically and mentally exhausted you feel. In this chapter, we look at some of the common problems and negative feelings that many mothers have during the early weeks of their maternity leave.

This is not to say that maternity leave is a bad time for everyone – it can also be the best few months of your life: getting to know your new baby with ever-increasing delight, enjoying the different pace of life at home, strolling in the park with the pram, meeting other mothers. If this chapter reads negatively it is because there is not much to say to the lucky mothers who find that everything goes splendidly – but if you are one of the women who finds the adjustment difficult then you need the reassurance that you are not the only one to feel like this, along with the good news that this stage usually passes quickly.

Many mothers in our sample, however, felt that maternity leave did not live up to their expectations:

> **Instead of sitting in a rosy glow, contented baby gurgling in a basket at my feet, having time for things like baking, sorting out cupboards, writing a novel, or catching up with friends I'd lost touch with, there I was the slave of this baby who never stopped crying. I didn't have time to have a bath, or even drink a cup of tea while it was still hot, my days were just full of feeding and nappy changing. When my husband came home in the evening he would ask me what I had done today – and I'd have to say nothing – I hadn't even managed to start supper!**

There is no evidence that working mothers suffer more from postnatal depression than mothers who have not worked, but being a working mother does bring its own dimension to the problem. There is a stark contrast between a busy, rewarding life and the repetitive, isolated treadmill of looking after a small baby.

When you are at home with a small baby, the job is never done. You've just finished feeding and changing the baby and stuffed some washing into the machine when the whole pattern starts again – and again. You may find you haven't got time to read a magazine, or even simply to get dressed. If a friend or colleague rings, you may feel unable to chat on the phone, as the baby always chooses that particular moment to clamour for attention.

If you have thought of yourself as an efficient and organised career woman, used to being in control and being able to meet the most difficult challenges, this may come as a shock, especially as nobody says 'well done' after an endless day of drudgery with a new baby, who can't even yet reward you with a smile. This is why many working mothers we talked to or who wrote to us went back to work after their maternity leave with a measure of relief.

> I think I suffered from postnatal depression, but it went in part, by going back to work. I think that for somebody who is a professional person, the trauma of having children is very substantial, completely under-estimated, and you make the mistake of tackling motherhood as a professional task which you're going to excel at. So you set yourself far too high standards, whereas what you ought to do is relax into it.

Coping With Exhaustion

This is a problem which besets most new mothers (and fathers!). Do not underestimate the amount of time it will take you to recuperate from the physical strain of labour (let alone recovering from a Caesarean). The older you are, the more this will take out of you. Some doctors say a mother does not get back to normal until a year after the birth.

On top of this physical exhaustion, you will have to cope with sleepless nights.

> Tiredness was my worst thing. My babies were all bad sleepers. I could have crawled under a hedge and gone to sleep many a time, given the chance. The twins were the worst. I think I was lucky if I got four hours' sleep a night for two years. My husband didn't share the feeding because he is a HGV driver and it would not have been so good for him to fall asleep at the wheel. These days my greatest luxury is to go to bed of an evening when I feel tired, on occasions 7.30-8.00p.m. When it's cold, with my hot-water bottle, it's sheer bliss.

Here are some suggestions to help you cope with tiredness:

* Arrange with your partner to sleep apart occasionally, even if only for one night, perhaps at the weekend when he does not have to go to work the following day, and ask him to handle the night feeds on those nights, so that you can have one unbroken night's sleep. If you are breastfeeding, you can express some milk which can be fed to your baby in a bottle, or you may decide to provide a bottle of formula. Several bottlefeeding mothers we heard from regularly shared the night feeds with their partners.

* If your partner isn't willing, perhaps your mother, or another relative or friend would come and spend a night occasionally to give you a break. Or perhaps you can afford to pay for a maternity nurse for a week or so.

* If you can't help hearing your baby cry no matter where you are in your flat or house, consider leaving your baby at your mother's or friend's for a night, or go and spend a night at someone else's house, or even in a hotel.

* Snatch some sleep during the day when your baby sleeps. Forget the chores. One mother decided she was so exhausted she was not doing anything constructive during the precious hours when her baby did finally drop off, so she deliberately set out to catch up on her sleep by lying down each time her baby fell asleep, no matter what time of day.

* If you can't sleep, find a few minutes to lie and practise the relaxation exercises you learned in antenatal class. This will help refresh you – or it may help you drop off to sleep.

* As one doctor who wrote to us said, 'Accept any help from friends who volunteer to come round during the day or occasional evening, especially if the baby is restless. They can walk, soothe, rock or amuse a

wakeful baby – and offer company and moral support.' They may even offer to mind the baby while you take a nap!

* Arrange for a babysitter or childminder in the afternoon who will watch your baby for a couple of hours while you sleep.

Maternal amnesia

Like many mothers, in the period immediately after the birth of a baby, you may experience something that can only be described as your 'mind going soft': loss of memory and concentration, a lack of interest in what is going on in the outside world, perhaps a loss of concern for all the things that interested you most before you had the baby. You may feel you are sinking into a mindless primitive maternal state where all that matters is how many ounces of milk the baby drank, and how often you had to change the nappy.

For some working women, this can be taken as an unwelcome sign that they have become inadequate and stupid, and that they will not be able to return to a job they felt confident in before. But this maternal amnesia is a very temporary side-effect, a trick your body plays on you after the upheaval of labour, as a way of making you focus on the baby. Enjoy it: don't worry about it; you will find your brain soon regains its former sharpness.

You and Your Baby

Blaming yourself

Contrary to most new mothers' expectations coming home with their new baby is not always a bed of roses. Many babies cry a lot. Many simply do not seem to sleep. Some have feeding problems. Some have colic. Some are ill.

These problems are beyond the scope of this book, but it should be reassuring to know that many, if not most, babies have one or more of these problems, that they are quite normal – and that they pass. Above all, *it's not your fault*. Popular psychological theories in the past have made many a mother feel she is to blame for any disturbance in her baby's behaviour. What you should accept is that although it upsets you, there isn't necessarily anything wrong with a baby who cries a lot. There is no point in worrying about that row you had with your husband when you were six months pregnant, in case it traumatised your baby in the womb! Do everything in your power to settle or soothe your baby, and try not to imagine some sinister underlying physical or emotional problem. (Also, see *Further Help*.)

> I was pretty depressed. Because my baby was so miserable she never stopped crying. I wondered if my milk was all right. I felt terribly responsible. I worried desperately about everything and we had terrible nights. I was so tired. Also I didn't ring up my friends as much as I would have liked to, because the baby was so miserable. I didn't want to impose that on other people, and anyway, I didn't have any time to phone anyone, and I had nothing to say. You feel your life is taken over, it's not your life any more. It was hard on my husband, too, but it was awfully nice to be able to share it with him. There was one night she cried fourteen hours non-stop. We finally rang the hospital, who told us to ring our GP. Of course just as the GP appeared, she stopped crying and fell asleep. We were both hysterical by then. But perhaps if they cry a lot at that stage, they seem to cry the devil out in a way. My daughter is much jollier now than any of the other two-year-olds.

All new mothers worry about something: many breastfeeding mothers, for example, worry about not having enough milk for their baby, often to the extent of disbelieving the evidence of their baby's chubby wrists and the clinic's scales. If you are worried about anything, do something about it: go to your GP or health visitor, look up the problem in a book, talk to other mothers. But don't add to the burden of your worry and doubt by blaming yourself when anything goes wrong, or less than smoothly.

Problems bonding with your baby

Many women are helped through this difficult, tiring period by the fact that they have fallen instantly in love with their babies: the best compensation for the sleepless nights and the strain. But the much-vaunted 'mother love' is not, contrary to popular belief, an automatic and instant emotion for all women. With all the emphasis on 'bonding' immediately after birth, it is hard for some thoroughly read-up and prepared mothers to find they do not instantly fall in love with their babies, no matter how much they want to.

Don't feel guilty and upset if you are in this situation, listen to other women who have been through it, and relax. Love grows, and it will between you and your child – if not in the first few days, or even in the first few months, then perhaps when he rewards you with his first smile, or much later even, when he first calls you 'mamma'. In the meantime, some mothers have found it helpful to compensate for the lack of emotional bonding by concentrating on physical bonding with their baby: a lot of extra cuddling, stroking and rocking. This is all a young infant will expect from mother love anyway, and it will help you feel closer to the baby.

It is reassuring to know that other mothers have these feelings:

> It was rather horrifying that when I first had the baby I didn't find I fell in love with him or anything. I felt extremely resentful of this child who'd taken over my life, and I felt very disappointed. I think a lot of mums feel that – disappointed that they don't match their own, and society's expectations. I simply couldn't get a grip

on this baby. In a way, going back to work, which I knew about and understood, was a tremendous relief.

You and Your Partner

* I think the relationship with your husband changes dramatically when you have a child. You are not a couple anymore, you are a family. You obviously have the shared joy of the child. But you don't have so much time and energy for each other.

* After my first baby was born I felt guilty about my husband – that I couldn't give him the attention that he had before, but at the same time I was so tired and out of sorts that I couldn't really be bothered to make an effort for him.

Many mothers find a change in their relationship with their partners when they have had a baby. Added to the loss of sexual drive (for many women, getting the sexual 'go-ahead' at the six-week postnatal check-up raises, at best, a hollow laugh), you may also experience a temporary emotional indifference to your partner.

This happens to some women because they are so overwhelmed by their new loving and protective feelings for the baby that they may exclude any other relationships, especially that with their partners. Others have partners who become jealous of the babies who, they feel, have displaced them – causing tension between the parents. Other women are just too tired to make an effort with anyone for a while – partners included.

Many working mothers on maternity leave also find themselves in the unexpected position of feeling out of step with their partners because of the sudden difference between their daily lives. While you were both working, you may have met in the evening to exchange shop talk and gossip about work, or you may both have been equally disinclined to talk about the day's events and relieved to be able to talk about other things or sit companionably in silence.

But on maternity leave you may find yourself envious of your partner's working day and excluded, which will reinforce your sense of isolation and dullness.

> I used to laugh, but was also upset about it. We often had the classic situation of me having been with the baby all day, him not coming home till late, and then me wanting to tell him about my day where the great events were that we went to the park and the sun shone. It's not that he wasn't interested, but combined with the fact that he was trying to start his own business, he was so stressed and exhausted by the time he did get home that he just wanted to go to sleep. So there was a dissonance between us, and we did have arguments about it. When your husband comes home in the evening – that's your time to talk. You're looking forward not only to adult company, but to your *husband's* company, and it's hard if he doesn't want to talk. I have to say that maybe I wasn't quite as interested as usual in what his problems were either . . .

Your relationship may also change if you find you resent being financially dependent on your partner and having to ask for money now.

As you both start to settle into your roles as parents and you become used to the new pattern of your lives, your relationship will adjust accordingly. It helps if you have an understanding partner: and you should be understanding too – bear in mind that he is tired as well, and also has emotional adjustments to make.

Controlling Your Time at Home

One of the difficult things for a first-time mother to accept is that you are not in control of your own time with a small baby. Babies are unpredictable creatures: you are lucky if yours feeds, sleeps and excretes to a set pattern – whatever your mother says!

Our own mothers and grandmothers were brought up to schedule babies from birth: most of them seem to believe in putting babies 'down' and leaving them to cry if four hours have not passed since the last feed. Today, it is hard to resist the 'feed on demand' philosophy, and very few mothers we have spoken to can listen to their babies crying for any length of time without picking them up. Here are a few suggestions for coping with the fact that, for a couple of months at least, your time is not totally in your control.

Don't try to do too much

Don't expect to achieve too much. Accept that your home will be less than pristine for a few months (or years!) and don't try to carry on your life exactly as before. For example before the birth, you may have been capable of shopping for a dinner party on your way home from work, cooking a cordon bleu meal, laying the table, tidying the living room, and getting yourself ready for guests by 8.00 p.m. Now, remembering to defrost tonight's supper may very well prove beyond you. Don't entertain others: let them invite you round, even if it means bringing the baby. You deserve the break.

Keep your baby with you

If you have the kind of baby that simply does not like being left alone and cries whenever put down, don't fight it. If you keep trying to put your baby down to sleep in another room, you will find yourself constantly having to drop what you are doing to answer calls of distress. Instead, keep your baby with you while you go about your tasks around the house – in a baby sling or propped up in a baby seat or bouncing cradle near you.

71

Organise your priorities

Make a list of all the things you have to do in a day, and those you would like to do. Then cross out all those that are not important, and drop them until you are feeling more in control. For example, keeping the house tidy, painting the baby's room, hoovering, cooking non-convenience food meals, ironing, writing thank-you letters for all those flowers and baby gifts, the work you brought home from the office to catch up on, reading your book, or the daily paper, and so on.

Getting dressed, bathed and ready

Some mothers say it can even be hard to find time between the morning feeds and nappy changes to get dressed and ready to go out. One mother suggests that you have your bath and throw something on before your partner leaves for work in the morning, so that he can mind the baby before you are left on your own. If you leave it until later, you may find you are still in your dressing gown when he arrives home in the evening! Or you may find it easier to have your bath or shower in the evening, when your partner is around again.

Getting out of the house

With a small baby it is easy to become totally housebound, a prisoner in your own home. One of us certainly remembers those first few weeks out of hospital as being a time when the world stopped at her own front door, when she felt frightened to leave the warm cocoon of her own home even just to pop out to the corner shop.

But for the working mother maternity leave is a precious time of freedom, which can be used constructively to meet neighbours and other mothers you do not normally have time to see during the day, and to start building that local network of goodwill which is so important to the working mother later.

Once you feel up to it, take your baby to the baby clinic regularly, or join a postnatal group or mother-and-baby group, or take the pram to the park, so that you can meet other mothers with small babies.

This is also a time you should use to start investigating childminders, nurseries, playgroups, nursery schools, if you haven't already. In many areas, it is never too early to think about primary schools, either – to put your child's name on schools' waiting lists (this applies to local authority schools, not just private education) as demand often exceeds the number of places available in the good local schools. Several mothers told us they used their maternity leave to find out about schools, and visit them.

One problem with any outing that involves a small baby is that it often seems impossible to get ready to leave the house at the time you plan to (for example between feeds or naps), because at the last minute the baby will invariably need changing or be sick over the two of you – meaning you *both* have to change all over again. One mother gave us this tip:

> If you want to get out of the house, prepare a bag the evening before with all the things you'll need – keys, money, nappies, wipes, change of clothes for baby (and for you, if you have that kind of baby!), dummy, rattle, bottles etc. – and leave it by the front door so at least you won't get caught in a last-minute panic trying to find things. It is also a good idea to put out clothes for your baby and yourself the night before.

Try to get some time for yourself

If you feel trapped by the baby's demands, it is a good idea to make some time for yourself, and get away for a while.

* Leave the baby with a relative or minder for a few

hours while you do something you like on your own, such as shopping, going to the hairdresser, to a keep-fit class, to the cinema – even just taking a walk by yourself, or going into another room to read a book.

* Find a babysitter so that you and your partner can go out in the evening, to visit friends, to a restaurant, to the pictures – or even to a hotel to renew your sexual acquaintance undisturbed by the baby!

Postnatal Depression

Depression after the birth of a baby is the biggest blow to any new mother. You are prepared, if you are realistic, to feel tired and over-stretched when your baby is very young – but you rarely expect to feel seriously depressed, and if you are one of the unlucky ones you can feel that your life has turned into a nightmare.

Recent research indicates that postnatal depression is much more common than was previously thought: at least 15 per cent of women suffer from severe postnatal depression and 90 per cent of women suffer *some* depression after the birth. One-third of all stay-at-home mums of under-fives are on tranquillisers. When you consider that some women will not seek help from their doctors at this time, and therefore never make it into the statistics, you can see the problem is common.

We are of course warned, in pregnancy books and in antenatal classes, that we shall probably experience the 'baby blues' in the first week after birth, usually on the third day when, like clockwork, a release of hormones causes many new mothers to dissolve into tears and misery for a few hours. But surprisingly we are not generally warned that for some mothers postnatal depression can come on much later than this, in the form of insidious creeping depression which often remains undiagnosed because it is difficult to distinguish from the 'normal' exhaustion and anxiety that follow the birth and in the first few months of motherhood.

This depression can range from mild to psychotic, and can last for many months. Its cause is often physical, probably hormonal, although many other factors are bound to contribute to it, in view of the enormous disruption of normal life patterns caused by a new baby: lack of sleep, isolation at home, perhaps anxiety and stress over a colicky, sick or just crying baby, or a resentful partner.

Postnatal depression can happen after any pregnancy, even if you have had children before and not suffered. One woman who wrote to us had seven children in all. Her first son was handicapped, her last two were twins, yet it was only after her third child was born that she suffered a particularly severe bout of postnatal depression that lasted years. She wrote, 'I suffered from agoraphobia as well as claustrophobia. I could not walk out of the gate, let alone ride on a bus.' Now, she claims, happily, to be 95 per cent better. This is an extreme case, but it proves that there is, in a sense, something arbitrary about postnatal depression, and it in no way reflects on your natural instincts or abilities as a mother.

Is it depression?

You may not even realise that you are suffering from depression in its milder form, and even your partner or doctor may not recognise it for what it is. Look at the list of the symptoms listed below: virtually any new mother will recognise one or two of these in herself. But if you suffer from a combination of three or more of them, or if they are becoming worse, then you may well be suffering from a form of postnatal depression:

* Exhaustion not cured by sleeping.

* Insomnia.

* Crying bouts.

* Feelings of inadequacy about handling the baby.

* Loss of confidence generally.

* Indecisiveness.

* Lack of concentration.

* Anxiety about going out of the house, and about meeting people.

* Loss of interest in your appearance.

* Loss of appetite or over-eating binges.

* Loss of identity.

* Emotional indifference – even to the baby.

* Listlessness.

* Loss of interest in sex which continues after your body has returned to normal.

* Excessive worrying about everything – including world affairs.

* Anxiety about your own health, unexplained pains.

* Anxiety about the baby's health, or others'.

The causes

If you have been suffering from any of these symptoms, your feelings of depression are likely to be compounded by shame or guilt. This is especially true if you have longed for this baby, planned for it, and have a healthy child and a caring partner. You may think 'How can I be feeling so bad when this is what I wanted, when it is all so perfect?' You may feel that you have turned out to be a terrible, heartless mother, a selfish and ungrateful partner, and a failure to yourself.

Hormones

It should help you to know that the cause is often a physical one, that it is your hormones acting up, and that these feelings will gradually disappear – they are not with you to stay.

Other factors

* Sheer physical exhaustion after the birth can lay you low. The lack of sleep is a major contribution. Sleep deprivation is a tried and tested form of torture, and if torturers had the free use of a screaming baby, they would really have an easy time breaking their prisoners' spirits!

* Loneliness and isolation at home.

* Anxiety and stress over a colicky or sick baby, and jealousy from an older child or your partner.

Psychological factors

There are also, of course, psychological factors that contribute to depression. Here are some of the common ones, as recognised by doctors:

* Bad experience during labour.

* Problems bonding with the baby.

* Jealousy of partner's interest in the baby.

* Fear of being less sexually attractive now.

* Unresolved sibling rivalry in your own past, which can be transferred to the baby.

Severe depression

Professional help must be sought for severe cases of postnatal depression. The symptoms are more intense than the ones described above, though similar:

* You can't sleep at all, or can't keep yourself awake.

* You think you are cracking up.

* You feel suicidal.

* You are frightened you might do harm to your baby.

* You suffer from a continuous severe undiagnosed pain or other feeling of illness.

* You can't stop crying.

If you have any of these symptoms, you must get help from your doctor. Fortunately these feelings won't last forever, although you can't be expected to be able to 'snap out of it' by force of will. It is pointless to go on dragging yourself around feeling terrible when help is readily available. If you can't face going to a doctor, ask for a home visit. If you feel your doctor is unsympathetic, think of changing to another doctor. Try to confide in someone close to you, or contact one of the organisations listed in *Further Help*.

Treatment

Severe depression is most commonly treated with anti-depressant drugs, which are not addictive (unlike tranquillisers) and you'll only need to take them for a limited period. If your doctor thinks that a hormone imbalance is the cause, you may be prescribed artificial hormones to correct any imbalance caused by pregnancy and giving birth.

Self-Help

If you feel depressed, there are some things you can do to help yourself. Even if you are not feeling depressed, these suggestions are useful for coping with the normal anxiety and stress that beset even the most even-keeled mothers of newborn infants.

Eat a balanced, healthy diet

There is scientific evidence that certain foods can cause or exacerbate depression, as can hypoglycaemia (low blood sugar).

Avoid

* Convenience foods with additives.

* Refined sugar.

* White flour.

* Caffeine (remember it is found in tea as well as coffee and also in colas).

Eat plenty of

* Fresh fruit and vegetables, raw as much as possible.

* Remember to drink a lot of liquids (milk, water or unsweetened fruit juice) especially if breastfeeding.

Avoid going on a stringent diet

You will probably find you lose weight simply by cutting out sugar and fat and living off a varied, healthy diet.

To avoid the sudden mood swings associated with low blood sugar (hypoglycaemia):

* Eat small quantities of food often during the day: don't go too long without eating anything.

* Choose high protein snacks like a glass of milk, nuts or cheese, instead of sweets, biscuits or cakes.

Try to get adequate sleep and rest

Don't automatically go back on the Pill

This can cause or exacerbate depression. You can get advice on alternative methods of birth control from your GP or family planning clinic.

Physical exercise can lift the spirits

Ask anyone who is addicted to aerobics or jogging about the high they get from exercising. Instead of making you feel more tired, physical exercise will magically give you new funds of energy. As an added bonus, it will help to get your figure back!

* Try to find a postnatal keep-fit class where you can bring your baby.

* Ask your partner, relative, friend (or minder) to look after your baby while you go swimming, play tennis, go to dance or exercise classes, or whatever you enjoy. Go swimming with another new mother — you can take turns watching the babies while the other swims.

* If nothing else, go for a brisk walk while pushing the baby in the pram.

Talk it out, get support

Whatever is troubling you, it is always helpful to express it to someone else. Obviously the first person most women turn to is their partner if they have one, but he may not be able to help. For example, he may feel upset at not being able to help you 'snap out of it'; the same may go for your mother or other members of your family, or the people at work, who may not be able to muster the necessary sympathy.

In this case, other new mothers sharing similar experiences and emotions are the best people to talk to.

* Get in touch with the women you met in hospital or at your antenatal class or NCT group. Even if they seemed frighteningly well-adjusted and self-confident you may well find that when you start talking you share many feelings and insecurities. They will also probably be longing for some sympathy and understanding.

* See if your local NCT group runs a postnatal support group, or ask your GP or health visitor.

* Contact organisations listed in *Further Help*, who specialise in putting new mothers suffering from depression or isolation in touch with each other.

Paid help – and unpaid

If you are depressed and feel you simply can't cope, see if you can afford to start employing someone now, before you return to work, to relieve you of the whole burden of looking after your baby. If you are planning to use a childminder, nanny or mother's help when you go back to work, find one now – a childminder may agree to start helping you out on a part-time basis. Even if you can't afford this, you may be able to pay for the occasional babysitter. Maternity nurses can be hired by the week – sometimes even by the day, but they are an expensive option (see Chapter 10: *Nannies, Mother's Helps and Other Help in Your Home*). Alternatively, a friend or relative may offer to help out. Instead of getting someone to help you with the baby, you could consider getting a cleaner to relieve you of the burden of the house and the laundry. Don't hesitate – or be too proud – to accept any offer of help – a neighbour who will do your shopping while she is out anyway, a friend who offers to bring round a ready-cooked casserole.

Other ways to overcome depression

Earlier in this chapter, we covered a number of pieces of advice from other women who have been through it which are particularly relevant if you are suffering from postnatal depression, so they are worth repeating:

* Don't try to be a super housewife and do too much.
* Don't set yourself impossibly high standards in your relationship with your baby or your partner.
* Get out of the house – with baby, and without.
* Make some time for yourself.

Go back to work

One message that came over loud and clear from the questionnaires and interviews for this book was that for many, *depression was cured, or at least helped, by going back to work*. This solution may not be the one for you – after all, the women we consulted are not a representative sample, as we only heard from those who *did* go back to work, not from those who gave it up. But we do suggest you read the next chapter, which examines the decision to go back to work, before you make up your mind about this one way or the other.

CHAPTER 4
Going Back to Work

The Big Decision: Keeping Your Options Open

Nobody – not even you – can predict how you are going to feel about going back to work after your baby is born. You may be convinced that you will wish to return to work after maternity leave, but when it comes to the crunch you find you simply cannot face leaving your baby in someone else's care. Alternatively, you may be sure you would like to stay at home and be a full-time mum, but once you have been at home for a few months, you long to be back at work. All you can do is keep your options open, and not burn any bridges. If you are entitled to maternity leave it is probably best to act as if you plan to go back and not make any final decisions until you have to.

Don't listen to others

In the immediate postnatal period, when you may be feeling insecure in your new role as a mother, worried about your temporary loss of memory and concentration, or even downright depressed, you may be overwhelmed by a flood of well-meaning advice. Try not to be influenced by what others think: this is an important decision that only you can make for yourself.

Try not to listen to your mother telling you that *of course* you will give up your job – after all, a child needs its mother. Nor to your boss confidently predicting that wild horses won't be able to keep you from the excitement of the office. Don't take your friend's word for it when she tells you that because she knows you so well she can assure you that you simply couldn't leave your baby when it comes to it. As for your partner: ideally, whether you go back to work or not should be a joint decision, but even so the ultimate deciding factor should be how *you* feel about it, not whether he thinks you need the extra income, or whether he feels more comfortable with the idea of his child being looked after by its own mother.

As one woman, who works as a senior chartered physiotherapist, wrote:

> I needed to get back to work – not financially – but for my own sanity! I needed stimulation and interaction with other adults – a baby can't do that.

Don't give up your job before you have to

Don't be tempted to give up your job before your maternity leave is up. Give yourself every chance to recover from the birth before you make a final decision about returning to work.

Employers may not like it if you eventually decide to leave your job – after all, it would be more convenient for them to know *now* if you are not coming back, than in six months' time. But unfair as it may seem if you look at it from the employer's point of view, the law is there to protect *you*; to give you the time to make up your own mind. At six weeks, going back to work may seem impossible; at eight weeks, it may start to look possible *and* appealing.

Your decision to go back to work may be temporarily affected by postnatal depression, and you may imagine things are going to be more difficult than they actually turn out to be. For example, you may worry about finding childcare and see it as an insuperable obstacle until you actually take the plunge and start looking:

> I was very unsure about going back to work. I worried I wouldn't be able to find the right nanny. In the end, I forced myself to advertise. My husband and I promised each other that if we couldn't find anyone we both adored I wouldn't go back to work. Of course the second girl we saw was perfect, and from then on my doubts disappeared.

Deciding not to return

The basic statutory maternity pay is yours to keep whether or not you return to work. But if your employer has paid you more than the legal minimum you may find you are obliged to pay back the additional pay if you decide not to return to work. You should check what it says in your firm's maternity agreement, or in your letter of employment. If you do have to repay this money, you will be able to reclaim the tax on it – though not the National Insurance. Contrast this with sick pay – which a man can receive, but doesn't have to give back if he doesn't return to his job! The Equal Opportunities Commission says it is questionable whether this is lawful under the Sex Discrimination Act. If you want to fight this, you should get in touch with them. If you are not sure about going back, it is probably wiser to avoid spending too much of this money during the time you are at home.

If in doubt, give work a try

A BBC local radio reporter who wrote to us said emphatically:

> I feel strongly that women should at least try working and motherhood if they have the slightest inclination towards it. If they don't like it they can easily give it up. It's not quite so easy to start up again once you've had that break. People say you can't have your cake and eat it, I disagree!

Things usually look very different when you are back at work, once you have found a suitable form of childcare and become used to leaving your baby. Tell *yourself* (not your employer!) that you are only going back for a few months to see how it works out, but that you can always give in your notice if it all seems too much. You may find that once you are back at work you want to stay. On the other hand, you may want to quit – but at least you'll be able to tell yourself you tried it.

A part-time farm secretary, and mother of a four-year-old, wrote:

> The positive thing about returning to work was that it made me get organised, get a routine going, get fit, get some make-up on again and go out into the world. I'm sure that without my job my postnatal depression would have been so bad I would have needed psychiatric help.

Financial Considerations

'I knew I had to go back to work as we had used up most of our savings in the eight months I was unpaid,' one teacher wrote to us.

If you are your family's main breadwinner, or if you and your partner rely on the second income to make ends meet, you probably do not have a choice about going back to work. Whatever anyone else says about suffering some financial hardship in order to stay with your child, if you are reading this book you probably do not relish the challenge of bringing up a child on a subsistence-level income, or on social security, if you have the choice.

But if money is the *only* reason you are thinking of returning to work, do think very carefully. As Elizabeth Squires, who is a personnel manager, wrote:

> **An observation I have made in my job is that women who return to work only for the money can be made very miserable and resent having to do it. I think this makes them feel guilty and therefore they have the worst of both worlds. Whereas those who enjoy their jobs (whether or not they need the money) at least have another reason for carrying them over a bad time.**

Calculating the costs

If financial considerations play a large part in your decision to return to work, it is worthwhile sitting down and examining your family budget with and without your salary.

The cost of working with a small child at home is *very* high: do not imagine that your wage packet will cover the extras it did before you had a child. Most of the women we heard from with pre-school children spent between one quarter to one half of their weekly take-home pay on childcare: some spent considerably more (one mother even paid her nanny more than she was earning herself – but presumably she and her husband could afford this). To see whether it is worth your while working on a purely financial basis, add up all the extra expenses involved in going out to work, for example:

* Cost of childcare (childminder, nanny, nursery).
* Your fares to and from work, plus any fares to and from childminder or nursery.
* Your lunches.
* The cost of buying clothes for work that you

wouldn't wear at home (for example, business suit, tights, and so on, if you work in an office).

* The extra cost of convenience foods for the baby and your family (if you would puree your own vegetables for baby, and cook cheap cuts for the rest of you if you stayed at home).

* The cost of disposable nappies (if you would wash terry ones if you stayed at home).

* The cost of a cleaner.

* Extra work-related expenses, like office whip-rounds for birthdays, engagements, people leaving; buying rounds at the pub, union subscription, and so on.

Compare the total with your weekly take-home pay, and see what is actually left over.

Keeping your financial independence

Many women who have been used to earning their own money prefer to go back to work to retain their financial independence. Even if in theory all your money is shared, it can be very hard to have to ask your husband for money. Two women we talked to thought this was very important.

* I have enjoyed having my own money in my own bank account again. I hated having to ask for cash when I was at home and broke, as I have never had to be dependent on another for money before, for day-to-day shopping etc.

* If I didn't earn any money myself, I would find it very difficult to spend any money at all, because my husband doesn't earn enough. Not that I'm particularly extravagant, but I would feel neurotic and guilty about spending any money on myself!

Your Happiness and Self-confidence

More than 95 per cent of the women who contributed to this book said that they would work even if they did not have to (although many did say they would prefer to work fewer hours, given the choice). Of course there are many women who love staying at home being a full-time mother and housewife, and some of our correspondents had stayed at home when their children were small, and did not regret having done so. But most of the women we heard from felt they were happier back at work:

> * Because I had worked full-time for many years I had a real shock when the baby was born. I panicked, felt trapped at home and couldn't wait to get back to a situation I could cope with! I feel that my return to work (part-time) has really helped me adjust to my baby better by providing me with a link to a secure feeling of friendship and familiarity with my friends at work. In fact I feel better in many ways. I really do think that part-time working is the best thing for me as a new mother.

> * Going back to work actually helped with my postnatal depression. I felt more like an individual person – I felt like 'me' again. I have something to talk about – not just nappies, bottles, teething etc.

Here are some reasons why you might feel happier back at work:

* Interest in your job; job satisfaction; intellectual stimulation.

* Communicating with other adults; friendship with co-workers.

* Self-confidence and self-esteem brought by paid

employment (unfortunately, our society sets very little store by the unpaid work of a housewife/mother).

* Financial independence; fewer worries about money.

* Avoiding the loneliness and isolation of being trapped at home with a small child; the boredom of days filled with domestic chores.

* Coping better with problems at home by being able to distance yourself from them – for example, if your baby cries a lot or is difficult in some other way.

* Structuring your day: it is one of life's paradoxes that the more you have to fit into a day, the more you are in control of it, and the more you seem to be able to achieve in the time available.

* More equal relationship with your partner.

As the mother of a six-month-old baby, a partner in a small PR agency wrote:

> Having been so fit during my pregnancy I didn't appreciate how much the birth, then attending to a newborn baby, night feeds and breastfeeding would take out of me. I found work and baby a struggle physically at first although work provided almost a relief from the strain of being a mum.

The Effect on Your Career

You may have a job you enjoy. You may have trained long and hard to qualify for your present position. You may be on a particular career ladder. In these days of high unemployment, you may feel you are lucky to have a job at all.

In these circumstances, there is much to be said for keeping your job and returning to work after maternity leave. Even though the maternity legislation's protective powers have been eroded in recent years, it is still there to protect your career, because it recognises that working women having children are heavily penalised in our society. It can be hard to find a new job later if you postpone your decision to go back to work and give up your present job for the time being.

Here are some of the things you will have to fight if you do give up your present job but still plan to pursue your career at some later date:

* *Prejudice against mothers*. Many employers, whether consciously or not, are prejudiced against employing women with small children because they are suspected of being unreliable, unfair as it is. At least if you continue in the job you had before, you'll have a chance to prove yourself.

* *Your self-confidence*. The 'I-am-just-a-housewife' syndrome can start gnawing at your confidence in your own professional competence from the first few months of maternity leave; it can get worse the longer you stay away from the working environment. It is amazing how fast an efficient career woman can turn into a domestic nobody in her own eyes – someone else's mother, someone else's wife – when she stops proving to herself as well as to others that she has professional or organisational abilities, a brain or a specialised skill. Persuading someone to give you a job, or even bringing yourself to apply for one, when the old self-confidence has been eroded, is not easy, as many child-gap career women have found to their cost.

* *Losing your value in the job market*. If you work in a field where in order to be effective or competitive you

need to keep up with the latest developments, (new research or new skills, making new contacts), staying away from work for any length of time is going to damage your value as an employee and your career prospects, no matter how long you have trained or how experienced and qualified you are.

* *Being forgotten.* It is also important to keep in touch on a personal level with your colleagues and contacts: in many businesses and professions, out of sight is out of mind. Unless you make an effort to stay in touch, even if you have left work with a good reputation and high esteem, when you re-enter the job market after an absence you can find that your colleagues and former employers have forgotten you.

However, many women do return to work successfully after a career gap, even though it is harder. See the chapter on *Finding Work*.

The mother of a two-year-old, who works as a supply teacher, wrote:

> Going back to work made me feel a person again, with self-respect and my own identity. I became introverted while at home, which is not me at all.

Timing Your Return to Work

Within the framework of the time you are entitled to take off for maternity leave, you may wonder when it is best to return to work – for your baby, for yourself, and for your career. Some mothers naturally want to spend the maximum amount of time they are entitled to at home with their baby, money permitting. But the end of your maternity leave period is not necessarily the best time. As one mother of two said:

In general I have found that leaving a small baby is much easier than an older child. My theory is that if you return to work before the baby is much older than three months they are used to more than one person looking after them and accept it. If you leave it for six months or more they begin to recognise you as a person and expect your continued presence.

Best time for baby

A good solution is to try to achieve a balance between spending enough time with the baby to establish a good relationship and routine, and returning to work while your baby is still young enough to be adaptable.

A very young baby needs to be changed, fed, played with, rocked and cuddled – but it does not much matter who does it. If the baby becomes used to being looked after by more than one person at this stage, then it will continue to be acceptable later. The end of statutory maternity leave, however, often coincides with the stage at which a baby starts to become very attached to you. It can be difficult to leave your baby for the first time if you have been the only constant caregiver and sole companion up to then.

If your baby is at the stage of suffering 'separation anxiety', any departure of yours may be greeted by screams of distress, even if you have just moved out of sight in the same room. This has led experts, such as T. Berry Brazelton, to state that a baby should start to be left by the mother either at four months, or else not before about eighteen months, when this separation anxiety is supposed to subside. But the experts don't seem to be able to agree between themselves on what separation anxiety is exactly – or to pinpoint when it occurs. Nor can it be shown that just because a baby protests when the mother leaves the room that any real psychological or emotional damage is done.

Any childcarer will tell you that each baby is different:

they do not go through the same stages at the same time, so it is impossible to anticipate the precise moment your baby will go through this phase.

Most babies are adaptable. Attached as they are to the familiar, any new situation will, given time, become familiar and hence acceptable to your baby, as long as the new situation is reassuringly consistent, and your own attitude to it is consistent, too.

As Penelope Leach writes in *Babyhood* (Penguin):

> There is a considerable amount of research which shows that children in this age group [six to twelve months], who protest bitterly if their mothers leave them either alone or with a stranger, remain calm, or protest only minimally, if they are left with a known (and presumably liked) person. Data also show that such separations cause least distress if they take place in completely familiar surroundings.

Best time for you

The best advice is to be flexible about when you wish to return to work.

You may be depressed and bored at home with your baby: do consider in this case returning to work before your maternity leave is up, if your employer agrees. On the other hand, you may have promised your employer to be back after three months, but find you are not yet ready to leave your child in someone else's care. Do not ignore these feelings, and adjust your plans accordingly.

Whatever you decide, leaving your baby for the first time may be very hard, but it will soon get easier. Some mothers of small babies said they physically missed their infants when they left them, especially if breastfeeding. Rosemary Kirk, for instance, a part-time social work assistant from Northern Ireland, who has four children, found leaving the youngest as hard as ever, but soon got over it:

I missed him while at work for about two weeks, and every time I thought about him my boobs leaked, so I just had to keep changing the breastpads. But it was okay after two or three weeks. I realised one day that I had been at work for five hours and had not even thought about him. So I've been fine since.

And a part-time secretary from Lincolnshire, writes:

Looking back now it was a horrendous thing to do, leaving a nine-week-old baby with a minder. However, at the time it didn't seem so. I was quite happy with my two minders and as the baby slept most of the time, it didn't matter who was around to feed, change nappies etc., as long as someone was. I missed him, but it was a physical thing. I used to rush off at the end of the morning to give him a cuddle and then spend all afternoon holding him.

For many mothers leaving their children becomes progressively easier, particularly when they are assured of their children's happiness with the arrangements. But some mothers of older babies, leaving their child for the first time, are more affected by their child's emotional distress, and may miss their company more. A woman from Northern Ireland told us she finds it harder to leave her eldest child than her baby, because 'she can now do things I'd enjoy helping her with – jigsaws, playdoh, etc – she chats incessantly and I find her a great wee pal.'

Best time for your career

The advantage of going back to work fairly quickly after maternity leave is that you will have had less time to lose the thread of what was going on at work, less time to lose confidence in yourself, and there will have been less time for your colleagues to feel resentful about your absence. But you may be doing neither your career nor yourself any good if you have not sufficiently recovered from the physical and emotional upheaval of the birth.

If you are suffering from sleepless nights you may be a lot less effective – even a downright liability – at work, and you can't expect a lot of sympathy and consideration from your colleagues. In this case, it may be better to postpone returning to work until you are more rested and more your old self. As a teacher from Exeter reports:

> I was very surprised that no allowances were made for me on days when I had had only three hours' sleep or less. I was still expected to give as much extra out-of-school time for meetings, lunchtimes, etc., as before. I appreciated that I would still have to do a proper job, but it still surprised me that no one seemed to appreciate that I had other commitments now.

Exploring the Options: Flexible Working

If there is any flexibility in your work you may be able to arrange to go back part time at the beginning, slowly working your way back to normal hours.

This will give you and your baby a chance to become used to the new routine and will gain you some time in which to overcome any teething problems in your childcare arrangements.

Many women think about switching permanently from full-time to part-time work once they have had a child. Certain employers are very good about this – some companies even have it written into their maternity agreement that you may be offered the option of an alternative part-time job, or job-share, within the firm.

But this is not a given right, and many employers are unable, or unwilling, to offer this option – or regret it when they do.

Phyl Driffield, who worked full time as a deputy ward sister in York, negotiated an agreement that she could go back part time when her baby was born – only she didn't have this agreement in writing.

> Following a change in senior management, I was refused this just before returning to work. The man who refused to let me work part time did me a big favour, as I realised on returning full time that I could cope (despite everyone telling me otherwise). I found that my daughter was just as happy, I was better off financially, I had returned to a career that I loved, and eventually got promotion that I would never have got otherwise.

Part-time work may sound like the ideal solution when you are a mother. It certainly has the obvious advantage of giving you more time to spend with your child – but it also has drawbacks, in terms of pay, promotion and employment rights, which are explored in Chapter 16.

There are of course other ways of cutting down your hours, or having more flexibility and freedom during the day. It may be possible to arrange a job-share with another mother, or for you to go on to flexitime. If you have a special skill which you can carry on from home, consider going freelance or doing temporary work where you will at least be able to avoid being committed to working when it is not convenient for you (for example, when your child is ill). These alternative options are discussed in more detail in Chapter 16.

What About my Child?

Most working mothers will experience some anxiety about having to leave their baby, and about finding the right kind of childcare. You may feel guilty wanting to leave the baby (or having to) to go back to work. Perhaps others will make you feel worse by their disapproval. You may even feel guilty about not feeling guilty!

Again, Phyl Driffield's experience is common:

I felt *so* guilty that I made a point of telling everyone that I *didn't* feel guilty about working, before they could say anything. I find it amusing (and feel angry) to think back to my feelings of confusion then. If only *one* person had said to me, 'You'll enjoy work and your daughter will be fine' I would have felt better. Only nobody did.

If this sounds like you – and it is a rare mother who feels no guilt at all – read and believe the chapter on guilt. Show it (or quote from it) to family, friends or colleagues who may be making you feel even worse, or more unsure about your decision to return to work.

Finding the right childcare

The most important thing for your baby, as well as for your own peace of mind, is to find a childcare arrangement you feel happy with – someone to replace you during your working hours whom you like and feel you can trust. Read the chapter on *Childcare for the Under-fives* for an assessment of the different options, and also the detailed chapters on each method of childcare. Start looking for a childminder, nanny or nursery as soon as you can, and don't be embarrassed to be choosy: only the best is good enough for your child. Don't leave it too late: you don't want to have to make any hasty decisions because your maternity leave has run out.

Arranging for a gradual handover to your childcarer

There are two factors, pinpointed by the experts, which will make it easier for your baby or toddler to be parted from you on a regular basis:

* Being left with a familar and liked person.

* Being left in a familar place.

Many mothers confirmed the importance of a running-in period for childcare arrangements. For example, a doctor from Belfast wrote:

> I felt it was important to have childminding arrangements going well in advance of returning to work. Domestic anxiety must be reduced to a minimum. The first day I went out on my own and left baby with Nanny No.1 I felt a bit sniffly but once I got used to the freedom I didn't mind.

And a teacher from Elgin in Scotland, who really hated leaving her child, also felt a gradual handover with the childminder helped:

> Many a night I cried myself to sleep at the thought of leaving Lisa. Grandparents do not live nearby so she had never been left for any length of time with anyone else. The earlier you can find a suitable childminder the better. It puts your mind at rest and means child and minder can get to know each other before the awful day of parting.

Handing over to a childminder or nursery

The minder or nursery may let you bring your baby in occasionally for an hour or so in the weeks before you are due to return to work, and let you stay with your child at the beginning. This will allow your child to become accustomed to the new environment, and to explore it and the people around from the safety of your knee, reassured by the friendly atmosphere between the new caregiver and yourself. This also gives you the opportunity to observe the daily routine in more detail than at your initial interview, so that you will have a sense of what your child's day will be like. You will also have a chance to see anything you don't like, which may give you second thoughts about the arrangement before it's too late to change!

Children in a clingy phase can be left for a short period –

an hour or two, so that they can grow accustomed to being left – and be reassured by the fact that you come back soon. Finally, you can leave your child for a whole morning or afternoon.

Often it is harder for you than for your baby. It is worth taking a tip from another teacher who lives in Scotland. She told us how she coped with leaving her baby with a minder for the first time:

> I chose a day before I had to return to work. My husband took a day off work too and we went out to lunch to a restaurant we had always wanted to visit. It was much easier than sitting at home worrying about how she was getting on.

Handing over to a mother's help or nanny in your home

If you are leaving your baby with a nanny in your own home, at least there is not a new environment for your child to get used to. But try to arrange for the nanny to start work a week or so before your return to work, so that you have a chance to show her your baby's daily routine and the way you like things done around the house. It will also give you a chance to show her the neighbourhood and introduce her to the neighbours; all this time your child is getting used to her.

During that week you may wish to take the nanny around with you for the first few days, then leave her alone with the baby for short periods to see how she copes and how the baby reacts. In the end you can leave her for a whole morning or afternoon while you treat yourself to an unencumbered expedition to the hairdresser's or to the shops, or even a social visit to your place of work to help you get used to the idea of starting work again.

Leaving your child

The first time is the hardest. Many mothers never find it easy – especially if the baby cries when left, or the child is not well. Sometimes it is hard even if your child is very happy and looking forward to an interesting day, which you would like to share, but can't! However, as soon as you have gone a sad baby or a screeching toddler almost invariably cheers up.

In the vast majority of cases, it is the moment of parting itself that is upsetting for your child, not your absence after that. Then, when you return, your child may recall the morning's indignation at being left, and start crying again: but this does not mean that he or she has been miserable all day.

A baby is too young to be deliberately manipulative, but even so we hear over and over again from childminders, nannies or nursery workers that howling babies are soon amiably sucking their fists after mother has departed, and the inconsolable toddler is found playing happily three minutes later, all distress forgotten.

Their mothers, on the other hand, can be disturbed and distracted with guilt and worry all day! As one London civil servant told us:

> I felt terrible. Of course what babies do is scream the minute you leave them, but as soon as you are gone they shut up. But when you get back in the evening they start crying again, so you feel dreadful. I kept ringing up the minder when I first went back to work. She was obviously quite used to neurotic mums like me. She kept telling me, 'She's all right now!'

And as Elizabeth Squires writes:

> My eldest daughter was a model of a working mother's daughter – never objected to my leaving her. Number two, however, can cry and look pathetic when I leave,

particularly when I'm in a tearing hurry. Howls and sobs at my heartlessness stop, I am assured, the moment I shut the door!

Here are some tips if your baby or toddler is upset when you leave:

* Develop a handover routine, and stick to it every morning. Build in some extra time so that you don't have to shove your child over the threshold and rush away. Go in and spend a little time settling your child with a book or a toy or another child.

* Make sure your child has a favourite toy, or some other familiar object for security. Leave something as a reminder of you during the day: give your baby a hankie sprayed with your scent; a toddler can be given your special pen and asked to keep it safe for you until you return later.

* If your child is old enough, explain that you are going to work, and what that means: how you get there (by bus for instance) and what you do there (talking on the telephone for example) so that your absence is not a frightening mystery. Promise a time that you will be back – so long as you are sure you can stick to it.

* Don't go in for protracted goodbyes: when the time has come to leave, cuddle and kiss your child, say goodbye firmly, then close your ears to any screams and go. You can make the parting more upsetting for both of you by dragging it out, coming back for another hug, trying to comfort your child. It is a mistake to let children feel that they have the power to delay your departure by making a fuss, or even to prevent you from going at all. The sooner you leave, the less time your child will have to get really worked up.

We have not heard of any children who remained inconsolable all day after their mothers had left, but should you be in this unusual situation you may be wise to reassess your childcare arrangement: perhaps there is something wrong that needs sorting out.

Of course, leaving your child can sometimes be worse for you than for your child, but Marie Burke, a full-time teacher with three children, who lives in Manchester, found it became progressively easier:

> **The worst time of my life as a working mother was when my first child was a baby. I cried and cried at the prospect of returning to work. Michael survived very well, so when it came to leaving William I felt a lot more confident about the situation. By the time I returned to work after Kim's birth I had very few qualms about leaving her. My main regrets were concerned with what I was missing.**

However, when a teacher from Merseyside had to part with her three-year-old and seven-month-old baby after her second maternity leave, she found it as difficult as the first time:

> **I was absolutely fine until I had to 'hand the baby over'. My daughter had run in ahead glad to be back with the childminder. I stood outside the house holding the baby and sobbing – it was as if by crossing the threshold I was leaving the children forever. However I did cross the threshold, and the next day and the next were much better.**

There were also quite a number of mothers who reported a sense of relief and freedom when they left their babies for the first time:

It was like a weight had lifted from my shoulders. I felt so free and light leaving the house without all the paraphernalia of stroller, nappies, change of clothes, bottles – being able to sit and read on the bus without being interrupted, shopping in my lunchtime without having to worry about how much I could carry plus managing the baby, etc.

Losing your child's love?

As soon as you have found a childminder, nanny, nursery or other form of childcare you are happy with, your guilt feelings will lessen. Once you have returned to work and your child is happy and thriving you will feel even better.

But working mothers have another fear. That is, that their children will become increasingly attached to their carer, and that they will lose their place as the most loved person in their children's world.

A number of the mothers in our sample told us that they soon realised this fear was unfounded:

At first I felt terrible. I felt jealous that somebody else was looking after my baby, until I realised that nothing and nobody can replace a mother, and even though he didn't cry when I left him, he was, and still is, always pleased when I pick him up.

Slotting Back into Work

It is lovely to return to work after maternity leave and find you are welcomed back with open arms, like this educational psychologist from Northern Ireland:

I enjoyed being back at work. I found that I had been missed. I found that being a mother made my advice much more acceptable to other mothers – it also gave me a lot of self-confidence.

However, it is as well to be prepared for the fact that you may find you no longer feel the same about your job, as having a baby can change your perspective. Also, be prepared for the fact that not all fellow workers and employers are going to be cheerful, kind and understanding about your having been away for such a long time. As the head of a department in a publishing company says,

> You get this lovely generous maternity leave, but it's not as simple as that. I knew I had to tread warily when I got back to work. For instance in my case, my deputy had taken over in my absence, and then suddenly she's being told to go back to her place. And then there were the people who didn't understand about the agony and hard work of having a baby and looking after it, who'd be thinking, 'Well, here she is, having buggered off for five months, sitting around at home with nothing to do on full pay, now she decides to swan back . . . ' You've got to come back and deal with that sort of attitude. And my brain was scrambled from exhaustion. But it was alleviated by the fact that I was in a place where I could have a conversation, where I could deal with things I was used to, where I could get some intellectual stimulation, where I wasn't just exhausted from the sheer physical grind.

It can come as a shock to find that your fellow workers are not sympathetic to you in your tender emotional and physical state, and that other women can be downright hostile, as a Yorkshire woman who works in a doctor's surgery describes:

> Some of the girls I work with were awful at first, especially the girl who took over from me when I was on maternity leave. She felt I shouldn't have returned to work and taken my own job back from her. It took a few weeks to settle back in again. None of the girls have or want children, and nearly every day there were snide remarks about people leaving their children and how they would rather have animals than children. This

went on until the day I erupted and lost my temper. Everything has been okay since.

If this attitude shocks you, imagine how you would feel if you were asked to do a more senior job for six or seven months, often at the same salary as you were earning before, or to do someone else's job as well as your own without being paid for it, and then being unceremoniously shoved back into your old job when that someone came back from maternity leave. It is undeniable that there are unfairnesses associated with the maternity leave system, and if you find yourself in this position, try to be as tactful and considerate as possible – and show fellow workers who have had to step in for you that you appreciate it.

Not all co-workers are unsupportive, however, as reported by a nursery officer from Preston:

> My line manager (a spinster) wasn't very willing when I first went back to work and asked for half a day off each day for two weeks just while Lauren was settling in. She let me take the time because I put a good case forward and my colleagues backed me.

Also bear in mind that although some fellow workers may be passionately interested in your baby, many people at work are bored or hostile when it comes to talk about babies and children.

Many of the mothers who contributed to this book were sensitive to this, and made it a rule not to bring up the subject of their child at work unless they were specifically asked. As Kristine Band writes:

> Don't ram your baby down your colleagues' or clients' throats! Anyone who is anti working mums is waiting for you to put a foot wrong.

CHAPTER 5
Breastfeeding and Working

If you have bottlefed from the start, or have been looking forward to returning to work so that you can give up breastfeeding, this chapter is not for you.

But if you enjoy the closeness and convenience of breastfeeding, the return to work may come before you are ready to wean your baby off the breast, or before your doctor thinks the baby has had maximum benefit from breastfeeding. Many mothers are concerned to carry on breastfeeding to continue protecting the baby with their own antibodies. And some babies are allergic to cow's formula (although there are substitutes, such as soya milk). If you come from a family with allergies such as eczema and asthma your doctor may well advise you to keep your baby exclusively on breast milk for as long as possible.

Most of the childcare and breastfeeding books imply that working and breastfeeding are not compatible. It is the experience of many working breastfeeding mothers that they are wrong. A number of women who wrote to us continued to breastfeed for quite a while after returning to work – one woman went back to work when her child was fourteen weeks old, and continued to breastfeed until he was nearly seventeen months.

If your milk supply is well established there is no reason why you should not continue to breastfeed your child, fully or partially, for as long as you wish. It partly depends on how old your baby is when you return to work. If, as is most common, it is after three months and you have been breastfeeding successfully, it is very unlikely that your milk supply will dry up, even though you are no longer feeding on demand.

One of the reasons given for not continuing to breastfeed on returning to work is that after an exhausting day at work you will not want to breastfeed at night. But there are few new parents who can say they do not suffer from broken nights whether or not the mother is breastfeeding. You may very well find that it is much less tiring to take the sleepy, just-awoken baby into bed with you for the late night or early morning feed, and perhaps doze off together while the baby is feeding. This can be better than the palaver of getting out of bed and into a cold kitchen, preparing a bottle, heating it and then feeding the now unhappy and impatient baby! One mother wrote to us:

> My main problem was being so tired, especially as the baby wakened at night so much. I ended up bringing him into bed to sleep and he fed himself and was much more settled.

Another advantage of continuing to breastfeed is that you don't have the hassle and expense of sterilising and preparing feeds. However, if you express your milk, or the baby will be partially bottlefed by your childcarer, you are obviously still going to have to sterilise bottles (and pump).

The trouble with most breastfeeding books, as well as the advice meted out by hospital and community midwives, is that they make it sound so complicated. For most women, breastfeeding is a natural ability, and with faith in yourself and your baby (as well as a dose of commonsense), you can usually find a way of continuing to breastfeed after you return to work.

When I was debating whether or not to return to work a couple of months after my baby's birth, one of the things that worried me most was that I might have to wean my baby early. People told me my milk would dry up, and that it would be terribly exhausting. In the end, I thought I'd give it a go, and it all went very easily. I went back to work when my baby was three months old, and at the beginning I fed the baby twice in the morning before leaving the house (at about 6.00a.m. and again just before leaving at 9.00a.m.). I then expressed my milk with a handpump at the office (I was lucky to have my own office so that I could just close the door and pump while reading correspondence or making business phone calls!) – twice to start with – and brought the milk home for my nanny to use the next day. She would usually have to give him one bottle of my milk and one or two bottles of formula during the day. I would get home at 6.00p.m. and kick my shoes off and feed the baby again immediately, while enjoying cuddling him and catching up with my nanny's news, and then I'd feed him again at about 9.00p.m., and once at midnight before going to sleep. Soon, however, he started needing fewer feeds, but I continued to pump once a day at work until he was six months old as I wasn't totally confident that I wouldn't dry up if I didn't do this. Weekends I tried to breastfeed on demand as much as possible. When he was about six months, I thought the hell with it and stopped expressing. I continued breastfeeding him in the mornings and evenings without any problem until he was about eleven months old, when I was starting to think that it was about time to stop. An upcoming week's separation (I had to go on a business trip) prompted me to wean him then.

There are several different ways of continuing to breastfeed while working full time (we assume that part-time workers can arrange their schedule to fit in with their breastfeeding times – if not, one of the options below will apply):

Full Breastfeeding

Baby comes to you

It may be possible to arrange for your baby to be brought to you at your place of work when a feed is due – this obviously requires a co-operative childcarer, plus an understanding employer and fellow workers, and a comfortable, private place to use for breastfeeding. One woman who wrote to us is a musician, and while she was breastfeeding, her baby and minder travelled with her so that she could feed when necessary 'anywhere, preferably quiet and not too public!'

You go to baby

If your place of work is near to your home or childminder – or if you are so fortunate as to have a creche at work – you may be able to use your tea and/or lunch break to feed your baby. A GP who wrote to us told us she expressed milk for some feeds, and visited her childminder in her lunch hour for a midday feed.

Expressing

You can express enough milk during the day and night to provide your child's caretaker with enough bottles of milk for the next day's feeds while you are out. You can either express at home at the end of each feed, and/or at work. Again, this requires a private place at your place of work to express – and preferably the use of a fridge to store the milk.

Partial Breastfeeding

If you are confident of your milk supply this is a good

option. Most of the full-time working mothers who wrote to us chose this way. Some of the mothers with older babies arranged for them to eat solids and drink juice when they were not around to breastfeed. Others let their babies be given a bottle of formula. If you have no objections on moral or medical grounds to feeding your baby partially on cow's milk formula, you may consider breastfeeding your baby mornings, evenings and weekends, and bottle feeding with formula while you are not there.

Some mothers compromise by partially breastfeeding, and expressing some milk for bottles, allowing their own milk to be supplemented with formula for additional feeds.

Expressing

There are several reasons for learning to express your milk:

* You are determined not to feed your baby anything except breastmilk.

* Your baby is allergic to formula.

* You are concerned about keeping up your milk supply (breastfeeding works on supply and demand, so if your breasts are not stimulated enough they may not produce enough milk for your baby at the times you are able to breastfeed).

Expressing milk for your baby's needs while you are out

This depends on how many feeds your baby needs during the day (which in turn depends on how old the baby is). If your baby is less than five or six months old, you'll probably need to express at least two feeds-worth of breastmilk per day. This will mean pumping once or twice at work, and may also mean pumping after your baby finishes feeding in the mornings and evenings. Some women find they have most milk at the early morning feed, so express to empty their breasts after the baby has had enough. It is also a good idea to lay in a small reserve supply in a freezer for emergencies, and you may wish to start collecting this a week or so before you return to work.

Keeping up your milk supply

The law of milk supply is one of supply and demand: the more you stimulate your breasts, (that is, the more your baby demands from them) the more milk you produce. Many women find that their milk supply will adapt itself to a working schedule: they will produce plenty of milk at the times they usually breastfeed their baby (for example morning, evening and night) without suffering from uncomfortably full breasts during the day, so long as daytime feeds are phased out over a number of days. Many working mothers continue this kind of partial breastfeeding until their children are toddlers. However, if you fear that by cutting out the day-time feeds you risk losing your milk supply, it is a good idea to express during the day at work, to make sure your breasts have extra stimulation.

The best stimulation for your breasts is your baby suckling; the next best is an electric pump; the third most effective method is a hand pump. Hand expressing is the least effective method of stimulating your milk supply.

So first of all try to spend as much time as possible while at home with the baby at the breast. This will be the best way to remind your breasts to produce plenty of milk at the right time of day. It may have the added benefit of making you feel better about leaving your baby while you are at work, as you know that you are in frequent skin-to-skin contact with the baby when you are together.

Second, express your milk, preferably with a hand or

electric pump, during your lunch hour and/or tea break when at work. How often you do it depends on how much extra stimulation you feel your breasts need to keep your milk going. You may find that pumping once, in your lunch break, is sufficient.

If you are seriously worried that your milk supply is drying up, despite plenty of breastfeeding at home and expressing at work, there are several easy ways to restimulate your supply. For full details you should read one of the specialised breastfeeding books listed in *Further Help*.

One of the best ideas is to take twenty-four hours, or a whole weekend, and spend it in bed with your baby, devoting the whole time to restimulating your milk supply. This will involve suckling on demand, at least every two hours, drinking plenty of liquids, and resting and playing with your baby in between, while your partner waits on you as if you were an invalid. What could be a nicer way to spend a weekend after a hard week's work?

If none of these methods work, other ways should be discussed with a La Leche League or NCT counsellor. (See *Further Help*)

Breast pumps and hand expressing

There are three ways of expressing your milk:

Hand expressing

This is the most convenient way if you just want to relieve over-full breasts, because it requires no special equipment. On the other hand, it has the disadvantage of not being the most efficient way of stimulating your breasts to produce more milk. Perhaps you were shown how to hand express at the hospital, otherwise you could ask your health visitor to show you, or look at one of the specialist books.

Basically, the technique involves cupping your breast in

your hand, thumb on top, and rhythmically squeezing around the edge of the coloured areola of the nipple, while simultaneously pushing your fingers back into the chest. Work right around the areola, and alternate breasts every few minutes.

The trick is to locate the milk producing glands (like a circle of small bumps) which are situated around the edge of the nipple areola. Some women find it useful to stimulate the let-down reflex with a warm wet flannel. If you want to collect the milk, you need a sterile, wide-necked receptacle (preferably plastic) that you can lean over, from which you can decant the milk into a sterilised bottle. You should, of course, wash your hands before you start.

Hand pumps

There is a variety of these on the market, which are inexpensive and available in most chemists. The cheapest type is the rubber bulb pump, which looks a bit like an old-fashioned car horn, but is probably the least effective and hygienic. The most popular type is the piston or syringe type of pump. It works by creating a suction vacuum around the breast: you press one cylinder against your breast, while with the other hand you pump the interlocking cylinder up and down. Most mothers who have used one find it very effective. Some of these pumps have receptacles that can be used as bottles, but if you are expressing milk to take home for your baby it is more practical to decant your milk from the sterile pump into a sterile bottle, to enable you to clean the whole pump and use it again.

Electric pumps

These are the most efficient for emptying and stimulating your breasts. However, they are also extremely expensive and quite heavy and bulky. If you find you are able to express using one of the other methods outlined above, it is questionable whether you'll find an electric pump necessary. However, if you can afford it, feel it is worth the expense, and you have somewhere to keep it at work, you may wish to investigate buying one.

Find out how to get one through your hospital or health visitor, your local NCT branch, or La Leche League representative. The advantages of an electric pump include efficiency, speed – and it leaves at least one hand free to do other things!

If you work in a large organisation that employs a large proportion of women and which shows benevolent concern for its employees, you may wish to suggest that the firm purchases an electric pump for the use of breastfeeding employees. Talk to your trade union or staff representative about this.

It is also possible to rent or hire these pumps – but again this is an expensive option. However, you may have reasons to use this measure short-term (such as wishing to restimulate your milk supply). Your local hospital, NCT or La Leche League may even have a pump that can be lent free of charge to mothers who can't afford to pay.

Pumping methods: the pros and cons

	PROS	CONS
Hand expressing	No special equipment; nil expense.	Not very effective for stimulating milk supply. You need both hands and collecting milk may prove tricky.

	PROS	CONS
Hand pumps	Inexpensive, portable and discreet. Usually efficient for stimulating milk and collecting expressed milk.	Need both hands, can get tiring. Pump needs cleaning and sterilising.
Electric pumps	Efficient at stimulating milk and produces quick results – leaves one hand free.	Very expensive; not easily transported. Takes up room, needs electric outlet, cleansing and sterilising.

Hygiene

If you express your milk to feed to your baby in bottles, you'll have to follow the same basic rules of hygiene as mothers of bottle-fed babies. Don't be put off or intimidated by overly technical instructions from hospitals, midwives or books – commonsense should prevail. Obviously, breastmilk will go off as easily as cow's milk, and if you allow it to spoil or collect bacteria it may make your baby ill. But there's no need for these precautions to be complicated.

When I went to the lecture about feeding at the antenatal classes at the hospital, the nursing sister made a big fuss of showing us an elaborate sterilising and bottle-preparing routine, after first having scrubbed up with clinical precision. I was intending to breastfeed, but I thought I'd like to be able to give a bottle as well, especially as I planned to return to work quite quickly. When I put my hand up and asked whether she had any advice for when I happened to be away from home with the baby without access to a steriliser (which after all was only a plastic container with a lid, for water and sterilising tablets!) expecting her to suggest improvising a steriliser or boiling the bottles in water, she turned on me fiercely, asking me how soon I expected to go away with my baby, as if this was an unforgivable, unmaternal thought. She added that there was no alternative to the half-hour sterilising routine she had described, and made it quite clear that if we didn't follow it (and presumably if we didn't lock ourselves up with our babies in our own homes for the first year) we would be bound to give our babies gastroenteritis, or worse!

All you really need to remember is to keep hands, pump and bottles clean, and to store the milk correctly.

Sterilising pump and bottles

A steriliser, in which you use sterilising tablets or solution is probably the easiest method of sterilising. You use this after thoroughly cleaning your equipment (it is necessary to use a bottle brush, as breastmilk really sticks to the sides of the bottle). You may want to keep one at home and one at work for maximum convenience. Otherwise, it is perfectly acceptable to take bottles you have sterilised at home to work in a clean container.

If you have a dishwasher, the temperature of the water and the heat of the drying air is generally high enough to sterilise effectively your bottles and pump (but dishwashers are very hard on latex bottle teats – you will find they will not last long).

If you can find them, you can use Playtex bottle liners, which are disposable plastic bags, already sterilised, which you can freeze and which fit into a special bottle. After use you throw the bags away. This is dearer than using ordinary bottles, but more convenient.

Keeping the milk cold

You must keep your breastmilk as cold as possible from the time you express it until you get it home. It is best if you have access to a fridge at work. If you are embarrassed about keeping bottles of breastmilk in the fridge, you can always disguise them in a bag or other container.

If you haven't got a fridge at work the milk will probably be all right in a wide-necked thermos which will accommodate your bottle of breastmilk, except on the hottest days of summer. Alternatively, you can use an ordinary thermos, which will take the breast milk but not the bottle. If using either kind of thermos, you should make sure it is thoroughly clean and cooled. You can cool it by filling it with ice cubes (made with boiled water) before you leave in the morning, which you tip out before putting in the breastmilk, or bottle of milk. You can also put your bottle in an insulated cool bag filled with an icepack or two which you freeze at home at night. For transporting the milk in the evening, a thermos or insulated container is useful.

Basic rules to remember

Make sure your childcarer remembers these rules too – don't assume she knows, no matter how experienced she is:

* Breastmilk won't keep for more than 24–48 hours maximum in a fridge. If you store more than one bottle, clearly mark each bottle with the date and time.
* Frozen breastmilk will keep in the icemaking compartment of your fridge for one week.
* Breastmilk will keep in the freezer compartment of your fridge (star rating **) for not more than two weeks.

* In a deep freezer which reaches a temperature below 0°F (star rating ∗∗∗) it will keep for a year or more.

* If you freeze your milk, do so very quickly after collecting it, in plastic containers (glass may crack), or special plastic bottle bags marked with the date and time. Don't fill the container to the top, to allow room for expansion.

* You can freeze milk in ice cube trays, then keep the cubes in a plastic bag, so that you or your childcarer can unfreeze small top-up amounts of milk without waste.

* Thaw breastmilk by putting the bottle in tepid water. When it is thoroughly defrosted, hold the bottle under a warm running tap; don't heat it on a stove.

* Partially defrosted breastmilk should never be refrozen. Thawed milk must be used within a couple of hours or thrown away.

* Once you have warmed it up, use it at once or throw it away.

* Breastmilk separates when it's been standing so shake it up.

Dress

The same rules of dress apply to women who express their milk at work as to breastfeeding mothers in general: dress for easy, discreet access. This probably means separates, with loose-fitting tops for maximum comfort and discretion, or front-opening blouses or dresses (but these will leave you more exposed than the loose T-shirt or sweater that you can pull down over your pump). Or keep a loose shawl at work – useful for throwing over your shoulders to hide the pump. As one busy professional woman found:

> Soon after I went back to work, I had been successfully expressing my milk at the office until the day I realised that the only way I could get access to my breasts was to take off my smart new knitted tube dress completely and sit in my room in my bra and knickers hoping no one would come in by mistake!

Washable clothes where possible are also essential: 'It's amazing how my baby always managed to posset on my shoulder the minute I got home, before I'd had time to change into my slopping-around-the-house-with-baby clothes . . .'

Finding a place to express or breastfeed at work

Expressing at work is not a new phenomenon. Working breastfeeding mothers have done it for years. Sarah Litvinoff's mother, Cherry Marshall, wrote about this in her autobiography *The Catwalk* (published by Hutchinson). It was 1946, and she was mother to a three-year-old and a baby, and had just started work as a house-model for a high fashion house:

> I hadn't told anyone about my two children. I was breastfeeding the baby as I believed bottle-fed babies were undernourished and deprived. In the morning I would give him his six o'clock feed, and my husband would give him bottles during the day. At night I'd dash home like a madwoman so that I could give him his evening feed and so salve my conscience. In theory it was fine; in practice it was disastrous. The beautiful, perfectly fitting clothes that cost hundreds of pounds looked fabulous when I modelled them in the mornings, but when nature decreed it was feeding time again I would swell visibly to everyone's horror. I'd bought myself a little breast pump which I could use in the privacy of the toilet. But at the crucial hours I was always wanted in the showroom, and I could see and feel my breasts blowing up by the minute. The vendeuse, that most elegant and precious of women, would stare

at me in horror as I burst over the top of my strapless evening gowns, while I'd pray that my waterproof bra wouldn't let me down. No one ever said a word to me about it. I think they were too horrified for words, and I was embarrassed and ashamed.

More recently, another woman told us that she would escape into the boardroom at work to use her breast pump, telling only her closest female colleagues what she was doing, fearing that the men would find it distasteful. The pump made a rather breathy squeak as it worked, and one day a friend of hers saw one of the men loitering outside the boardroom with a perplexed expression on his face. He called her over and said, 'Do you hear what I hear? I think we've got mice in the boardroom. I think I should call the pest-control department at the council.'

You may be lucky enough to have a private office with a door you can shut at your own discretion. If not:

* Enlist the help of your union or staff representative, personnel manager, or your firm's nurse or health and safety representative. They may be willing to find somewhere to put at your disposal for the half-hour or so required. For instance, if your office or factory has a first aid room or infirmary you could arrange to pump or breastfeed there.

* There is always the ladies' toilet, although we can't recommend this if there is any alternative: it depends on the state of your ladies', but it is unlikely to be very hygienic. Also, you won't be very popular if you block the loo for twenty minutes at a stretch!

* If you can't find anywhere suitable – don't give up. Start thinking laterally. Do you have a relative or friend living near your place of work, who might allow you to come over during your lunch hour to express at their home? Can your health visitor, GP,

local NCT representative, La Leche League chapter, help with any suggestions?

Above all, don't be embarrassed or apologetic about your desire to continue breastfeeding when you are back at work. If all breastfeeding mothers politely but firmly insisted that breastfeeding facilities should be as commonly available in public places as toilets, the message would eventually trickle through. If your employers or fellow workers are embarrassed by your breastfeeding think it's their problem, not yours!

Getting Your Baby Used to a Bottle

Some experts say you should start getting your baby used to taking milk from a bottle with the occasional bottle of expressed milk in the first couple of months of life, to make sure it won't be rejected when you return to work. Others say that you mustn't try a bottle during the first two months as this will endanger your milk supply. A sensible compromise is to try a couple of ounces of milk once or twice to see whether your baby takes to the bottle easily. If so, you probably won't have to worry about it further until perhaps the week before you return to work.

If your baby refuses the bottle:

* Offer a bottle of breastmilk, so the baby doesn't have to get used to the new taste of formula as well as the container.

* Let someone else offer the bottle, and wait until your baby is hungry. Your baby may associate your smell with the breast, but may be happy enough to take milk in a bottle from someone else.

* Experiment with different shaped bottle teats (some are shaped to imitate the nipple), the temperature of the milk and the size of the hole in the teat (perhaps the milk is coming out too slowly, or too fast).

* Some babies refuse a bottle, but will take milk from a spoon or cup.

If you are worried your baby will prefer the bottle to the breast and reject you:

* You may prefer to offer expressed milk (or formula) from a cup or spoon.

* Make sure that the teats you're using have small enough holes so that your baby doesn't have to work harder at the breast than the bottle.

Conclusion

The best advice working women with breastfeeding experience can give to others is, 'Don't let it become an obsession.' Don't let your anxiety to produce enough milk or keep up your milk supply come between you and your baby. One mother became so obsessed with squeezing out enough ounces of breastmilk for her baby's needs while she was out at work that she would express some milk *before* feeding her baby, preferring to leave her baby frustrated and hungry at the breast rather than fail to collect the desired number of ounces for the next day! For most mothers, the main benefit of breastfeeding is continuing that closeness between you and baby – so cuddle and nurse as much as you can in the hours you spend at home, and don't worry too much if you can't produce enough ounces to keep your baby fully fed while you are at work.

If your milk does eventually dry up, remind yourself that

at least you breastfed your baby this long (probably much longer than the average woman), and the therapeutic benefits of the antibodies in your breastmilk are greatest when your baby is small. The chances are that you would have given up at the same time even had you not gone back to work.

CHAPTER 6
Working When Your Child is Young

Practical Considerations

Going back to work when you have a baby or young child is tough. The advice from many of the mothers who contributed to this book is: keep your housekeeping routines as simple as possible. Many mothers pointed out with astonishment (and pride) just how little housework they could get away with. With limited time at your disposal, you have to select your priorities, and many choose to spend more time with their children or partners.

As Lesley Schatzberger, a musician from York, says:

> Try to remember what's really important: time with your child or polished furniture and ironed bedding. A child doesn't need a pristine or impeccably tidy environment to be happy.

Shirley Conran liberated a whole generation of women from the tyranny of housework in her book *Superwoman*, by proclaiming that 'Life is too short to stuff a mushroom.' Life is also too short to make beds, wax floors, dry up dishes, hoover and dust every day. Turn to *Your Home and your Partner* for general tips on making things as easy as possible around the house.

Here are some extra pointers specifically for those with small babies or toddlers at home.

Disposable or terry nappies?

Disposables are much more convenient – you stick them on and you throw them away – no messing about with nappy pins, no soaking, washing and drying. One of the excuses fathers use for not changing nappies is that they can't manage the fiddly safety pins – but sticking on a disposable takes no manual dexterity!

But are disposables more expensive? If you work out the initial outlay on terries, plus the cost of plastic pants, nappy liners, sterilising solution, soap powder and electricity or the cost of a launderette, you may very well find that there is not really that much difference in the cost, and the time and effort you save with throwaways is well worth the difference if you can afford the weekly cost.

Certain big stores, including Boots and Mothercare, will deliver a month's supply of disposable nappies to your home, saving you the effort of carrying them, if you have the space to store them in bulk.

However, there are also good environmental reasons for preferring terries. If you have moral objections to disposables, or you can't afford them, or if your baby gets a rash from them, as happens in a few cases, here is a tip from Rosemary Kirk from Northern Ireland:

I used terry nappies because I couldn't afford disposables. To save the washing I used a very large flip-top bin as a nappy bucket. It can hold about twelve to fifteen nappies and took about three days to fill, so I didn't need to put them in the washing machine so often. Although you are supposed to change the sterilising liquid every day, I find they are okay. I put them in a rinse cycle and then a hot wash and two years later they are still lovely and white.

Or, as Betty Shepherd, another Northern Ireland mother, suggests, 'Find a baby minder who will do the nappies!'

Easy-care clothes for your child

Life is certainly too short to handwash delicate baby woollens and silk smocking. Stretchy terry bodysuits (the kind with poppers at the crotch for easy changing) are the most practical for babies from birth until they are crawling, and are appropriate for any season and either sex. The more you have, the less often you will have to wash them. Dark colours are especially good as baby stains can be hard to remove from whites and pale pastels. To extend their lifespan, slit them open at the toes when they are tight.

If you receive gifts of any baby clothes that need handwashing and ironing, you'd be well advised to stuff them into the back of a drawer – just bring them out when the donor comes to visit!

For older babies and toddlers, too, you will save a lot of effort and time by getting machine-washable tops and trousers or dungarees. Tracksuits are especially good as they come in all shapes and colours for boys and girls: they are warm, comfortable, hardwearing, and never need ironing.

When your baby starts feeding himself, one plastic pelican-type bib which has a lip for catching spills and which you can wipe clean is much more practical than laundering fabric bibs.

Easy-care clothes for you

Babies are messy creatures, so it is a good idea to wear machine-washable, no-iron clothes yourself as much as possible. Many mothers also become used to carrying a cloth (a muslin or 'burp-rag') for mopping up messes immediately. One executive mother of a six-month-old baby and a two-and-a-half-year-old gave this tip:

> On working mornings, I get myself all ready bar my suit or dress. I do my hair, make-up, put on a slip, then cover it with a dressing gown until two minutes before leaving for work. Otherwise I'll invariably get the baby being sick on the shoulder of my best suit at the last minute, or loving sticky jam fingers all over my skirt.

* Tip: To get the sour smell of baby's milk or posset off your clothes, dab at it with a damp cloth dipped in some bicarbonate of soda.

Baby food

One of us says she'll always remember, during the long period that her baby was only interested in food that came out of a glass jar from the supermarket, her feelings of guilt, shame and frustration on hearing a working friend tell how she spent time at the weekend making marrowbone soup to give to the minder for her baby, and another who explained how she and her nanny had worked out a detailed balanced daily diet for her child which included lentils and liver at least once a week.

By all means spend time cooking special foods for your baby, if it makes you feel good, or if you enjoy it. If you don't enjoy it, or if your child does not, ask yourself why you do it. If it is out of a sense of guilt because you go to work, it is simply not worth it. There is a wide range of baby foods on the market which will give your baby all the essential nutrients: look for those labelled 'no added salt, sugar or preservatives'. They can be prepared in a matter of minutes, so you need never keep your hungry baby waiting. Leftovers keep for forty-eight hours in the fridge, so there need be no waste either. It is true that your child may become used to the blandness of convenience foods, but that stage passes. It is better to put up with this than become too anxious and emotional about the whole subject of what your child eats and does not eat:

> I recognised that when I had devised a nice little homemade nutritious mush for my baby I became offended and het up if she didn't like it, or stopped eating after a couple of spoonfuls. That was when I'd be trying to force it in when she had clearly had enough. I was far more laid back about the tinned stuff, and realised that I may be setting up eating problems if I continued to be too emotionally involved with her rejecting 'my' food, so I kept on with the commercial stuff for a while until she began to show more interest in other foods.

If your baby does like home cooking, you may find it quite easy to offer mashed-up portions of whatever the family eats, and you may decide to use part of your weekends to cook up quantities of mashed food to freeze. A good tip is to freeze small dollops in an ice tray, so that you can defrost and use them in exactly the right quantity without wasting any.

A teacher from Devon with an eight-month-old baby suggests storing your child's frozen meals at your minder's (if she has a freezer):

> I make Paul's meals at the weekend and freeze enough for the week, then take it to the childminder. I know he is getting fresh food and I don't have to grab a packet each morning.

The best thing for a working mother's conscience is a minder or nanny who cooks a fresh, balanced and wholesome meal at lunchtime so you can be sure that your child is getting at least one square meal a day!

Your Relationship With Your Child: Quality Time

The concept of quality time, like most child-rearing pronouncements, is something of a double-edged sword. What it means is that it is not the *quantity* of time you spend with your child that is important, but the *quality* of your time together. This is very reassuring for the working parent who feels guilty about the small number of hours per day that are left to devote to the children.

Quality time is a label for something that naturally happens in the lives of working parents and their children. It's a pleasure to see someone you like and love after a day apart, and you genuinely want to chat, cuddle and give each other your attention.

If you feel guilty about leaving your child while you go out to work, ask yourself how much undivided attention you would give if you did not work. Would you really be the perfect mother, with nothing on your mind all day except devising fun and amusement for your child? Or would you, like most of us, try to park your child in a corner with a toy, while you got on with your chores? Or would you spend some of that time nagging or shouting?

Experiments have shown that mothers at home all day do not spend more quality time with their children than working mothers. One experiment showed that children with mothers at home spent about 5 per cent of their waking hours interacting directly with their mothers – and the children spent almost that long – 4 per cent of their waking time – interacting with their fathers, who were out at work all day!

The negative side of the quality time concept is that we are all human. There are days when you come home tired and stressed and in a foul mood. Pity the person who wants meaningful cheerful interaction from you in that mood, be it the bus conductor, your partner – or your child. What you want then is to do nothing at all, or else you find yourself spoiling for a fight, seconds away from explosive irritation. There are also the days when your child is a little monster, disagreeable and fretful, turning all your good intentions sour with the kind of behaviour every parent dreads. If you are too obsessed with the idea of quality time, believing that every moment you are together with your child should be positive and stimulating, you are inevitably storing up a lot of guilt for yourself.

What we advocate is obeying the spirit rather than the letter of the law of quality time. Be available as much as you can: most of the time seeing your child in the evenings and mornings is a great pleasure, and you will spontaneously want to spend time together and have fun. But it is not a duty. Your child must learn along with everything else that people get tired and irritable, but that it passes. You are not doing any irreparable harm if on the odd evenings you just want to lavish quality time on yourself.

What your child needs from you

If you provide good substitute childcare, you can rely on your child receiving essential physical and practical care: clean body and clothes, food and drink, warmth, exercise and naps. Your childcare arrangement will also provide some intellectual stimulation and play. A good mother substitute will also give your child some cuddling and even love.

But when it is your turn to be with your child you will want to provide plenty of your loving attention to reinforce your relationship, to show that 'mummy loves you and is proud of you', even if you can't be there all day. This will give your child emotional security. There are no rules about how you should show this loving attention: you can go on outings together, play games, teach something new, make things, have a cuddle or a romp, read a book, sing

131

songs. If your child is old enough you may simply want to talk, and find out about what happened while you were not there, discussing fears and fun. Quality time does not necessarily mean a rigorous learning-to-read session with flashcards: if you are tired, it can just mean cuddling on the sofa, listening to music or watching a favourite television programme, so long as your child feels that you are sharing this time together.

How to find time

Every working mother we heard from managed to find some regular daily moment in her hectic schedule that was her special time with her small child. Some women are very strict about this. One London editor told us that she was so anxious to see her two-and-a-half-year-old in the morning that she would sometimes wake him, 'to have enough time with him', and in the evening:

> Between collecting him at six and bed at eight, that time is solidly devoted to him, I won't even answer the phone, I don't want to be disturbed by anything. Although it's feeding, bathing time, it is very much a time when he gets our full, undivided attention.

Not many working mothers will have as much time to devote to their children as this part-time farm secretary with a four-year-old:

> Every afternoon is 'Stephen's time' – we play or read books or go out to play with other children. He also helps me when I bake or do the cleaning. I tell him stories in the bath and read to him in bed. I take him for his riding lesson and we go swimming each week – we are about to start a gym class.

But even a mother with a full-time job can fit a number of these same activities into her schedule, with some planning.

However, small children can be very demanding and have no concept of time. They often nag you to do things with them while you are busy. The same farm secretary writes: 'I don't think he has suffered from having a working mother, although he sometimes says I'm always saying "wait a minute" and that I never do things when he asks me to.'

Every parent will recognise the 'not-now-maybe-later' automatic reply to a child – it is bad only if it means you are indefinitely putting off paying attention to your child. If you hear yourself constantly saying 'in a minute', and 'maybe tomorrow', make sure you carry out your promises eventually.

As a systems analyst from Preston writes, 'Give your child your attention, rather than the chores. Tell yourself that a perfect home means that no one is demanding your time – and that is lonely.'

On the other hand, don't let guilt drive you to believe that you must always drop everything because your child wants your attention. Sometimes later is better if there is something you have to do, or you want to put your feet up first.

Here are some suggestions for finding time:

Get up early

If you are bright in the morning and have trouble getting back to sleep after your baby's 5.00a.m. feed, or if your toddler insists on waking you at dawn, don't fight it. Try to go to bed earlier to get enough sleep, and use this early morning time to be with your child, whether it is to cuddle and play in your bed, or to get up and do puzzles, play with Lego or playdoh, or have a friendly intimate breakfast before the family morning scramble begins.

Hazel Coates writes that her two-year-old wakes at 6.00a.m., and 'it is playtime with mum and dad until 8.00.'

Involve your child in your routine at home

On the days that you don't have a spare half-hour to set aside, involve your child in what you are doing. You can chat or sing to your baby – who can be propped up in a bouncing cradle watching you – while you get on with preparing supper. A toddler will enjoy following you around with a duster or splashing about with water in a bowl while you do the dishes (but you'll have to tolerate the mess!). You can talk to your child anywhere: 'He'll come and chat to me when I am on the loo and he loves to help wash mummy's hair!'

Adjust your child's bedtime

There is no law that says a small child should be in bed by six or seven, never mind what anyone else thinks. A mother who is at home alone all day with a difficult baby or lively toddler can put her child to bed by six with a sigh of relief, thinking that she has deserved a bit of peace at last (a consequence of this early bedtime is that there are many fathers who never see their children except at weekends).

But if you do not get home until six, do you really want your child to go straight to bed? Several mothers told us that they had adjusted their child's bedtime to give them at least a couple of hours between coming home and going to bed. Jane Lee, from York, gets home with her four-year-old at about 5.45:

> Then I cook the meal, bath her, have cuddles and talk and play. I get her into bed by 9.00p.m. which a lot of people think is far too late, but what else can you do when you're working full time?

If you fear your child is not getting enough sleep, you can always ask your childcarer to make nap-times during the day. As Heather Lockett, a teacher from Merseyside, says:

134

> Don't put your children to bed too early – otherwise
> you'll hardly see them. I'd rather they sleep during the
> day and have more time with them.

If you have one of those children who refuses to go to bed,
you may want to make the best of it. Rather than spending
every evening in a battle of wills, you can make the official
bedtime an hour or so later, and use the time for quiet
activities together.

But no matter what time you establish as your child's
bedtime, try to be consistent and stick to it. As one of the
women we interviewed reported,

> I know one working couple who will get their daughter
> up after she's been put to bed if one of them comes home
> late, as they feel they haven't seen her all day. No
> wonder their child has sleeping problems!

Make a daily special time

Many of the working mothers who wrote to us have a
regular daily time with their children, more often than not
the tea-bath-story-bed routine. Many mothers share this
routine with their partners: one entertains or bathes the
child, while the other gets supper ready; one plays a last
game, the other reads the bedtime story.

A London mother who works in publishing, a very
sociable field in which after-work drinks and cocktail
parties are a regular part of the working day, told us that
she makes it a rule to refuse all cocktail-hour invitations:

> I always try to get home by six, and the next two hours
> are sacrosanct. I'm quite happy to go out again after the
> children are in bed, so I do often go out for a working
> dinner instead.

Weekends and family time

Working parents often feel torn at the weekend: it is

probably your only time to clean the house, do the garden, do the shopping – yet it also represents your only real free time for activities with your children. Weekends also offer an opportunity for all the family to do things together.

It can be fun to have regular family time, outings and activities which you can all enjoy while your children are small. As they grow older and more independent, they may not wish to spend so much time in shared activities.

Nevertheless it is common to start off with good intentions but find that time is taken up by household chores, or that you and your partner are both too tired to do anything except slump on the sofa. Listen to a London executive:

> We usually make a New Year's resolution to do something interesting with the children on Sundays, and it usually fades out about February . . .

One way round this is to do normal weekend activities together. The Saturday weekly shop can be turned into a family outing, with a treat at a cafe, or even lunch out. Gardening can be turned into a family activity if you all enjoy it. Even little ones will like having their own special patch to dig. The odd family meal can be turned into a special memorable occasion by simple innovations like dining by candlelight, or by turning it into an indoor picnic complete with toast cooked on the living-room fire.

Sometimes these simple things are better than a special planned occasion, which may turn out to be a letdown when it has been anticipated for too long. But when these work they can form the best childhood memories. This woman, a divorced mother of three from Preston, wrote of one such day:

> Make use of a special day off or weekend every so often, forget the cost, spend the money necessary to make it different. It was one year to the exact day their father walked out. I took them to London – the train fare was

peak hour (I hadn't checked which trains could be used so we arrived for the wrong one). I then just said yes to requests for drinks, food, ice-creams, tube rides etc. Expensive; but we all remember mum's 'yes' day out.

Time for yourself

It is also important to keep some time for yourself, and not let your free time be totally taken up by your children. Some parents take it in turns at weekends to do something with their children while the other is freed to do something else. A London mother says:

> We stand in for each other at the weekends, for example my husband will take my daughter into the garden or out for a walk. It means that occasionally I'll get an uninterrupted hour or two, to catch up on work or just to sit and read the paper.

A set bedtime for your child helps to give you time with your partner. As Hazel Coates, who is a physiotherapist from Belfast with a two-year-old, points out:

> It's important that the child understands that Mummy and Daddy need time alone. We aim to get Suzanne to bed between 7.30 and 8.00p.m. – she gets very unsettled if she is up later and then it takes her a long time to get to sleep.

Coping with poor quality time

When things do not go smoothly with your child, or you are too tired and harassed to spare much time, don't punish yourself for it. If you set yourself impossibly high standards about quality time, you'll only feel guilty if you do not live up to them. Every family has its rows and irritations, and every mother shouts and nags at her children sometimes. Every mother has moments when she wishes she could divorce her children. You may not always be a model of patience, and after a strained day at work you will not always be able to summon up attentive fascination for your child's complicated story about what happened in playgroup today. All we can do as parents – whether we work or not – is to do our best, most of the time!

If you have been irrationally snappy or irritable you can apologise when you are feeling better, or if your child won't understand, give a loving cuddle later. Children who are a little older appreciate a warning, 'I'm feeling cross today,' or 'I'm in a bad mood' or simply, 'I'm too tired.' Remember to add that this is because of what happened at work, or small children are likely to feel that they have caused your irritation or tiredness.

Don't demand too much of your child, either. You might want to do something 'stimulating', such as a puzzle, while your child may just want you to watch daring leaps off the sofa, again and again . . .

Once quality time becomes an effort and a chore it is meaningless. If you are relaxed and enjoying your children it shows – and requires no special skills or equipment.

As your child grows older quality time as such becomes less relevant. Older children would probably be somewhat offended if they suspected they were being allocated set times. Sometimes older children need much more sustained time and attention from you – although just because you have cleared a nice little space in your day, it doesn't mean it is necessarily convenient for your child, who may be longing to watch television or too busy with school friends and hobbies to fit you in!

CHAPTER 7
Childcare for the Under-fives

Choosing Your Childcare Option

Which sort of childcare you choose for small children or babies is the single most important decision you have to make as a working mother. Some lucky women have relatives or friends who are happy to look after their children; for the rest of us finding good, quality care for our children while we are out at work is a major headache.

You have to be resourceful and determined to track down the kind of care you want, and you may have to compromise when you find that there is little provision for pre-school childcare in your area – yet it is possible to arrange something you are happy with if you are persistent. Unless you are very lucky indeed you will also have to be prepared for the fact that it will take a large slice out of your earnings after tax. (If childcare were tax-deductible it would not only be financially easier for us, we would also be able to pay our childminders and nannies more – which they deserve as working women who have very long hours.)

What the women in our sample chose

A number of women who completed our questionnaire

skipped the childcare section, because they had not worked when their children were small. Of the others, about 40 per cent had used childminders, 10 per cent had nannies or au pairs, 12 per cent used day nurseries, and 13 per cent had relatives who looked after their children while they worked. The rest mainly used the part-time cover provided by nursery schools and playgroups combined with help from relatives, neighbours or minders (but these women had children over three, and usually worked part-time).

The women we interviewed were a much less representative group: the majority had used nannies, with about half that number using childminders. Only one had used a private nursery, and another had an unemployed partner who looked after their child.

The national figures are rather different. The following are statistics provided by the General Household Survey, April 1991–March 1992, (they do not specify whether the mothers were working full or part time, or indeed used a nursery school or other facility even if they weren't working). Seventy per cent of those responsible for under-fives used some form of childcare; 21 per cent used a nursery school; 20 per cent had their children looked after by unpaid family or friends; 14 per cent used a private or voluntary scheme (creche, playgroup or day nursery); 9 per cent used a childminder or nanny; 6 per cent used a local authority scheme (presumably also creches, playgroups or day nurseries); 1 per cent used a workplace facility. (The total comes to 71 per cent, because some used more than one form of care).

Childminder, nursery or nanny?

Your choice of the type of childcare you decide on is limited by a number of factors:

* Availability

Much depends on where you live. For example, in an area like London and the South East, the demand for childminders and nursery places often exceeds the supply, but young girls wanting to work as mother's helps or nannies are flocking in from all over the rest of the country. In an area of high female unemployment, on the other hand, it less of a problem to find a childminder or even a nursery place.

* Your circumstances

Wherever you live, you are unlikely to find your child is eligible for a local authority day nursery place unless you are at least a lone parent. In many areas, even that will not guarantee you a place, as places are often reserved for families with greater social problems.

* Cost

For many this is the overriding factor. Most working mothers spend a high proportion of their take-home pay on childcare: on average, between one-quarter and one-half according to our sample (though it is not necessarily representative). But we also noticed that there seemed to be a relationship between how much a woman earns and what proportion of her pay she is prepared to spend on childcare. We found that the women in the higher-paid professions tended to be the ones who spent the highest proportion of their net pay on childcare – up to two-thirds in several cases. The most extreme examples were a woman who spent 90 per cent of her salary on her nanny, and another who claimed to have spent more than she earned for a few years when her children were small (but we assume that in each case they and their husbands could well afford this luxury). This can be explained by the fact

141

that for these women the work is probably more important to them than the money, whereas the lower paid need every penny they earn to make ends meet.

It is difficult to generalise about cost (there are great fluctuations round the country and many exceptions). Roughly, help in your own home (nannies and so on) is the most expensive option; followed by private day nurseries, then childminders, then publicly funded nurseries.

However, a nanny or mother's help need not *always* be the most expensive option. If you share a nanny with another family you may find it does not cost much more than a childminder. If you have several children under five, or if you also have an older child for whom you have to pay to be cared for after school, a nanny or mother's help may cost the same (or even less) than a minder or nursery, where you pay per child (although some minders and nurseries offer a small reduction for a second child).

Other Factors Affecting Your Choice

Your child and your feelings

A lot depends on your own feelings, and those of your partner – sometimes also the personality of your child. Some parents prefer the idea of their child being looked after by one person in their own home; some like the idea of a substitute family environment and mother-figure as offered by a childminder; others worry about their child becoming too attached to one single caregiver, and want their children to make friends, so prefer a group situation as offered by a day nursery.

Convenience

Do take practical considerations into account. You may be

so dazzled by the modern facilities of that private nursery that you ignore the problem of getting your child there on two separate buses (complete with stroller and paraphernalia) in the opposite direction to your office! A childminder round the corner, so long as you and your child like her, may save a lot of wear and tear on your nerves and stamina in the long run. A live-in nanny will save you or your partner from having to do any taking or fetching at all, with the possible added bonus of having some household chores done in your absence.

On the other hand, if there is no one in your house during the day, it will be as tidy (or untidy!) in the evening as you left it in the morning, and it won't be your carpet that gets covered with baby food and toilet-training accidents!

Holidays and sickness

A day nursery or creche may close down during student holidays (especially if it is attached to a college or similar); so may a nursery school or playgroup, which you may use to supplement other childcare arrangements. Even if they don't follow school terms, the holidays are likely to be inflexible.

A day nursery will keep going in spite of the absence or illness of staff – whereas a childminder or nanny who falls ill, goes away, or wants to stop looking after your child, can leave you without anyone to fall back on.

A nanny will be able to look after a sick child at home, but a childminder or nursery may well refuse to take a sick child (especially if the illness is contagious).

If you are very undecided about what care to choose, we recommend that you read each of the following sections on childminders, nurseries and nannies.

CHAPTER 8
Childminders

A childminder can be a very good choice for the working mother. As a mother herself, looking after your child in her own home (often with her own children around), she can be the closest possible substitute for you, and your child is being cared for in a family environment. As a local mother she can potentially provide the most continuous care for your child – right up to school age and beyond, because she has her own reasons for staying in the area. She has experience with children of the most practical kind: she has learned by doing it herself, and as a working mother too she will be sympathetic to many of your problems. The joys (and the drawbacks) of a childminder are summed up by the mother from Merseyside who wrote to tell us that she has a child of three and one of seven months, both looked after by a minder, along with another child of eighteen months:

> My children have all the experiences they would have at home and probably more – such as cooking (my three-year-old often tells me that she has helped to make cakes and pastry), going to the shops, 'helping' to tidy up, and so on. I think my children benefit because although I love them dearly I'm not what I would call a 'natural mother' – I need my professional life as well.

My childminder seems to be a natural mother and is able to give my children the things I never could. There are, however, good and bad childminders. When I first returned to work after my eldest's birth, I had put her with another childminder. I didn't feel happy, and she didn't seem happy. I was, however, fortunate enough to find the one I have now and I moved her after three weeks. We have never looked back. The only problem is I do wish I didn't have to travel so far with them. She would willingly look after the children if they were ill, but one can't drag children out of bed and take them on a twenty-five-minute car ride if they are sick.

Technically a childminder is a person who, for payment, looks after children, other than those of a close relative, in her own home, for more than two hours a day. Including her own children, she is allowed to look after three under-fives (only one should be under a year, though exceptions are sometimes made – for twins, for example). Since the new Children Act, which came into force in 1991, the ratio of under-eights is also controlled: she must look after no more than six under-eights – that is, she can look after three extra children on top of the three under-fives. All childminders should be registered with the social services department, and are then given a certificate of registration.

We are interpreting 'childminder' rather more loosely, to include women who are prepared to come to your house at least some of the time; relatives – like your mother or mother-in-law; or friends who have perhaps not yet got round to registering. We are also taking a look at the option of becoming a childminder yourself if you need money, want to stay at home with your own children, and like the idea. It is worth reading that section anyway, because we go into more detail about what is involved, and it can help you in making your choice when you are looking for a childminder for your own children.

It hardly needs to be said that there are good and bad

childminders. Everyone is familiar with the bad stories of overcrowding, neglect and cruelty. Stories like these are probably responsible for putting off many mothers from even considering the option. This is a great pity, for of course childminders come in every shape and form, and some of the most glowing testimonials we received came from women who used minders. Heather Lockett's was just one, quite typical example:

> My children's faces light up on arrival at 'Auntie Carol's' – even the youngest, who doesn't like most people, quivers with excitement when she sees her face – and that's after only two weeks with her.

Some women are lucky enough to find a childminder they and their children are happy with quite easily. But obviously this is not something you want to leave to luck. If you are determined to avoid the barely adequate or downright poor childminder, there is nothing like starting to look as early as possible – even while you are still pregnant, when you may not even be sure that you want a childminder. Otherwise you can find yourself in the situation of a teacher we talked to who left her child with a minder she mistrusted because time had run out, she was due to go back to work, and there was no other choice. In London and other cities it is particularly hard to find a registered childminder who has room for any new children at all. It is not quite so bad in other parts of the country, and in areas of high female unemployment minders may have vacancies. But if you want to find a woman you trust and like, you should start your search as early as possible.

How to Find a Childminder

Social services department

As all childminders must register with the social services department, this is a good first stop to find out what is available. They hold a list of registered childminders in the area, and may know which ones have vacancies. However, at the time of revising this book, many areas are experiencing delays in registration. Under the Children Act, all childminders are having to be re-registered, even if they have been registered for many years, which is causing a log jam, as registered childminders queue alongside new childminders for registration. This means that your department might be out of date.

Even so, it is worth a try: ring to ask for someone who deals with under-eights. Each department is likely to have a different title for this officer. Don't expect to speak to the right person straight away – like all conversations with council departments, it can take time.

Many women have been fortunate enough to find the right minder through the social services. As one contented mother who lives in Manchester wrote, 'She was the third of the three I visited on the list nearest to home. I took to her straight away.'

Although each social services department is likely to operate differently, it is worth being aware that some are inclined to pre-select – just giving you one or two names of childminders close to you. Ideally you want to know every name on the list so that you have the maximum chance of choosing the right person. On the other hand, lists date, and if you receive a complete list you could find that some have given up.

Do ask for more names if the minders you have visited near you are not what you are looking for. Many of us would prefer the inconvenience of a longer journey if it meant going to a minder we liked and trusted, rather than someone round the corner that we didn't.

It is important to realise that registration is no guarantee of quality. Virtually anyone can become a childminder, so long as she is a 'fit' person, which usually means little more than that she doesn't have a police record, has never had a child taken into care, and that her home meets the required safety standards. The onus is on the social services to prove that she is 'unfit', so although many areas, backed by the Children Act and childminding associations, are trying to tighten up selection, it is up to you to vet carefully.

Marie Burke has had good experiences with the childminders she has used, except one:

> The only childminder recommended very highly by a health visitor turned out to be quite unsatisfactory. She was mainly concerned with keeping her house immaculate and as a result rarely spoke to my son. I know personally of three other mothers who have employed her to their great regret.

Doctor/clinic/health visitor

Being more intimately concerned with the mothers in the area, these people are more likely to be up to date with the state of vacancies; they may know the minders personally and be able to give you some background information. Use the frustrating waiting time at the clinic to talk to other mothers and ask what they know about minders. You may find yourself sitting next to one, or someone who is considering doing it herself.

Childminding organisations

If there is one in your area you'll find the address through the social services department or at the local library. These groups are likely to be of more help than the social services because they will be in touch with the availability of vacancies among their members. Some have a counsellor who will liaise between parent and minder.

You can also find out about local childminding organisations through the National Childminding Association (NCMA), which will also know of lone childminders who do not belong to a group but have joined the association (see *Further Help*).

Word of mouth

Ask, ask, ask – wherever you are. Let everyone know you are looking, and you might find the right childminder through less conventional means. Anneliese Young found her childminder before her baby was born because she was sitting next to her in the choir:

> I mentioned one day that I was going to return to work after the baby was born and would have to find someone to look after him. She said she would love to do it. [She had never done it before and wasn't registered.] I urged her to become registered before she started to mind my second child.

Heather found the wonderful 'Auntie Carol' mentioned earlier because she taught Carol's child: 'I noticed that her child had a lovely nature. Her mother – an ex-teacher, and now a registered childminder – likewise.'

A woman who lives in Elgin, Scotland, was also happy with the registered childminder she found by asking around, who turned out to be a friend of a friend. 'Living where I do, with its small population, word travels fast.' One London woman had fixed herself up with a registered childminder through the social services who let her down at the last minute:

> I actually went round all the local shops, desperately saying: 'Look, I've got to find a minder, otherwise they'll sack me, I'm already a month late back to work.'

So this chap in the newsagent said: 'Oh, I'll ask Margaret, she knows everything.' And this wonderful Margaret said: 'I'll have her!'

Creating your own – relative or friend

If you find the right person to mind your child it shouldn't matter that she is not already registered – she can always apply once you have come to an agreement. If you know of someone who is prepared to look after your child – a friend, a woman you met at the clinic, a relative – and you feel she is the right choice, you can help her make arrangements to become registered.

Registering is a formality, even if it takes a while. It allows the minder to take other children within the agreed ratios, if she is so inclined, and gives her access to help and useful literature. You will find the NCMA a great help, and it is worth both of you joining as soon as you make the decision (membership is not restricted to childminders). Their literature raises points about pay and conditions you might not have considered. It will also make sure that your childminder knows how to place herself on proper terms with the tax office before she starts. It is worth drawing up a contract (which the NCMA provide, and for which we give suggestions later in the chapter). This way you can talk about issues before they happen and so know where you both stand.

A part-time doctor's experience of a friend as childminder shows how ideal this can be. Sheila Paul's arrangement was made while she lived and worked in West Germany, but it could equally have happened here:

> My closest friend was my childminder. She had children exactly the same age as mine, all best friends and all going to the same kindergarten, school, gym club, swimming etc., so she had to make the same journeys anyway. Even when I could get away, my two older children preferred lunch with the childminder to lunch with me – because her children, their friends, were there.

150

A primary teacher who lives in Devon eventually found the childminder who looks exclusively after her eight-month-old son because she was recommended by a friend, but she had previously asked the social services, visited various childminders, and asked the health visitor's advice. The minder is not registered, but is becoming so.

A woman who also has an eight-month-old baby says, 'My childminder is in fact an old friend – which is very reassuring. I hoped money wouldn't be the only consideration – I'd pay over the odds for peace of mind.' Her friend is not registered – which of course is illegal. She looks after her own baby and two school-age children as well as our correspondent's baby.

> She has a little girl six weeks older than mine – I think it's a big plus to have another child around rather than spending days with an adult only (they're still a bit young to play together, but it will be good soon). It worried me that it could spoil a good friendship – but it has in fact worked extremely well so far. I suppose it's the idea of paying a friend, 'employing' her, that's a bit sensitive.

She could find that if her friend registered and they drew up a contract, this area would become less sensitive – though the social services department might be reluctant to register her to mind two young babies.

Needless to say, using a friend can sometimes backfire. One mother wrote to tell us about an arrangement she made with a friend. Her children were at school, but the pitfalls would be the same at any age:

> Having decided to do a three-year teacher-training course at a local college, I got a friend/neighbour to look after the children twice a week after school. I had known her for years, and was paying her. To my great surprise the arrangement was a failure. She kept my kids apart from her own, which I found strange as they had often played together in the past. She lectured them on

151

how 'good children' should behave, and they always complained of hunger when I brought them home. I tried to give her a way out by saying it was too much for her, but she wouldn't hear of stopping the arrangement. Eventually I had to tell her outright that I was not happy, and they would not be going to her any more. She was very annoyed and avoided speaking to me for some time, although we eventually got back on speaking terms – though with reservations on both sides. The moral of this tale is to be very careful when asking friends to look after kids – you may find you didn't really know them at all.

Using and paying a relative

Other mothers wrote to tell us about using relatives as minders. This is something you are likely to have thought of anyway if you have family who live close by and are available during the day. Although these women are not technically childminders, many of the working mothers decided to pay them anyway. Recognising that it is a job that deserves to be paid puts the relationship on a formal footing. Your relative is not, therefore 'doing you a favour', which means she is more professionally committed, and it allows you to make your own wishes clear without offence.

Phyl Driffield's sister-in-law is her childminder. 'She worked part time before and I said I'd pay her the same money for looking after Kerry. She was overjoyed but initially refused payment. She now accepts it when I pointed out that if she didn't look after my daughter I would only have to pay someone else.' Sisters-in-law are probably counted as close relatives, and therefore don't have to register, but this should be checked with your local social services department first.

Rosemary Kirk's mother minds her youngest son, and she finds the arrangement ideal:

My parents are retired and love Michael, so that is great.

My father never had the pleasure of looking after a young child even when we were young because he was working long hours and had poor holidays, so that I know both my parents are happy with this arrangement and I am content. They would look after him for nothing, but I insist on paying them.

Although close relatives do not have to register, it does give them the option of taking in another child or two if they want to, and they can benefit from whatever the social services have to offer childminders in the area. Sharon Foor's mother minds her youngest daughter. She has registered and chosen to take in other children too. Sharon pays the same as the other mothers. Sharon's daughter, at four, is the eldest, and isn't particularly interested in mixing with the others, but the arrangement works well. 'Rachel doesn't call my mother "grandma", she calls her Mary, as the other children do.'

One woman, who works part time and lives in Lincolnshire, has a minder who looks after her four-year-old son most of the time while she is at work, supplemented by her mother:

My mother looks after my son one morning a week. She offered to do this before he was born, but I pay her (and have always paid her) the same amount as my other minder. This I feel stops any arguments. I'm pleased she sees him so regularly. My childminding arrangements are very flexible, and each minder swaps with the other if necessary. They are both very conveniently sited, so I don't have to travel far. Because they both look after him in their own home they are free to do their own chores, if they wish, so long as my son is okay, and in fact they both let him help with jobs – which he loves, and which I don't always have time to let him do. It is a fresh environment for my son on certain days, which is good, and I know he will always be warm and dry in winter – while I'm saving on fuel at home! I don't see how it could be improved – it has worked very well for nearly five years.

Advertising

If you have no luck finding a childminder through the ordinary channels it is worth advertising. A notice in the newsagent will probably bring in a few replies, or you could try the local paper, and noticeboards at the doctor's surgery, clinic, post office or local school. You are likely to see advertisements in these same places from childminders with vacancies to fill. Remember, of course, to interview the minder and check references as carefully as you would if you found her by some other means.

A correspondent from York says, 'There are few registered childminders in the area, but most people advertise and then arrange for the minder to become registered with the social services department as necessary.'

A woman who lives in Bangor, Northern Ireland, chose a childminder because 'we wanted our children to be the only children in a homely environment.' She advertised in the local paper and found a woman whose own family had grown up and was interested in having some more little ones around:

> I think that our set-up is very good in that the children are at home during the day sharing their time with a (lovely) mother figure and not yet having to contend closely with other children from outside the family. As the minder's family is now grown up, she and her husband are thoroughly enjoying a second chance at having babies around and probably put more into their entertainment than most parents have eneregy for.

What to Look for in a Childminder

We all hope that the childcare we provide for our children will be perfect – even though, being imperfect ourselves, we know that this is just a dream. However it does no harm to fantasise about a paragon, the 'ideal' childminder; you may then have a better idea of what you are looking for. Your fantasy could include the following elements:

* She'll be very like you – without your faults. Temperamentally she will be placid, smiling and patient.

* She will love the children in her care and have a (secret) soft spot for yours, even when they are going through a difficult phase or being noisy and irritating.

* She will do the minimum of household chores, but miraculously her house will always be spotless. When doing housework she will allow your children to help – even if that means mess.

* Her house will be perfectly safe, with fire-guards, fire-blankets, stair-gates, and so on. It will be so child-proof that your children can roam happily – and the minder won't have any precious items that can't be touched, or furniture that will be ruined by being climbed on.

* She will have plenty of toys, and will encourage messy games, such as painting, modelling and water play.

* She will have a garden or take them out to the park when the weather is fine. She will know about all the activities in the area.

* She will be endlessly patient: playing games, reading stories and singing songs; will encourage imaginative play, such as dressing up; and some activities will be educational.

* Her television will be switched off except when there's a particularly interesting and educational children's programme.

* She will have a quiet place for your children to rest.

* She will take your children to the library.

* She will have been on a course for childminders and will be clued up on all aspects of childcare, and trained in first aid.

* She will be linked to a childminder's group – and will take part in activities with other minders and their children.

* She will cook good nutritious food, offer healthy snacks, such as fresh fruit, and discourage sweets, fizzy drinks and chips.

* If weaning or potty-training, she will do it perfectly.

* Your children will learn nice manners and good behaviour.

* When you collect your children, she will tell you all about their day, their new achievements and funny stories.

It can be difficult to grill another woman about the way she looks after children, and to inspect her home with a less-than-polite, assessing eye – but this is what you have to do. It obviously pays to be well prepared. It helps to have a list of things you want to ask and look for, so that there is no chance of finding out too late about something that is unacceptable. If your childminder is experienced and registered it will make the interviewing much easier – she will expect you to ask questions, and will respect you for doing so. If she is used to drawing up a contract with the parents who employ her, so much the better – she will probably raise the issues that you need to discuss.

However, if your childminder is new to the job you can't rely on her for this. The following is a list of what you should look for and ask.

Visiting her home

Ask to see the rooms where the children will be. Use your commonsense when you look around. Anything too pristine should cause alarm bells to ring, because a home with happy children never looks perfect. An ordinary amount of mess is okay, while dirt is obviously not.

Pam Jones, of the Wandsworth Childminding Association, an excellent ex-minder herself, recommends paying more than one visit. 'Anyone expecting someone can put an act on,' she says. 'You should rely on your instincts. Mums do know. Pay more than one visit, and try to vary the times at which you call. Go at lunchtime, for instance, and see what kind of food she is serving and how she handles the other children. Call in during the afternoon when there is a play session.'

Pam Jones recommends making the first visit purely social, so that you can soak up impressions. You can ask the things you want to know at subsequent visits.

The first visit will tell you certain things immediately:

* Does she smoke, and do you mind?

* Are there any pets, and if so, are they hygienically kept?

* Is there enough room for the children to play?

* Is there somewhere for them to nap?

* Is there a garden?

* Is the home well-placed or not – a high-rise flat, for example?

* Do the other children seem happy?

* Do you like the way she deals with them?

Casual chatting can tell you much more than the childminder even realises. How does she talk about the other mothers and children? If she complains a lot, the story is likely to have two sides. Which age-group does she seem happiest with? Some minders obviously adore babies; others have an affinity with toddlers; still others are best with older children. Minders who take your child as a baby, however, usually develop a fond relationship that continues through the stages. What are her family circumstances? Does she have a good relationship with her husband? Is he unemployed, and therefore around? Do *you* like him? (One mother only found out when her son began to talk that his childminder's husband beat her up in the kids' presence!) Does she seem a contented person, with friends close by and an interesting and varied social life with the children?

What to ask

If you have any special needs, you will obviously be prepared with the questions you have to ask. These are the points likely to be common to all mothers:

* What hours does the minder work? Will they realistically fit in with your working day? If not, will she be prepared to look after your child for longer on an overtime basis?

* What does she charge? If you work part time or shifts, you might want to work out a fee by the hour or the session.

* Do you have to supply baby food, milk, nappies? Or, if she is prepared to arrange this, how much extra will it cost?

* Can you take your child for a few hours on the odd day over a fortnight or a month for settling-in purposes? Most experienced minders will offer this anyway. If she doesn't like the idea, you should beware.

* What is her daily routine? For instance, does she take the children out every day?

* What sort of food does she provide?

* What kinds of things does she do with them at home?

* Will she take an older child to playgroup? Who pays the fees?

* When does she take her holiday? Can you take yours to coincide?

* Will you pay during the time you are away but she is still working?

* Do you pay when your child is off sick?

* Do you pay for odd days off, bank holidays?

* What happens when the minder is sick? Some minders, especially if they belong to a group, have an arrangement with other local minders to help out in an emergency.

* What are her ideas on childrearing?

* Does she have strong views on things like potty-training, nutrition, discipline, and do they coincide with yours?

A childminder is unlikely to change her way of doing things to suit you, so the best solution is to look for someone with whom you broadly agree on most matters. There will inevitably have to be some compromises. As this London mother of a two-and-a-half-year-old daughter wrote:

> The good things about the childminder arrangement manifest themselves in my daughter's character. She was a very difficult baby. Now she loves people, is open, friendly and enthusiastic. There's no doubt, though, who she loves most — thank God! She meets a

> completely different set of people with a different way of life, and isn't ignored or dismissed. The bad things are that there is little room for manoeuvre on the schedule, which makes for wear and tear on my nerves! Also the odd bad habit picked up — her accent, some swear words, too much telly-watching.

A good experienced childminder will almost certainly interview you, as well. It is equally important to tell her everything she needs to know about your child, and your own views on childrearing.

What to expect from a childminder

Just as the needs of working mothers vary, so does what a childminder is prepared to do. On top of looking for the personal qualities you want, you need someone who is prepared to work the hours that suit you. Sheila Paul, who was so lucky having her friend as childminder in West Germany, now find that back in England she needs three separate childminders, because no one person can fit in with her shifts.

A childminder who looks after only your child or children is likely to be more flexible; if she takes other children, whose parents work different hours, she is likely to want to standardise her own hours.

Looking after your child

There may be appointments you want your child to keep or activities that you would like introduced. For instance, you might need your baby to be taken to the clinic for check-ups and injections; an older child might benefit from attending a playgroup or one-o'clock club, and so on.

If the minder looks after only your children she might be prepared to take them when they are mildly ill, especially if it is just a slight cold, or they are feeling under the weather or recuperating from an illness. But, understandably, most minders won't want to look after a very sick child, and if they have other children they may even refuse to take a child who is only slightly unwell. That's why, like all working mothers, you need contingency plans of your own.

One Manchester mother, whose three-year-old now attends a nursery but used to be with the minder who now looks after her one-year-old exclusively, is aware of this problem amongst the joys:

> During troublesome times when the kid is cranky, the problem is shared. She's been through it all and puts problems into perspective – I take them less seriously in consequence. She's more patient than I am. They get told off less than they would if I were at home all day! My children have learnt to love one extra adult very easily. My first child had an older child to relate to because for her first year the minder's son wasn't yet at school – so it was very much a family atmosphere. All in all we are very lucky to have a like-minded mum, who loves the kids, handles them intelligently and is considerate about my feelings when leaving them. She herself returned to work after her first child was born – that is extremely useful, as she knows what I'm feeling and is sensitive to it. I worry that she might leave the area – I put consistency of care very high on the list of priorities and I've been lucky so far. We have a back-up system (another minder who the children know socially) but I still worry when she is ill.

What to Pay

What you pay is between you and the childminder. The NCMA were reluctant to quote any figures for the revision of this book, because they date quickly. Certainly the women who wrote to us reported considerable variations. Fees are often calculated by the week, though if your hours are odd you might prefer to work them out by the day, hour, or morning/afternoon. Minders will often make reductions for subsequent children. In many areas childminder groups agree fees between themselves, so that there is no shopping around for a cheaper minder. Obviously, if you did find someone who was cheaper than the others you would want to ask yourself why, and whether the saving was worth it. A few areas have introduced salaried childminders paid by the council. This is good news for the lower-paid, who may not be able to afford childminding fees. The parents' contribution is worked out in proportion to their earnings, and the council makes up the rest. Sometimes the social services department will help with fees anyway. Unfortunately, these subsidies usually only apply to families with children 'at risk'.

If you want the childminder to work particularly early or late, you will almost certainly have to pay extra.

An experienced minder is likely to have her rates worked out, and you will either agree with them or not. If the minder is new, or she is someone you know who is becoming a minder, it is worth getting the guidelines and contract from the NCMA. For instance, you will have to agree whether you are going to pay when your child is absent through sickness or holiday – and whether it will be the usual rate or a proportion of it. If you are happy with your minder you will probably feel it is worth paying a retainer while you are away on holiday if she would otherwise think of finding another child to fill the place.

Settling your Child

It is ideal from everyone's point of view if you can manage to leave your child for trial periods with the childminder before you return to work. It'll make you (and your child) feel better on your first day back if he or she is not suddenly plonked with a stranger, but is handed over to someone who is becoming familiar, in a house that is not unknown territory. It means that you can first experience the wrench of parting (not to be under-estimated) knowing that you will be back soon. It allows you to practise what it feels like leaving a child who perhaps cries and clings – which is a wretched experience and takes some getting used to. Most importantly, it also allows you to see if there are any problems that you hadn't thought of before, and whether you have made the right choice of childminder.

To make settling in as easy as possible, send your child off with the favourite toy/security blanket/dummy of the moment. Your minder will probably tell you what else she would like you to bring. At least one change of clothes is usually a good idea; if your child is a baby, then you will probably bring disposable nappies, made-up bottles, possibly home-prepared food.

Your childminder will need to know:

* Your work address and phone number.

* The numbers of anyone else she can contact in an emergency.

* Your doctor's name, address and phone number.

* A record of your child's illnesses, immunisations, allergic reactions.

It is probably worth writing in the (relative) calm of your home, a list of any other details about your child that might help the minder: likes, dislikes, preferred temperature of food, things that frighten (like vacuum cleaners or dogs), things that soothe (like a particular record). With an older child a 'dictionary' of own private words and what they mean is helpful. Your childminder will learn these quickly anyway, but it will help over the first few days.

Of course, if for religious or health reasons your child has a special diet or customs that must be observed, you will have discussed these at the interview stage with the minder. Add them to the list anyway.

Prepare for the fact that your child might well cry when being left, or behave badly when being collected. This really doesn't mean things haven't gone well during the day. As one mother wrote:

> For the last two months, now that Lisa is coming up to two and a half, she has objected to being left in the morning. She is fine as soon as I have gone. We try speaking about all the exciting things she will do during the day. She even assures me that she won't cry when I go away – but we still have the inevitable tears.

It is not these moments that tell you whether your child is happy or not with the minder. More important clues include difficulty in sleeping, nightmares, or a change in behaviour or personality at home. If your child is not happy with the minder, he or she is likely to show unhappy behaviour at other times, and continue to be extra-clingy when you would have expected more settled behaviour. This obviously needs looking into and you should talk to your childminder about it.

Your Relationship with Your Childminder

It is important to get on well with your childminder. Liking and respecting you will affect her feelings towards your child. If there is friction between you, a good childminder will try not to feel differently towards your child, but she is only human.

It is most important to keep scrupulously to your side of the bargain. Pay on the dot, and pick up your child when you say you will. Mothers who arrive late create bad feeling. After all, childminders regularly work ten hours or more per day looking after the children, and still have their own families to see to. If you are going to be late, at least telephone to let your minder know in good time if you possibly can. It eases the irritation somewhat if you have agreed to pay overtime when you are unavoidably late.

If you can make friends with your childminder there will be benefits for all of you. First, the likelihood is that if you feel real friendship for her she is likely to be on the same wavelength as you, and therefore a good substitute for you. If she is a good choice, she will probably grow fond of your child, and your child of her. Most childminders prefer it if you collect your child and leave quickly at the end of the day so that they can get on. But some like it if you stay for a coffee and a chat – and if yours does, jump at the chance, even if you are in a hurry to get home. It is the best way of finding out how things are going and what went on during the day. Otherwise, develop the habit of making a convenient time to have a long chat with your minder; perhaps invite her and any kids of her own over to you. Pam Jones says that when she was a minder she would invite all the mothers of her children round once a week in the evening, so they could talk together about problems, or simply have a good chat. If your childminder thinks this is a useful idea you could try it yourself – or offer your own home as a venue, or take it in turns with the other mothers.

The all-round benefits of having a nice childminder who turns into a friend is clear from Anneliese Young's warm report of the childminder who looks after her two boys:

> Our childminder has become a good friend, although not in my age group. She has three sons of her own – seventeen, sixteen and twelve years – so she is used to boys. She has enduring patience (unlike me), is very easy-going and flexible and it suits her to be paid to stay at home. She puts my children's needs before her housework, saying it will just get done when it gets done! Maybe my sons do not get enough discipline from her but they get a lot of love and she calls them sons. I do not interfere with what she does with them during

their time with her. It's my choice to work, I can't be part of every minute of their lives but have to accept that they will have experiences I cannot share. I remember telling the childminder that one of my sons had reached a certain milestone and she said she had noticed before I had, but hadn't wanted to mention it so that I could be the first to remark on it. That is typical of her selfless personality, and her help over the past five years has been so good that working, knowing I have her, has been made so much easier. I dread the thought of losing my childminder because she is so much part of our lives – she is my sons' 'Auntie Beth' and she remembers birthdays and Christmas, just as they remember 'Other Mother's Day'.

When things go wrong

Even with the best childminder there are likely to be minor irritations on your side and hers. Try to discuss difficulties as soon as they arise. The most important thing is the happiness and well-being of your child, and you should let that be your guide. If you feel your child is not happy, then you must take action quickly. Make an appointment to talk it over with your minder and see if she knows what the problem is. Unwittingly, it could be your fault. Pam Jones talked about one difficult baby she minded whose problems, she felt, stemmed from the mother's guilt feelings: 'When she was persuaded to relax and let go, the baby settled down quite happily.' Older children who sense your guilt can try to play you off against the minder, which can cause tensions if you are not alert to this.

If the problem is caused by something the minder is doing – or not doing – make every effort to sort it out. If you like her, and have a decent relationship with her, you can probably work out the solution together. If possible, don't take your child away without trying to improve matters first. It is best for your child to have the stability of a constant substitute for you, and switching from minder to minder could make the problem worse. If you need outside help, contact the local social services department and ask if their childminding adviser (the job-title varies from area to area) will mediate.

Of course, if you discover that the minder is negligent or cruel you must take your child away immediately, whatever difficulties this causes. But most problems are less serious than this, and can be dealt with satisfactorily, given tact and patience. One mother had trouble when her daughter wouldn't eat. It turned out that the minder was forcing her to the point of making her sick:

> We were adamant that nothing should be forced on her, only offered to her until she began to want food of her own accord. It was fairly ghastly for a while, as my daughter had obviously got herself into a real state. She still eats minimally chez the minder – perhaps because the food is disgusting!

If the minder merely does things differently from you but your child is happy, there is a strong case for leaving things as they are.

One mother describes her mixed feelings over the childminder's way of potty-training her daughter:

> Nicky told me happily that she was rewarding my daughter with sweets every time she performed in the potty. I didn't like the idea of this at all, but Nicky's handling of her had always been right up to that point, and she was very happy with her. I didn't want to clash with Nicky over this – after all, she was the one clearing up the 'mistakes' – so I thought I'd wait a while and see what happened. As it turned out, my daughter was completely clean within a fortnight and showed no signs of either demanding sweets to perform or any more sinister psychological symptoms. Eleven years later, I can still say it didn't seem to do her any harm at all!

If you have regular talks with your childminder you can be quite straightforward about anything that bothers you. If you let things fester, and then suddenly blow up, it will create bad feeling between you and won't be good for the child.

Becoming a Childminder Yourself

I became a registered childminder when my first child was one year old. The little boy I minded was two and a half and I enjoyed his answers and suggestions and getting stuck into messy play. My son wouldn't sit still for a story but I knew he enjoyed it when I heard him repeating the animal sounds from across the room. I might not have continued reading if I didn't have the older child. My son is now at school and my daughter is nearly three years old, and I can evaluate the enormous benefits we have gained. Both children learned to share with ease. My son can cope with a wide range of behaviour from other children at school. My daughter has overcome her fear of loud aeroplanes and other adults through watching children around her cope. I am amazed at how little I need to intervene. The children offer suggestions for play activities and sort out how even the little ones can join in. New children seem to settle very quickly, and my two look forward to a new child's visit.

Obviously it isn't all rosy. The children fight and argue, but I find it's not much quieter or less messy at the weekend! I do feel that minded children have their parents fresh and eager to be with them at the end of the day when I am wilting.

I spend time at the end of the day with each child. I also rely very heavily on my husband, who does shift work, so is often at home during the day. He will give our children a bit of special time, taking one for a walk or sharing a nice long bath.

I can't imagine family life without other children around. We seem to have all the benefits of having a large family without the financial pressures. It's hard work, but so satisfying and rewarding.

Becoming a childminder is a good option if you want to stay at home and like kids. But it won't make you much money, and won't give you any officially recognised skills, however experienced you become.

Being a childminder is a job. It is not an extension of being a good mother: looking after other people's children is different from looking after your own. Your hours are likely to be long, say 8.00a.m.–6.00p.m. if the mother is working a standard day and has to travel far to work.

If you are minding the children on your own you will probably only be registered to look after one or two (you are usually allowed three under five, including your own, and rarely more than one baby). You could be allowed up to three more between the ages of five and eight, including your own. So the amount of money you are likely to make will be little more than a 'useful extra' once you have deducted expenses. However, a friend or neighbour can register to help you, in which case you will be allowed to take on more children, though the number varies.

Some local authorities employ salaried minders. This has advantages if you are lucky enough to get the job. You continue to work from home in the same way as other minders, but your wages are paid by the council (so you don't worry about late payers). You also receive holiday and sickness pay, maternity leave, and all the usual benefits of the employed. More common is a subsidy scheme, whereby the council pays the fees for the children, but you are not salaried. However, some minders report that they have to wait a long time for this money.

Registering

By law you must register with the local social services department if you receive payment for looking after one or more children under eight who are not related to you, in your own home for two hours or more per day.

You can find the address and phone number of your

social services department under the name of your local council in the telephone directory. Ask to speak to the person who registers childminders, and you will then be told what you have to do.

These departments vary in the way they register, and what it is they look for, although this has started to become more standardised under the Children Act. All of them will visit you at home and give you the necessary forms to fill in.

Virtually the only legal requirement is that you should be a 'fit person' (in the sense of being fit to look after children), and the authorities have to prove that you are unfit if they refuse your application – which means that almost everyone who is determined to register gets through.

Certain social services departments are increasingly concerned about standards of childminding, and they make things slightly harder in the hope of weeding out women who are unsuitable. Some do this by having 'pre-registration' meetings or courses, which you must attend. Women who don't attend or drop out seldom get as far as registering. Other departments have their own quirks; for instance, one won't register smokers because it says they are unfit.

The visit

The childminding visitor is supposed to check that you have a safe, warm house, with room for the children to play, and that your kitchen and toilet facilities are adequate. At this stage the visitor might discuss childcare with you, and let you know exactly what the job involves; at some stage she will talk to you about why you want to do the job.

Safety

The visitor might make recommendations about items that could make your home safer, such as fire-guards, stair-gates and fire-blankets. It makes absolute sense to follow these, and do everything you can to child-proof your house – for the children's safety, and to preserve your own sanity. If your own child is still an immobile baby you could be unaware of the hidden dangers lurking in a normal home. Similarly, if your children are long grown-up, you may well have forgotten what these are. The following are some of the things to look out for:

* Electric plugs and sockets – are they broken or over-loaded? (You can buy safety covers for sockets not in use.)

* Check flexes and leads – children can pull on them with tragic results.

* Cookers: even tinies can reach up and pull pans down on top of themselves. A cooker guard gives you peace of mind.

* Fires: are they properly guarded?

* Poisons: bleach and cleaning materials should be kept up high, out of reach. So should medicines.

* Sharp objects, such as knives and knitting needles, should be out of reach. Sharp corners of furniture and radiators may have to be padded if you have a lurching toddler.

* High chairs and child-seats must be absolutely stable.

* Stairs should be cordoned off with a stair-gate.

* Small objects that babies can swallow or choke on should not be left around.

* Large expanses of glass (like french windows) should be covered with a shatter-proof film, or decorated with cut-outs so that children know they are there.

* Plants should be kept out of reach, or the kids might chew on the leaves. Check whether they are poisonous, and the correct treatment if this does happen.

Other requirements

Each authority designs its own registration system, but anyone who applies has to answer a few questions about herself and any other person over sixteen who lives in the same house. Questions cover your state of health, and ascertain whether you are able to provide warm, secure care. They will also want to know whether anyone in the household has been involved in cases of abuse to children or violence. Checks may also be made through the police. A doctor's reference, and sometimes other references may be required.

Waiting for your certificate

Like anything bureaucratic it can take months for your registration to come through, which is why it is worth applying as soon as possible. It shouldn't take more than six weeks, but in practice it can take as long as six months. It is illegal to mind children until your registration does come through, but many women are driven to go ahead by the delays. Councils are unlikely to prosecute if they have approved your registration and are simply waiting for the paperwork. They usually only prosecute women who persistently refuse to register.

The advantages of registering

One of the best reasons for registering is that you cannot

be covered by the insurance that protects minded children and their property unless you are registered. It is also illegal to mind children if you are not registered, unless you are closely related to them. An unregistered childminder is first served an enforcement notice. If she fails to respond, she will be fined – and it can be around £2,000.

But there are more positive advantages, too:

* You are entitled to a third of a pint of free milk every day for each child you mind. It is your only legal right, so the NCMA particularly urge all childminders to claim it. The application form (WF/DN) is rather complicated, and some minders have had their claims returned because they were incorrectly filled in; but the childminding visitor should be able to help if you are in doubt. You are also required to keep proper attendance records of the children before you can claim it. The Children Act also requires records to be kept, not just of attendance, but also behavioural notes. Although these don't have to be formal, it is wise to do so, and helpful for the parents of the children.

* The childminding visitor should continue to visit you from time to time. This is not to snoop, though she will obviously be concerned with how you are managing. Most childminders find her help invaluable. One minder wrote to the NCMA newsletter to say that her visitor was always prepared to help out in a crisis even out of working hours – and would listen to private problems, too.

* In many areas you will get practical help from the social services department with loans of toys, first-aid kits, expensive safety items such as fire-guards, or other equipment, such as double buggies. If schemes of this kind don't operate in your area, ask why, and join with other childminders to lobby for them. Most

173

councils are well disposed towards helping registered childminders.

* Similarly, many more councils are introducing courses for childminders, and you may have the opportunity to attend one. These include lessons on childcare and development, educational play, and discussions of problems faced by childminders.

* Once you are registered the social services department will put your name on the list and send mothers who want childminders to see you.

* It is only when you are registered that you can advertise your services.

* Some social services departments arrange group meetings for childminders, and you will find getting to know the other women invaluable. Some areas have drop-in centres where the children can play; this allows the kids you mind to get to know others, and you can make friends with other minders.

Finding children to mind

Except in areas of high female unemployment you will have no problem finding children to look after. If you do not already know of someone who needs your services, you will be put on the registered minders' list, and mothers will start coming to see you. You can also advertise – a simple card in a newsagent's window will usually bring you more enquiries than you can handle.

In this sense, you are in a much better position than mothers looking for a minder, and you should take advantage of this. You are entitled to vet the children and the parents as thoroughly as they vet you. After all, you may well be looking after the children concerned for years, and it is important that you all like each other.

You want your own child or children to get on with any

other children you bring into the home, and unless you are experienced, you probably don't want a child who is very difficult and will take a disproportionate amount of your time. One minder accepted a child whose mother had come to her in despair after having been left by a succession of nannies: 'I suspected strongly that they left because the *mother* was difficult, but the end result was a disturbed little boy, who took months of careful handling.'

It obviously helps if you and the mother think alike about discipline. The NCMA supports EPOCH's 'no smacking' campaign, and at least one capable and experienced childminder was de-registered by the council for continuing to administer the odd smack which, the council said, was against the Children Act. Therefore, if the child is used to being smacked, you may find that your own gentler form of discipline doesn't work, or alternatively, you might believe in a 'good smack' but the mother doesn't, and reports you to the social services. One childminder found she got on extremely well with all her mothers, except one: 'I couldn't even call her by her first name. My children didn't like her, my husband avoided her like the plague. She resented me, so she put me down, and though I was looking after her child she said childcare was something anyone could do.'

Pam Jones says, 'You should be able to have a relationship where you can be quite honest about anything you don't like. Even if the mothers get upset initially, or you slightly resent what they say to you, as long as you can always talk about it things will turn out all right.'

Knowing what to charge

There is no standard rate for childminding, and rates vary from area to area. It is worth finding out what the going rate is locally, which the social services department will tell you. But in the end it is between you and the mother.

Some women charge by the day, others by the hour, the

week or the session. If the child is going to come to you five days a week at regular times, it makes sense to charge a weekly rate. If there is a lot of chopping and changing, you may prefer one of the other options. There is no reason why you have to charge the minimum if you know that the child comes from a higher-income home, and you are providing meals and quality care.

Other considerations

When fixing your charges remember that you will incur a number of expenses in doing your job: food, heating, lighting, wear and tear on furniture and furnishings, toys, equipment and outings. You must in any case keep a note of these, as they are tax-deductible. The NCMA provides a useful cash book for you to log these things, as well as an attendance register. You can, of course, use any notebook to record these details, but some women find that having a special book inspires them to keep on with what is essentially a boring chore.

When fixing your rate, decide:

* Are you going to charge a special rate for unsocial hours: before 8.00a.m., after 6.00p.m., weekends? (Many minders do.)

* What to charge for absences – sickness or days off when the parent is at home. (Many minders do charge for these.)

* What to charge if you are sick. (Usually no charge.)

* Will you charge during the parents' holidays? (Many minders do.)

* Will you charge when you are on holiday? (Usually no charge.)

* Will you charge for bank holidays? (Many minders do.)

* Will there be a separate charge for main meals (sometimes), disposable nappies (usually), other special items for babies (usually), special outings (usually), playgroup fees (usually)?

* Will you make reductions for children from the same family?

It is important for the parents to be aware that what you are doing is a job, and if their children don't come for a day or more you can't be expected to take a drop in earnings.

Asking for payment in advance often helps avoid problems about late payment. Fixing it for the mother's payday is another good idea if you sense there might be a problem. Some parents try to make deductions for the days their children did not turn up. You should not allow this, and payment in advance usually helps stop such arguments.

Drawing up a contract

If you don't use the NCMA's contract, you should draw up your own. These are the details it should include:

* Agreed hours.

* Agreed days.

* Agreed fees – including overtime.

* Charges for:
     sickness
     occasional days off
     child's holiday
     childminder's holiday
     bank holidays

* Agreed payday.

* Who is to pay playgroup fees.

* Agreed period of notice.

* What the parents have agreed to supply.

* Any other special arrangements.

This should be signed and dated by both parent and childminder. Contracts have been successfully upheld legally. The Citizens' Advice Bureau will give you advice on pursuing a breach of contract through the small claims court, and the NCMA could advise too.

Your own family

This is one job that affects your entire family. It is their home too, and you should discuss it with them all, however young. Your children will have to become used to sharing you, and their rights must be respected. Their toys should not necessarily be communal. Outgrown toys can be added to the minded children's playthings, but not new or precious ones. Your children should be encouraged to put away any toys that are precious to them, or anything they don't want touched.

Your partner must also be made to understand that what you are doing is a job, which means that he cannot expect the same standards of housekeeping and cooking as before. One women, whose mother became a childminder, reported that her retired, sick father became very irritated when the children were around, even though one of them was his grandchild: 'But the house was big enough for him to get away.' If your partner is ill or unemployed, and the house *isn't* big enough, you will clearly have to think twice about whether it is really possible.

Pam Jones had six children of her own, and began minding when the fifth was born. The older children weren't bothered one way or another by having the other children around, and her eldest daughter positively loved it: 'She could do anything I could – and better – when she was thirteen and older.' But her youngest boy became jealous when she took on a difficult child to whom she had to give a lot of attention, including having him at night and weekends. 'The older he got the more I realised that he didn't like me looking after other children. I had to miss a lot of his school events because of minding very young children that I couldn't take with me. One day I realised I had gone in too deep.' At that point she gave up childminding and took a job with the local childminding association instead. From her own experience, Pam Jones recommends all minders keep a careful eye on their children. 'If your own child is showing difficult behaviour you may have to give up.'

Starting up

You make everything a lot easier for yourself if you are absolutely professional from the start.

Keeping financial records

Keep careful records of all money received and expenses incurred. Because a lot of expenses are tax-deductible, including 'hidden' costs, such as heating, childminders usually find that they do not make enough profit to have to pay tax. But if you are haphazard in your accounting and are hazy about what you have spent out, you may find that the Inland Revenue estimate that you are liable to pay tax. What is worse, if they only find out about your existence years after you started working, you may find yourself with a heavy backdated tax bill with no means of convincing them that their estimate is unfair.

Tax, National Insurance, and the impact of childminding fees on benefit payments

The NCMA are the best people to contact about this. The

following information is taken from their literature. If your local tax office has not had much dealing with childminders they may not be up to date about what is allowable. Do check all of this information first, as it can date.

1. *Expenses you can claim*

At the end of each week, write down which of the following expense have come out of your childminding earnings. What is left is your profit for the purpose of calculating tax, NI and so on.

* Food for the children (unless paid for by the mothers).

* One-third of heating and lighting bills.

* Any money spent on outings.

* Toys and other equipment.

* One-tenth of rent and rates.

* Wear and tear on furniture (one-tenth of income).

* Petrol and other travel costs.

2. *National Insurance*

The NCMA estimate that most childminders do not earn enough after expenses to be required to pay National Insurance. That does not mean you can just forget about it. You should contact your DSS office and ask for a 'certificate of exception'. It is important to do this, or you might be asked for back payment.

Higher earners will have to pay class 2 contributions (the self-employed stamp). Refer to NCMA's leaflet or the local DSS to find out about current earnings limits. In 1992/3 you had to make a profit of £3,030 (£58.27 per week) after all your expenses had been deducted from your fees before needing to pay a stamp of £5.35 per week. With profits of over £6,120 in 1992/3 you also had to pay class 4 contributions (the stamp of the higher-earning self-employed) – which is rare in the case of childminders.

3. *Taxation*

Childminders earning less than a certain amount per year will not have to pay tax. In 1992/3 it was £3,445 after expenses for a single person or married woman, £5,165 for a one-parent family, but the figures may have changed by the time you read this. The NCMA updates its leaflets whenever there is a change. Your local tax office will also tell you what the current earnings limit is.

4. *Income Support*

The NCMA point out that if you or your husband claim Income Support, only one-third of your earnings as a childminder is recognised as income. So although your Income Support can be reduced because you are childminding, as the reduction is calculated only on part of your earnings, in most cases it is still worth continuing to childmind.

5. *Family Credit*

This is assessed on a six-monthly basis, so if you start minding a child within that period you should continue to receive it, though not afterwards.

Insurance

As soon as you are registered, take out an insurance policy to cover accidental injury to the children and their property. Registered childminders have to accept responsibility for the children in their care, and large damages can be awarded against them if a child is injured while in their care, or a child damages other people's property while in their care. The NCMA has a block liability insurance for members.

Keeping a register

Record the name, address and attendances of each child, including basic information such as date of birth and doctor's name and phone number, as well as a record of everything you need to know – previous illnesses, treatment the child has received, any allergies.

Emergency list

Keep a list of emergency numbers by the telephone (doctor, hospital, work numbers of parents, anyone else you can contact, such as grandparents, neighbours). Include on this someone you can call to take over from you in an emergency – ideally another childminder.

Accidents

Keep a well-stocked first-aid box. It is also extremely useful to take a course on emergency first aid. With the best care in the world, children still have accidents. One concerned minder wrote to the Wandsworth Childminding Association newsletter about this problem. She said that if a child had an accident she would inform the parents, take the injured child to hospital, and if necessary sign a consent form for treatment if the parents could not get there in time. Her worry was that the hospital might not accept her authority. She discussed the situation with one of her mothers, who wrote to the local hospital to find out what they thought about it. This was part of the reply:

> . . . should parents wish their child's childminder to have any of the rights normally held by the parents concerning treatment it is best that the childminder has in her possession a written authorisation, preferably drawn up on the advice of a solicitor, giving an account of the rights the parents wish the childminder to have in the event of an emergency, with particular thought given to situations such as blood transfusion, minor operations, major operations and life and death situations. Childminders with such authorisation will be permitted details of the condition of the sick child in their care should they come to the hospital in person. Where a child is in urgent need of clinical treatment the doctors will treat them regardless of either parents' or childminders' wishes, as they have a legal and moral obligation to do so . . .

Although some parents and childminders sign a form drawn up by childminding associations giving the minder the right to look after the child in case of accident, some hospitals might not consider this enough. Parents may not like discussing the possibility of serious accidents, but you would be well advised to do so at an early stage.

Your other role for your clients

Good childminders usually find that their work is not confined to looking after the children in the hours stated. Mothers who have grown to like and respect you tend to feel that you can do anything. Pam Jones remembers that she often had to mother the mothers:

> I was told about every kind of marriage problem, and asked for my advice on solving them. Parents sometimes phoned me in the middle of the night if their child was ill and asked me what was wrong. I said I couldn't possibly tell as I wasn't there! But they assumed I knew

everything, and I often found myself having to guess at a diagnosis when symptoms were described to me.

Joining an association

Childminders can suffer the same feelings of isolation that all at-home mothers share, and those who have made friends with other minders are very much happier. In some areas there are self-help groups and associations run by the local childminders. The social services are likely to know of them. As one minder said:

> I found joining my local group a great help. Childminders use one another to talk though problems, because they have all experienced them, and can come up with solutions. You can pair up and help one another out if you are ill, and meet up regularly with all the children.

The NCMA will also be able to tell you if there is a group in your area, or you can join the association as an individual member. The group rate is even more favourable. The benefits are much more than social:

* You have the opportunity to join the block Public Liability Insurance Scheme. Registered childminders who belong to the NCMA are covered by a policy that pays out legal fees and damages. The cover operates whenever the children are in the care of the minder, and also covers minded children being temporarily left in the care of another adult during an emergency. The cost is calculated per childminder rather than per child. Claiming is not complicated, and the NCMA helps with formalities.

* You receive copies of the quarterly NCMA magazine, which covers topics relevant to childminders, and includes letters about problems and solutions and good ideas from other minders.

* You receive annually updated leaflets which cover guidelines on pay, and conditions and tax and benefits as they affect childminders.

* You can call on the help and advice of staff and elected regional representatives, many of them ex-childminders.

* They give up-to-date information on any small grants that are available.

* For someone starting out, the contract form for drawing up an agreement between parent and minder is very useful, as is the registration form, register of attendance, and accounts book, which you can buy at a reasonable price.

CHAPTER 9

Nurseries and Other Forms of Group Care

I personally feel happier about leaving my baby (ten months) at a nursery than with a childminder, which I feel might be a confusing situation for a baby – another 'mum', another 'home', too like her home and mum here. She can't confuse the nursery with her home situation, and the other children and staff provide a constant source of interesting things to do and see.

In this section we want to say something about all types of group care for the under-fives. There is a big difference between day nurseries and creches on the one hand and nursery schools and playgroups on the other.

Day nurseries are a genuine under-five childcare option for the working mother: they are usually open all day and the hours reflect the needs of working parents. Nursery schools (or classes) and playgroups have a more social and educational purpose: they are usually only available half-day, and are no more geared to the parents' working hours than schools for older children. A number of the part-timers who wrote to us took advantage of the limited hours per day nursery schools or playgroups offer, but this was usually by supplemented other childcare. It is only a possible alternative if you work very short hours which coincide with the school's hours, and your home is very close.

Neither type of group care is widely available in Britain. Statistics from the Early Childhood Unit show that in 1990 there were only 0.9 local authority day nursery places per 100 children under five (down from 1985 at 1.0 places); 1.8 private registered nursery places; 24.5 places at nursery schools and classes, and 33.2 places at playgroups. It is hardest of all to find places for the under-twos. Few local authorities even keep records of which nurseries in their area cater for under-twos. There is little formal policy about this age-group, and what there is is often negative: many authorities are *proud* of the fact that they don't provide much in the way of group care for babies, because they believe it is not good for the children. Often it is left up to individual council officers, or the director of each day nursery, to decide whether to provide a 'baby room' for under-twos.

With less than 25 per cent of four-year-olds in any form of nursery education, Britain's record compares poorly with other European countries. Take France, for example, where there is universal state nursery education from the age of three in the *Ecoles Maternelles* supplemented by *haltes garderies*, which are additional childcare facilities to fill the gap between the end of nursery school and the end of the parents' day.

Day Nurseries and Creches

Even though only a tiny number of women are able to choose to send their child to a day nursery, full-time day nurseries are a preferred option for many mothers. They like the idea of their children being cared for by trained nursery nurses in a safe, clean environment, surrounded by equipment and toys appropriate to each stage of development, with lots of other children to befriend. As more women are returning to work now than in the recent past, competition for nursery places increases. As one woman wrote about the situation in her medium-sized town:

> The social services run two day nurseries for fifty to sixty children who come from 'deprived' families. These nurseries are not a choice normally available to working parents. There are two small private nurseries offering full daycare from 8.30-5.30 to about twenty children a day. Both nurseries have long waiting lists.

One woman who lives in Hull and now has teenage children remembered their nursery days:

> I had just moved to a new area so didn't know anyone to ask about nurseries. I had to change my three-year-old twice before I was finally satisfied with the nursery.

The idea of chopping and changing now seems like unimaginable luxury to most working mothers, who might be so pleased to get a place that they do not look too closely at how ideal the nursery is. According to a study by the Thomas Coram Research Unit, only 15 per cent of the women in their sample who used a nursery felt that they had had a choice of nurseries.

In some areas being a lone parent qualifies you for preferential treatment in gaining a local authority day nursery place, but when there is a very heavy demand the 'deprived' children who get in are suffering genuine serious problems. To be guaranteed a place in heavily over-subscribed areas a woman often has to sign a form saying that she is likely to abuse her child; commonly these women don't work (your child is not at risk from you if you are out of the house all day!), and usually their partners are unemployed, too. Here is a typical example of the extent of the shortage of places: one woman got a job at a day nursery and needed a place for her own baby. She was told that the nursery was only for mothers 'in real need' – so she ended up having to scrabble around for an inconvenient arrangement with a childminder. You can understand the authority's interpretation of 'real need', yet it is galling for this working mother, whose need was genuine enough in that she could not start helping those other children without suitable care for her own child!

Finding a nursery

If you like the idea of sending your child to a nursery, start early. Find one and put your child's name down on the waiting list as soon as you can. Sometimes you may be told that there is no likelihood of a place, only to find that one comes free when another child drops out.

All day nurseries have to be registered with the local social services department, whether they are private or state-run, so you should be able to find out the addresses of local nurseries through their offices. There should also be a list at your local library.

What to look for

If you are lucky enough to find a nursery within reasonable distance of your home, with a place available when you need one, you will want to look at what is on offer very carefully.

One of your first concerns will be the hours the nursery is open, and whether this fits in with your working day, taking travelling time into account. You may find a nursery or creche near your place of work rather than your home – in which case you should also consider whether travelling during the rush hour with a child and assorted equipment like a buggy is going to be a problem for you.

You will want to know what the nursery costs, and whether your child is within its age-range. Places for babies are invariably restricted because they need constant care (and consequently more members of staff); very few nurseries will take babies under six months, and most only start taking children from the age of two.

The ratio of staff to children is another important factor, particularly if your child is a baby and will need regular attention. You will expect a minimum of one staff member to every three babies, and one to five for older children. Ideally the staff-to-child ratio will be even higher than this. Where there are too many children and too few staff you will only be able to count on your baby's immediate physical needs being looked after: feeding, nappy changing, attention when really distressed. After that the staff will not have the time to offer the kind of attention and stimulation that babies need if they are to thrive. Older children can amuse themselves and each other, but even they need a considerable amount of attention. Problems can arise where there are only a few members of staff, however well-intentioned – particularly as they can fall sick.

A visit or two will give you a good idea of the general happiness of the children at the nursery, and whether they are busy and contentedly engaged in various activities.

> As my child is the only one – and is likely to continue to be – a day nursery was the best choice with regard to her mixing. I did not want a childminder – felt it would be like a surrogate mother.

Facilities

A visit will also tell you what you need to know about the facilities. You will hope to find plenty of room inside and outside, with equipment such as climbing frames, sand trays, Wendy houses, a variety of toys, books, and opportunity for messy play with water and paint.

If the nursery has no garden you will want to find out whether there is easy access to a nearby park or square, and if not, whether the children are taken out every day for an outing.

There should be enough room in the nursery to provide children who need it a place to rest in the day. You will also be influenced by good light, fresh air, bright cheery colours, and evidence of the children's creativity pinned to the walls. Nurseries are regularly checked from the safety point of view, but you will probably want to look round for yourself.

If your child is under two, you will want to know if there is a baby room or whether the children are mixed together in 'family groups'. There was a move away from baby rooms, but many nurseries are reinstating them – a newly crawling baby, for instance, can be in danger from boisterous four-year-olds. On the other hand, a baby room that is small and in which the children do all their playing, eating and sleeping is not desirable.

Some nurseries are trying to create family environments, with sofas and carpets and ordinary furniture, which you may prefer.

Find out what kind of food is provided (sometimes depressingly unhealthy, as many mothers report) and whether you can give your child a packed lunch.

Staff

You will want to know whether the staff are qualified, what the qualifications are, and how many trainees/other helpers there are. The more staff the better. A study showed that nursery nurses, being subject to stress, were regularly off sick – and, because they were concerned not to let colleagues down, would return before they were completely better, setting up a vicious circle.

A visit will give you a general idea of how the staff manage the children: discipline, how they sort out quarrels, how far they involve themselves in the children's play and activities.

Unfortunately there is often a regular turn-over of staff, so it would be a mistake to take up a nursery place just because you were particularly impressed with one or two of the staff.

> We wanted our daughter to attend a day nursery to increase her contact with other children and to get her used to spending time away from us. We opted for a day nursery rather than a childminder because we did not want to introduce a third 'significant adult' into her life.

Policy

Talking to the principal can give you a good idea of what the general aims and policy of the nursery are, but each member of staff will interpret this individually. Some day nurseries are quite rigid in their scheduling of the day and noticeably old-fashioned in their ideas – believing that children should be timetabled (sitting six-month-old babies on the pot, for instance). Others are working to provide more homely, flexible environments, and trying to give the babies continuity in who looks after them.

Parental involvement

When your children are young you want to be as actively involved in their care as possible, given that as a working mother you are not around in the day. Therefore you will want to know what the policy is towards parental involvement.

* Do they allow you to have a reasonable hand-over period, when your child is distressed at you leaving? It *can* be irritating for the staff (who know how quickly your child perks up once you have gone) to witness a prolonged leave-taking, but they shouldn't make you feel that you are not allowed to do this.

* Can you visit a younger child during the day – for breastfeeding, or a purely social call? This may be

slightly disruptive for the members of staff, but they should be able to recognise the value of it for your child. (Some nurseries encourage all parental involvement.)

* Can your opinions affect policy? If you have strong ideas about food, discipline, or other concerns, do they welcome them – are they flexible enough to change, if other parents agree?

Activities

What kinds of activities are planned for the day? Are the children encouraged to have times of vigorous play mixed with quieter moments when they are perhaps read a story? Do they take the children on local outings regularly? Is there a policy of taking one or two children on 'ordinary' outings – to the bank, post office, shop, and so on?

Discipline and training

You will want to know how they handle naughty children, and if their ideas fit in with yours. Are they prepared to change nappies and potty-train, or will they only take children who are already trained?

Illness

It is also important to ask what their policy is on sick children. Is there a sick bay for your child to rest if unwell at nursery and you can't come immediately? Must children stay home if they have any infectious illness? (This is usually the case, and is a distinct problem with nurseries – also that your child is likely to catch every germ going from the other children.)

Hours and holidays

How flexible are the nursery's hours? Does it matter if you are ever a little late picking up your child? Is the nursery open all year round or does it keep to school holidays? What is the arrangement when you go on holiday or your child is ill – will you be expected to pay for those days or not?

Local authority day nurseries

These usually open at hours that suit most working mothers: weekdays from 8a.m. to 6p.m. is common, and they are open all year round, though some close for a couple of weeks in the summer. Fewer and fewer take young babies, and most don't take the children until they are two. The children can attend until they are five, and ready to start school.

Some local authority day nurseries are free, though many charge a small fee, and sometimes your income is taken into account.

The staff are usually qualified nursery nurses with NNEB diplomas, or similar, and trainees. Nurseries are regularly checked by the local authority, and standards of hygiene, safety, staffing levels and care, are good on the whole. The problem is that most of them are staffed only by the statutory minumum, and staff sickness means they can become under-staffed. Because many local authorities believe that group care is harmful for the under-twos and prefer childminders, morale can be low among staff who believe that their work is under-valued.

Bear in mind that the emphasis in day nurseries is on the physical and emotional care of young children. Although the trained staff will be familiar with the importance of play, they are not trained as nursery teachers, and you should not necessarily expect the level of educational activities of a nursery school.

You are very unlikely to get a place for your child in one of these nurseries unless your circumstances are unfortunate. One woman, who lived in York, was granted a place because she was a single parent, though her circumstances were otherwise fine. She paid a token amount for this marvellous nursery, which was open from 7.30a.m. to 6.00p.m., and there were four children to each nursery nurse:

> My only criticism is that if she becomes ill whilst she is there they ring me at work and expect me to collect her immediately. I feel that there should be some provision for keeping them there, such as a sick-room, until alternative arrangements can be made.

One possible drawback of a local authority nursery place is that you will lose your place if you move outside the authority's boundaries — for instance, in London if you move to an adjacent borough.

Another woman wrote about the day nursery her daughter attended in the year before starting school:

> It wasn't strictly a local authority nursery: it was a research-centre, but provided a similar service and was free. There were no entry requirements: they simply took any child who lived within half a mile of the nursery whatever the circumstances. I'm afraid to say that I gave the address of a friend because I lived far too far away to qualify. It was the most fantastic place. Neither of us could believe our eyes when we looked around the playground, with its climbing frames, sandpits, old tyres and children merrily splashing away with paint on easels. Inside was even better if anything: Wendy house, book corners, puzzles, toys, masses of supervised activities. My daughter had been very happy at her childminder, but she didn't know what happiness was until she started at the nursery! She was outraged that they insisted she was broken in gently and had to

attend mornings only for the first week. It was like
dragging her from paradise.

Private day nurseries

Since first writing this book, there has been a growth in
provision of private day nurseries, alongside the higher
profile gained by working mothers – who are now
recognised as providing substantial business. A number of
nursery franchises have been set up, as well as independent
nurseries.

Like local authority day nurseries, these open at hours
that are convenient for most working mothers. They are
usually run by private individuals as businesses so charges
reflect what they are offering, though some are subsidised.
Very roughly, you can equate private nursery fees with the
fees you would expect to pay for a private primary or
secondary school.

Private day nurseries also fall under the Children Act, so
you should expect standards to be in line with local
authority day nurseries. Not all the staff will necessarily be
qualified, however, so you should check this.

A number of women in our sample used private day
nurseries and seemed happy with the ones they had found.
Alison Downer, who lives in Cleveland, heard about the
nursery she sends her three-year-old daughter to from her
health visitor, but it was also recommended by other
mothers. The hours are 8.30a.m. to 5.00p.m., but slightly
flexible, and there are four members of staff to each child.
She says she realises that she was lucky to get a place, as
now it has a waiting list. She was very happy with the
nursery, and her child enjoys it, but she has one
reservation:

> The food at nursery is boring – the same menu week in
> week out. It seems to have taken her appetite for more

exotic food away. Now she's not keen to try anything new. It may well be a phase she'd go through anyway, but the slight guilt at working makes me blame the nursery.

Another woman wrote to us about the nursery her ten-month-old baby attends in York, which she heard about from a colleague. She went on the waiting list when she was six months pregnant, and her baby started at eight months. It is open 8.30a.m. to 5.30p.m., and is charged either by the morning, the afternoon, or for a full day. There is one adult to every three children, and the staff don't mind mothers visiting at lunchtime:

> At the moment I feel that my situation is very good indeed. The nursery is near to my place of work and the staff are wonderful, creating a happy atmosphere, never leaving a child to cry, being firm when necessary, etc. They get taken out on trips, walks, gymnastics, swimming, and generally have a good time. I consider myself lucky to be able to use such a good nursery for my baby. She seemed to settle there after just a couple of weeks, and this made me more relaxed and helped when I left her.

Jill Thornton from West Yorkshire was lucky enough to find a private nursery just down the road from where she lives, and her son (now two) started when he was thirteen months old. There is one member of staff to every eight children. The hours are 8.15a.m. to 5.45p.m.:

> I like this arrangement because the staff are all very friendly and take notice of any advice you may offer. They are all fully trained nursery nurses and have done or are doing first-aid courses. The children have substantial meals at lunchtime and have sandwiches in the afternoon to tide them over until tea time. They have parties when it is their birthdays. There is every sort of toy imaginable. The children are split into two age-groups – until two and a half, and two and a half till

it's a nice day there are paddling pools, a
and all sorts of outdoor toys. Bradley has his
friends, some I know and some I don't. He tells me
little things that have happened during the day. The
nursery help potty train and help with talking and table
manners. The girls take an interest in us as well as
Bradley which makes them seem like friends as well as
people looking after Bradley. I don't really think it can
be improved.

A woman who lives in Manchester, sends her eldest son,
aged three, to a nursery that was recommended to her. Her
youngest child is with a childminder. She had to put her
name down on the waiting list two years before she
wanted a place:

> There is a very good team running the nursery though I
> sometimes wish I had more opportunity to find out all
> that they're doing – Jonathan only tells what he wants
> to. But I know he's happy so I don't really worry – it's
> the beginning of him having an independent life. I'm
> also a bit critical of the menu at lunchtimes – I wish it
> were a bit more health-conscious – but I understand she
> has to go with what the majority like and Jonathan does
> eat the sausages and crisps like everyone else.

Workplace day nurseries

These may be provided by an employer or by institutions
such as a hospital or university for their staff or students.
The fees you pay for a place are usually subsidised by your
employer. Happily, since this book was first written this is
no longer considered a taxable perk, so long as the nursery
is registered and is on premises provided by the employer,
or, if off-site, the employer is 'wholly or partly responsible
for financing and managing the provision of care'.

A drawback may be that a workplace nursery place can
make changing jobs more difficult, though if you are

happy in your job (and secure) a workplace nursery can only be a bonus. One of the main advantages of the workplace nursery is that you can often have more say in the way they are run. Only one woman who wrote to us was lucky enough to take advantage of such a place. She is a lecturer who lives in Devon, and has children who are now eight and ten. When younger the children went to a nursery run by the student guild at work, which fitted in with her hours. She applied as soon as she knew she was pregnant:

> I wanted a nursery because then the children wouldn't suffer from one person's faults or the dangers of a private home. The nursery was inspected, the staff trained, sockets were out of reach, bleach etc. was locked up and there were more things to do and play with than at home. Also our home wasn't big enough for a live-in nanny and being out in the country there would have been problems with transport – we couldn't have offered a car.

Even if your place of work does not offer a day nursery, it is worth finding out if any others in your area do. Sometimes they may have a few spare places to fill.

This is what one woman who lived in York did. She heard that the local university sometimes took children from outside, and she put her daughter's name down on the list very soon after she was born:

> She started attending for two sessions a week when she was ten months old. We have been happy with the care she received there. We felt that the staff and parents of other children shared our outlook and values on life and childcare in particular (trying to operate a small non-sexist multiracial unit). We gradually increased our daughter's attendance at the day nursery to three full days a week as our work commitments increased. Initially I was very concerned about our daughter's physical safety at the nursery. As it happened, all the major accidents she has had have occurred in our care!

> The problems we found with this day nursery were that the hours were inflexible and the nursery followed university terms and closed down for a month during the summer and two weeks at Christmas and Easter. We had to take leave and rely upon friends to cover these holiday periods.

If you work for a large organisation with other working parents, you may want to investigate through your union the possibility of establishing a workplace nursery. The Workplace Nurseries Campaign was launched in March 1984 when the Inland Revenue decided to treat employers' subsidies to workplace nurseries as a taxable benefit to those parents who use them. Apart from successfully campaigning to have this lifted, the organisation also offers practical support and back-up to trade unionists and employers who are trying to establish new workplace childcare provision. They have now changed their name to Working for Childcare (see *Further Help*)

Voluntary and community day nurseries

Some voluntary groups are establishing community day nurseries. Some also join with local employers and/or the local authority to set up such nurseries. These are for local parents, who are also expected to be involved in managing the day nursery and making decisions about how it is run. This is a real bonus if you have strong ideas, know like-minded parents who share your views, and are irritated by the fact that it is usually difficult to impress them on conventional nurseries.

The charges are usually kept down because they are also funded by grants from the local authority or charities, and the fees may be means-tested. The facilities may not be as good as those in other types of nursery.

Jane Parkin from York had both of her daughters at the local community nursery for a short while: 'Both girls were happy there. It was cheap and cheerful but not ideal for full-time care as there was very little outside play.'

Part-time Nursery Care: Nursery Schools and Playgroups

These schools and classes will not look after your children for a full day and will present the same problems to the working mother as primary and secondary schools: that is, what to do in the long school holidays and half-terms, as well as coping with the short hours.

Many mothers like the idea of their children mixing with others and most children enjoy the educational aspect of nursery school, so even if it is not a satisfactory answer to your childcare problems, a place at a nursery school or playgroup can be a bonus for your child.

How to find one

Nursery schools are the province of your local education department, and they should be able to tell you what state or private nursery schools you can find in your area.

Playgroups are the responsibility of the social services department, which should have a list, or you can contact the Pre-School Playgroups head office, to find out about branches in your area (see *Further Help*).

Nursery schools and classes

These are provided by education authorities as early education for children of at least three or four. There are some separate nursery schools, as well as nursery classes attached to primary schools. It is well worth checking whether your local primary school offers such a class.

Many of these nursery schools are just open for two or three hours each morning or afternoon, though some follow the normal school day (9.00a.m. to 3.00p.m.). They are open during school terms, and are usually staffed by nursery teachers and nursery nurses.

One woman who wrote from Newtonabbey applied early for her four-year-old daughter to attend a local state nursery school after hearing about it from other mothers. It was open 9.15a.m. to 1.00p.m.; although she worked part-time, these hours didn't fit in with her job, so her parents-in-law had to collect her daughter. This suited her well: 'I am very happy with the arrangement and don't think it needs improving.'

A woman who lives in West Yorkshire sent her children (now aged seven and five) to a state-run nursery school. She applied a year in advance to do so. The staff/child ratio was 1:7, and the hours were 9.15a.m. to 3.15p.m. She said, 'I think nursery education is appallingly designed – how can working mothers finish at 3.00p.m.?' She was able to send her children because she employed a nanny, who would pick them up.

A woman who lives in Manchester sends her three-year-old to a state-run nursery school, which she found by enquiring at school and ringing round. It costs nothing, and the hours are 9.00a.m. to 3.30p.m. for full-timers. The childminder picks her daughter up at the end of the day. The child loves the nursery:

> The headmistress gave me preferential treatment as she believed teachers should help other teachers. I was extremely lucky. The nursery has an excellent reputation and I cannot praise them enough for their dedication, high standards and achievements with the children. My only complaint is that she goes to a nursery in the authority where I work and not in the authority in which we live. This means that she will not be going to infant school with the same children, which is a pity for her. There is hardly any provision at all for nursery places in Bury.

Private nursery schools

Private schools are run on similar lines to local authority schools. Some run for half a day only, others for the full school day. Charges vary widely from area to area.

As with any other form of nursery care you will find that there is probably a long waiting list:

> I rang up the local Montessori nursery school nearly two years before my son would need to attend. They told me that they were fully booked for years ahead and it was very unlikely that my son would find a place. I chatted on anyway to the headmistress, and told her how I had been a Montessori child myself, how marvellous I thought it was, etc. To my surprise at the end of the conversation she said that she would 'see what she could do' and that it might just be possible to squeeze my son in. It shows that it can really help making a personal appeal, and establishing yourself as a person with them, rather than being 'just another mother'.

A woman who lives in Belfast told us that she applied two years in advance for a place that her child took up at the age of four. Her daughter attends three mornings a week and absolutely adores it:

> I would prefer her to go five mornings a week, but it is not possible because of the long waiting list and they attempt to give everyone something rather than turn away. She has made good friends there and two others will be going to the same school in September.

Playgroups

Nearly every district has a pre-school playgroup within reasonable distance. The children who attend are usually three to five years old, and may stay with or without their parents. Under-threes are expected to have a parent or another adult with them. Playgroups usually open for two or three hours each morning or afternoon, rarely longer than four hours, and they usually follow school term times. They may be run by the local authority and/or a group of local parents, some of whom may have had training.

Parental involvement is particularly encouraged, which can pose a problem if you work full time, though nannies or childminders can deputise. You will usually have to pay a little. The sessions are usually held in church halls, youth clubs, community centres and similar premises that are also used for other activities.

Many mothers are keen for their children to attend, particularly if they are looked after by a nanny or childminder the rest of the time, so that the children can enjoy a wider variety of activities and start mixing with others in preparation for school.

One mother who lives in Bangor sends her children (aged three and four) to the local playgroup, which is open 9.00a.m. to 1.00p.m. There are usually around twenty-four children and five helpers (there is a parents' rota). Her freelance husband or childminder collects them:

> I feel that this is an excellent playgroup and the children get to do an enormous variety of things. I don't know where the leader gets all her ideas from. They are very caring and understanding and are thoughtful – they gave my eldest a card and crayons and colouring book when he went into hospital for a tooth extraction. They also lent me a book, *Going into Hospital*, to read to him beforehand.

Extended-day playgroups

Since first writing this book, the provision of extended-day playgroups has increased. The Pre-School Playgroups Association has over 1,000 full-day care groups, and over 250 extended-hours playgroups. Some charge is usually made, and meals are provided.

Mother and toddler groups, one o'clock clubs, etc.

These tend to be set up by local authorities or groups as an informal, come-as-you-please play and social facility for the under-fives and their mothers. Unlike playgroups, you do not usually have to reserve a place – just turn up when you wish. They are usually free, or there is a nominal charge. Although a one o'clock club may have trained staff on hand, children are expected to be accompanied by a parent or another adult who is responsible for them.

Again, these do not offer a childcare solution for working mothers, but they are well worth investigating if there is one near you. They are an opportunity for your child to play with other children, and for you or your childcarer to get out (even if your baby is small) to meet other women looking after children.

CHAPTER 10

Nannies, Mother's Helps, and Other Help in Your Home

Help in Your Own Home

We have always had marvellous live-in nannies. They have all been intelligent and educated, some of them have been postgraduate students, one was a guitar teacher. Now that the children are at school, the nannies can have another job during the day, or go to college, as long as they have enough time to do things I expect them to do, like the school run and the shopping. My sons have always learned something from their nannies: one taught them to play the guitar, another was a passionate iceskater and taught them to skate, and they get other things from them they don't get from us, like an interest in pop music.

Full-time London editor

For those who can afford it, employing a nanny or mother's help is an attractive childcare option. It means leaving your children in the security of their own home, surrounded by their own toys, favourite foods, friends, in the care of someone whose function it is to give them her full, personal attention. She is accountable only to you, so that you can expect her to follow your instructions about the way your children are looked after, disciplined, fed and entertained. It also has the advantage of convenience to you: it means you don't have to fit rushing to drop off your children and pick them up again into a hectic working day. There will also be less pressure on you to be home exactly on time, and there is the possibility of built-in babysitting or housework as well!

> I think my children gain by having a nanny because a nanny does all sorts of things you as mother don't do. My nanny socialises a lot, she's got endless nanny friends so they are forever going out or having other children to tea. She's much more creative than I am: making things, drawing with them, making music, taking them swimming, to the library, to the one o'clock club in the park. I'm useless at a lot of those things and wouldn't enjoy them. I'm better at doing things like reading books with them, so we complement each other.
>
> **Part-time London civil servant**

Some working mothers are put off by the connotations from another era that stick to the idea of a nanny. The word conjures up images from Victorian and Edwardian life – Mary Poppins or Christopher Robin's nanny – all starched aprons, nursery teas, faithful retainers below stairs – a world of class privilege. Around 1900, about half a million nannies were employed in England, but the Second World War did away with most of that 'Upstairs, Downstairs' world, including the world of the nursery. Although the traditional, uniformed nanny may still exist to cater for the whims of the privileged few today, the modern nanny employed by families in which both parents work is a completely different species. She is not a servant, but an employee, and she is respected as a professional, having either been trained as a nursery nurse or had a number of years' experience of looking after small children under her belt. She is most usually on first-name terms with her employers and charges, and wears a T-shirt and jeans (or whatever she likes) to work. She may live in or out, but in either case she expects to have set, regular hours, and to have most of her evenings and weekends off. If you feel guilty at the thought of employing a nanny, because it doesn't fit with your social principles, tell yourself that you are providing a much-needed job and helping someone come off the unemployment register.

> Most of the time I don't mind having my nanny around. I quite like talking to her and the children like her – I suppose they love her, but now they're older, not as much as they loved the first two. The first was really like a part of the family, like our daughter, the second one actually felt she was the children's sister, and acted like their sister.
>
> **London airline executive**

Nannies/Mother's Helps: What to Expect and Look for

A *nanny* is someone whose primary function is to look after your children in your own home. She can live in, come in daily, be part time or full time and she may also be shared with other families. She won't normally expect to do any housework except that which relates directly to the children in her charge ('nursery' duties). She will either be trained to look after young children (the most common qualification is the NNEB) or she will have a minimum of two years' experience of looking after small children. We have heard of one or two male nannies, but as they are still such a rare breed we shall refer to nannies as 'she'.

A *mother's help* is someone you employ in your own home to help you with the normal housework, including light cleaning, perhaps some shopping, cooking, and looking after your children. She is not usually qualified. Again, she can live in, be daily or part time. An older, more experienced (and more expensive) version of the mother's help – probably more responsible, too – may be called a *housekeeper*.

When people advertise for a *nanny/mother's help* they usually want a nanny who is also prepared to help around the house like a mother's help. Some agencies define a nanny/mother's help as a newly trained NNEB with no experience, or an untrained person with one year's experience of working in a family.

Qualifications

NNEB

The most common qualifications for a nanny is the nursery nurse's NNEB: a certificate from the National Nursery Examination Board. This is obtained after a two-year course, and because the course is very popular, most colleges now demand at least two or three GCSEs at entry. Many candidates have more, and some even have A-levels.

Three-fifths of the student's time is spent at college, learning about looking after children from birth to seven years old. The course covers such things as health; nutrition; the psychological, physical, emotional and social development of children; physical and mental handicap; the importance of play; changing patterns of family life (including the situation where both parents go out to work), and the relationship between a nanny and her employer.

The remaining two-fifths of the student's time is spent on short-term placements, gaining practical experience in day nurseries, in maternity and pædiatric wards of hospitals; and sometimes in families. They are usually placed in a family where the mother does not work, so they don't have 'sole charge' of the children and therefore this isn't usually a source of low-paid help for the working mum!

At least one-third of all trained nursery nurses go into private families as nannies, the others take jobs in nurseries, creches, hospitals (in non-nursing jobs), and infant schools.

Other training

There are courses run by the National Association for Maternal and Child Welfare, which are recognised as providing a qualification for a mother's help or nanny.

There are also the private, exclusive nanny colleges: the Norland Nursery Training College, The Princess Christian College and the Chiltern Nursery Training College. They train their students to take both the NNEB and RSH certificate (Royal Society of Health for nursery nurses).

The graduates of these colleges are trained to a high standard, but the Norland Nanny will expect a uniform allowance, and a grand house which provides at the very minimum a day and a night nursery, as well as her own room, and a high salary, which rules out all but the very few top-earning working mothers.

The National Council for Vocational Qualifications will advise on what new training courses are available and how to apply for them. (See *Further Help* for all addresses)

Related training

Young women trained as teachers, social workers, playgroup leaders, or nurses sometimes turn to nannying for variety and relief. Obviously, any one of these qualifications may be useful.

Are qualifications really necessary?

If you go out to work all day and plan to leave your nanny in 'sole charge' of your child, it is not unreasonable to expect her to have either some qualifications or some experience of looking after young children. Some of the mothers we spoke to insisted on having a trained nanny:

> I was determined they would have experience, and I wanted an NNEB. I did try half-heartedly experimenting with a posh Norland nanny, but they took one look at our unposh house and fled. But I did want someone who understood about childcare, knew about first aid, about child development, who'd be willing to sit down and help with reading, writing, drawing, jigsaws, someone who could cook them a basic meal, that sort of thing. In the end, I don't think I ever got a nanny who measured up to all those wishes – but I always did get qualified ones.

But most of the mothers told us they wanted qualities that can't be acquired through training:

> * I wasn't really looking for qualifications, the main thing I wanted was somebody who was really interested in looking after children and surprisingly, that is not all that easy to find.

> * I think it's important for the nanny to have something of the child about her, so that she can relate to your child on his own level, as well as having the usual things like a sense of responsibility. The other things will come with experience. After all I didn't know everything before I had a child – I don't have qualifications either.

Indeed, it is dangerous to rely too heavily on qualifications: they are no substitute for instinct, and training is no guarantee of commonsense, a sense of responsibility, or reliability.

> Our previous nanny was a qualified nurse, but she was the one who let my daughter drink a whole bottle of Calpol, just by not being very clued in! It was a disaster: the child had to have her stomach pumped.

As Anne Babb, who runs Swansons Agency in West London, told us:

> I feel an NNEB girl hasn't proved her worth until she's lived with a family long-term, and can show that she can survive within a family unit. The training doesn't provide the natural talent and commonsense that has to be there, although it does show a certain commitment to the job on the nanny's part.

On the whole, most mothers feel that it is important for the person to whom they entrust their children to be warm, loving and fun, with lots of commonsense and a highly developed sense of responsibility. The training is an extra, a bonus, but it can be very reassuring for the new mother:

> I found it reassuring, as a first-time mum, to have someone who had actually been trained, simply on things like diet, or recognising the kid was ill, whether to take him to the doctor or to say, don't panic. Second time around, you're more experienced yourself, you don't worry so much, so training doesn't seem that important now.

Experience is often more useful than training, particularly when you get the impression that she has a continuing warm relationship with her former charges, or if she comes from a family with younger brothers and sisters in whose care she was actively involved. The knowledge that she is trained in first aid is reassuring, but you can always encourage an untrained nanny to go on a first-aid course when she is working for you.

> Our nanny is full time but lives out. I insisted on NNEB training and inclination to newborns. Sarah has experience of three newborn babies already, so is mature at twenty-three. She looks after the baby from 9.00a.m. to 5.30p.m., and doesn't do housework or anything. It is quite expensive, but it is so worth it to us because she is so trustworthy, efficient and obviously

adores the baby. We *tried* to choose someone who would be as like us in her ideas as possible – not possible totally but we succeeded in part. She offers advice, but tactfully, and does anything I specifically ask her to do regarding Chloe.

> Kristine Band, Bedfordshire,
> full-time partner in PR agency

Some different types of nannies/mother's helps

If you advertise for a nanny, you may be surprised at the wide range of types of people who apply. Here, for the first-time employer, are some examples of what you can expect.

Young nannies or mother's helps

Most commonly nannies are young girls with or without an NNEB. Many nanny agencies refuse to take girls under eighteen as they think they are too young for the responsibility.

If you are looking for someone to have 'sole charge' of your child, you should consider that a young nanny may suffer from homesickness if she is leaving home for the first time. Some nannies leave their employment after a very short time because of this.

The relatively young girl may have the advantage of being more flexible than an older, experienced nanny, less set in her ways, and will perhaps be more readily prepared to follow your instructions to the letter. But young girls tend to move on to the next job very frequently: many stay an average of only six months in one job, a year at the most.

Older Nannies

Older nannies may be more experienced, which is reassuring for the first-time mum: they also have a tendency to stay longer in one job. Some have been nannies for years, but these are in a minority, as many nannies eventually move across to another career like nursing or becoming a playgroup leader. Others are ex-nurses turning to nannying as a relief from the strains of nursing sick children.

You are less likely to find an older nanny who is happy to live in. As Anne Babb says, 'After about three years of living with a family, most girls want to move out and have their independence.'

As she is more experienced, the older nanny might be more set in her ways, which can possibly lead to conflict with you over how your child should be treated, and in matters such as discipline.

Nannies/mother's helps from abroad

Many Australian and New Zealand girls come over to the United Kingdom for limited periods to work as nannies/mother's helps before going on to see the rest of the world.

They make popular nannies: that little bit older than average, and they tend to fit into families very well. Even if trained they are not as concerned about their status as some British nannies, and tend to have no problem mucking in with the housework as well.

The drawback with girls like this is that their main objective in coming to the UK is rarely to work with children, but to earn some money to travel round Europe. You'll have to make sure that they don't up and leave without notice when their boyfriend joins them – which has happened to several employers we know! Also, if employing someone straight from her home country, you won't have the opportunity to interview her before she arrives in England.

Other mothers

You may find a local mother who will act as a nanny for you and come to your house to look after your children.

She can earn more this way than as a childminder. She may long to look after a baby or toddler again because she has children who have left home; she may have children at school; she may even have a child of her own the same age as yours. If you have no objections, she could bring her child to your house which would be fun for your child as well (although you may want to take into consideration the extra wear and tear on your house, extra cost of food, and the possible cost of extra equipment, for example a double buggy or extra highchair).

Nannies live in or out?

> The first nanny we had was more like a sister. She lived out to begin with, but when we moved she lived in during the week and had weekends off. We had no rules, and she ate with us, although she had her own television. We would always put a boyfriend up for the night (in a separate room!) if requested and encouraged her friends to come to the house.

Whether you go for a live-in nanny or a daily nanny depends first of all on whether you have a spare room: the minimum standard of accommodation for a nanny or mother's help is a room of her own. Another consideration is the area: if you live in a big city or town, finding a daily nanny won't present many problems, but if you live in the heart of the country you probably will have to have someone living in. Live-in nannies are paid less than dailies, because their board and lodging are included. If you employ a daily nanny or mother's help in an expensive area such as London, you will have to take into account the fact that even basic bed-sits are rather expensive, and she has to find money for bills, food, fares and so on (unless she lives at home). Therefore, you are going to have to pay a salary that will cover those relatively high living expenses.

LIVE IN	LIVE OUT
You'll have to give up a spare room.	You'll have to pay higher wages to cover her rent, bills, food and possibly fares.
Your household expenses will be higher: an extra mouth to feed, higher electricity, phone, heating bills, additional petrol and possibly higher insurance if she has to use the car.	Your household expenses will still be higher than normal during the week as you'll be providing a daily's main meals while she's on duty, and the extra cost of heating, lighting, car will still apply if she is in your house with the children all day (but not weekends).
Constraints on your privacy: a stranger will be a witness to your rows or happy times, and when you are both in the house there is a possible conflict of authority for your child.	When you're at home, she goes home: early mornings, evenings, nights and weekends are for you and your partner to have 'sole charge' of your child.
As she is in the house, she's unlikely to keep you waiting in the morning, and if you are late back from work, she is less likely to be inconvenienced.	She may be late in the morning and she may have to leave punctually in the evening.

If she is mildly ill, she'll probably be able to manage as she's on the spot.	If she's ill she may not be able to manage the journey.
She'll be more available for babysitting, and you won't have to rush home by a certain time as she can simply go to bed.	Babysitting will have to be arranged in advance, and you'll have to get home at a reasonable time, and probably take her home or pay for a taxi.
Possible problems with anti-social behaviour and irritating habits (from hogging the bathroom in the morning, leaving dishes in the sink, to playing loud music).	These problems won't affect you as you don't have to live with her and she is only in your house during working hours.
Possible invasion by her friends, or boyfriend, or getting involved with her emotional problems.	These are less likely to intrude as she isn't living with you.

Finding a Nanny/Mother's Help

The ideal nanny doesn't exist, of course: neither does the perfect mother. But there's no harm in dreaming a little of what qualifications the perfect nanny would have. This list may help you make up your mind, before you start, about which qualities in particular are going to be the most important to you in a nanny.

* She will love all children – yours in particular; she will be gentle and affectionate with your child, but won't usurp you.

* She will have boundless energy and infinite patience.

* She will have a great sense of humour and a cheerful disposition.

* She will be a joy to have around the house, but will never intrude on your privacy.

* She will have lots of good ideas for play indoors on a rainy day.

* She will read and sing songs with your children and only put the TV on for pre-selected, educational programmes.

* She will encourage your children to make friends, and will meet up with other children and their nannies or mums.

* She will organise interesting outings but will always let you know where she is taking the children.

* She will be punctual – but never mind if you are a bit late coming home.

* She will be sociable and independent, but will be available when you need her, and will be glad to babysit.

* She will cook your children healthy, appetising, balanced meals, and will not allow too many sweets.

* She will share your ideas about discipline, manners, snacks, potty training and so on.

* She will gladly lend a hand without being asked when she sees a job that needs doing around the house.

* She will never be ill.

* She will take her holiday at the same time as you.

* She will never betray the trust you have placed in her and she will be open if there are any problems.

* You will be confident that she could cope in a crisis.

* She will stay long enough to provide security and continuity – but not too long, so there is not too much trauma when she leaves.

When to start looking

Ideally, you should allow yourself six, even eight, weeks to find someone, although in practice it may not take so long. However, if you advertise it may take two weeks for your ad to appear from the time you send it in. You should also give yourself time to re-advertise if the first advert should produce no satisfactory results.

From the day your advert appears you should allow yourself two weeks for applicants to write in and to arrange interviews (it will take less time if you give a phone number instead of a box number).

After that, your chosen nanny may well have to give as much as a month's notice if she is presently employed elsewhere, although mothers we talked to found that many applicants are often ready to start straight away.

Advertising nationally

The traditional place to advertise for a nanny or mother's help (or other domestic staff) is *The Lady*, a weekly magazine which conjures up all those cosy, old-fashioned Mary Poppins images, but which is filled with pages and pages of nanny adverts.

Another place to advertise is *Nursery World.* Buy a copy of each to get an idea of the advert you should place. (See *Further Help.*)

These magazines are especially useful for advertising live-in posts. If you are interested in a newly qualified nanny, the summer months at the end of the academic year are probably a particularly good time to advertise. The only bad time to advertise for a nanny is in the period just before Christmas, when few people are looking to change jobs.

Phrasing your advertisement

The longer your advert, the more it will cost, so it is worth spending time composing it carefully, and making sure it covers all the important facts. Some adverts in *The Lady* are full of effusive prose, but it is useless trying to lure nannies with the prospect of a 'lovely house' if you do not say where it is. All nannies will assume all parents think their children are the most lovable in the world, so it's a waste of good money to spend too many words there. As for stipulating the kind of personality you are looking for, this may help to create the right atmosphere in your advert, but it isn't actually going to help you find someone who is as fun-loving, warm, friendly, cheerful, charming or responsible as you wish her to be. You cannot logically rely on some poor girl to eliminate herself on those grounds!

Here are the most important points you should consider covering:

* What type of help (nanny, mother's help and so) and whether there are any special duties involved (for example, some cleaning, cooking for the family, or walking the dog).

* Where you live.

* How many children and their ages.

220

* Whether the nanny will have 'sole charge' (many nannies like this — there is no interfering parent around during her hours of duty, so prefer working for families where both parents work).

* Live in or live in out (it's probably useful to specify things like 'own room', 'TV', or 'use of car' and so on).

* Whether you want someone part time, or if you work unusual hours.

* Whether you are looking for a nanny to share with another family.

* Whether you want qualifications or experience, and references.

* Any other special requirements, for example 'non-smoker', 'driver's licence', or if you have a set idea of the age the nanny has to be.

* You may wish to include other facts which might make your job sound more attractive, for example, some families put in 'local nanny network', or 'daily cleaner kept'.

* Salary is not usually included in the advert, because you will probably wish to stay flexible according to the candidate's experience, qualifications and expectations. However, if you are offering a very low salary and can't raise it under any circumstances, you might consider putting it in to avoid a lot of wasted time all round.

* How to contact you: although most prospective employers just give a phone number, the best and safest method is to take a box number, although it is more expensive and more time-consuming. The candidates who take the trouble to write in may be fewer than those who will phone, but they are likely to be more serious, and you will get some useful

pre-interview information from their letters. If you decide to give your phone number, indicate if you can only be reached at certain times. If you give your phone number at work, give an extension number rather than your name. *It is not a good idea to give your name, address or the first names of your children in an advert if you also give your phone number or address.* We have heard of several cases of crank phone calls to parents and even to children, which have been traced by the police to adverts in *The Lady*.

Advertising locally, and word of mouth

An advert in your local paper, your local job centre, or in a newsagent's window (or at the clinic or surgery if they allow it) may be a good idea if you are looking for someone to come in on a daily basis.

This way you are more likely to find someone who already lives in your area. The problem with daily nannies is that they sometimes try to find a job before they find somewhere to live, and this can be difficult for them and inconvenient for you. Looking locally may even produce a local mother.

Another good way to find local help is asking around. If you have a friend who already employs a nanny ask her to mention it on the grapevine to the local 'nanny mafia' (in many areas, nannies form informal social networks): that way you may find a nanny whose job is coming to an end (for example, her charges may be about to start school) and who wants to stay in the area.

Agencies

There are many employment agencies for nannies/mother's helps: most of them advertise regularly in *The Lady*, or in the Yellow Pages. You may find an agency local to your area, but many of the agencies will find you a nanny wherever you live. (See *Further Help* for a limited list.)

How they work and what they charge

Agencies do not come cheap, and they make their money from you as the employer, not from the nannies. Indeed, most agencies confess that their greatest struggle is finding well-qualified and experienced girls: finding employers is no problem at all!

Some work on a list basis, which means that they charge a small fee for mailing you a list of available staff currently on their books. Others will take your particulars and then try to match their girls with you, sending those that they feel suit your requirements.

Charges for a sucessful placement vary widely, but you can expect to pay between two and five weeks' salary to the agency for finding you a permanent nanny. Most agencies will offer to replace the nanny free of charge, or refund all or part of the fee if things don't work out and the nanny leaves within a set number of weeks of starting employment.

What do agencies do for you?

You can expect the agency to vet and select nannies for you and check their objective references: for instance, qualifications and their last personal references. They can supply you with a short-list and save you all the initial sifting that you would have to do if you placed an advert. As agencies' standards vary, it is probably a good idea to ask them how they select their girls. The best ones will insist on seeing and interviewing each candidate at the agency before recommending them, although in practice this may be difficult if the candidate lives in another part of the country or comes from abroad. However they should all check references scrupulously, by phone as well as by letter.

The limitations of agencies: a word of warning

Although agencies are convenient, you should not rely on them totally and take on a girl just because she comes recommended by the agency, no matter how reputable.

You must always interview a candidate personally, and also check her references personally, even if this seems like duplicating the agency's work.

No matter how careful the agency is, unsuitable candidates may still slip through, and it is up to you to check that the nanny of your choice understands the details of the job and your particular standards and requirements.

When an agency is most useful

Agencies really come into their own as the working mother's lifeline when temporary help is necessary. For instance, when there is a time-gap that needs to be filled between going back to work and your chosen permanent nanny starting; or between nannies; or to supply a maternity nurse.

Nanny colleges

If you are interested in employing a newly qualified NNEB, find out from your local library which local colleges offer NNEB courses, and get in touch with the college. It may also be a good source of temporary help, for instance during the college holidays.

Telephone interviewing

Although we recommend taking a box number if you have the time, most prospective employers give a phone number when advertising – so this is a suggested strategy for dealing with telephone replies to an advert. If you have given a telephone number, you will in effect be conducting an initial interview over the phone before deciding whether you wish to interview the applicant face-to-face.

Keep a checklist of questions by the phone, together with a notepad and pencil, and write down all the applicants' answers in sequence. This will help you decide which ones to interview, and you'll be able to compare them easily.

Don't rely on your memory: if you have a good response, you are unlikely to remember each phone call. Keep the notes for when you interview the candidates. Keep your notes on those you decide not to see first time round too, in case you need to call on them if your initial round of interviews produces no result.

Avoid committing yourself to interview every person who rings up – get some idea of the general response first. The response to an advert can fluctuate wildly, nobody seems to understand why. One advert one week produces eighty replies, while another the following week gets no response.

If advertising in *The Lady*, you can expect the bulk of phone calls in response to your advert on the first Wednesday, Thursday and Friday after the issue comes out. After taking down each applicant's details you can simply promise to ring her back later, or the following day, if you want to arrange an interview. If you commit yourself to seeing too many candidates you may find that making a choice becomes much more difficult than if you see a selected number – and you must consider your precious time!

Suggested questions for telephone interviews:

1. Name, address and phone number.
2. Age, experience and/or qualifications, does she comply with the requirements in your advert?
3. What salary does she expect to earn?

4. When will she be available to start work?
5. Why did she leave or is she leaving her last job?
6. If advertising a live-out post, does she have somewhere to live and is it near enough to your house?

Interviewing in your home

Interviewing nannies or mother's helps is often a daunting prospect. Even if you are used to interviewing staff at work, you will find that choosing someone to whom you'll entrust the life of your child and the safekeeping of your home is a much more emotionally fraught situation. It will help to make sure you have plenty of time for each candidate, and to be well prepared with all the questions you want to ask, your exact requirements, and the terms and conditions you want to offer.

Arranging the interview

To make sure your chosen candidates are not offered other jobs before they come to you, you should arrange the interviews quite swiftly. You may have to take a day or several days off work. Give each candidate an appointment, and allow at least an hour for each interview, with a half-hour gap before the next interview. This helps if the interview runs longer or if the candidate is late, and gives you time between each interview to make notes while your impressions are fresh, or to discuss her with your partner if he is also present.

Some parents arrange to see the candidates together. In other families the mother arranges the initial interviews, and then selects a short-list to come back for a second interview which the father will attend; others just ask their favourite candidate to come back and meet their partner.

It is useful to have your children available for a short time during every interview.

Make sure every person you invite to an interview has

your address and telephone number (in case she wishes to cancel the appointment). If she has far to come, offer to reimburse her fares.

Preparing yourself

Make a list of all the questions you want to ask, and number them so that you can easily take notes at the interview and have answers to the same questions from each candidate for comparison.

Also write down, as a reminder to yourself, *the exact details of the job*: the terms and conditions you are offering, and any special requirements you have. This will help you to avoid the situation where you *think* you mentioned to everyone you saw that you expect the dog to be taken out for a walk twice a day, but you can't remember *for sure* whether you mentioned it to the person you've decided to employ.

When making a list of all your requirements, try to think ahead: most families prefer nannies to stay at least one year, and hope they'll stay longer. At the moment, for example, your child may be a baby, and all the nanny will need to know about cooking is how to make up a bottle of milk. But in six months' time, when you find out that her idea of a freshly cooked meal is fish fingers, tinned peas and Smash, you may regret not having asked at the interview whether she could cook and what her ideas on nutrition were!

Similarly, if at any stage during your prospective nanny's employment your child will start nursery school or school and is going to have to be driven there, it is worth looking for a nanny with a driver's licence, even though you don't need her to be able to drive for a year or two yet.

The interview

At the start of the interview, the candidate may be nervous.

Do your best to put her at her ease by asking simple questions first. It will give you an oppurtunity to relax, too: after all she is assessing you, and your house and family as well!

* Start by checking the questions she has already answered over the phone (any inconsistencies will be suspicious).

* Ask her about her training, if any, and find out which part of the course she particularly enjoyed. Ask about her student placements, her knowledge of first aid.

* Ask about her experience: get her to go into detail of previous jobs (or babysitting), including where they were, how many children she looked after, what the conditions were, what she earned, and most important, why she left (this can tell you a great deal). Try to find out whether she got on with her employers – if there are a lot of complaints you may become suspicious, but if she speaks of her former charges with affection, and reveals perhaps that she continues to visit them from time to time, you may well be right to feel encouraged.

* Find out about her personal circumstances: is she married or engaged, does she come from a large close-knit family? As Anne Babb says:

Try to suss out how sympathetic their home life has been: whether they've been used to helping at home, for example; if they're from a loving family. If you get a girl from an unhappy background, she's not going to understand the basic rules of family living. And it's also a good idea to ask about boyfriends. I have more girls leaving to go back home because of boyfriends than anything else.

* If the nanny you are interviewing comes from far away and has never been away from home before,

discuss how she feels about leaving home, whether her parents are happy about her leaving, whether she has thought about feeling homesick. It is quite common for a young nanny to leave a job after a couple of weeks because of homesickness.

* Ask for her views on nutrition, discipline, potty training, smacking: see if her attitudes fit in with yours. To short-circuit her from giving the answers she guesses you wish to hear on a sensitive issue like discipline, ask her how her own parents disciplined her when she was a child, and if she would do the same if she had children of her own.

* Ask her about hobbies, what does she do with her free time: try to get an impression of how important her social life is, boyfriends, and so on. If you are looking for a live-in nanny, this is an area of potential conflict and irritation.

* Ask her what she would do with your children during the day when you are out, apart from the obvious routines: give extra marks for ideas about going on outings, to the library, if she inquires about local playgroups or one o'clock clubs, or if she wants to take them swimming, dancing, and so on.

* Make sure she has understood your advert properly and that she is prepared to do any domestic work you require, that she conforms to your special requirements: ask her to confirm that she's a non-smoker, for example, and if you require a driver, make sure she has a clean licence and ask how long she has been driving. If you want her to take your children swimming, can she swim?

* Discuss any other matters that may be important to you: religion, for example, or politics, or pets, or what she eats. Ask her how she feels about drugs, about drinking.

* Ask about her health.

* Tell her about the formalities of the job you are offering: the salary (including the actual take-home pay if you are planning to deduct tax and National Insurance), hours, holidays (and whether you expect them to be taken at the same time as yours), time off, whether you want her to stay for a minimum period, notice period, sick pay, and so on.

* Show her around the house. If live-in, show her her room, the bathroom, and so on. Discuss whether you wish her to eat her meals with your family, whether you have rules about friends, boyfriends in the house, use of phone, car and so on.

* Introduce her to your children, and watch the way she responds to them: she is bound to feel self-conscious, and your children may deliberately misbehave. But try to tune in to your intuitive feelings when she is with them. If she pays more attention to your child than you, it's probably a good sign! Ask older children to show her their rooms; if you have a baby, you may want to ask her to do a change or handle a feed. No matter how young, trust your children's instinctive response to the candidate. If they don't seem to like her, don't consider taking her on, no matter how good her qualifications.

* Make sure you have the names, addresses and phone numbers of at least two referees, and if she has worked before this should include her last employer.

* Finally, give her plenty of opportunity to ask questions about your family and the job: these may turn out to be revealing. For example, if she asks a lot of questions about evenings off, holidays, or whether it will be all right to have friends staying, you may start wondering whether her social life is going to be more important to her than the job. On the other

230

hand, if she can't think of any questions, it may be because you have covered everything or you are too intimidating, but it may also show a lack of initiative and interest.

References

When considering employing someone in your home, and entrusting them with your child's life and your house and possessions, it is essential to take up references. It is all too easy, if you have found someone you think you really like, to feel superstitious and fatalistic about it – not wishing to hear anything negative about the person chosen because you have already made up your mind to employ her. But to give in to this would be pretty foolish. Even if the person comes recommended by an agency, you should still check her references personally.

Written references are not enough

Do ring up and have a chat with your prospective nanny's former employers. A nanny agency told us that sometimes a candidate can have a glowing letter of recommendation, yet when they ring up the referee and ask the right questions, serious problems can be revealed as the former employer loosens up and is assured of the confidentiality of the conversation.

Obviously, if you discover problems, you have to weigh them against your own assessment of the nanny. There are two sides to every story, and perhaps the employer was in the wrong, or expected too much. But if your chosen nanny does have short-comings then you should be forewarned.

One mother we spoke to took on a nanny with glowing references from a prestigious London agency, and did not follow up the references herself. The girl was delightful and the kids instantly adored her, but it was only some weeks after the nanny had made off with some treasured family possessions that the mother found out that this nanny had actually served time for theft, and had tricked several other families and agencies with false names and references. Perhaps if her references had been taken up alarm bells would have sounded!

Asking questions

These are the kind of questions you should consider asking when phoning former employers:

* What was the nanny like as a person?

* Was she punctual? Was she ever ill? Was she always reliable?

* Did she ever have to cope in a crisis?

* What was her relationship with the children, and what sort of things did she do with them?

* What was she paid, did it include tax and NI? What holidays did she take? What hours did she work? Did she do any housework? Was she tidy?

* Were there ever any problems or irritations?

* How long did she stay with the employer?

* Why did she leave?

* Do they fully recommend her?

Remember (or remind the employer you are speaking to) that *references are privileged*. This means that if asked for a reference, you can say anything that is true and is said without any malicious intention, without fear of being sued for defamation.

Offering the job

Deciding whom to employ is a serious decision. If necessary, ask your favourite candidates back for a second interview, preferably with your partner present if he was not at the first one.

If you find it difficult to make up your mind after having evaluated all the candidates' qualities, experience and qualifications, try asking yourself: 'Will my child like her? Will we mind having her around every day? Do I feel I can trust her? Do *I* like her?' Sometimes, you can be so bogged down with other considerations that you may forget to ask yourself the most obvious questions.

> **We had to learn to share our lives with a seventeen-year-old, who was vulnerable in her own way, as well as with a new baby – after seven years of marriage and doing our own thing. We gave her her own room which had its own washbasin, and added a TV, easy chair and kettle, to try to give her some privacy. She also brought friends in from time to time, and we enjoyed meeting the new people. She still visits occasionally – turns up when off-duty and 'mucks in'.**

When you have made your choice, ring up the candidate and offer her the job. If she accepts, discuss how soon she can start. Follow this up with a *letter of employment*, or a contract: you are required to do so by law. (The Working Mothers Association provides sample contracts, see *Further Help*.)

In the letter of employment, you should cover the following points:

* What the job is (nanny, mother's help, etc.).

* Live-in or daily, hours, agreed time off, babysitting.

* Notice period, and any agreed trial period or minimum leaving period.

233

* The date you have agreed for her to start work.

* Holidays, sick pay and so on.

* Salary (specify whether net or gross of tax and NI).

Send the nanny two copies of the letter, and ask her to sign both copies. She should then return one copy to you and keep one for herself.

Some employers recommend giving your new employee a second, less formal letter when she actually starts work, in which you specify the exact details of her duties as you have agreed them at the interview. This may help you to avoid misunderstandings and conflict later on. The most common reason for discontent among nannies and employers is housework. It is better for you to make it clear right from the start, in black and white, that you expect her wash up your breakfast things, for example, than to throw baleful looks at her and the breakfast cups in the sink when you get home in the evening (the same cups have probably been annoying her all day as well).

Anne Babb advises:

> It's a good idea to write down everything that she's expected to do, so that when she's finished she knows she can relax. I made a whacking great list of duties for my last nanny. She later told me that she had liked us at the interview but when she saw the list, she nearly changed her mind! But then, after a couple of weeks, she told me, she really got into the routine, helped by the list, and she always had the housework done by 11.00a.m. She found it wasn't daunting and the children were not abandoned either!

Other mothers suggest writing down a guide to your children and the house, to make things easier for the first few days. This can include preferred food, toys, nap times, where to find things, and so on. This is essential if you haven't been able to have an initial overlap period with her so that she can learn from you what your child's routine and idiosyncracies are.

When you have found your nanny, do not forget to inform the other girls you interviewed that you have decided to offer the job to somebody else. You may prefer to do this by letter if you feel badly about phoning them. But it would be inconsiderate to leave it altogether, as many employers are tempted to do.

How to be an Employer: the Basic Facts

> **Our nanny is trained, single, aged twenty-seven. We 'head-hunted' her from her previous position. She's a great success, calm, competent, caring. Travels about twenty miles each way to our home daily, and works roughly thirty-eight hours a week. She has two half-days off and in return works late occasionally (to let us out for a quick early evening meal together) and also occasional Saturday mornings. We pay her what we consider to be quite a good salary and in return get first class service from a committed person.**
>
> **Belfast GP**

Salary

How much: This depends on where you live, on whether the nanny or mother's help lives in or not, on her training, experience and expectations. It also depends on what you can afford!

Nannies do not expect to be paid more for looking after several children than for looking after a single child in one family (it is different where two families share a nanny). This is a question of preference, some girls prefer looking after one baby, others prefer to look after several kids of different ages. However, if a new baby arrives after a nanny has been working for you for a time, and was not employed in the knowledge that another baby was on the way, it may be fair to offer her a rise.

We have decided not to give suggested salary figures in this edition of the book, because it is not useful when they date. Find out from other local mothers, or nanny agencies, or the Working Mothers Association, what the current band of salaries is.

Temporary or part-time nannies are often paid hourly and normally work out more expensive than full-time permanent employees.

When: Nannies are usually paid weekly. If you are paying her tax and NI, you will find that even though you are paying her weekly, you can send the PAYE and NI to the Inland Revenue quarterly.

Rises: You should expect to give a rise after your nanny has been with you for a year; some families give one after six months. You may work out a percentage increase based on your own wage increase, or you may simply put up her wages by a fixed amount. Some mothers recommend stating in your letter of employment the date on which you plan to review her salary, so that there is no room for misunderstanding and she knows where she stands.

Bonuses/additional payments: some families give their nanny an annual bonus; one employer told us she always shared her own Christmas bonus with her nanny. Others just mentioned gifts at Christmas and on birthdays. Some nannies are paid overtime for babysitting or are given time off in lieu.

Trial period, minimum period of employment, and notice

It is a good idea to suggest an initial trial period of one or two months: this gives you a chance to assess your new employee on the job. Also, many families stipulate that they expect their nanny to stay at least one year.

Several working mothers told us their nanny was on a twelve-month contract. It is not a bad idea to plant the idea in the nanny's mind that you expect her to commit herself to staying at least that long, as you will be hoping for as much continuity as possible for the sake of your child.

How much notice should be given on both sides when the nanny does want to leave (or if you don't want her any more) should be discussed at the interview and you should put it in your letter of employment.

Obviously, you can't stop someone from simply walking out on you, and as most nannies are paid weekly, by law they need only give a week's notice. However, you will wish to insist on a least four weeks' notice (some families ask for six weeks or two months).

If your nanny is a responsible person, she will recognise that you must have time to find a replacement and that you rely on her not to leave you stranded.

Hours

Even if a nanny (or mother's help) lives in your house, she will expect to work regular set hours.

Usually, she will come on duty shortly before you leave for work, and clock off after you get home. Adding together your working hours and your travelling time, plus a handover period (see below) this can often mean a very long day for your nanny. If you work full time, she may be working a fifty-five-hour week or more (especially if she babysits as well). It is therefore important, if you wish to keep your nanny, to respect the hours you have agreed with her.

Hand-over period

When working out your nanny's hours, try to work in a half-hour's hand-over period at the beginning and end of each day. This means she starts work half an hour before you are due to leave the house, and goes off duty half an hour after you get home. This gives you time to catch up on her plans for the day, the day's news, to sort out any problems, leave instructions, exchange general chat. It also provides a calmer, more relaxed atmosphere for your child during that crucial, and potentially upsetting, period of the day. It is hard enough for your child to cope with the daily goodbyes without being bodily shoved at the nanny as you pass each other on the doorstep in the morning.

When your children go through the stage of 'separation anxiety' it really helps to have the time to settle them with the nanny and a favourite book or toy, or entice them with the prospect of an outing to the park with the nanny, before attempting to take your leave. One mother told of her experience:

> The problem with the last nanny was that we never had time to talk, she had a busy social life, and she'd be watching from the window and start dialling for a mini cab as soon as she saw my car coming down the road. Sometimes two days would go by before I'd managed to remember to ask her whether such-and-such had happened. With my new nanny I insist that for about fifteen minutes she's able to sit and talk to me about the day. My son doesn't like it either when one of us rushes off, the nanny or me.

Punctuality

Don't be too lenient about lateness at the beginning of your nanny's employment. You may be quite happy to leave for work a bit late when you first go back to work, and your employer may be tolerant of your lateness at that stage, but it will prove extremely difficult to persuade your nanny to get into the habit of coming in on time once she's become used to coming in later.

You should make it clear to your nanny that you rely on her to come in on time in order for you to keep your job – and her job depends on yours! If your nanny lives in, this is probably not such a problem, but one mother told us that she'd established a rule that her live-in nanny must be home before a certain time in the evenings before working days, to prevent late starts the following morning!

If you expect your nanny to be on time in the morning, you should also try to be punctual for her in the evening. As one mother pointed out:

> She is totally punctual, and I have never once been late for her either. I feel if I'm going to be late for her, she's got every right to be late for me.

Part time: unusual hours

If you do not require a nanny all day every working day because you yourself are part time or because your child goes to playgroup or school, you may want to find someone part time.

However, bear in mind that according to our sample, part-time nannies are often paid proportionally more per hour than full-time help. We noticed that the families who employed nannies more than half the normal working week (but less than the full week) often end up paying as much as families employing full-time nannies, especially if the nanny found it difficult to fit in another job for another family.

If you can afford it, you may wish to employ your nanny more or less full time, or for longer than your own working hours. A part-time London civil servant told us that she goes to work on Monday, Tuesday and Wednesday, but she employs her nanny four days a week:

the nanny works for another family on Fridays. On Thursdays, the mother is at home with her children and the nanny, which means she can go to the hairdresser or dentist without children in tow, or is able to take one child shopping, leaving the other behind. As her husband helps at the weekends, this leaves her just one day a week on her own with children:

> On Friday it's just me and the kids. It's the only day of the week that I'm like an at-home mum. I try to devote the day to the children, not to do any housework except their lunch, putting some laundry in etc. – and I'm a nervous wreck by Friday night!

If you need the part-time services of a nanny because your child goes to school in the mornings, you must take into account what you will do during the school holidays or if your child is ill. One London woman, a full-time airline executive, has two children at school in the mornings and employs a daily nanny. She has devised an ingenious solution to this problem:

> I specified in the contract that her hours are any time the children are not at school from 8.30a.m. In fact, she normally only comes in at 2.00p.m. and picks up the kids from school, but I can call her to come in all day if they're ill, when the teacher's strike was on, or during the holidays. She'll also come in early if I ask to let the gas man in etc.

Others have more complicated arrangements:

> I work four days a week from nine to three, except one day when I work until six. I tried to make my nanny's hours as uniform as possible even though my own hours are weird. She comes in every day at 8.30a.m., even on my day off, to allow for an emergency happening at the office, so that I know she'll be there just in case. She works until 4.30p.m., except on the day I stay late, so I let her off at 2.30p.m. on my day off to compensate.

Night duty

On the whole, live-in nannies do not expect to do night duty, and working parents with live-in nannies whose children have sleeping problems can't expect help from that quarter. If you do want to be relieved at night occasionally to get a good night's sleep, you should negotiate this at the interview.

Maternity nurses will expect to do night duty with small infants – they will also be paid a lot more to do so. Some of the working mothers we interviewed had jobs that involved travelling and had negotiated with their nannies that they take over for the occasional night or nights while they were away. One had a live-out nanny who agreed to spend a week living in once a year (even though she was married) in exchange for extra time off.

Days off

On the whole, nannies expect to have their weekends off. A couple of women indicated to us that they were very happy to have a live-in nanny who went home to her family when they were not working. Others want their nanny to be on duty occasionally at the weekend – Saturday mornings, for example, to give them time to do the weekly shop and other chores. The minimum you should give your employee off is a day and a half a week and a full weekend every month. But most nannies have every weekend off, so you may find it more difficult to keep a nanny if you often expect her to give up time at the weekend.

Evening babysitting

Live-in nannies usually expect to do some babysitting as they are on the spot anyway, but most of the women we spoke to who employed daily nannies had also negotiated some regular babysitting with their nannies as part of their employment conditions.

Whether or not you pay extra is a point for negotiation. A common solution is to agree as part of the employment conditions that she will babysit one or two evenings a week and that this is covered by her regular salary; after that you'll pay the local going babysitting rate for any additional babysitting.

Some families pay a different hourly rate for babysitting according to whether the children are in bed or not. It does seem fair to pay extra for babysitting at weekends, especially for daily nannies who will have to make the special journey to your home. You should probably also offer to drive her home, or pay for a taxi, if you are home late, as you would any babysitter (unless she agrees to spend the night occasionally at your house).

Several mothers complained that although their nanny had agreed to babysit when they were first offered the job, in practice it caused resentment: 'The present nanny pulls a face a mile long whenever I ask her to babysit although it was part of the conditions that she should babysit one evening a week.'

Anne Babb gives this advice:

> Try to make it clear from the start how much babysitting you're going to need, and try to stick to it. If you say at the interview you'll expect two or three nights a week, it is important to establish that routine in practice when she first starts working for you, even if it means only going to the pub with your husband. If you never call on her to do it at the beginning, she'll resent it when you do need her to sit for you later on, even though she agreed to it.

You should also try to give your nanny as much notice as possible of your babysitting requirements every week, and to respect the fact that she has a right to a social life too. One nanny we talked to said she had finally left the family she had lived with for five years because it happened once too often that she was waylaid on her way out, with: 'Oh you're not going out are you? I'm afraid you can't because *we're* going out this evening.'

If you employ a nanny you'll probably prefer to use her as a babysitter, rather than a stranger. But if you go out a lot, she may start feeling exploited: remember her day is very long already. You should find a back-up babysitter who lives near you and whom your child can get to know, so that babysitting doesn't become a major area of conflict between you and your nanny.

Holidays

How much paid holiday you offer your nanny depends on your own holidays and whether you expect her to take her holiday at the same time as you or not. Many families offer their nanny the standard three or four weeks' paid holiday, (sometimes three weeks in the first year, four weeks thereafter), plus bank holidays, ideally on the understanding that she takes her holiday at a time to suit them — usually when the family goes on holiday. This is the most satisfactory arrangement, and if your nanny is a single girl without other commitments, if can often work well.

> We usually plan our holiday dates about nine months in advance, so there is plenty of advance notice for her to book a holiday at the same time. We had a problem with the previous nanny because her boyfriend was an accountant, and his busiest time of year was June, when we'd planned to go away.

Things are more complicated if your nanny cannot arrange for her holidays to coincide with yours, as few working families can afford to give their nanny a holiday on full pay and pay the wages of a temporary replacement.

If you want your nanny to come on holiday with your family to help with the children, you should not count this as part of her holiday entitlement.

Sickness and sickpay

A sick nanny can be a major disaster for the working family. Most nannies will drag themselves to work rather than leave you in the lurch, but every working mother's nightmare is the nanny who comes down with a long-drawn-out illness such as glandular fever. For suggestions on how to cope when your nanny is ill or away for any reason, turn to *Illness and Other Crises*.

You should agree at the outset what you are going to do about paying your nanny when she is ill. Some families offer one or two weeks' paid sick leave, others tell us that they will rely on being able to pay and claim back from Social Security Statutory Sick Pay (SSP) if they are paying the nanny's stamps. However, you should know that this is not paid for the first three days your employee is off sick, so you should be prepared to pay her for the first three days at least.

> In the contract I send out, I state that I allow one week's paid sickness: after that, the state has to take over because we simply couldn't afford it.

If you wish to continue paying your employee her full salary during her time off for illness, you will have to make up the difference between that and SSP, which is a flat-rate payment.

If you do agree to pay your employee's full wages for a long absence, you should consider whether you can afford to do so if you are also going to have to pay a temporary nanny or take unpaid leave yourself.

If your nanny is self-employed and has been paying her own NI stamps, she should contact the local DSS office to claim sickness benefit or supplementary benefit.

If your nanny is earning less than the lower earning limit for SSP (under £54 per week in 1992/3) or if for some reason her stamps have not been paid up, you will have to decide whether you want to continue paying her wages, and for how long. If you can't afford to pay her, she can claim Income Support.

How to claim SSP for your nanny: if you are paying PAYE and NI for your nanny, you can claim Statutory Sick Pay if she is away ill. You will probably have a booklet from the DSS about how to do this, which you were sent with all the other bumph. SSP means you pay your sick employee a flat rate amount according to her normal salary. In 1992/3, if her normal weekly wages were between £54 and £189.99 SSP was £45.30 per week. For a salary of £190 or over SSP was £52.50.

You will be able to claim this amount back in full from your quarterly PAYE/NI payments. Do keep a detailed record of your nanny's absences and reasons given, in case you need to tell the DSS. She does not need to provide a doctor's certificate for the first seven days she is away sick, and after that the law leaves it up to you as the employer whether you require to see a doctor's certificate.

Tax and National Insurance

Employer's responsibility

If you pay your nanny or mother's help more than a certain amount a week, you will be responsible for:

* Deducting income tax from her wages under PAYE (Pay As You Earn).

* Deducting her National Insurance (NI) contributions from her wages.

* Paying a separate NI contribution as her employer.

Cost of tax and NI on a nanny's weekly wages

N.B. these figures are to be used as an example only. They are based on rates during 1992/3 tax year, and on the assumption that the employee is a single woman with no dependants.

Gross weekly pay (per week/ per annum)	Tax	Nanny's NI	Employer's NI	Net pay (in hand)	Total cost to employer
			contributions		
£100/£5,300	£8.44	£5.22	£6.60	£86.34	£106.60
£110/£5,720	£10.94	£6.12	£7.26	£92.94	£117.26
£120/£6,240	£13.44	£7.02	£7.92	£99.54	£127.92
£130/£6,760	£15.94	£7.92	£8.58	£106.14	£138.58
£140/£7,280	£18.44	£8.82	£12.04	£112.74	£152.04
£150/£7,800	£20.94	£9.72	£12.90	£119.34	£162.90
£160/£8,320	£23.44	£10.62	£13.76	£125.94	£173.76

Check with your tax office or Social Security office what the current pay thresholds are; as a guide, in the 1992/3 tax year, the lower earnings limit above which an employee was liable for tax was £66.25 per week, and the National Insurance lower earnings limit was £54.

The law says that you as the employer are responsible. Even if the tax man doesn't come and ask you for it, it is you, not your nanny, who will be asked to pay any arrears if you neglect to pay tax and National Insurance, and further penalties may also be imposed.

> I ended up having to find hundreds of pounds because I got behind with the tax payments. Even if you pay on time, three months' tax and NI can add up to a hefty sum. I now put aside the nanny's tax and NI into a separate account every week to make sure I don't get taken short again.

This is a heavy burden for the working mother, and most mothers think it is unfair. It is not just the effort involved – after all, you are an individual already pressed for time, not a company with a wages office – but also the fact that, as you are paying your nanny's wages out of your own salary which has already been taxed, you end up in effect paying tax twice.

Most nannies think in terms of their net weekly pay, and they are often unprepared for the large bite deductions for tax take out of a weekly paypacket.

To avoid any misunderstanding from the beginning, it is tempting to offer your nanny a round sum as a net, in-hand salary, then calculate the tax and NI on top of that. Unfortunately the tables the tax office provides do not help you to do this. If you want to start with a net salary and work out the tax and NI on top of it, ring your tax office and ask them to help you. The table above will give you some idea of the relationship between the gross salary, the net salary, and how much the whole thing will actually cost you (this is more than the gross salary, as you have to pay the employer's NI contribution on top).

Here is an example (based on 1992/3 rates): if the maximum you can afford to pay in total is £120 per week, you'll have to tell your prospective nanny you can offer her a gross salary of £112 per week, which will mean about £94 in her hand. On the other hand, if the girl you are considering says she wants £100 per week net, it means paying her a gross salary of £120 per week, which will cost you a total of £128 a week.

Advantage to your employee

Explain to your nanny that it is important for her sake that her tax and NI are deducted, so that she can be eligible for unemployment benefit, statutory sick pay, even old-age pension. If you pay her less than the lower earnings limit, try to encourage her to keep her stamps paid up. If she wants to, she can make voluntary NI contributions. She should contact the DSS office about this.

Self-employed nannies

Some nannies claim self-employed status, and take responsibility for paying their own tax and NI. If she only works for you part time and she has several other jobs, she *might* be able to do this. However, to be safe, you should clear it with your tax office, as there seems to be no clear across-the-board ruling at the Inland Revenue about this.

If your nanny is self-employed, you are of course under no obligation to give her paid holidays or paid sick leave – although you probably will still wish to do so. But as the offering of these things is a determinant of employee status, the tax office could well argue that she is not self-employed.

How to pay PAYE and NI

> I didn't know how to fill in the forms and the whole thing fussed me. In fact, it is extremely easy. I wrote to the tax office and they sent me all the explanatory stuff. They have subsequently, regular as clockwork, sent me the cards, the envelopes and reminders. You only pay once every three months, in arrears. They send you reminders so you don't even have to remember to do it. It's terribly simple.

Most of the women employing help in their home had found out how to pay their employee's tax and NI from their tax or DSS office, and confirmed that although the prospect was daunting before they had started, they had found it quite easy in the end.

Under the Simplified Domestic Scheme, (also called Simplified Deduction Scheme, Domestic Scheme or QD Scheme) you just need to sit down once every three months to work out how much to send to the tax office, which

collects both tax and NI, and to fill in a fairly
straightforward deductions card.

Call your local tax office (under Inland Revenue in the
phone book). Tell them you are taking someone on and
wish to pay their tax under the *Simplified Scheme* (or
quote the other names if the officer you are talking to
doesn't seem to know what you are on about!). They will
want to know what you propose to pay, her NI number if
known, and her P45 if she has worked before.

Some tax offices are more helpful than others: if many
women in your area employ nannies they will be used to
similar enquiries. But when we were revising this book,
one local tax office we talked to claimed that there was no
such thing as the Simplified Domestic Scheme, or any of
the other names – so be prepared to persevere!

> I have been dealing with the tax people for my nanny for
> years. A friend told me that it was easy and that they
> were very helpful, well I guess it depends on which tax
> office you deal with. I have often found them unhelpful.
> I always have to chase them to send me the right forms
> and the prepaid envelopes. They don't pay any attention
> when I inform them that they always get our names
> wrong. When I am a bit late with paying I get
> threatening form letters. I do the best I can, but I find it
> quite hard even after all this time to understand their
> language and to work out exactly how much I owe. One
> day I'll get a letter saying I've underpaid £100 and the
> next day I'll get a letter saying that I've overpaid in the
> previous year. I wish I could just tell them what I'm
> paying my nanny and that they would send me a bill!
> Sitting in the kitchen late at night trying to work it all
> out when I already have so much on my plate –
> sometimes it seems like the last straw.

The tax office will send you:

* 'Simplified Deduction card' (P12). This will record

your nanny's tax code and 'Free Pay' – this means her tax-free allowances, the amount she can earn before she needs to start paying tax.

* Instructions card (P16) telling you how to fill in the Simplified Deduction card on one side, with simplified tax tables on the other. These tables enable you to see at a glance how much tax is due according to the 'taxable pay' (this is what is left after you deduct her 'free pay' from her total weekly pay – her gross pay).

* Tables for working out the NI contributions (CF 391): against a column indicating her gross pay, these tables will tell you what her NI contribution is, and what yours is.

Once a quarter you fill in the columns on the Simplified Deduction card with her pay, deductions for NI and tax, and your own NI contributions. It is then relatively simple to add up the columns and send off one cheque for both tax and NI to the tax office, using one of the payslips also provided.

At the end of the tax year (early April)

The tax office will send you a new Simplified Deduction card, and will ask you to return the old one. You will also receive a P60 form to give to your employee. This will give her a record of how much tax has been deducted on her behalf over the year.

If your nanny leaves

You will be required to complete the Simplified Deduction card up to her leaving date and send it off with all the money due, and also a P45 form which she needs for her next employer.

Household and car insurance

You should check with your insurance company whether your normal household policy covers you if you employ someone to work at home, in terms of security and your liability in case anything happens to the employee while she is on your premises. If you are going to let her drive your car you should make sure you have a comprehensive insurance.

*Living With Your Nanny –
Happily Ever After*

Your nanny's duties: 'nursery duties', housework and more

> Nanny makes the children's breakfast, gets them dressed, does the playgroup run, makes lunch and feeds the children in the evening before we get home. This last is *very* important and has made for a much less stressful homecoming. She also does all their washing, reads to them, plays with them, keeps their rooms tidy and does a bit of a tidy-up in the living room and kitchen before she leaves.

The average nanny will expect her primary occupation to be childcare, but apart from looking after your children's physical needs and playing with them, she will normally accept to do the following domestic tasks, grandly called 'nursery duties':

* Cooking your children's meals while she is on duty and washing up afterwards.

* Possibly light local shopping for her own food and the children's, mainly for last-minute 'extras'.

* Washing, ironing and mending the children's clothes and bedding.

* Tidying the children's rooms, including making beds, sorting out toys and so on.

* Tidying up after the children and herself in the rest of the house.

If you employ a mother's help, on the other hand, you will generally be able to expect her to do any household tasks bar heavy cleaning (such as washing windows).

Many families in our survey expected their nanny to do tasks other than those outlined above: some did the whole family's laundry, some did the ironing, or cooked the odd meal for the whole family, looked after pets, or did the cleaning.

> Her duties are all those necessary to our daughter and her health and cleanliness: tidying up her room, complete maintenance of her clothes including mending (actually, she doesn't do that often), ironing, washing etc. She also does our washing, at least our clothes (not things like sheets). What is very helpful is that she washes up all the breakfast things. Frequently, she does much more than I ask. She would also do a little shopping for me if I asked her, but I'd only ask her to get something for their lunch, etc.

We even talked to parents who found a nanny willing to take on extra tasks like looking after horses, taking dictation and typing, or answering the phone. Kristine Band, who is a partner in a PR agency in Bedfordshire, also had an unusual request:

> Sarah was taken on on the basis of relieving me at the office if required, i.e. if I am not busy she will man the office and I can go home. She will do it, but she does prefer looking after the baby. She also covered for me at the office for a month or so after birth.

The important thing is that if you do have extra requirements you make those very clear at the outset. Of course, some nannies are very helpful and don't need to be asked to do odd jobs around the house, but to save hassle it is probably better not to count on it.

Do bear in mind, of course, that the more you expect your nanny to do around the house, the less time she will have to pay attention to your child, and you should make sure she realises that your child is your primary concern. But if, for example, your child is at nursery school in the mornings, you can probably expect your nanny to do more around the house.

> **Duties:** to organise the social and school life of the children, to provide them with good balanced meals, to supervise the playroom and their bedrooms, cook, mend, clean for the children. Nothing for us, officially, although in practice she does some washing up, clearing up for us as well.

Servant, daughter or friend?

> Although she doesn't live with us, when she's here, she's absolutely one of the family. I think if you are paying someone to look after your child and you think they are worthy of the responsibility you're not going to treat them like a servant. I regard her as my friend.

How should you treat your nanny or mother's help? Will she be part of the family? Will you expect her to sit down to meals with you and your partner – and in front of the telly afterwards? Will you invite her to join in when you are entertaining family or friends? Or will you want her to vanish discreetly into her room whenever she is not on duty? What rules should you set, if any, about her using the phone, about her entertaining friends at home, about having friends to stay the night, about staying out late – or all night? What about boyfriends? Use of the car?

I think she feels part of the family, but only up to a point. Like a lot of nannies these days, she's an independent person with a professional job, and she doesn't particularly want to be totally immersed in our family. She only ate supper with us when she was new. Then she discovered her own circle and now we never see her.

Here's what Anne Babb advises:

Do respect her privacy. I think a live-in nanny has as much right as anybody to set times which are stuck to. It's quite a demanding job, and they get pretty tired at the end of the day. After all, we mothers find it totally exhausting ourselves, and if they're in a household where the children are allowed to knock on their door at all hours, and people keep popping in for chats, it's wearing. Sometimes all a girl wants to do is shut her door, turn the telly on, read her book.

It is useful to have thought about these issues before you take somebody on, so that you can try to ascertain at the interview whether there is likely to be any friction. Even if employing a daily nanny you would be wise to give some thought to this.

For example, your daily nanny may use the phone a lot during the day, which can be inconvenient if it means you never get through when you try to ring home, quite apart from the expense. And daily nannies may also be visited by friends, or boyfriends, during the day.

We have no rules of the house, just the assumption that everyone will stick to reasonably civilised behaviour. I did tell her that although she can have friends to stay (she has a little flat of her own at the top of the house), a succession of men won't be very acceptable. A steady boyfriend is a different thing. I told her to observe basic discretion with regard to the children, I don't want them initiated into the facts of life quite that young!

Anne Babb comments:

> Although it sounds terribly mean, I always recommend
> to employers to make a rule to begin with that she
> should have no boyfriends in the house. If a girl has a
> steady boyfriend, it may be a different matter. But if you
> are relaxed to begin with, the situation can get out of
> hand, and you can't then suddenly turn around and start
> being awkward. You can always relax the rules when
> you know your nanny better.

Friendship, loneliness and the nanny mafia

If your nanny is new to your area, it is important to help
her meet up with other nannies, mother's helps,
childminders or mums. The problems of isolation and
loneliness that beset the mother at home with small
children can affect nannies in the same way, and a
depressed, lonely or homesick nanny won't be very good
company for your child. If she can find friends in the same
area who also look after children, you will probably find
that your child benefits by becoming part of a group of
children who meet regularly.

> For security reasons, you must insist that they don't
> invite casual acquaintances round to your house. They
> must be taught to make a distinction between the friends
> they make among other nannies, for example, and
> people they've just met in the pub.
>
> **Anne Babb**

There are ways to help your nanny make contact: take her
to the local one o'clock club, mother and toddler group or
playgroup; introduce her to the nannies of acquaintances
or neighbours, and to the neighbours themselves; make
enquiries of your health visitor or your child's nursery
school teacher, who may know of other families
employing nannies in the area.

Here is what one woman who lives in West Yorkshire
wrote about this:

Our first nanny's biggest problem was boredom – her duties were fairly light as we didn't want her to be a domestic drudge, but until she made friends through a mother and toddler group it was quite a lonely working life. Once she had made friends she would go out a lot and the girls would play with her friends' children.

If your nanny falls into the local nanny network, you may find that she and your children are sucked into a busy social whirl of lunches, teas and outings. On the whole the mothers we spoke to saw this as beneficial both for their nannies and their children, who became used to mixing with a group of other children. Nannies are also more likely to do really interesting and exciting things, like taking the children to the zoo or on a picnic, with another nanny than on their own.

There were some complaints about the endless gossip in which the 'nanny mafia' sometimes indulges:

My nanny is in a circle of eight nannies with children who flow between different houses on a daily basis. She'll say, 'I've got three children coming for lunch tomorrow, and two nannies,' and we discuss what I should get for her to cook. My daughter gets a Cordon Bleu cooked lunch every day, and it has made her used to eating in company. But they all gossip and complain about their employers, and that does drive me crazy. You'd think we were all absolute demons. Ultimately it's a bore to have to listen to the horrors going on in the other nannies' households – always things like having to work longer hours then agreed, mothers cooking awful food like fish fingers every day of the week, or being grumpy or moody. I have stopped encouraging this kind of conversation. I don't mind hearing about the other children, but not about their ruddy parents!

Anne Babb comments:

If it's a good group and they're having lots of fun on their time off, the nanny mafia works very well. I think it's important that the nanny has friends, but the friends can sometimes be very undermining. For instance, they all tell each other what they earn, and what they're expected to do: this can of course lead to discontent and resentment.

Responsibility and trust

> She makes her own rules with the children, e.g. no drinks in the lounge, tidying up toys etc. The only thing I would not have is for her to smack the children. I do not smack them myself and I think this has been communicated without anything being said.

The happiest employer/nanny relationships are founded on mutual respect and trust. This means that although you should establish clearly at the beginning what your standards and expectations are, you must be flexible enough to show your nanny you trust her and let her take her own decisions about how to handle unexpected situations. She will probably do her best, if she is any good, to imagine how *you* would handle it and act accordingly.

This means giving your nanny time to get to know you and see you in action: how you deal with fights or tantrums, for example, how you like things done around the house, how you use the neighbourhood amenities.

Once your nanny is in charge, you should be careful to avoid undermining her authority in the eyes of your children. For example, don't overrule her if she has forbidden a snack before teatime. Many families have a rule, clearly understood by the children, that the nanny is totally in charge during her hours of duty, even if a parent is around.

Your children will soon sense if they can play you and the nanny off against each other. If you ever have to criticise her, it is better to save it for when the children are not around.

We asked working mothers whether they knew where their nannies took their children, and whether they felt they should know what they did all day.

Some were relaxed and did not worry about it:

> I don't know where she is all the time, but I trust her, and I know she'd ring me with any problem. I think that basic trust is something one should establish with one's nanny, and if she feels you're breathing down her neck it's probably a bad thing.

But most mothers expected to have some idea of the nanny's movements, and where she could be reached in an emergency.

Some families keep a calendar in the kitchen, in which the nanny records where she is going, if, for example, she is taking the children out for tea at another nanny's house, and also keep a list of her friends' phone numbers.

Most mothers make time in the morning to go over the day's coming events with the nanny, and some insist that she calls them at work if she is taking the children out anywhere unusual.

> At first she often used to take the children out on long trips to town without letting either of us know where she was going. On several occasions we phoned up or popped in at home to find no one there – we were left wondering what had happened – accidents or worse. Eventually she came to appreciate the importance of letting us know when she planned to take the children out.

It is probably wise to set standards from the beginning about what places and activities you find suitable for your child, and what you would not accept. You may want to specify, for example, that she takes your child swimming every week, or to the library, or that they should go out for at least one walk in the fresh air every day. And although you may be happy for your nanny to take your children to McDonald's once in a while as a special treat, you may not be pleased, as happened to one mother we spoke to, to find that your nanny regularly met a boyfriend in a pub for lunch, child in tow!

The most sensible approach is that any activity or outing is acceptable as long as it is safe and enjoyable for the child as well as the nanny. If the nanny is having fun, the chances are that your child will have a good time as well.

However, it may be as well to remind your nanny subtly from time to time that as she is paid to keep your child amused, (not just safe) her first consideration must always be your child.

Praising your nanny

It may sound too obvious to say that you should remember to praise your nanny from time to time. But according to several nannies, this is a courtesy that many employers forget about! A nanny will feel happier and more self-confident in her work if you generously give credit where it is due. For example, show her that you have noticed her efforts to teach your children manners or that she has trained your child to pick up the toys. Nannies work a very long, exhausting day: sometimes it is nice for them to hear just, 'I don't know what I'd do without you'!

> I try to treat our nanny as part of the family and a good friend – and give her as much responsibility for running the house as possible. For example, ordering coal when needed, making lists of groceries needed. She uses the telephone when she wants – although she always asks first.

Keeping track of your child's daily life

One problem a working mother can encounter, especially if her child is not yet talking, is how to impress upon her nanny that she wants to know what her child has been up to during her absence at work – for her own interest and peace of mind, not because she is prying, or because she doesn't trust the nanny:

> I have this voracious *need* to *know* what has gone on during the day, to fill in the gaps of my son's life between when I wave goodbye in the morning and when I greet him in the evening, and I'm afraid my nanny (though not unwilling or particularly secretive) just doesn't satisfy my curiosity by simply answering 'We went to the park today.'

If you can't find time at the end of the hectic day to sit down with your nanny, perhaps over a cup of tea, so that you can chat and draw her out about the big and small events of the day, you may want to imitate one mother who bought a page-a-day desk diary, and asked her nanny to help her write in it. The mother records any special instructions for the day (for example, 'shepherd's pie in the fridge for lunch', or 'don't forget to pay the milkman'). The nanny records where they have been, what the children did, what they had for lunch, details of any symptoms of illness, whether they had a nap, upsetting incidents, funny things they said or did. The mother on her side keeps the diary at weekends and during the holidays, so that the nanny has the same continuous overview of things that go on in *her* absence.

This makes the mother and the nanny into a proper team, and gives the nanny greater job satisfaction.

> As a bonus, I have a detailed record of my youngest's early years, day by day, including all those cute first words you always mean to write down. When A. first came she found it quite difficult – I'd started the diary with my first nanny – and her entries were quite short. But now she's got used to it she writes funny stories in it and really seems to enjoy writing it.

Household kitty

> We have a purse in the hall, into which I put a few quid.
> I check it from time to time and top up if necessary. I
> don't ask her to keep a record because I think she should
> be trusted like one of the family. My principle is that I
> pay for everything, for instance if they go to
> McDonald's for lunch as a treat, I pay for my nanny's as
> well as my daughter's meal.

Most of the mothers who employed nannies confirmed that even though they did the weekly shopping themselves, they gave their nanny a weekly float or allowance for miscellaneous expenses, including treats, outings, fares. It may not occur to you that it is necessary if you have a small baby, but do budget for some weekly spending money if you are employing a nanny to look after older children.

> I give her a weekly allowance and I don't ask for every
> penny to be accounted for because I expect her to have
> spent it on the children – not always wisely, not always
> as I would wish it to be spent. Off and on I do get on at
> her about not giving them too many sweets.

Love and jealousy: the emotional relationship

We asked the working mothers we spoke to whether their children loved their nannies, and whether they, the mothers, ever felt jealous of the emotional relationship between the nanny and their children.

Although it is normal to experience the odd pang of jealousy when your child runs to your nanny for comfort, or enjoys a private joke with her, the general consensus was that a loving relationship between nanny and her charges was desirable, even necessary: 'I'm very pleased that the kids so obviously like the nanny – and I would feel less happy if they didn't get all that love from her.'

One mother confided that she was worried that her nanny didn't love her child *enough*, or at least that she didn't *show* her affection enough:

> I'm not jealous of her relationship with my daughter, but I do worry that she doesn't show my daughter enough physical affection. She's the perfect nanny in every other way – she knows all these super games, and builds playhouses and shops for her – but she doesn't cuddle her enough.

If you are secure in your relationship with your child, there is no need ever to fear that the nanny might in some way alienate your child's love for you.

> I'd only feel jealous of the nanny if my husband seemed terribly enthusiastic about her! I have always felt that a child's love is not like a piece of cake, that they have just so much love and have to share it out between everybody. I feel that the more love they have, the more they can give. So if they can love one person they will love another. When I was last ratty, my daughter said, 'I don't want you as my mummy any more, I wish Jackie [the nanny] was my mummy.' Surprisingly I didn't feel hurt or devastated by that. I just thought to myself, 'Serves you right for being so horrible!' I was reassured that she likes the nanny so much.

One mother seemed less secure about her relationship with her son, which made her feel somewhat threatened when he developed a strong bond with his nanny:

> I did have some feelings of jealousy over my previous nanny. I was very fond of her, but she had a very strong character, and she had such an influence over my eldest – she was quite possessive – that there was a slight struggle between us over him. He never rejected me in favour of her, but I would say he probably felt *as much* for her as for me.

It is unlikely that your nanny will wish to come between you and your child: most modern nannies are very conscious of their professional status and try to keep a certain distance. But if you feel that your nanny is being too possessive about your child, discuss your feelings with her and give her a chance to explain herself. Comfort yourself that research has shown that although children can develop a close relationship with others, they will, given the choice, overwhelmingly prefer their parents to any other beloved adult in the long run.

Children soon learn that nannies come and go, but that their parents are a permanent fixture in their lives. If, like all the working mothers in our sample, you make a real effort to spend regular time together with your child on a daily basis it is really not possible for a nanny to replace you in your child's emotional life, although she may add to it and enrich it.

When things go wrong

You must air any problems as they come up, rather than let resentment fester until it suddenly explodes and you find yourself firing your nanny – or she walks out on you. Experts agree that continuity of care is important for small children, and many of the mothers we spoke to were inclined to put up with their nanny's imperfections for the sake of the children, who would be disrupted and upset by a change of nannies.

> The family we were sharing our nanny with had much higher expectations of the educational things she should do with the children, and wanted to get rid of her. They are very well off, and got a Norland nanny in the end. But we decided that it was far more important for our daughter to have the continuity. She was very fond of the nanny – and I kept her on in spite of certain failings.

Of course, you may discover something unacceptable

about your nanny's behaviour. If you feel your nanny, by her actions or neglect, is endangering or damaging your child in some way, or that you can't trust her, you should feel no hesitation about sacking her. These are fair grounds for dismissal. On the other hand, if you sack your nanny because she doesn't keep the linen properly, say, or because her boyfriend stayed the night, she might well have legal redress for unfair dismissal.

Always listen to her point of view first, and if you feel you can still believe her, and trust her, it may be best to give her another chance.

> I found out by accident that my nanny was leaving my daughter with her own mother while she attended occasional classes at a local college without my knowledge. My first impulse was to sack her, I felt I couldn't trust her any more. But we had a good long talk and a lot of things came out, and I felt I had not made everything as clear as I should have done. I decided to give her a second chance, and I haven't had cause to regret it. She has stayed two years so far, and we are very happy with her now.

When your nanny leaves

If you have had a good relationship with your nanny, you may feel hurt and upset when she gives in her notice. But most nannies today feel they have to move on after a year or two.

Sometimes they move for more money, or sometimes just for a change. After all, it must be difficult to live the life of your employer's family for too long, no matter how much you like them.

Mothers who have been through several nannies confessed that it had been a blow when the first nanny handed in her notice, but that they had since found that nobody was irreplaceable!

Our first nanny stayed three years. I think that's too long, you get tired of each other. Even though we're still very close friends, and she still takes the children for holidays at her parents, I think the relationship is better now than it was at the time of her employment with us. Two years is about right, in my opinion. The second nanny left after two years, she wanted to do something different and went to work in Zimbabwe. The third stayed for seven months. We didn't fire her, though her friends thought we had – she just upped and left for Canada. We were quite relieved. In all the panic of finding a replacement I suddenly thought to myself, 'What's the worst thing that could happen? That she decides to *stay* after all!'

Of course if you find you have lost six nannies in as many months, you want to step back and analyse if there is a reason why they don't stay. If you are not paying enough, they will probably have told you. But is your home too cramped to accommodate another person comfortably? Does your nanny suffer from a lack of privacy? Is your house too chaotic and messy? Most nannies prefer to work in a neat, orderly house. Or do you expect too much housework to be done on top of the burden of childcare – are your expectations of what can be achieved in a day unrealistic? Is it possible that you are too interfering, or that you don't know how to make your nanny feel appreciated?

When your nanny leaves: the impact on your child

If your child has had a close and happy relationship with the nanny, her leaving can have a considerable impact, especially if your child is at a vulnerable clingy age. In extreme cases, the departure of a loved nanny can affect children almost like a divorce. Put yourself in the child's shoes: there is the feeling of abandonment, and if things are not explained, the child may feel to blame.

It is also possible that your child will develop a real, if irrational, fear that if nanny can leave, you or your partner may do the same, so it is important to make it clear that these fears are groundless.

There are ways that you and the nanny can help soften the blow and ease the pain of her leaving. Both of you should explain that she is leaving for a specific comprehensible reason unconnected with your child, (for example she has to earn more money, she is getting married or she wants to be nearer her own parents). Try to get your children, if old enough, to talk about their feelings for her, so that both of you can provide reassurance and support, emphasising that although she is leaving she still cares.

If possible, arrange for your new nanny to overlap with the departing nanny for a few days, so that your child will have time to get used to the new face. See if your departing nanny will agree to come back and visit your child occasionally, rather than abruptly disappear. If she is moving far away, you may be able to ask her to write a postcard, or telephone your child from time to time. Many mothers we talked to seemed to take it for granted that their ex-nannies remained friendly with the family.

Sharing a Nanny

I decided to employ a trained nursery nurse to collect Jo from nursery school late morning until I arrived home from work. Coincidentally a work colleague with a child about the same age was interested in a similar arrangement, so we decided to employ someone jointly. We advertised the post at the local college that trained nursery nurses and employed a newly qualified nursery nurse. We experienced a few teething problems with our employee, but she has been excellent with the children and they have both grown very attached to her. My husband employs the nanny. He works out her wages (tax and NI). The other couple pay their contributions monthly. We employ the nanny for longer hours than the other couple, so we work out her pay on two rates: a higher rate for caring for two children than the rate for caring for just one.

The couple we share with have longer holidays than us. They pay a retainer for the nanny (half their usual payments) when they are on holiday. The arrangements are flexible for all parties but the nanny has a guaranteed minimum pay and four weeks a year leave entitlement. We each keep a kitty for the nanny to use for day-to-day expenses (like bus fares). The children spend half the week at each house (the same days each week). We try to keep in close contact with the other couple and try to resolve any difficulties that arise jointly. I have found this arrangement most successful as far as my work is concerned because it is flexible and I have been very happy with it.

Social worker, York

Sharing a nanny between two families is a way of getting the luxury of a nanny at a little over half the cost (shared nannies do usually expect to earn a little more than the average going rate to compensate for the additional complications and extra work).

When considering a nanny share bear in mind that it's bound to be a little less convenient for your family than having your own nanny. On the other hand, if you have an only child he or she can benefit from a regular playmate.

Splitting a nanny's time

If you do not require a nanny's service all the time because you work part time, or because your child is at school in the morning, you can try to find another family with whom to share, whose needs mesh with yours. In this case you can find a nanny to work part time, separately, for each family. She can live in or out, or with one of the families.

Shared day

A mother who works in the mornings could share with another who works afternoons, or with one who works full time with school-age children who need to be picked up from school in the afternoon and supervised until the end of the working day.

Shared week

If you work only certain days of the week, you may find another mother who needs a nanny on the days you don't.

Shared school year

A teacher with pre-school-age children can combine with a mother in another job who has school-age children. Between them they can employ a nanny who will look after the teacher's small children during term time. During the school holidays, while the teacher is free to look after her own children, the nanny will cover for the other family, solving their school holiday problem. If considering this option, do check that the teacher's and children's school holiday dates coincide.

Nanny sharing

A proper full-time nanny share means that you find another family living near you, with children of compatible ages with yours, and between you employ a nanny who will look after both families' children at the same time, in one or other house. Some find more than one other family to share with, but in this case the nanny is required to register as a childminder, under the new Children Act.

A part-time speech therapist's arrangement shows just how flexible such an arrangement can be:

I share a nanny with two other mothers who also work part time and live near me. We have five children between us, but we make sure the nanny never looks after more than four at any one time, and even then not for more than a morning at a time. She lives with one of the others, who arranges her tax and NI. I pay her separately, on a daily basis. We are all great friends, and the nanny is wonderful – she has been working this way for us for years. It may sound complicated but it's good because it's so flexible. As we all work on different days there is never a problem about holidays and sickness, so we can all stand in for each other and the nanny if necessary.

How to find another family for a nanny share

Although you can employ your nanny first, having made it clear from the start that you will be looking for a family to share her with, it is more convenient to find another family first, and then to advertise for a nanny together.

Some nanny agencies provide a nanny share service for a fee: they will attempt to match you with another family, then with a nanny.

Many Working Mothers Groups, which belong to the Working Mothers Association, also operate local nanny share registers.

If nothing like this exists in your area, you can advertise for another family in your local paper or NCT newsletter, or ask around at your child's school or playgroup.

Some women find others to share with while they are pregnant, at their antenatal classes. You might even look through the adverts in *The Lady* and ring up any families who live near you and are advertising for a nanny, and suggest to them they consider a share with you.

If you already employ a nanny but find the financial burden too heavy, discuss with your nanny the possibility of finding another family to share her with. Some nannies positively enjoy the variety provided by working with several children for two families. The extra money may also be an incentive. If she agrees, you could advertise for another family to share her services.

Checklist for a successful nanny share

Proximity

Ideally, the family you share with should live very close to you. Remember that one of the parents will have to drop off their children at the other house in the mornings and collect them in the evenings. If the nanny is expected to spend some days at the one house and some at the other, the closer they are the better, especially as you may have to transport equipment back and forth.

Children's ages

It will probably be easier for one nanny to cope with one infant and one or two toddlers, than with two small infants who will need to be changed and fed at the same time (not that this is impossible – as mothers of twins assure us).

Many families have a preference for sharing with a child who is slightly older than their own, as they feel this will provide additional stimulation and interest for their child. But sharing with a baby or younger child may help prepare your child for the emotional upheaval of a baby brother or sister. Consider whether any difference in ages will prevent the children from enjoying playing together, or whether the nanny will find it difficult to give her charges equal amounts of time and attention.

Also think about how the nanny is going to get out and about. If you expect her to look after one small baby and two toddlers, for example, she'll have to manage with either a double buggy or a pram with pram seat – but she won't be able to manoeuvre both at the same time. If she is going to do the school run, consider the maximum number of child safety seats and carrycots you can fit on the back seat of a car (not many).

Equipment

You may have to share the cost of a double buggy with the other family, unless you happen to have compatible buggies that can be clipped together, or you may have to buy a pram seat, or extra car safety seats. You may also need an extra high chair, a spare cot for naps, and so on.

Which house?

Some families always use one home for the nanny and the children to stay in; others alternate houses weekly, monthly, quarterly or half-yearly.

If you swap homes regularly, consider how you are going to transport any extra equipment between the two houses, and whether there is enough room in each house for the extra equipment you need. The family whose house is being used benefits from the convenience of not having to drop their child off, and also of having the nanny on the spot to do household chores. Against that you should weigh the extra cost of heating, electricity, telephone and so on, plus the extra wear and tear on the house and its contents and additional use of household necessities (for example, coffee, tea, milk, loo paper and so on).

If you swap houses regularly, these things will balance out, but if not you may consider agreeing that the family whose house is used pays a slightly lower share. As for food and drink, you can budget it and contribute to a joint weekly kitty, or, if changing houses regularly, you can simply agree that food is provided by the host family. You should also consider whether each family will provide its own nappies and so on, and whether the nanny will be expected to do both families' children's washing.

Holidays, sickness

It will be important to arrange for both families and the nanny to go on holiday at the same time, so that no child is left stranded while the nanny is away. This will need careful planning, probably a long time in advance. If this is not going to be possible, you should discuss what you can do about it. Also discuss alternative arrangements and contingency measures you will make if the nanny is ill, or when one child comes down with a contagious illness.

Notice

It is wise to agree in advance what happens if one of the families decides to withdraw from the arrangement, and agree a notice period between the families as well as between both of you and the nanny.

Compatibility with the other family

Women who have experience of nanny sharing emphasise that it is most important to find a family with similar ideas, standards and aspirations as yourselves – if possible, you want a couple with whom you can be really good friends. It will be necessary for you to see eye-to-eye on everything from nutrition and education to potty training, discipline and suitable activities for the children. For example, you cannot reasonably expect the nanny to cook different meals for each child, nor to be encouraged to provide one child with sweets and deny them to the other.

To avoid friction and forestall problems, it is a good idea for the two families (or mothers) to get together regularly to discuss how it is all going and to air any problems: you should ask the nanny to meet with you occasionally as well.

Au Pairs

> I don't want an au pair – I've been an au pair and I
> know one really isn't interested in the children. You're
> there to learn the language and find out about yourself,
> being in a foreign country, away from home for the first
> time. You're not really committed to looking after
> children. It would be different if I was a mum at home,
> just needing someone to help me.
>
> **Mother with live-in nanny, London**

Au pairs are not really a childcare solution if you work
full time. They are usually foreign girls who come to live
with an English family, but sometimes young British girls
also work as au pairs in Britain, filling in time between
school and college.

According to Home Office regulations, an au pair is a
single girl aged between seventeen and twenty-seven from
a Western European country who can stay in the country
for a maximum of two years. The idea is for her to have
the opportunity of living with a British family to learn
English.

You can expect her to do no more than five hours a day
of light domestic work (up to a total of thirty hours
maximum a week) – for example, hoovering, ironing,
dusting, washing up, loading and unloading the washing
machine, some shopping, perhaps some cooking, and
childcare; plus two or three evenings' babysitting a week.
In return, you pay her substantial 'pocket money', provide
full board and lodging (au pairs will expect to live as a
member of the family) and give her the chance to attend a
local college or language school for daily English classes.

Even if your au pair is not strictly an au pair in the
Home Office sense, it is wrong to use her as a cheap
substitute for a nanny or mother's help, and give her sole
charge of your pre-school children for more than a few
hours a day. If you employ someone to do more than the

minimum outlined above, and she is happy to do the work you have detailed in advance, fine – but don't call her an au pair, call her a mother's help, and pay her accordingly. Sometimes, au pairs who do more than the minimum are called 'au pair plus' by agencies.

An au pair can be a solution when winding down an expensive nanny or mother's help when your children have started attending school. Picking up children from school and looking after them until their mother gets home would seem to fall well within the five hours' daily limit, giving the au pair the chance of attending college in the mornings. But do consider what you are going to do during the school holidays and when the child is ill.

As Marianne Walsh, who runs Mar's Au Pair Agency in West London, told us:

> I don't place au pairs with families where both parents are working full time, because I don't think it is suitable. If they want someone for children who are still at school, I always ask what will happen if their child is ill, or during the school holidays. If they expect an au pair to take over, it's just not on, unless it is spelled out and agreed in advance, and they offer to pay extra for these times, and the au pair accepts those conditions. Then they should check whether the holidays of the college where she is studying English and their child's holidays are the same.

Here are some other points to bear in mind if considering employing an au pair:

* If you employ someone direct from her home country, you will not have the opportunity to interview her face-to-face before she arrives.

* If your au pair does not speak English very well you may not be able to trust her to cope in an emergency when you are not around. Will she be able to make

herself understood with the police or ambulance service, for instance?

* Most au pairs stay for quite a short time: usually it is between six months and a year. A high turnover of au pairs may be disruptive and upsetting for your child.

* Many au pairs are living away from home for the first time, and may be very homesick and lonely. You may find you have to cope with her emotional problems and you may feel it is more like being responsible for another child than like having someone to help you. It helps if you live in an area where there are other au pairs from her home country for her to meet up with.

* Some au pairs are marvellous helps around the house, and wonderful with children (especially if they come from a large family and have been used to helping out with younger siblings). However, others may never have been expected to lift a finger at home, and may prove worse then useless. Different cultural standards, for example towards food or hygiene may also create problems.

How to find an au pair

There are many agencies specialising in bringing au pairs over from the continent: look in your Yellow Pages, or in the adverts in *The Lady*. If you have contacts abroad, you may consider asking them to advertise for an au pair locally.

In this case, do familiarise yourself with the Home Office regulations if employing someone from a country outside the EC to make sure she is not denied entry into the UK on arrival. You should also investigate the English language classes available in your area for non-English speakers at local adult institutes, colleges or schools.

Maternity Nurses

A maternity nurse is either a qualified nurse or an NNEB nursery nurse who specialises in young babies. As they usually work on short contracts – often a month to six weeks when a mother first comes home from hospital with her baby, but rarely more than three months – they are not a long-term option for looking after your child, except if you are as lucky as one London barrister who prevailed upon her wonderful maternity nurse to stay on and be her nanny.

As they are very expensive (you can expect to pay twice as much as for the average nanny) they are out of the question for most mothers, but sometimes a generous grandmother will offer to pay for one.

If you are fortunate enough to be able to afford one and if you are very worried about having to cope with your newborn baby (or the sleepless nights!) a maternity nurse, with her reassuring experience of small infants, can be a great boon. She will usually consider her duties to be limited to the new baby and can't normally be expected to look after older siblings.

The most appealing thing about a maternity nurse is that she will be prepared to handle the night feeds. Some breastfeeding mothers have their babies brought to them at night already changed. They feed the baby themselves, then have the baby taken away again to be burped and settled by the nurse while they sink back into well-earned sleep. Often, the maternity nurse sees her goal as having the baby sleeping through the night by the time she leaves at six weeks.

Of course, this is not every mother's idea of heaven: some would prefer to have someone take all the other household duties off their shoulders and pay attention to any older children, so that they can give their undivided attention to the new infant. In this case, a daily cleaner, nanny or mother's help (if there is no willing relative to hand) is probably a more satisfactory option.

A temporary maternity nurse, if funds allow, is also an option to be considered if you need a break or if you are suffering from exhaustion or postnatal depression. Some agencies are prepared to supply maternity nurses on a daily basis, though many stipulate a minimum of one week.

If you are covered by a private medical insurance scheme like BUPA and there is a medical reason for special care of yourself or your baby, you may be able to claim the cost of a maternity nurse back from your insurance.

How to find a maternity nurse

Look in *The Lady* for agencies advertising maternity nurses. Your GP, health visitor or maternity hospital may be able to recommend someone, or you could just find someone through word of mouth: many good maternity nurses are passed from mother to mother on personal recommendation.

CHAPTER 11
School-age Children

For many mothers this is when the practical problems really start. Mothers who have previously stayed at home with their children often decide that it is the moment to find a job again, and the mothers who are already working find that their excellent childcare arrangements are no longer adequate.

Your child is at school for just a few hours each day. Arrangements have to be made for the end of the school day until you come home – unless your hours coincide; some women are unable to take their children to school and have to find somebody to do it for them, and even if you work part-time, you have to cope with the long months of school holidays.

Because there is no established system for coping with children before and after school and during the holidays the women we spoke to and who wrote to us had lots of different ways of coping.

Choosing a School

Even those of us who don't put our children's names down at birth for a public school start thinking fairly early about where we are going to send our children to school.

Certainly in parts of London many mothers find that if they want to get their children into the best local authority school they have to register well in advance – sometimes when their children are two or three, or younger. It is best to ring your own local education authority to find out the situation in your area, and how many schools you can choose between.

Even if you don't have to put your child's name down early, you will probably have decided a year or so in advance where you want to send your child – probably partly based on what local gossip says is the best school around.

For many people in many areas the choice of school is a foregone conclusion – it may be a toss-up between two local schools, or there may simply be only one school nearby. But those who live in larger towns and cities may find the choice bewildering, and those who have just moved to a new area will even find a choice of two unknowns difficult.

Your two main considerations will probably be the standards at the school and the ease of journey from your home.

The quality of the school

You will obviously want to visit the local schools and talk to the headteacher. This gives you a certain impression of the school, but it can be misleading. A school in a beautiful building is not necessarily better than the one that is older and dilapidated. A head may be plausible and enthusiastic, but it is his relationship with his staff that really makes the difference. When choosing it is worth looking a little further:

* Some schools allow you to visit when lessons are in progress, and it is worth taking a day off if you can to do so. This will give you an idea of the standard of

teaching and the atmosphere as well as the general behaviour of the children and the relationship between staff and children.

* Other schools invite you along to an open day. This tells you less about the school, but gives you the opportunity to talk to other parents with children at the school and hear their views.

* Do listen to local talk about the schools – it tends to be rather negative and lurid more often than not, but somewhere in there is truth.

* Talk to as many other mothers with children at the school as possible. If you simply talk to the mother with a chronically shy child who is being bullied at the moment, you may form a lop-sided picture.

* Try to make time to stand outside the school on a few occasions at going-home time. Observation will tell you quite a lot about the atmosphere of the school. Are the children rowdy, rude and loutish as they emerge? Happy and chatty? Subdued until they think they are out of sight and earshot of the staff?

Convenience of the journey

It is ideal if the school you like the best is close to home. That means that when you judge that your child is ready he or she will be able to walk alone to school. (It rarely *is* alone, because local children tend to walk to school together in large gangs.)

Otherwise you will be looking at the ease of journey: whether it is convenient for you to drop your child off on your way to work, either by car or public transport. One mother chose a school that was apparently furthest away from home – but it was connected by a good rail service. 'The two nearer schools were harder to get to: one you could only reach by walking (a twenty-minute walk) the other was served by a very unreliable bus route.'

Other considerations

It may suit you to choose a school that takes children early: a preparatory class that takes them at four rather than five. A lecturer in Devon has this tip:

> If you can, search out fee-paying convent schools run by nuns. You don't have to be RC – in fact most aren't – but they have numerous advantages with regard to working mums.
>
> 1. Our local one took rising four-year-olds – the state schools were post-five-year-olds.
>
> 2. The convent school was *much* cheaper than the day nursery – about 60 per cent of the cost.
>
> 3. The term was longer though the day was shorter.
>
> 4. The children are not 'dismissed' at the end of the school day. A sister stands outside with them and then takes them all back into school. It means you don't have to worry about them being left alone – a nightmare for the working mum. Sometimes I was an hour late, but they were safe.
>
> 5. Ours was a good school with a wide social mix, boys and girls, and always spotlessly clean.
>
> I realise it raises other problems – shorter day for some people, longer holidays, but I had the holiday problem anyway as the day nursery only ran for the student terms.

Compatibility of schools

If you are considering sending several children to different schools do check on the compatibility of the schools' hours, half-terms and holiday dates. These can fluctuate widely from school to school.

After-school care

Some schools do much more for their children after the school day ends, and this may influence your choice, especially if after-school is going to be a particular problem. Some keep staff on to supervise playgrounds, run clubs or play-centres in the classrooms. Your local education department will know which schools do this.

Starting School

Some children slip into the routine of school quite easily. If your child has been looked after at a nursery or at a busy childminder's, or has regularly attended a playgroup and is used to lots of people around, the change may simply seem exciting. But many children find the first experience of school quite difficult. If your child is at all shy or nervous, or if you are only now returning to work, or your child has been used to a nanny or has been the only child being cared for in another situation, school may seem bewildering at best, and threatening or downright frightening at worst.

You are the best person to gauge your child's ability to fit in and to adapt to the big change of school. There are all the other children to cope with, most of them much older, and there are rules to learn, however simple. There are also many more children with whom to compete for the teacher's attention in class.

You will probably want to be around at the beginning and end of the first day, at the least – so that you can give your child moral support and hear all about it. (This will be the first of many occasions when you have to decide whether or not to take time off officially for school events!) However, you might also possibly feel that your child needs more support than this. If you suspect that your child will be particularly nervous and disturbed about the big change, you may feel it is worth arranging in advance to take some holiday at that time.

Depending on how much support you think your child will need you can do these things:

* Arrange to go in to work later for a time, so that you can take your child to school and wait around in the playground (or wherever) until school starts. This way your child can chat to you if he or she hasn't yet made friends. You can also start to get to know the other mothers and children.

* Arrange to leave work earlier for a while, so that you are there at picking up time. That is when your child is most full of what has been happening, and if the day has been miserable or difficult for any reason you are there to cope with it immediately. This is also the very best time to meet and talk to other mothers, who tend to congregate early. You can pick up gossip about the school, the teachers and the routines, and perhaps start to make the friends who will be invaluable to you as a working mother.

* Take a week or two of holiday and involve yourself in the school day if your school encourages this. Some schools positively welcome mothers coming in for a morning or afternoon to help with reading, dinners, or practical work such as sewing and painting. This allows you to sum up the other children and the teacher, and to get to know the school. One mother found that doing this made a real difference:

> As I am freelance I was able to arrange to come in a few mornings a week during the first term and help in my daughter's classroom. In fact she is a gregarious happy child, and although she was very pleased and proud to have me there I don't think she actually needed it. But I found it invaluable. I recognised that the teacher liked quiet shy girls the best, I got to know the other children and worked out who were the troublemakers, and knew the layout of the classroom and school backwards. All this was very helpful to me later. When my daughter seemed to clash with the teacher I understood why, and was able to be of more use helping her cope with it, and I wasn't fooled by the angelic faces of the bullies – I

believed her when she told me what they had done, and was able to steer her into happier friendships. But knowing the school was one of the most important benefits of going in. Five-year-olds aren't very good at explaining clearly – they assume you know what they are talking about when they tell you snippets about their day. As I had come to know the routine, layout and jargon of the school I was able to understand what she was telling me – double-dutch to anyone else – and actually have a conversation about it, instead of just saying 'Yes, dear'.

Bad behaviour

Some mothers report that spending this unusual extra time with their children causes them to play up. Depending on whether your child does this – and how badly – you may decide that it is better to keep away. On the whole though, it seems worth putting up with the embarrassment of a bit of bad behaviour for the benefits you both gain in the long run.

Fitting the School Day into your Working Day

Getting your child to school

Getting your child to school can be a problem if your day starts early and you have a long trip into work yourself. If both school and work are local then you probably won't have a problem dropping your child off on the way, or there may be a school bus. Some schools open their doors early for children whose parents have to rush off early; if your school doesn't, it is worth lobbying to get them to do so.

Some women have nannies that they have kept on for the school-age child, or who is now looking after a younger child, and obviously she can do the school run if she lives in. Some women have partners who start later or work for places that are more flexible about time-keeping. Glynis Day, a part-time teacher, describes her solution:

> I am extremely lucky in having a very supportive husband. When I am working I have to leave the house at 7.45a.m. My husband stays at home with the children until it is time for them to go to school and then he arrives at work an hour late. Luckily his boss does not mind as long as he stays an hour later in the evenings which we consider fair. After school my children are picked up by my childminder who brings them to their own house and stays with them until I arrive home, usually about 4.45p.m. My childminder and I have known each other since we were pregnant together, the children look upon 'Auntie Carol' almost as a member of the family, and her daughter enjoys coming to our house to play after school so the situation suits everybody.

If you have problems taking your child yourself you may want to consider these options:

Finding someone else

* Some childminders are prepared to do the early morning run. Even if you don't have to use a childminder for the end of the day or holidays, you may find one who will take your child to school and is happy for you to drop your child off as early as you need to.

* Another parent or neighbour may be prepared to take your child in. Most mothers who have to make the school run anyway find it no bother to take another child along too.

* A responsible teenager who goes to the same school, or a nearby school may take your child for you. Either

the teenager could come to your house to wait with your child, and lock up when they leave, or you could drop your child off at the teenager's house.

Sharing the early morning run

If you find other mothers in the same position you can share the run. Arranging to come in late one morning a week when it is your turn may be quite acceptable to your employer.

Going to school alone

If you live near your school your child may be able to walk alone, or with other children from the same school. A responsible older child may also be able to catch the bus or train alone. Although this is less risky than coming home alone, your child still needs to be very well prepared. You should thoroughly explain road sense in general, and how to handle the school route in particular. There is less chance of a child being abducted on the way to school, but your child should still be told to be extremely suspicious of any strangers, or even of acquaintances who suggest a diversion before school.

After School

School ends between three and four in the afternoon, and for the first term or so many schools send the new children home at lunchtime. Clearly this gives the working mother a new problem: how to bridge the gap between your child finishing school and you returning home. Some of you may work shifts that allow you to arrive in time for the end of school. Others may have an obliging relative who is prepared to pick up your child. Otherwise you may want to explore some of the other options.

Childminders and nannies

If a childminder or nanny has been looking after your child up to now then you have probably already considered continuing the arrangement. Nannies often like the extra free time that they gain, and if you have another baby or plan to have one soon, keeping on your nanny or finding another one is even more essential.

Most childminders are happy to continue looking after your child once school starts, especially if they have become fond of each other. One of the plusses of using a childminder is the continuity of care that many of them offer – from babyhood to well into schooldays. If your child has been at a nursery or similar until now, or you have only just gone back to work you may also want to consider finding a childminder to pick up and look after your child.

A childminder is still limited in the number of over-fives she can look after. She can take on up to an extra three who are under eight. It is quite common for a childminder to look after three under-fives for most of the day, and then to pick up a few schoolchildren when school ends.

Of course, you will want to choose your childminder carefully. School can be quite a strain for a young child, particularly to begin with, and when your child is just starting he or she may be very short on stamina and need a quiet time at the end of the day; later on there may be homework to do. If a childminder has too many children to look after at this time your child may become over-tired and irritable by the time you arrive.

These are the things you will probably want to look for when you are choosing a childminder to look after your school-age child:

Someone who likes older children

Some childminders adore the baby stage and are not so good at handling the bigger ones; they find the more independent-minded school-age child an irritant.

Someone who sympathises with school problems

This usually goes with the above. Ideally you want someone who will listen, reassure and be sensibly involved.

Someone who restricts the numbers

Too many other children around can be fatiguing after a full day at school, although in the holidays it might not matter so much. Your child alone would be ideal, although you may have to compromise with just one or two others.

A place to rest

Some children can recoup in front of children's television, others may actually need to lie down for a short while after tea.

A quiet place to do homework

An older child who has homework to do needs to be in a separate room if there are other children around playing together or watching television.

Finding a minder

For more information see the chapter on *Childminders*.

* Ask the social services department, or local childminding group, whether there are any minders near you who take older children. Interview her carefully, just

as you would for a younger child. Check how many children she takes and ask what she proposes to do with them until you arrive to pick up your child.

* You can 'create your own' childminder. This is easier for children over eight as the minder doesn't have to register. You may find a 'granny' who would like to pick up your child and go back to your own house. This is what Jane Parkin did:

> When Sally started school I found a minder who could fetch her from school. This worked well, although she wasn't registered. Most people thought she was Heather's grandmother.

Similarly you could pay the mother of a schoolfriend to act as childminder and take your child back to her house until you are ready to collect. That is what this mother did:

> I asked around at school and was told that a woman with an older child than mine would sometimes mind a child until the mother was ready to collect, for a few pounds a week. At that time she wasn't picking up any other children and agreed to look after mine, along with her daughter and baby boy. She took my daughter home with them and gave her tea, and then she would let them play or watch television until I came to pick my daughter up. She never minded if I was a bit late. She just let them amuse themselves while she got on with what she had to do. I kept up this arrangement for a year and it worked perfectly well. My daughter wasn't *particularly* friendly with the minder's children, but they got on okay. I think it was better than if she had gone home with a friend. At that age they are always rowing and breaking up friendships and going off with someone else. Being with children who were of a different age and not special friends was less emotionally fraught.

If you do ask a mother of a schoolfriend to take your child home on a regular basis it is usually better all round to insist on paying, even if she is reluctant to take money. Working mothers, who can rarely repay in kind, feel better when the arrangement is on a financial footing. It is very difficult to feel continually under the obligation of a favour.

* You could put up a notice on the school notice board saying that you are looking for a minder.

* Ask the headteacher to include the fact that you are looking for a minder in bulletins sent out to parents.

* Ask mothers of other pupils at the school whether they know anyone who wants to mind your child for some extra money.

Au pairs

Once all your children are at school an au pair becomes a real care option if you have a spare room. She can also take your children to school and be around much of the time during half-terms and holidays. Continuity is less important when your children are school age (although you will prefer not to have too rapid a succession of girls), as is the fact that the girl won't be able to speak much English. After all, what you mainly want is someone responsible around to give your children tea at the end of the school day and oversee them until you return home. It certainly takes the anxiety out of rushing at the end of the day if your children are being looked after at home and you don't have a deadline to pick them up from somewhere else.

During term time the au pair will have the whole school day to herself to pursue her English lessons and anything else she wants to do. You should not expect her to take over the entire care of your children during half-terms and holidays: you will almost certainly have to combine her presence with one or more of the other options suggested. See the chapter on *Nannies, Mother's Helps and Other Help in Your Home* for details on finding and giving a home to an au pair.

Neighbour

A close neighbour may be prepared to pick up your child from school, or be at home to let your child in at the end of a school day.

Older school children

A responsible teenager may be happy to pick up your child and go back to your house afterwards for the equivalent of a babysitting fee. The teenager can prepare tea and then get on with homework while keeping an eye on your child until you arrive home. You will want to choose a teenager you know well and trust, or who comes highly recommended by other parents or teachers.

Other arrangements

Look at *Half-terms and Holidays* for other ideas.

As your child begins to make good friends at school, other mothers may begin to issue after-school invitations. Obviously you can't rely on them for all after-school care, but if you, your partner or a relative is able to reciprocate from time to time you may feel quite happy about asking another mother to help out occasionally.

Out-of-school schemes

More and more of these are being set up all over the country. Many of them collect children from school and take them to a play-centre or community centre where they are fed and looked after until around six o'clock. Your school ought to know if there is a scheme nearby, or you may be able to find out from the local education department or your local recreation/leisure/youth and community department. The Kids Club Network (see *Further Help*) may also be able to tell you about facilities in your area.

These can be marvellous if your hours mean that you are able to pick up your child by six o'clock.

Starting an out-of-school scheme

The Kids Club Network will give help to any group which is considering starting a scheme. The majority of working mothers would almost certainly find the prospect of setting up something like this far too daunting or exhausting, as you have to find premises, staff, and arrange the financial and legal side; but it is worth trying to gather support for the idea. Taking charge of one aspect – sorting out the insurance, say, may be possible when you know that other women are taking care of the rest of it. Among the parents of children at your child's school there is very likely to be someone who likes a cause and has more energy, push, commitment and time than perhaps you do.

Before you become too deeply involved in the practical side of setting up a scheme you will want to know what the demand is. Again, the headteacher is likely to have a good idea which children have mothers who work and have problems with after-school care. You could put a notice on the school notice board, in the school magazine or ask the head to circulate a note with the other regular school bulletins. Ask the other mothers to contact you and perhaps arrange one meeting for interested parties. You'll soon know if the interest is great enough, and how many other working mothers will be prepared to help.

School provision

Some schools have clubs or schemes for looking after their children after school: supervised playgrounds, evening youth clubs, play-centres within the classroom itself. You'll know by now whether your child's school does this. If not, and the local education authority tells you that another school nearby has similar schemes, you could ask whether they will take children from other schools.

Coming home alone

If school is in easy walking distance, and you are going to be at home yourself or arriving soon after, or you consider your child old enough to cope, you might decide to let him or her come home alone. An older child may be able to manage public transport alone.

You will know when your child is ready for this, but you must take certain precautions:

* Go over the route thoroughly with your child, making sure that you explain how and when to cross roads. Do this a number of times before you allow your child to try it alone.

* On at least one of these occasions walk a good way behind your child so that you are too far off to give reminders, and see how well he or she manages to remember the rules.

* Impress on your child about not talking to strangers, or going home with *anyone* unless you have arranged it first.

One woman writes,

> I remember the first time they walked home from school. I had to stop myself picking them up. It was *their* request so to do. I was a cat on hot bricks all afternoon and zoomed home to find them quite unimpressed by my arrival – too engrossed in TV and drinks.

If your child regularly has to spend any time alone at home, see also *Fostering Independence* and *Alone in the House*, later in this chapter.

Child coming to your place of work

If you work near school and it is permissible, your child could come to your place of work and sit quietly (!) until you finish. This obviously works better with older children who may be able to spend fairly long stretches in quiet play – reading or drawing or doing a puzzle, or even homework when the school starts to set it. However, most employers would not like this at all; you can only consider it if you work for yourself or in the kind of set-up where this would be tolerated or welcomed.

Changing your hours

If you work shifts or part-time, or are able to take work home, you may be able to alter your hours so that you can pick your child up. One full-time lecturer writes, 'I bribe the timetabler to leave me free at four onwards. My job is flexible, and I can and do bring work home.'

Half-terms and Holidays

These are perhaps the biggest problem for a working mother, apart from the lucky ones who are teachers or married to teachers. Children have about four months' holiday per year, so even if you have as much as a month's holiday yourself, that still leaves roughly a quarter of the year when you have to make alternative plans. Many mothers muddle through making a number of different arrangements.

Most of the women who wrote to us had untypical arrangements. Almost all the mothers took their main holidays during the long summer recess and then cast around for other help. Some had a member of the family nearby who did not work and could help out some of the time. Some had husbands who worked shifts and shared care with grandmothers. Some mothers invited their own parents or in-laws to stay during the long summer holiday, giving them a break, and also providing free childcare. Mothers who could arrange it worked at home for part of the time. One mother who worked as a sales rep would take her children with her when they were younger. Others sent the children round to various members of the family – two or three days here and there.

One woman, with the advantage of being the vicar's wife and therefore knowing the local community well, sometimes employed responsible teenage girls to look after her children. A few women called on friends to help out, and older children were sometimes left alone or went to stay with friends.

These are the more conventional ways of coping with the holidays:

Childminders

If you have a childminder who picks up or takes your child to and from school, you may want to make an arrangement for the holidays too. Even if you make other after-school arrangements you may well decide that a childminder is the best bet for holidays. Childminders do not have to be registered to look after over-eights, and they can take on as many children as they want. You will want to choose a childminder for the holidays as carefully as you would a minder for a younger child. If your children are quite young, you would probably be wise to avoid someone who takes in too many children and has little time for them individually.

Employing a student

Jane Parkin, who works part time in York, employs a student to look after her two daughters aged seven and five during the holidays. 'I've found the nursery nurse girls

295

from the local tech to be reliable and keen to get the experience – and cheap.'

A student teacher from a local college may also be interested in looking after your children.

Nanny

If you have used a nanny until this age you may wish to keep her on, at least for a while until you have made other satisfactory arrangements.

Even if you have not had a nanny up to now, you may want to consider sharing with a schoolteacher. This has worked successfully for at least two women.

The teacher has the nanny during term time, and during school holidays, when the teacher is off work, the nanny comes to you. If this appeals, it is obviously worth asking at your child's school if there is a teacher who would consider doing this. Otherwise you could write a letter to the local paper.

Holiday play schemes

If there is an after-school care scheme in your neighbourhood, the chances are that it includes holiday schemes. These schemes suit the slightly older child best, as younger children might find the relentless all-day fun rather tiring!

Barbara Herbert, a part-time market researcher in Paisley, wrote about her local scheme:

> Last summer holiday our Community Education service ran a summer play scheme between nine and four in the local high school during the school holidays, which was a great success. The scheme organised games and a room or two was set aside for painting and making models, keep-fit and outings were also arranged. It cost very little per child, with outings extra. I found it invaluable as did many other working mothers around here. It is

hoped to do the same this year. It was run by one or two paid leaders and the rest were volunteers. Obviously a scheme like this is given a grant from the local authority so it depends if the cash is available or not.

For some mothers the fact that Barbara's scheme ended at four would rule it out if they could not find someone to pick up their child until they came home. Another mother who lives in London sent her child to a holiday play scheme:

It was open every day of the holidays, 8.00a.m. till 6.00p.m. There were indoor and outdoor activities and special outings. All you had to pay was the normal school-dinner fee, after that only special outings were extra. All the kids loved it.

Your local department called Recreation, or possibly Leisure or Youth and Community, or a division of the education authority, should be able to tell you about schemes in your area.

Sending your child away

Another alternative is to arrange for your child to go away, at least for some of the holiday. You may have relatives in another part of the country who would be pleased to have your child for a while. For older children there are supervised activity holidays. Travel agents and tourist information centres will be able to give you the details of the holidays currently on offer.

Playbuses

These are organised by groups affiliated to the National Playbus Association (see *Further Help*). They are usually run by voluntary groups, and will visit specific areas such as housing estates on a regular basis. The buses are converted inside, and sometimes have a mobile library. Obviously they don't offer continuous care, but if one comes to your area it offers an occasional alternative to your usual plans.

Play parks/adventure playgrounds

If you have one of these in your area it may be supervised at holiday times. However the supervision mainly takes the form of seeing that the children come to no harm while they are there – the supervisers won't take responsibility for stopping your child from leaving at any time. The local parks department will be able to tell you what kind of care is on offer.

Letting your child stay at home alone

Clearly this is a desperate measure, and few mothers have to resort to this when their children are young. Even mothers of teenagers are usually reluctant to leave their child completely unsupervised for days at a time. (But read *Alone in the House* to see how other mothers have coped with this, and recommended safety precautions.)

Participating as a Parent in School Activities

Parents' meetings

Parents' meetings keep you in touch with how your child is doing and give you a chance to get to know the teachers. They also allow you to impress yourself on the teachers and correct any misconceptions. As one woman wrote to us:

My son, in his mandatory essay on family life, wrote

298

that I worked in Manchester and earned a lot of money doing the sex act. I actually worked for the Equal Opportunities Commission and he couldn't spell discrimination! I did have to explain my job to the teacher.

Unfortunately in some schools few of these meetings are arranged for evenings. If your school schedules the meetings for afternoons, it is worth trying to make them reschedule them for the evening. If a number of other parents work too you may be able to drum up quite a lot of support. Perhaps the headteacher would consider holding some evening meetings specifically for working parents. If there are not too many of you these meetings would not take too long. And if there are a lot of you then they should see that there is a real case for holding all meetings in the evenings.

Otherwise your options are limited, unless you work part time, are able to arrange your time around the meeting, or if you are freelance or have control of your own hours, or can take work home. If your hours are strict, you may have to take a day from your holiday, or arrange for time off in lieu. Sadly, some women feel their only option is to call in sick.

A few women who wrote to us had to give meetings a miss. Others had partners who were able to attend, or took it in turns with their partners to take a day off.

Some schools are very bad about giving notice of meetings or other school events. If you only know the week or day before it can be harder to make whatever arrangements are necessary. If this is the case with your school explain the problem to the headteacher, and see if there is any way that these meetings can be timetabled a term in advance so that you know your commitments right at the beginning of term.

Open days and fêtes

These pose similar problems to parents' meetings. Even if your school holds its parents' meetings in the evenings it is unlikely to do so for these special school occasions. Similarly concerts, plays and sports days are rarely held in the evening. A teacher (whose name we'd better not mention in this context) wrote to us angrily about her experience:

> Just before Christmas I wanted half an hour off so that I could go and watch my little girl's nativity play. She was an angel. The only member of staff available to help me out refused point blank which really upset me. Needless to say, she has no children of her own. I was doubly angry as my attendance is very good, and the four days I have been sick this year is the most time I have ever had off. Because of this lack of co-operation I went sick for a day when the nativity play was repeated, which meant that the school lost a member of staff for a day instead of half an hour. I had to put my child's happiness first. In fairness, she is the only colleague in eleven years who has been anything but kind and helpful.

Another woman wrote:

> I often feel as if I'm a bad mother because I have missed church services, sports, etc. I've also not had time to get involved in things like fund-raising activities for nursery schools, primary schools, etc.

You have to make the decision whether you can take a whole or half-day off to attend one of these functions. Another alternative is to ask a relative to go, or the childminder, or a friend that your children know. From the children's point of view it is often enough to have someone there specially for them, even if it can't be mum or dad.

Helping at functions

Non-working mothers get brownie points for being able to help out with the jumble sale, manning a stall or organising the fête and other activities. This kind of participation is usually beyond working mothers, but if you feel your child or the teachers will mind if you don't participate, there are other things you can do:

* Donate jumble.

* If you are a baker, make a cake or a batch of biscuits for the function.

* If you are very pushed for time, give a bottle for the raffle or a bought cake or biscuits.

* Offer to sell raffle tickets at your place of work.

If you *are* taking the day off anyway, it is worthwhile offering to help behind scenes if only for a while. It is the best way to get to know the staff – and hear things about the school that you might otherwise miss.

Joining the PTA

Not all schools have a Parent and Teacher Association (PTA), but if your child's school does you will be considering whether to join it. For some mothers (and fathers) this could be the last straw – having yet another thing to do in the middle of a tiring week; possibly having to arrange and pay for a babysitter to free you for an evening that could be deadly dull.

As one mother said:

> I just couldn't face joining the PTA. I don't think it would have made a lot of difference if I had, but occasionally when I found myself grumbling about something or other to do with the school it crossed my

mind that if I had belonged I might have been able to do something about it.

The PTA will mainly concern itself with fund-raising and school events – another thing that could deter the working mother whose free time is desperately limited. But other business does come up too, and it is an excellent time to learn about school policy and to make your feelings known.

A number of the women who wrote to us belonged to the PTA. One, who must have boundless energy, is a full-time lecturer with two children of eight and ten. Her husband works away from home, and she regularly brings work home to do in the evenings and weekends but still manages to be chairman of the PTA and a school governor! Sandra McDonald, who works full time as a tele sales and sales admin clerk says, 'Being secretary of the PTA has enabled me to get to know the staff very well indeed and I have an excellent relationship with them all.'

Another woman, a local government officer who also works full time, believes it is very important to belong: 'I have always been a member of the PTA at primary and secondary schools. I feel it is a way of sharing their school-life if you know the teachers and the building and are involved in fund-raising etc.'

What may help tip the balance in favour of you joining the PTA is if there are things you very much want to change about the school. If you are hoping to provoke interest in an out-of-school scheme, or you want the school to open earlier in the mornings, or to reschedule meetings for the evenings so that working mothers can attend, you can be assured of a more powerful audience at the PTA. Building up goodwill by participating, even to a limited extent, in school events will mean that your views are respected and you are not simply looked upon as a troublemaker. Now that more and more schools are self-governing and have control of their own budgets, parent-members are more powerful than ever before.

If you don't want to join, it is worth cultivating someone who is a member. That way you will at least get to know what is happening, and perhaps channel your views through that person.

You and Your School-age Child

Helping with homework

> We cannot help with homework now as it is too difficult, but we do take an interest and praise high marks and nag if they could be better!
>
> **Mother of two teenage children**

Few schools give homework before the children are seven, and many wait until the last year when they are ten. The exception is reading, which many schools like the child to practise at home, and hearing your child read is a pleasurable chore.

Our reason for including this section on homework is that many mothers feel guilty when they haven't the time (or energy or desire!) to help with homework, particularly if they are told that other children get a lot of help, or have it done for them. Some schools expect you to oversee it and check that it gets done (possibly signing it afterwards), but few expect more than that. One mother ruefully wrote that she was far more involved than she wanted to be, admitting that she sometimes did some of the work, 'and I hate the Latin!'

Many mothers lose sight of the fact that the point of homework is to teach the children to find out how to do the work unaided and to practise. You can help them by pointing them in the right direction and encouraging them, but if you actually do it for them you are not helping them at all – even if they think so. The emphasis should be on the children doing it unaided – not on getting it right, or getting high marks. Too much helping can ultimately rebound on your children at exam time.

On the whole it makes sense if, from the beginning, what you do is help your child develop a routine in which homework has its place, and show him or her how to organise well and work systematically. You should be aiming for a time when your child does whatever homework is required as a matter of course without your help and preferably without you nagging. Long-term this will be much more useful than giving your child the answers or becoming emotional about handwriting or marks. This may not be possible, but certain things you do will make it more likely.

Helpful attitude to homework

* From the time your child first has homework to do – however short or pointless it may seem – take it seriously.

* Discuss together the time it should be done: on arriving home, or after children's television, or after supper; take your child's views into account. Until your child has developed a routine you will have to remind him or her every day that the time has come to start the work, switch off the television, and so on. If your child is reluctant to do it at the time agreed you can insist it is done *today* at that time, but that you will agree a new time for tomorrow and the rest of the week.

* Encourage your child to sit at a table or desk, rather than sprawl on the floor or on the sofa.

* Try suggesting that your child does homework in a quiet, separate room. If he or she really loathes it and feels banished, don't insist – or you'll find the work is

304

more likely to be rushed. But don't let the television remain on while work is being done.

* If your help is asked for, don't just provide the answer. Look for the answer together in a book or (if it is something like maths) ask your child to try to remember the teacher's explanation and tell it to you. That way your child may either come up with the answer alone, or you can clear up any misunderstanding. In any case, as the work becomes more complicated the answer is likely to be beyond you, so helping your child to find out in other ways is by far the most useful thing you can do.

* If handwriting is dreadful, or your child is setting about something in the wrong way, try not to criticise, but offer tips and suggestions. If you are too involved, or take over, your child is likely to abdicate responsibility for homework, which is the last thing you want.

* Strike up general conversations about the day and what your child has learnt. Don't home in on marks or achievements, but show interest in the content of the lessons.

* Praise the fact that homework has been done at the right time and with care. Resist the temptation to look through it unless your child asks. If you *are* asked, don't be too impatient or critical if you don't think it has been done well; constructive suggestions before homework is started another time will do more good. Don't withhold praise if the mark is low: you don't want your child to feel that it wasn't worth the bother.

Once your child has come to see homework as something that must be done, and is his or her responsibility rather than yours, then you should not have to give it much thought or time. Certainly, you should not feel bad if you do not involve yourself. As one single mother wrote, 'I try to be involved in homework as necessary but because I'm busy I often can't create enough time, and then I feel guilty.' Another mother's attitude is perhaps more useful, 'Beyond showing an *interest* in homework, school activities etc, I do not become involved.'

If your child is underachieving, terminally lazy or aggressively anti-homework, and the school is worried too, then you will probably have to become more involved. But this is not primarily a homework problem. Nagging, punishment and force may work to a certain extent but unless the underlying cause is sorted out it may become an increasingly frustrating area of conflict.

After-school hobbies

As your children become more independent-minded and start to develop talents and interests, you'll find that they may want to join out-of-school clubs or similar. This takes some getting used to, as with younger children you have taken it for granted that most of the evening is yours to spend as you wish. It can also make life very complicated. As one woman – a full-time educational psychologist with four children under eight – wrote to us:

> Both my husband and myself involve ourselves fully with homework and extra-curricular activities. For example, both boys attend swimming classes, one boy goes to cubs, one boy goes to boys' brigade, one girl goes to girls' brigade, one boy goes to piano lessons, one girl goes to gymnastics, one boy goes to hockey coaching. I have a timetable on the kitchen wall to remember all their activities. My husband collects and delivers them mostly. Also neighbours and relatives help in turn.

Luckily, most parents won't have quite this much to

contend with, although even one child with one strong interest can seem too much at times, as this single parent wrote:

> At eight my daughter suddenly showed an exceptional talent for gymnastics. The club she belonged to 'promoted' her to the advanced group, which meant going three evenings a week for four hours, and Saturday afternoons. I was rather unhappy about the whole business as the hours seemed excessive and they were training them seriously – gymnastics is a young sport and the children are treated much as adult athletes are. I had misgivings about what it could eventually do to her body. But she was terribly keen and committed and she wasn't tired by the training. I felt that stopping her doing something that she loved and was very good at might be damaging to our relationship so I put up with it. Then the club moved and soon after that *we* moved. Getting there was a one-hour journey on public transport (I don't have a car), so I had no alternative but to sit and watch the lesson. Not only that, it was a real hole in my pocket – fares and class fees. But when she went to secondary school she started to find the training irksome and began to question her ambitions. Soon after she gave up of her own accord, which thrilled me. I know that if I had insisted while she was still keen she may have always felt thwarted.

Most parents feel that the extra cost and the time spent is worthwhile. A child with a strong interest outside school is often able to cope well with the ups and downs of school life. It also helps increase feelings of independence and makes your child more self-reliant. Many parents find it can enhance their relationship with their children, particularly if they are involved themselves in the activities. Barbara Herbert, who works part time, and has two boys of seven and ten, says:

> On Thursday evenings we go to the cubs together. Both boys are cubs and I'm a cub leader of the same pack. We all thoroughly enjoy this and the various activities that

emanate from this. We also go to our local sports centre, which is five minutes from our home – and in particular during the school holidays when the centre organises special programmes called family recreation – where you can spend a whole morning using all the facilities, such as badminton, squash, trampoline and team games.

The evidence is that working mothers spend at least as much time as at-home mothers participating in their children's extra-curricular activities. Perhaps because we all continue to feel a little guilty about what we *can't* do, we make that much more effort.

> The boys play rugby, so they train during the week. My husband is one of their coaches so plenty of advice and encouragement is forthcoming. I try to watch them play in matches. I take them to galas for swimming, to cubs etc.

It can make things easier if you become friends with other parents whose children also take part in the same activities. Then you can take it in turn to pick up each other's children and deliver them home.

Sometimes you will have to resign yourself to spending more time than you would like at the place where your child pursues the interest. One divorced mother, a full-time physiotherapist, wrote:

> I try to encourage sport and have spent a lot of time and money (which I don't feel is wasted) taking my three children to various activities and waiting around for them. (I would take a letter to write or mending to do, or even read the paper.) It's difficult when there is no one to share the job at times. Fortunately they see their father on alternate weekends and he also does activities with them.

As your child becomes older your involvement may simply be confined to picking up at the end of an evening session.

Time with your school-age children

> We enjoy our garden. The children help us with that.
> We do all the usual things outdoors: garden games, golf,
> tennis over the washing line, barbecues, picnics. In
> winter: TV, jigsaws, games, cards, dominoes, darts. We
> have just got a snooker table. In the days when we had
> no car we got the children ready for church every
> Sunday morning for the 9.10 bus. We never missed,
> winter as well. We had three toddlers and me pregnant,
> but we did it and thought nothing about doing it. We
> still go to church as a family every Sunday but we have a
> car now.
>
> > Mother of three children still at home,
> > the youngest eleven

All mothers, working or stay-at-home, find that as their
children grow older the time they spend talking and doing
things together gets less and less. Certainly, with more
than one child, individual time can dwindle to almost
nothing during the week. As one operating theatre
technician says about her two sons, 'We spend less and less
time with the children these days as they both have their
own interests and tend to be out most of the time in the
evenings.'

Traditionally, mothers give their main attention to their
children when they come home from school full of the
day's events, triumphs or traumas. For the working
mother, this usually happens when *she* arrives home –
often before she has even taken her coat off. Julie Howell,
a full-time bank cashier with two boys of ten and seven, is
typical:

> I do find it difficult to give everyone some attention as
> soon as I return from work. I always sit down with a cup
> of tea before I do the dinner in order to try and listen to
> everyone at least for five minutes each. I still find that
> everyone wants to talk first though so there are

difficulties. It is also the time when I find the children want a cuddle. On these occasions I sometimes find dinner is later than it should be. Cuddle time is sometimes immediately after dinner, so causes friction due to lateness of bedtimes. If you don't take time for everyone you feel guilty or selfish. If you do take time you also feel guilty as jobs don't get done, or times for certain things become unreasonable. Whatever you do, you do wrong!

As they grow older, most happy and occupied children don't seem to mind having less time individually with their parents; there are too many other things they want to do – sometimes we mind much more. But even though making yourself available for 'quality time' and playful interaction becomes less relevant, the older your children grow the more they call on your emotional support. The younger school-age child, and any child going through a difficult patch, does want and need time and attention, and problems become more complex and less easily resolved with a cuddle and sympathy; they may need talking through, sometimes over a period of days or weeks, as in the case of school problems such as bullying. Sometimes, inevitably, teenage children cause the most problems of all:

> My sixteen-year-old daughter had a difficult couple of years at school. I would get very distressed phonecalls at work: she truanted a lot and was bullied. She'd wake up in the morning feeling unhappy and depressed, not wanting to go to school. It was emotionally draining and I had to take time off work to sort it out. I went through a bad patch myself worrying about her, and I felt it affected my work. I suppose I blamed myself. At least we get on very well together, and had long, complex conversations about it all. This is the difference between having little children and having teenagers: one is dealing with adult problems.

Working mothers perhaps have to be particularly alert to the child whose reaction to stress is to withdraw. One who gets into a bad mood or ostentatiously sulks is easy to spot, but the one who causes no trouble and just becomes extra-quiet needs watching.

There isn't the space to go into this in detail, but here are a few ways that you can keep tabs on increasingly busy children and have time to sort out problems together.

Bedtimes

> Since the girls have grown up they stay up later and I'm often asleep before them. I find I've no time on my own in the house. Because I'm teaching, the girls are home when I am.
> **Mother of two children aged fifteen and thirteen**

Spending time with each child at bedtime is probably the best and most popular opportunity for talking. Children of different ages can have their bedtimes staggered so that you have time alone with each, and if you have a partner you can take it in turns with different children. Many children welcome this long after the age of needing practical assistance or stories and songs, sometimes until they are quite grown up. It's a chance to hear about good things as well as worries, or clear up disagreements.

Chores

Asking one child at a time to help you with different chores, such as cooking, washing-up, gardening, or tidying their rooms is another opportunity to give a child time alone with you. This is particularly worth pursuing with the older child who may prefer not to have a bedtime chat, or who goes to bed around the same time as you do. Other children are less likely to want to join in, as work is involved. Sometimes you may find 'difficult' conversations easier carried on like this. Talk of sex, periods, molesting strangers, violence, or drugs carry less of the air of a lecture if you are both clattering saucepans or sorting out clothes that have got too small. If your child has something awkward to say it can also seem easier when you are not having a face-to-face confrontation. Even if it is just chit-chat and jokes it makes for an easy atmosphere and opens the lines of communication.

Family time

If possible make a regular time when you are all together – one or two evening meals a week, for instance. Suggesting that these are the occasions for raising grievances or problems after the meal is over is a useful idea. Allowing group decisions – within reason – makes your children feel respected and listened to, which also helps when one of them is having a bad time. It can be very informal: in the cosy-sounding home of Wendy Wass, who has three teenage children still at home, she says, 'We all talk together non-stop whenever we're all in together; they follow me around talking.'

Weekends are obviously the best time of all for the family to spend time together – on outings, as well as at home at mealtimes.

Time out together

Finding ways of being out of the house with one child at a time is also a help. Intermittent treats are a good idea, as Rosemary Kirk with four children under twelve discovered:

> When our last baby was born he was (and still is) a rotten sleeper. He was taking a lot of our attention, especially when he was very young. We realised that our other children were losing out and we hadn't even the time to talk to them individually. So for a year my husband John and I took one child in turn out on a Friday night for tea to a shopping centre nearby. This cost a few extra pounds every week and it was only for two hours but this way the children got one-to-one

attention – and also the shopping was done for the weekend. The children loved it and it became known as 'my treat'.

Wendy Wass has a similar solution:

When the children need clothes, shoes, etc., I've always made a point of taking them to town on their own when possible so that I can give them all my attention. I have four and they all would get their turn individually. We go and buy whatever they need, and go to a cafe for a snack. The kids love it as we are away from the hassle of home where everyone is trying to talk at once.

Helping round the house

In an ideal world all members of the household would pull their weight. But the majority of working women find that even their partners are reluctant to do more than the minimum, and good intentions to train the children to help often go by the board. The problem is that we get so used to doing everything for them while they are young and helpless that it requires far more effort to train them to help than to carry on as we have been doing.

The value of them having their own jobs, helping with housework and maintaining their own clothes and rooms hardly needs to be stated. But the breakages, slap-dash work, surly attitudes and other irritants more often than not lead the harassed mother to give up trying to get the help that should be hers by right. The senior educational psychologist with four children under eight has an admirably tough attitude:

My motto as a working mother is NEVER DO ANYTHING ANYBODY ELSE CAN DO. For example, I don't waste time doing menial tasks like peeling vegetables, washing or drying dishes, ironing clothes – because these are jobs anybody else can do. As time is so valuable to me I only spend time doing those jobs that only I can do. For example: preparing a more elaborate meal or baking something; sorting out clothes which fit the children (those which are too big, too small, need transferring from one child to the next); clearing out drawers and cupboards, etc; generally organising the smooth running of the household – that is, delegating as much as possible. All this allows me that most important time – the time to spend with and talk to the children.

But whether any of these chores are taken over by the children, she doesn't say.

Susan Lumb, who works part time and has three boys aged fourteen, eleven and nine has a similar attitude:

I only do work which is necessary in the home when I have worked all day. I delegate jobs to the boys, getting the meal started, emptying waste bins, making their own beds and being responsible for keeping their bedrooms straight. I feel that if I am prepared to work for things for them, they should be willing to contribute also. I feel it gives them a sense of responsibility, and in some ways they appreciate what we are trying to achieve for them. It is cheering when I come home to find the boys have done all I have asked of them. They notice I am tired and they tell me to sit down and make me a drink of tea. The funny thing is, they never say the same to their dad, who has a very physical manual job. He is usually greeted with, 'Will you mend my bike? Are you ready to take us to rugby training?' I think they have discovered my weak spot. They can usually worm anything out of me after a good cup of tea.

If you do plan to succeed whether others have failed or have been only partially successful, here are some tips:

Start early

It's maddening, but up to the age when they begin to be able to be really helpful, children love to help. Once they are reasonably competent they don't want to know. To produce children who help as a matter of course you have to let them do things when they are only a hindrance, causing mess and chaos and extra work for you.

Give a regular job

Give each child a regular job within his or her capabilities: setting the table, putting out the rubbish, vacuuming. These jobs should always be done, barring illness. Young children will be pleased and proud to be given the responsibility, but the novelty soons wears off. If you are to succeed later, don't let your child give up a job just because it becomes routine.

Be consistent

You may decide that it is time your deft nine-year-old son ironed his own shirts because he can do it as well as you. But if, when he does it badly, or doesn't do it for a while and goes out with a crumpled shirt, you mind enough to do it 'just this once', you can be quite sure that the job will end up yours again. A similar thing will happen with any chore, such as cleaning the bathroom or tidying their rooms. If you are going to care when your standards are not met and then do it yourself, your children will spot the easy way out. In the same way, avoid threats you can't keep. One mother said that her son wouldn't be allowed to bath unless he cleaned it afterwards. He thought this was a wonderful way to avoid the bath, and she had to give in.

Make a rota

With a larger family a rota of jobs is useful. Include yourself and your partner. If everybody gets a share of the nasty and the easy jobs it will at least be seen to be fair. Try to discourage too much swapping and bargaining with jobs. A clever older child may find lots of ways of off-loading the worst jobs on younger children, and bad feeling can build up. Or, like Rosemary Kirk, you can find that good intentions fizzle out:

> At one stage I had organised a work rota for the children to 'do' two rooms each every Saturday morning. This lasted about six months but died a death when they began rushing out on a Saturday or getting the easy rooms like the hall and rows started over this. So now I just do the house when I can and try to accept lower standards.

Know yourself

Your success in getting your family to share the chores depends a lot on your attitude. It's a question of whether you see all housework as 'yours', so that you are asking (or nagging) them to 'help' you. If you genuinely and guiltlessly consider the work to be 'ours', then you can more forcefully get across the idea that it is everyone's problem to see that it is done. Children sense the difference in attitude and may come to use 'helping' as a weapon or bribe.

To pay or not to pay

You may decide that having the chores done is worth paying your child for, or you may think this is a bad idea. Paying can either be an incentive or a bribe. If you have children who really like earning money it may be a good idea – but it can rebound if it establishes a situation where the housework is seen to be *your* responsibility and they can opt in or out depending on whether they want or need the money. Barbara Herbert makes pocket money conditional on chores being done by her two boys aged seven and ten, 'The kids help by setting the table and drying the dishes. This gives an incentive to work for pocket money at the end of the week.'

Controlling the mess

Even if getting them to help with chores is difficult, you can compromise with certain rules that make things easier for you. A full-time maths teacher with a nine-year-old girl and a seven-year-old boy suggests, 'Don't let the children untidy more than one room at a time, and as soon as they are old enough make them put toys away.'

Fostering Independence

Working mothers may be no better than other mothers at getting the children to help, but force of circumstance often means that we produce children with a good sense of independence. Our children learn to be more independent because we are not always there to pick up after them and sort out their scrapes. This may cause us agonies of guilt earlier on, but it soon becomes a source of pleasure. As one woman wrote, with understandable pride:

> Working gave me independence and confidence in myself, and also for my children as they grew up. They are friendly and outgoing and quite capable and willing to look after themselves. Should I drop dead tomorrow, although they would miss me as a friend and confidant, I know they would cope. That means a lot to me. I wish I could say the same for the 'old man'. I have failed miserably with him. He would be in a right tizzy wondering what to do with the dirty socks. The chippy and take-away would do a good trade from him.

Children whose mothers have been working are usually the ones who go to school already knowing how to do up their shoes and go to the loo by themselves. Being used to a variety of people they can usually understand different

317

accents and the strange, non-family words and phrases used by teachers and other children. Often we are fostering their independence quite unconsciously, because there isn't enough time to do anything else, but there are a number of ways we can promote it.

Let them try

From a young age let your children do things for themselves when they show interest – even if it means mess or lost time: such as feeding themselves when little, or putting on difficult clothes; selecting and paying for things in shops when they are older and start to count. When they are older still, encourage them to try further, as Susan Lumb and her husband do: 'If a bike is broken for example we get them to think what is wrong, how it can be repaired, and to at least try to repair it, to be independent rather than relying on someone else.' There are many little ways each day that you can do this.

Make them think

Help your children to learn to make decisions for themselves and develop independent judgement. A classic way to start with younger children is to give them a choice when privately you know you would say yes. Alternative phrases when permission is asked could be, 'You decide about that', 'It's up to you', 'Whatever you think best'. Feeling trusted and respected makes your child want to be responsible. Give praise when your children use their initiative – perhaps making a decision when you are not there to help. Stop yourself from putting them down when the decision is wrong: point out why, say what you would have done, or what you recommend next time, but acknowledge the courage shown – many children simply dither when there is no one around to ask.

Teach safety

As your child becomes older it helps to teach how to use the dangerous items in the home rather than banning them entirely. If, under your supervision, your child regularly lights the gas, handles the electric kettle and so on, these things will seem less glamorously adult, and there shouldn't be the same temptation to do them surreptitiously. Also, when the time comes you can feel more confident that your child is able and competent to do these things if you are not around.

Keep them involved

Let your children participate to a degree in family decisions: allow them to express opinions and disagree. Don't just overrule them, but explain why things can't be done their way: not enough money or not enough time. Be prepared to sympathise with grievances or strong desires, even if you can't do much about them. Let them know when there are problems such as lack of money, looming redundancies or discussions about divorce. They'll sense something is going on anyway and not telling them offers no protection from their own fears or feelings of guilt.

Handling money

All children spend money like millionaires when they have the chance. It helps if you give them some money of their own to handle – and let them make their own mistakes. To save your sanity, you should obviously not give too much until they have proved themselves able to cope with what they have. A weekly amount that has to cover all comics, sweets and crisps is good to start with. If it all goes on the first day, don't bail them out. Later this can be increased to cover fares. As your child slowly learns to budget and shows signs of being responsible you may want to include lunch money and clothes allowance. This is about the only way to learn what money really means and does, and your child will have more sympathy with your own attempts to make ends meet. Withdrawing the money for a misdemeanour is counter-productive, though obviously if you fear it is being used for alcohol or drugs that is something else – and not the province of this book.

Out and about

Sooner or later your child will be going out and travelling around alone. Since nearly every day there is a horror story in the newspapers about a child who has come to harm, our instinct is often to shield our own children totally and perhaps bar them from going out alone, particularly if we live in a city. Of course, this is impractical and wrong and our children will resent it. We can't, unfortunately, protect our children forever. What we have to do is make sure that they are fully prepared: alert and knowledgeable about possible dangers and well-versed in how to handle them. You can't start preparing your children too early, even if it is many years before you allow them a certain amount of freedom.

Talk about the dangers

There are so many different dangers that this is clearly not the subject of a one-off lecture. It should be one of the topics raised regularly in your household, and can continue right through childhood as your children become more sophisticated and can understand more. If you have a very happy, well-adjusted, trusting child you may feel distressed about having to introduce subjects that will disillusion and may disturb, but it has to be done. A little one needs to know that 'stranger means danger' but learning the slogan won't do much good unless it has been backed up by a few conversations that illustrate the truth of it. Similarly, road sense takes time to learn, knowing the rules is not enough.

Opportunities to raise the subject of dangers are numerous. Children from quite an early age pick up on news stories that relate to other children, and often ask questions. Your aim should be to alert your children, but not to frighten them. In fact, most children are rather ghoulish and not easily disturbed by horror stories. But if you sense your child is worrying too much you must be reassuring as well: put the dangers in proportion or your child will become over-fearful and paralysed by the thought of independence – which is also dangerous.

Teach road safety

Make sure that your child knows the rules well in advance of venturing out alone. Any journey together – on foot, in the car or on public transport – can further your child's knowledge. You can ask questions like, 'What should we do here?', 'Why was that man very silly?', 'How can I tell when it's safe to cross?'

Teach people safety

'Stranger means danger' is one slogan, but this must be backed up by your own observations, such as that bad people can look and sound nice. Teach your child to be on the alert for people who look at them too fixedly, or move oddly (such as drunks), so that they can skirt danger before they are approached. Delicate subjects like sexual abuse, particularly if the abuser is someone your child knows (or a relative) are especially hard to raise. One way to do this with a young child is to get hold of one of the excellent storybooks on the market dealing with the subject, such as *We Can Say No* by David Pithers and Sarah Greene (published by Hutchinson). Older children will begin to hear about such things from other kids and on the news –

it may be embarrassing for you to talk about the subject and answer their questions (particularly as most of us feel sure it could never happen to our kids) but it is irresponsible not to. Teach them that they can and must say no (and very loudly too) to any adult who wants them to do something they know or sense is wrong.

Teach money safety

Show your children how to carry money safely, how to handle it without dropping the lot or advertising how much they've got. It's as well to have an emergency supply for fares – down a sock, or in a hard-to-get-at pocket, in case the rest is lost or stolen. It also helps for emergency phonecalls – a phonecard is even better.

Know your own area

A child's first journeys out alone will be close to home – to the shops or to the local school, or round the corner to a friend. Make sure that you and your child know your area and its dangers well. This is important not just for road sense, but for other trouble spots: perhaps a particular pub, a shop with an odd owner, a bookie's, or a games arcade should be avoided. Maybe there is a certain person with a dodgy reputation of whom your child should be wary, or a short-cut you know to be dangerous.

Using public transport

Make sure that your children know how to use public transport sensibly and safely: not hopping on or off before the bus reaches a stop, for instance. Discuss the best places to sit: near the conductor or driver on a bus, or in the first carriage of a train or tube with access to the driver, or near the guard or ticket collector. Your child should choose a carriage with plenty of other people in it (particularly women!) in preference to an empty or near-empty one. Tell your child that the communication cord is there to be pulled in the case of harassment, but in a tube he or she should wait until the train reaches the next station. Your children should also be encouraged to change carriages if there is anyone who disturbs them, or to alight at the next station and find a member of staff.

Asking for help

Make sure that your children know who and when to ask for help. A policeman is the obvious choice; it is also better to enter a shop, where there is likely to be a telephone, than to stop a passerby in the street.

Develop safety strategies

In the course of quite unfrightening conversations you can ask your children what they would do 'if': posing some likely (or unlikely) dangerous situations. Discuss your children's ideas and add your own. Develop together the best and most effective ways of dealing with the hypothetical situation: when to run, when to shout loudly, when to search for a policeman, when to pull the communication cord etc. If your child has mentally worked through how to behave in these situations, then the chances are that he or she will instinctively do the right thing if it happens.

Arrange a code or password with your child that you will give to any adult who comes to pick up your child without prior arrangement. Alternatively, tell your child that you will never arrange for someone else to pick him or her up unless you phone the school office first and leave a message. This is a good general safety rule.

Keeping in touch

When older children regularly go out and about alone and spend some time away, such as at a youth club or friend's house, get them into the habit of phoning you wherever you are so that you know when they have arrived, when they are leaving, or any change of plan. If your area is well provided with telephones that take a phonecard it is worth giving one to your child: this ensures that telephone money won't be frittered, and there is a higher chance of finding an unvandalised telephone.

Make sure that your children have all essential phone numbers if they travel alone at all: work, grandparents, neighbours who are usually in, etc. One mother, whose children travel to and from school alone, writes all important phone numbers on the flap of her children's satchels. This is a good idea: you can add your doctor's surgery number in case of accidents.

Veto anything dangerous

Older children who have become used to some independence may insist that they are perfectly able to look after themselves. Don't be intimidated into agreeing to let them do things you continue to believe are dangerous – such as coming home alone in the dark through a deserted alleyway, or similar. This may mean that you have to insist on picking your children up from late dos, such as parties or discos, even if it is inconvenient for you and embarrassing for them.

Check up

Children often tell white lies about such things as what other parents allow, security arrangements for a party, or the fact that a friend's parent is giving them a lift. Don't be afraid to check up if you are suspicious or unhappy about any arrangements: parents are often relieved to find that other parents feel as they do. Checking up is easiest if you are on moderately friendly terms with your children's friends' parents anyway, and can be done apparently in the course of a general chat.

Alone in the House

When the children are alone in the house, we have a code for phoning them so that they know it's us (or grandma, or a friend) and they don't answer otherwise. The door is always locked and they don't open it to anyone they don't know. The eldest boy has recently started doing their lunches during the holidays, but up till then I used to leave sandwiches for them. They are not allowed to have friends in if we are not there. In an emergency they can go to the neighbours, or ring me, my husband, my mum, or any other member of the family.
Mother of two boys aged fifteen and twelve, Sheffield

No mother wants to leave her children alone at home, but sometimes she finds that there is no other choice. There is no point in going into the rights and wrongs here; we must accept that it happens, and look at it from the practical point of view. 'Latch-key kids' is an emotive phrase, a negative image exploited by the media. There have always been sensibly trained older children who have been trusted by their parents to come and go on their own.

Except in rare cases most people don't leave younger children alone for more than the odd emergency hour. It surprised us to find that despite a popular belief that it is forbidden to leave children under the age of fourteen alone in the house there is no age below which it is *illegal* to leave your children alone, though the social services may apply for a care order if they find that young children are left frequently and therefore are in danger or grossly neglected.

The points here are mainly aimed at mothers with older

children who may be leaving their children regularly for longer periods: allowing them to come home and look after themselves after school for instance, or spending some entire days at home during the half-term or school holiday or when they are recuperating from an illness.

One divorced woman, a market research interviewer, who wrote to us has two teenage children living at home. She works a seven-day week and a ten-hour day, and has left her children on their own since they were small. She says:

> There is really nothing one can say except that I would not have left my children when they were younger without an Alsatian in the house. Also they don't open doors to anybody but their young friends. No one else – gas men, my friends, repair men – is allowed in. Neighbours or people they know are also not allowed into the house if I have not told them to do so, regardless of what happens. If the phone rings and somebody asks for me, they say I am in the bath or loo or wherever.

Make your home safe

Most mothers who regularly leave their children alone at home seemed particularly concerned about the dangers of people getting in. In fact this risk is much smaller than the chances of your child having an accident. It has been dinned into us that most accidents happen in the home, and it is obvious that a rash or enthusiastic child is likely to be more accident-prone than an adult. If you have to leave your child alone you must be specially careful to make sure that all obvious dangers are eliminated: frayed flexes, uneven stair carpet, bleach in an old lemonade bottle – each home has a host of such things, and no list we make would be complete. There is no substitute for looking around your home very carefully and doing something now about the things you have been putting off.

Make rules about use of equipment

> Sometimes just one child may be in but no cooking is allowed. They are told to go to a neighbour if anyone strange calls at the house, and only say when I will be back on the telephone if they know who's calling. They can phone me at work if I'm there and there is a problem.
>
> Mother of three children aged eleven, thirteen and fifteen, Preston

Be clear about which household gadgets you want to ban. Perhaps you don't want your children to use the cooker or have the fire on when you are not there. This is more likely to be adhered to if there are alternatives – soup in a thermos, for instance, or in a slow-cooker, ready-made sandwiches, or the ingredients to assemble them, perhaps the central heating set to go on at an earlier time.

Make your child competent

Once you have decided what your children can use in your absence you must make sure that they know exactly how to do so safely and properly. Ideally your child should have used/done the thing umpteen times under your supervision before it is allowed when you are not there.

> We live in a high-risk area for burglars etc, so the children have been brought up not to open the door if they do not know who is there. They also answer the telephone carefully and do not say we are out. I found the microwave a boon for the children to cook themselves a meal or a snack as it is so much safer than the chip pan. If there was an emergency there are five or six neighbours they could go to for help and they know our office numbers off by heart. I could be home in ten minutes and my husband in 30-45 minutes, depending on trains.
>
> Mother of two children aged seventeen and fifteen, Lancashire

Go through safety routines

Accidents can happen even when the most sensible child is in charge. An electrically caused fire, for instance, is nobody's fault. Your child must know exactly what to do in an emergency. Apart from knowing who to telephone, a child should know simple precautionary things like how to contain a fire: shutting the door at the very least, or using a fire blanket; how to turn off the water at the mains; how to turn off the electricity.

List emergency phone numbers

Keep a list of emergency numbers prominently by the telephone. This should include doctor, nearest police station, your work number plus any other numbers that may be useful, such as the next-door neighbour who could be on the spot to help in the case of an intruder.

> **If they are alone in the evenings and we are both out they do not answer the door to anyone. They keep doors locked, etc. We leave a phone number for emergencies.**
> **Mother of two children aged sixteen and thirteen,**
> **Londonderry**

Protection from intruders

A peephole on the front door and a chain are important. Your children should be taught not to let anyone in unless you have told them to beforehand. Some parents think it is safer not to open the door at all.

Rules about friends

You have to decide whether or not you are going to let your children have their friends in while you are out. Your children and their friends may be perfectly well behaved and cause little trouble, or they may be bumptious and need an adult's eye on them. At best highly excitable children can greet you with a mess to clear up – at worst they can egg each other on to break rules.

Other security

It is often safest if your children are evasive on the telephone about your whereabouts or time expected back. Some parents prefer their children to pretend they are in but can't come to the telephone at the moment. Certainly you don't want your children letting it be known to a casual caller that they are in the house alone for any length of time.

Other rules

> I sometimes leave them for ten minutes in the morning because they are not allowed into school before 8.50a.m. – but this is just when my husband is out or I have to leave early. The only rules are not to have the fire on or use anything electrical. The elder child locks the door and sees the younger one out. They only have to walk up the road to school.
> Mother of two children aged nine and seven, Humberside

You may have a list of things that you'd rather your children didn't do while you are out. You'll probably have to accept that it is unlikely that you will be totally obeyed. If you don't want biscuits eaten before the evening meal or the X-rated video watched it's better not to have them in the house at all; rules about not making long calls on the telephone or turning the central heating up full blast are less easy to enforce. However, so long as safety and security are respected you may have to turn a blind eye to some of the other things – and hope that the sense of responsibility you have instilled into your children curbs the worst excesses! As one mother told us:

> It's important for children to have responsibilites, not to
> be left to run wild. I don't like laying down the law in
> the house, but children can sometimes feel abandoned:
> if there are rules to follow, it is as if you were still
> present. I've always said, 'Ring me if you're not sure
> about something you want to do.' I try to reward the
> communication, even if I don't like what they've told
> me! I'd rather they told me than not.

Going out

If your children have to leave the house unexpectedly make
sure that they telephone to tell you why, where and how
long for, even if they are only going to the friend who lives
next door. If this is impossible because you can't be called
at work or are not near a phone, they should leave a
prominent note giving all the details. They should also be
in the habit of locking up securely behind themselves.

Teach key sense

If you give your children their own door keys they must
also be shown how to look after them properly. Keeping
them attached in some way – round their necks, or clipped
to a belt – is a good idea, though keys around the neck
should be worn hanging inside clothes, or they may
advertise the fact that your children could be letting
themselves into an empty house. You could also attach the
keys to elastic or string secured inside a schoolbag, though
there is the possibility that if the entire bag gets lost there
will be clues to the address of the house, which is a security
risk. Encourage your children to confess if keys are lost, as
it is usually sensible to change the locks in case they have
fallen into the wrong hands. It is as well to leave a spare set
of keys with a trusted neighbour for this – and other –
emergencies.

Secondary School

Most of the points covered so far apply equally to primary and secondary school children. There are clearly a host of new practical and emotional problems as your children grow older and become young adults with strong views of their own – but these are no different for the working mother. However there are a few separate considerations.

Choosing a secondary school

This is usually far more fraught than choosing a primary school because most of us feel that the choice will be a major factor in determining our child's future. In the case of state schools and most independent schools, selection is made in the last year of primary school, and many schools actively discourage parents of younger children even checking them out before then. This is not the place to go into the fine points of choosing a secondary school – but you should prepare yourself for the fact that in this year you will probably have to set aside quite a few days from your holiday in order to visit the possible schools. Most of them fix days for groups of parents to see around and hear about the school and these tend to be immovable – so you won't necessarily be able to fit them all into one week of your own choice. You may also have to accompany your child to an exam or have a private interview with the head teacher.

Be prepared also to feel glum and tense during this time: one school starts to look very like another, and it can be difficult to assess which one really would be the best. If for one reason or another your child does not get into the chosen school, the whole family may be depressed and worried, especially as there are months to wait before term starts. Remember that if the school turns out to be completely wrong for your child you may be able to effect a change in the second year. But with very few exceptions most parents find that once their children have settled in everything looks much better. Most parents we talked to look back with amusement on their own misgivings and worries about the move to secondary school.

Half-terms and holidays

After starting at secondary school your children may begin to have strong ideas of their own about how they are going to spend half-terms and holidays while you are not there. Older children may feel that they are now too grown up for out-of-school play schemes; similarly childminders and nannies may seem inappropriate to all concerned. It may be time to look at some of the other holiday arrangements suggested earlier, to see if any of the alternatives would be more acceptable. If you have always invited grandparents to stay during the holidays, or have a mother's help or au pair, your children may feel perfectly content with the old arrangements. If you have had no such casual in-house care you may find that your children will now push to be allowed to stay at home alone or have the freedom to join in with the activities of their friends.

There is likely to come a stage when you feel quite secure about your children staying at home alone. But there is a period of transition. You will probably want to break them in slowly: let them have the odd day or two unsupervised, or ask a willing neighbour to be in charge: overseeing in a limited way what goes on, and granting permission for other activities. Another alternative is to let your children spend the occasional day with friends whose mothers are at home: even once a week may be enough to make them feel that they have a little more freedom and leeway. Also spending the occasional day attending a sports or games centre where there is a certain amount of supervision has the same effect.

Exams

Older school children have exams, and the later ones are very important. It is a stressful time for your child and most probably for you, particularly when the exams affect your child's future career.

Helping to revise

Your child may be well organised about homework, but may need a little extra help from you when it comes to sorting out a revision system. If you don't have any ideas about this yourself, this is something that you can bring up when you talk to the teachers at the next parents' evening. You may need to involve yourself more than you do with homework, such as making yourself available for testing what your child has learned. If, for instance, the revision system involves your child making notes on the term's work, or copying topics onto cards, you can use these to ask questions.

> I devote as much time as my children want with regards to homework and I have always helped them both with revision for exams. My daughter is studying for nine exams at the moment and my husband has devised a revision programme with her. Their education is *number one priority* and we help and encourage them both in every way.
>
> **Mother of girl aged sixteen and boy aged thirteen**

Developing good habits

Some teenagers insist they can't revise without quantities of coffee or tea, or without the music blaring loud. They may start the revision late, and go on working into the small hours. Once these habits are entrenched there is very little you can do about it without adding to the tension by complaining or nagging. There may be nothing you can do about it anyway – except try to help your child form good sensible habits during the first ordinary school exams. Certainly starting the revision early enough before the exams helps, as there should be less frantic, frazzling last-minute late-night work.

Helping at home

Even if your children haven't helped around the home before now, this is the time that you will almost certainly start to resent it. In some ways this is rather unfair: if you haven't insisted on any participation before it is hardly likely that your children will suddenly decide on their own to start helping. But you have every reason to expect your children to help at home if you work, particularly if you work full time.

Suddenly to start complaining about lack of co-operation is not the best way to approach the matter. It is better if it is the subject of a family conference. It takes very disaffected children not to see the fairness behind your request for more help, even if they consider your so-called spare time less valuable than their own. Work out together how much time they can reasonably give to general chores, and which of their own personal chores they should take over entirely. A weekly rota, agreed to in advance, is more likely to be adhered to than a general agreement to take on certain jobs. This can be modified, or even waived at special times, such as during exams.

Part Two

CHAPTER 12

Why You Shouldn't Feel Guilty

During the writing of this book one of us went to talk to a small group of working mothers about what we were doing. They all had good jobs; they were were well-off, and most of them had nannies. They were politely interested to hear about the various topics we had researched, but the overwhelming impression was that they had coped marvellously with the practical problems of being working mothers on their own.

But then guilt was mentioned, and the atmosphere instantly changed. They wanted to know *exactly* what we had found out, what the experts said, and the conclusions to be drawn. It was clear that these women, so obviously in control, who knew that they were doing their best (and who were pretty convinced that their best was very good), needed reassurance.

Almost all working mothers feel guilty. You don't have to have a particular focus for your guilt: nothing may ever go wrong, things may go conspicuously *right*, but in our society it is widely felt that there is something unnatural about choosing to be a working mother, so it is inevitable that doubt, anxiety (and guilt) creep in. It is a no-win situation. As a housewife you are disregarded and undervalued for doing work that is accorded little respect, while if you work you are considered to be a bad mother.

In one poll, 80 per cent of those asked said that women with small children should not go out to work unless they really needed the money.

There is a time-bomb element to the issue. When can you congratulate yourself that you have done a good job with your children? Even if your children seem happy and well-adjusted now, can you be sure they will be so later? The fact that being a working mother is something you feel you have to apologise for, at least some of the time, puts this nagging doubt in your mind, and makes it hard for you to believe the evidence of your own eyes. Later in the chapter you will read that there is no evidence to suggest that the children of working mothers suffer, and plenty of evidence to show the reverse: that they thrive and gain from the experience.

But when there is a conflict, a problem, a crisis, your child starts acting up or being miserable or is ill (all these things happen to every mother, working or not) it is hard to be reasonable with yourself. *Would this have happened if I hadn't been working?* is the inevitable question. We, at least, take comfort from the fact that with the best will in the world it is *impossible* not to make mistakes with your children. Look at Dr Spock who guided millions of parents through their children's childhood, only to be forced to re-evaluate his methods later in the light of the way his children and others had developed. Look at the things in your childhood that *your* parents did wrong: you've probably vowed not to repeat them and you will probably succeed, but it is inevitable that you will make mistakes of your own. You can only do your best, and that includes doing the best by yourself: a happy and contented mother is usually a good mother, even if she is busy and tired. The fact that she maintains her self-respect and feels fulfilled means that she has a lot to offer her children, who in their turn are saved from the guilt they can feel when they want to branch out independently and leave a mother who has devoted her life to them.

On our questionnaire we didn't use the word 'guilt', but asked what were your feelings on leaving your child. Inevitably, guilt was the feeling that cropped up most frequently.

Julie Howell, now a full-time bank cashier, wrote very fully, describing the mixed feelings that are so common:

When I received a phonecall from my bank manager (three years after the birth of my second child) asking me to return to work part time, my initial reaction was excitement. I knew I was becoming a boring person, a cabbage. I could never be the TV commercial housewife, which is what I thought I should be. The TV brainwashes you to believe that you should be cooking all day in a gleaming kitchen, running to the family's every beck and call with a permanent grin on your face. Some women can do it. I couldn't. My second reaction was guilt that I should feel excitement – or even contemplate leaving the children. My next thought was money. We were on a very low income and I wanted to find out how much I would earn and how much a childminder would charge – if I had some left over then it would be worth while. My husband was dubious but was the first to say, 'Never mind the money, you need the job for yourself.' Going back to work has, for me, been the best thing I could ever have done. It has given me back my self-respect. I take more care of the way I look and I enjoy what I'm doing, which in turn makes me a much happier person. The children have benefited from my working in material things alone. They have pocket money, holidays and a better home. If I didn't work we would be living on a very low income. They have become more outgoing from meeting other people and mixing more at the childminder, which in turn I believe has made them less selfish and more caring as they find themselves helping the childminder with the younger children.

Why working mothers feel guilty – the background

The most common argument against mothers of small children going out to work is that 'children need their mothers'. The idea that 'good' mothers stay at home and that working mothers are therefore doing something wrong imposes the heaviest burden of guilt on most working mothers, a burden made heavier every day by the disapproval, expressed or implied, of relatives, neighbours, employers or colleagues.

However the idea that children need the concentrated twenty-four-hour attention of their mothers to develop normally, mentally as well as physically, is a very recent one. Motherhood did not come to be considered as an exclusive and all-excluding occupation in its own right until the ideas of Freud and Piaget filtered into the popular consciousness through post-Second World War childcare literature written by experts such as Dr Spock. In the past, children fitted into their mothers' lives in a more natural fashion. In rural and industrial communities, babies would be slung on a hip or on the back while women got on with their jobs, or would be left with an older sibling, grandmother or neighbour. Older children often worked alongside their mothers. In wealthier families children were generally looked after by servants and the most devoted mother would probably not see her children for more than a couple of hours a day.

Before the 1950s, advice in childcare manuals focused on the physical aspects of childcare and discipline. But then the effect of Freud's theories, coupled with Piaget's, and especially John Bowlby's, started to be felt. Bowlby's theory of maternal deprivation stressed the crucial and irreplaceable central role played by the mother – not only in the physical well-being and progress of her children, but in their long-term emotional, social and intellectual development. His findings came to be interpreted to mean that all adolescent misconduct and adult neuroses were Mother's Fault, and the most damaging thing a mother could do to her small child was to deprive him of her presence even for a few hours. Mother became the only person capable, in the pre-school years, of nurturing, stimulating and teaching her children. People interpreted Bowlby to mean that any substitute childcarer, even the child's father, was very much second best, if not tantamount to wilful neglect. This is the prevailing atmosphere in which most of us have been raised. No wonder we sometimes feel guilty.

But it has often been overlooked that much of Bowlby's work was based on children living in inadequate, understaffed, residential orphanages, where they may have been physically cared for but received no individual loving attention. Bowlby's theories were stretched to include any form of daycare, even nursery schools, for the under-fives, as it was assumed that it was psychologically damaging to separate young children from their mothers even for a limited period of time during the day, making no distinction between institutionalised orphans and children who only spent a limited number of hours per day separated from their mothers. Of course society owes a debt to Bowlby for pointing out that a small child needs loving and cuddling and a close relationship with one consistent adult, as much as food and warmth, but it is a pity that his theories have encouraged the popular misconception that young children should never be separated from their mothers at all.

Research carried out since then draws different conclusions from Bowlby. In spite of many studies designed to prove the opposite, no study has been able to show that separation from the mother is in itself harmful to the child, nor that daycare outside the home (or inside the home by someone other than the mother) causes psychological damage. And although the young child's attachment to one consistent and continuous adult presence is important, there is no proof that the adult need be the child's mother. Nor are there ill-effects from a child having several mother figures, so long as each provides good care and a stable relationship.

Researchers have found less sexual stereotyping in the ideas of children of working mothers. They have found the children more skilled at playing with other children, more friendly towards new faces, more comfortable in and better at co-operating in group situations, more willing to initiate and better at initiating activities for themselves and their playmates, and more capable of taking direction from others.

Here is one extract from more up-to-date research:

> A woman becomes a source of immense curiosity to her child. He wonders 'Where does mummy go and what does she do?' And because working mothers usually answer this question in affirmative descriptions of life at the office, their children develop an expectation. Like mother, they expect that people outside the family are interesting and exciting. Newcomers are faced eagerly and with great interest.

Why You Shouldn't Feel Guilty

The most important reason for not feeling guilty is this: if you are doing your best by your children, yourself and other loved ones, then you have nothing with which to reproach yourself. If this is not reassuring, then it is important to realise that no psychologist has shown, in test conditions, that there is any justification for your guilt – research shows that what you are doing is not harmful, and can be beneficial, for your children.

Here are the most common worries – and why the guilt is unnecessary:

Worry: 'My child will be emotionally or intellectually deprived if looked after by anyone but me'

You feel no one can love your child as you do, or understand your child so well. It seems impossible that anyone could provide the standard of care, stimulation and teaching you would provide for your child. But if you arrange good substitute childcare for the hours you are at work, there is no reason why your child should not thrive, especially as you and your partner are around the rest of the time to give your child your love and attention.

The experts say

Many studies have been carried out to see how day care affects the development of children. So far the conclusions are similar: good childcare has no adverse effects on the child's development – if anything, children in day care get extra educational input and stimulation, and perform better than children of the same age who stay at home with their mothers. (It has also been shown that any differences between pre-school children who have been in day care and those who have been looked after by their mothers at home disappear after the first years of school.)

The small child's wider social network plays a much greater role in the child's intellectual and emotional development than we ever thought when all attention was concentrated on the mother. Fathers, siblings, the child's friends and peers, and others involved in their care (nannies, childminders, grandparents, nursery teachers) all have a role to play. This not only lifts some of the burden from the mother, but also points to the idea that far from being harmful, there are positive benefits for a young child in being involved in the more wide-ranging social life that occurs when the mother goes out to work.

It is also recognised that in a modern society where a

child can be cooped up all day with one adult (the mother), perhaps in a high-rise block without access to play facilities or other children, the child suffers. It is a new phenomenon, as extended families scatter and isolation of mothers with children becomes the norm: previously children had daily, natural contact with dozens of other adults and children. They *need* this. In Europe, where childcare facilities are more widespread, it is recognised that the children need the stimulation and variety that this offers. These facilities are not primarily set up to make it easier for working mothers, but for *children*, who otherwise might be stuck in a unnatural one-to-one interaction with their mothers.

Other mothers say

Women who wrote to us found that their guilt feelings subsided once they saw that good care was working out and their children were thriving:

* One thing I have found difficult is coping with feelings of guilt. But I try to deal with it by simply looking at the children and realising how generally happy and well-balanced they seem. And perhaps they appreciate me more too.

* First time round I suffered the usual guilt – fear of the unknown and wondering what damage I was doing to him. As time went on I saw he was turning out well (so did everyone else – my parents, critical friends) and I began to relax.

* I do sometimes feel guilty because I tell myself that I would spend more time setting out paints for him, dancing and singing with him, or teaching him the alphabet, etc, than his nanny does. But she does other things I would never do, like taking him to the park everyday. He has a whole social life with her separate from me. And if I'm really honest with myself, I'm not

sure I *would* do these things with him – more likely to park him in front of the telly so that I could get on with the housework!

Worry: 'Without my protection my child may pine'

The desire to protect your child is a strong instinct, and it is common to feel that without you there your child will not be able to survive the hurly-burly of life outside the home. But it does children no favours to be wholly dependent on their mothers: in child psychology books it is shown that extreme over-protectiveness causes at least as many psychological problems as severe maternal deprivation. And young children gain a lot from learning to interact with other children and adults. Above all, they learn to be independent.

The experts say

Children in daycare are more socially at ease than children at home: they tend to get along better with other children and with strangers. They are also more independent. They demonstrate increased self-confidence and self-awareness.

Other mothers say

Many mothers wrote to tell us that their own observations bore out what the experts say:

* I feel my son is also benefiting because he doesn't totally rely on me, he is more sociable and independent.

* I think all my children have benefited from having a working mother. They are more independent. This was brought home to me recently after taking William (aged seven) swimming. I have been worrying for weeks that the other children let their mothers dress them, whereas

William wants to do it all himself. It only dawned on me yesterday that this is the way he has been brought up – it's those other mothers who have to 'baby' their sons who should worry, not me!

* I worried that my daughter was too sensitive to cope with the roughness of other children. Kids can be so cruel to each other. But I saw her toughen up in the healthiest way: she never became aggressive herself, but she learned how to deal effectively with aggressors. I was sometimes more upset than she was when she reported an incident, but when she *was* upset, we were able to 'talk it away'. If I had been there to shield and protect her all the time she would not have learned to cope, and it would have been a harder lesson to learn later on.

Worry: 'My children will grow away from me'

It is common to worry that your children may grow to prefer your substitute and may love you less when you are out at work every day, and that perhaps you will have a less close relationship with them as they grow up.

But none of us has a limited quantity of love that has to be eked out among the people in our lives. The more people your child can love the better – and you will never be replaced.

The experts say

Even Bowlby noted that most children brought up in an Israeli kibbutz (where they live in a communal nursery, but see their parents for two or three hours every day and at the weekend) develop normally and make their closest relationships with their parents.

Other researchers have shown that although a child may form a close relationship with the childminder, nanny, or other childcarer, this does not effect the emotional bond between the child and mother: 'They may also form an affectionate relationship with [the person] who is involved in their care for a substantial period of time, and this caregiver is preferred to a stranger, but day-care children still overwhelmingly prefer their mothers.' (*Day Care* by Alison Clarke-Stewart.)

Research also shows that older children of working mothers have a higher respect for the competence of women and that the daughters of working mothers have higher ambitions for themselves than those of non-working mothers: in other words, the increased self-respect their mothers feel has a long-term beneficial effect on their children.

Other mothers say

No mother wrote to tell us that she felt that her children loved her any the less because she was out at work, although some had feared that it would happen:

> I was terrified to leave my daughter. I worried she would grow away from me, prefer the childminder, loosen the bonding, stop eating etc.

All of them realised this fear was unfounded once the routine had been established.

It was also interesting to hear from mothers of much older children who felt that their relationship had definitely not suffered – or had been enhanced by the fact they were working:

> The most rewarding thing was that as my daughter grew older, she was able to understand life better – because as I was working I had a varied and more interesting life to discuss with her, and conversations were not restricted to just school, home, and everyday 'run-of-the-mill' things. Since she has left school and become a working girl herself, we find that we can share our work

experiences and the ups and downs of working, running a home at the same time. We have become more like sisters than mother and daughter, sharing the housework, helping each other, and my partner and I feel that we are a closer family unit than if I had not been working.

Other mothers asked their older children how they felt about them working:

> My son is now working in the 'Big City' (Aberdeen), sixty-seven miles from here and lives with my in-laws. He comes home for odd weekends and his holidays and he hopes in due course to transfer to Inverness which is nearer. He always seems glad to come home and when asked says that generally he didn't mind me being a working mum especially when old enough to understand the advantages. My daughter doesn't remember when I didn't work but says she never envied her friends whose mums didn't work.

This woman wrote about her relationship with her own mother:

> I found that becoming independent in my late teens was helped by the encouragement from my (working) mother. I saw that my friends who were having the most problems had mothers who had always been at home. I continued to have a good relationship with my mother, based on mutual respect: later I sought her company because I wanted to see her and found her interesting and her experience valuable. Some of my friends with non-working mothers had relationships that were far more fraught and dutiful: they saw them because they felt guilty.

Another woman had a similar experience with her own mother, who also worked:

> When I got to my teenage years, she wasn't as possessive as the other mothers. All my friends would say, 'Aren't you lucky that your mother isn't breathing down your

neck all the time.' I also relied on her advice because she was much more objective. I could go to her as a sort of friend, rather than just be given a mother's point of view.

Worry: 'My child will grow up to be a delinquent'

This worry is usually put into the head of the working mother by others influenced by the old idea that working mothers produce deprived children: 'latch-key kids', who roam the streets unsupervised and get into trouble. Now that it is recognised that well-cared-for children of working mothers are as well-adjusted as other children, it is time this myth was laid to rest.

The experts say

All recent research bears out the fact that this is a myth. Michael Rutter, a leading practitioner and research worker in the field of child psychiatry, says in *Helping Troubled Children* (Penguin):

> Although it has been claimed that the children of working mothers are particularly likely to become delinquent or develop some psychiatric disorder, there is abundant evidence that this is not so. Indeed, in some circumstances children with working mothers may be even better off, as this may mean that the mothers have an increased range of interests, are more content and so have more to give the family.

Other mothers say

Mothers of teenagers have the evidence of their own children's behaviour to prove this worry groundless:

> * I think it's important for the children to have responsibilities, not to be left to run wild. I give my children rules to obey: it makes them feel I'm still

present, even when they are at home on their own. My children are quite responsible, they don't do silly things, and I trust them. We've never had a great disaster. They look after the house – I can leave them alone and they're fine.

* Trust and responsibility feed each other. As my child has proved herself responsible and able to cope, so I have trusted her with increased independence. She wants to reward my trust with responsible behaviour, and so on. So far she's a pillar of society, rather than the reverse, always thinking sensibly on her feet in a crisis. At thirteen she was the person who organised an ambulance for a man who had been knocked over in the street, by barging into a bank and getting them to ring the emergency services, while adults were standing around ineffectually. She also once called the police to a burglar climbing into an upper window – who turned out to be a man who had just locked himself out. She was very embarrassed, but the police congratulated her and said that they wished more people would do as she had done.

Worry: 'I won't be able to spend enough time with my child'

What is behind this worry is that you won't be able to give your child adequate affection, attention and stimulation in the time that you have together. But what happens is that working mothers, because of this fear, make efforts to make every minute count. Giving your child your whole attention for a concentrated period of time ('quality time') is extremely valuable. A mother who is at home all day with her child may not feel the same inclination to give undivided attention.

The experts say

Studies have shown that working mothers spend about as much time in child-related activities as mothers who don't go out to work. One study showed that working mothers played with their children more than the mothers who stayed at home.

Other mothers say

On the questionnaire we asked the mothers how much time each working day they managed to spend talking to or playing with their children. Two or three hours was an average – with much more time spent with their children around but doing other things (like non-working mothers). Some gave breakdowns of the time, which included the minutes in the morning as well as the blocks of time in the evenings – and they made those minutes count. Some mothers were keen to use the time to educational purpose:

> They are sociable children with a wide vocabulary and the eldest [aged four] is learning to read. We are teaching him with flash cards. Because I work, the time I spend with them has to be significant and beneficial.

Others use the time for talking, playing or cuddling, and many make the point that weekends can be used for catching up with each other:

> Time spent with children tends to be communication time. Weekends make up for the week. We walk, play and attempt to get out together as a family in outside and sport activities.

Some women simply noted that they were better disposed to their children, so that time together was pleasant:

> * Apart from the material benefits I think our relationship is more relaxed now I am working. I do not get so ratty with the children (usually!) because I have an outside interest and come back to them tired but delighted to see them and ready to listen.

* The baby is always looked after by someone who wants to look after her – the childminder, during the day, and me in the evening. Because I don't see her all day I don't get fed up.

* When I come home I feel the baby gets more from me than at the end of one of my home days.

Worry: 'If I want to work because motherhood is not entirely fulfilling, I must be a bad mother'

Many women feel guilty that work means so much to them: that they actively enjoy it, and choose to go out to work rather than look after their children at home. They fear that this means they do not love their children enough, and therefore that they can't be good mothers. This is nonsense – nobody suggests that a man who loves his work cannot be a loving devoted father at the same time! You can adore your children but still need extra challenges, the stimulation of work, the company of other adults, and the extra self-confidence, self-respect – and money – that working brings. If this is what makes you feel good about yourself, then you will be a *better* mother.

The experts say

Tests have concluded that whether a mother works or not is less important to her child's development and to her relationship with her child than whether she is happy in whatever she does. A mother who goes to work for financial reasons but who hates her job or resents not being able to stay with her children – or a mother who looks after her kids at home but is bored or depressed and wishes she had a job – will both have a more negative effect on their children than the mother who goes out to work because she enjoys it, or the mother who loves nothing better than being at home with her kids: 'satisfied mothers – working or not – have the best-adjusted children.' (*Effects of Maternal Employment on Children* by Claire Etaugh.)

A neglected aspect of Bowlby's work on maternal deprivation is that he also saw that mothers who were unhappy to be at home, and therefore could not relate effectively to their children, had children who were almost as disturbed as the institutionalised sample. He said that his research showed, 'A child is deprived even though living at home if his mother . . . is unable to give him the loving care small children need.'

Other mothers say

Many mothers made the point that their contentment made them better mothers:

> * I enjoy my work and feel that the whole family has benefited, not only financially, but through my peace of mind at having fulfilled my ambitions and having some independence.

> * I needed to go back to work – not financially – but for my own sanity! I needed stimulation and interaction with other adults – a baby can't do that. Towards the end of my maternity leave I found myself going out to the local shopping centre daily just to see other adults. I felt very isolated. I now feel I am a better mother – able to cope with and stimulate my child and at the same time fulfill my own needs as a human being.

> * I wouldn't be sane if I didn't work and have my own money to live on.

> * Sometimes I feel like a juggler, trying to keep everything going, then a clown, trying to keep everyone happy. But most of all I feel torn between being a 'good' mother and fulfilling my needs as a person. I look at it this way – through working I feel I'm a better mother because it stops me from getting very depressed (which I would if I had to stay at home every day) and I appreciate the time I do spend with my child more.

Worry: 'What will people say about me?'

If you are surrounded by mothers who don't go out to work, or your parents, in-laws, friends, neighbours or colleagues disapprove, you may feel particularly guilty and unsure. This is where you need the advice and support of other working mothers most.

Other mothers say

The women in our sample varied in the degree that they were able to discount the ill-informed opinions of others:

> * I honestly feel that you have to do what you want and ignore other people's attitudes and opinions about working mothers. You will always get people who think it is wrong. I have never felt guilty about leaving my children to go to work. I have made good arrangements. Continuity leads to stability and security. I enjoy working and get great satisfaction from being able to do many things with my time. The children have had to fall in with what I do, but I feel they are happy, well-adjusted children who are not dependent on me to fill their time.

> * Other people tried to make me feel guilty about 'farming my child out'. I did feel guilty but tried to overcome it by talking to people with children who were already back at work.

You should also ask yourself if you are being over-sensitive:

> Perhaps I am too sensitive at times. The lady in the post office commented that she could tell that my daughter was on holiday from the nursery because she was not as tired as usual. I immediately interpreted this as a criticism of myself, when, in fact, it was an innocent remark.

If other people make you feel bad, try to find friends who are in the same boat as you so that you can face it together, as this woman does:

> I organise the situation on work days so I know I am doing my best for my kids – I can't do any more! With the second child I've hardly given it another thought. Experience gives you confidence and so many of my friends are now doing the same thing, I don't feel such a freak either. We support each other if we come under attack.

When Guilt Serves a Purpose

Some guilt is constructive: just as physical pain has a physiological purpose, warning you that something is wrong with your body, so guilt can be seen as a different kind of warning sign. It can act as a trigger to re-examine your routine: are you doing something wrong, or not doing something that you should? For guilt to work positively in your favour you should examine the elements that are making you feel guilty, and see if you can eliminate them. Continuing to feel guilty after you have done that is unproductive, and will not do you or your family any good.

Ways of combating guilt constructively

The most effective way of combating guilt is to analyse exactly what is causing it, and try to do something about it.

Firstly try to ignore vague guilt feelings induced by other people, if as far as you can see everything seems to be going well. Save worrying for when it is necessary – and then do something practical about it. Guilt feelings won't do anyone any good: practical action will.

These are some examples:

If your guilt is to do with worrying about what happens to your child while you are at work:

* Make sure your childcare arrangements are the best you can find, and that your child is settled in and happy with them.

* Make arrangements for your child after school or during the school holidays that give you peace of mind.

If your guilt is concerned with the amount of time you can spend with your child:

* Put aside some time each day that is for your child or children exclusively. It can be as little as fifteen minutes in the morning and half an hour before bedtime, but make it into a routine that you adhere to.

* Set aside a regular time at the weekend for your child to get your full attention (and leave the chores).

* Do your best to be with your child on special days or occasions when your absence would be most felt (first day at school, school concert/play, first dentist appointment, and so on).

* See *Quality Time*, p.130 and *Time with your school-age children*, p.309).

If your guilt stems from the worry that work divides you from your child:

* Don't cut your child off from that other side of your life: find ways to bring your work alive for your child. (see p.502, *Involving Your Children in Your Work*)

If you eliminate the major problems in this way, guilt

won't be a thing of the past, but should then only arise over specific issues:

> There was one ghastly occasion when he said, 'Oh please turn up for the church service' and I completely forgot about it. The next thing was I went to see his form school books at the end of term. I turned to a little essay written in his book saying, 'There was the Harvest Festival Church Service and my mummy wasn't there but I DIDN'T MIND', the implication being that of course he *did* . . .

Moments like these are heart-rending, but they tend to stick in your mind more than your child's, particularly as you are likely to do your best to see that they are never repeated.

Another woman (a barrister) told us of a similar instance:

> Oh god, it was his birthday last week, and I went into work. I would have taken the day off but I happened to be in court the next day with a very important case, and you can't really stay home the day before you're in court. So we had, 'Why are you going to work on my birthday?' I did feel bad about it, and in future if it's possible, I'll take the day off.

In fact, this woman also compensated by getting up extra early on her son's birthday and spending a couple of hours with him opening his presents and playing with him, and also by arranging a party for him on the following Saturday. Another solution is to give your child an 'official' birthday every year, which falls on the weekend following the day itself. Children love the idea of two birthdays and will only feel bad about this if your guilt is so obvious that they think they *ought* to feel bad.

Destructive Guilt

Guilt is destructive when it is either groundless or has no particular focus.

Destructive guilt often strikes women who question their own right to be happy: if they enjoy their work and are sometimes relieved to be leaving their children they may use guilt to punish themselves so that the pleasure is spoilt. They feel better about what they are doing if they are not entirely happy.

Another form of destructive guilt is entirely due to other people: if they think you should be feeling guilty, then you do, even though there is no particular reason for it.

This woman who wrote to us is an example of someone fruitlessly feeling guilty:

> My main feelings about leaving the children [aged fifteen and twelve] have been, and still are, ones of guilt at not being there when they come home from school, not always being able to attend school functions, not being there when needed. My children reassure me that they are fine, that without me working they wouldn't have nice clothes, computer, etc., and a nice house to live in, holidays. But the guilt feelings are still there. When I am at work in the school holidays I worry incessantly about them.

It is easy for an outsider to see that this woman is worrying needlessly. From other information given on her questionnaire it was clear that her children were competent and well-behaved, and of an age when they can stay home alone and look after themselves. She is obviously a loving and much-loved mother. She has only missed some functions at school, and she always has been there when her children really needed her (when they have been ill she put them first, even when this caused trouble at work). Above all, her children are happy, and tell her so.

This kind of guilt is usually sensed by the people around you. The ever-guilty, apologetic mother is the one who usually finds herself doing everything, because she feels she has no right to demand active participation from husband or children. This can spill over into work, where she finds herself taken advantage of by boss or colleagues.

If your guilt means that you are walking round with a sense of impending doom it is easy to blame anything that goes wrong on yourself. Certainly you should get things into perspective: because as a working mother you already feel extremely sensitive about the fact that you work, you can fall into the trap of blaming all problems and setbacks on that. All children have their ups and downs, regardless of whether their mothers work. No amount of time and effort will guarantee a completely happy, pain-free life for your children, however much you may wish it.

Self-induced Guilt

This kind of guilt is a product of the Superwoman myth that it is possible to do everything, and do it all well. The more high-powered and competent you are at work, the more likely you are to demand too much of yourself generally. A mother who would like everything to be perfect is not unnatural, but one who believes she can make it so is definitely unrealistic. Asking the impossible from yourself is bound to end up with you feeling guilty.

Child-rearing has its fashions, and much self-induced guilt is caused by attaching too much importance to following the current theories (often to the exclusion of trusting your own instincts) and thereby letting yourself down. This is not to say that the ideas behind them are not valid, nor extremely admirable – just that there are no rules, and there is *no competition* – some of the aims or ideas will be right for you, others won't.

These are the kind of things that cause avoidable guilt –

in other words, they suit you and your baby or not – and feeling guilty if they don't is a waste of emotional energy:

* Wanting to have a 'perfect' birth: no drugs, natural childbirth, active birth, and feeling guilty if you don't have the experience you planned, or had to 'give in' (see *Labour*, p.58).

* Breastfeeding: some women take to it easily, others have a struggle. If you believe that breast is not only best, but also essential, you can feel guilty if you can't breastfeed, or you hate it. As one woman told us: 'Breast is best should be banned. It makes you feel you're doing your baby terrible damage if like me you really can't manage it.' She took her baby to a specialist in a panic when he started bringing up blood: the doctor diagnosed the blood as being hers, and advised her to stop breastfeeding! She had gone through immense pain and agony for months because she was so convinced that breast was best. (One of the doctors who wrote to us confessed that she chose to bottle-feed because it was so much easier, and she was able to recover from the birth sooner.)

* Grandiose plans for what you are going to do during maternity leave and the first few months of your baby's life: for most, at best, this will just involve muddling through. Many women feel guilty that it takes them so long to adjust (see *Maternity Leave Blues*, p.62).

* Following the rules to bond with your child. Mother love doesn't come quickly to all of us, even if we do all that we are told to do (put baby to the breast instantly and so on). Many women find that it takes time to fall in love with their babies, which can be the cause for needless guilt (see *Maternity Leave Blues*, p.68).

* Educational theories, 'bringing on' your child's

intelligence by stimulating him or her with all the correct toys and flash cards at the relevant age. If you enjoy doing this, fine – it will be fun for you and your children, who love enthusiastic attention from their parents, whatever the reason. But if you don't like this sort of interaction you don't have to feel guilty:

I felt so guilty because my daughter was bright and loved looking at books – she showed signs of being ready to read – but whenever I tried to teach her I would get very worked up and irritated if she was dopey or hadn't understood. I decided that it was better to stop trying than to have this conflict, but I still felt that I was failing her in some way. Then when she started school my guilt fell away. Learning to read with the others was such an exciting experience for her. She was bursting to tell me every day the words she had called out that began with 'b' or something. The kids who could read already missed the fun. They were stuck in a corner with a book to get on with, and she used to feel quite sorry for them.

Other self-induced guilt takes the form of needless worrying about other areas of your life, such as your work. Many mothers interviewed worried that they were letting their work or their employers down in some way, because they had additional family responsibilities. But when questioned most turned out to have extremely high, perfectionist standards for themselves at work, probably higher than their standards for others, especially their male colleagues. Is this a new self-inflicted double standard? In the extreme cases this does show that working mothers are employees with a high sense of responsibility – an asset to an employer – but at great emotional cost.

The Best of Both Worlds?

It is good to be able to report on the working mothers who

have dealt effectively with their guilt, particularly as even the ones who have it under control are often superstitious about admitting that everything is fine. But some women frankly admit that they are getting the best of both worlds, and that their children are getting the best deal. This seems to us to be very healthy. Here is a selection from some of the questionnaires.

A radio journalist, a mother of a three-year-old and a one-year-old wrote:

> Jonathan is now taking a real interest in what I do – he enjoys a visit to my workplace, and tells his friends about it. He has thrived in a nursery with other kids – if I hadn't gone to work he wouldn't have had the same experience. We have money for outings and holidays – this sounds mercenary but they can enrich the experience of life. On a teacher's salary alone we would have had financial worries – and extra money doesn't stop us making things from cornflakes packets and having walks in the park! I need the company I get from work: I really like people around. My career matters – it is a profession that is very difficult to rejoin. I get a sense of achievement in doing both jobs, and they both benefit: having children made me more relaxed about my work. People say you can't have your cake and eat it; I disagree.

Another mother, who runs a teacher's centre, knows from her professional experience that having a working mother is no drawback for a child:

> I didn't feel particularly sad or glad about leaving my child. I was preoccupied with planning (and hoping everything would be all right) for all three of us; having worked for fourteen years it seemed only natural to be going back to work and I was utterly convinced my son would be fine. The key to this being (a) much experience over ten years of professional working mums where the children developed with very healthy attitudes to life; (b) my own belief that it isn't necessary nor always advisable for a child to be 'with mum' all day long.

Other women noted that because they felt so much better in themselves they knew it must be good for their children, like this doctor:

> Working gives me freedom! At least for part of the day. I also appreciate my children all the more because I come home to two happy well-cared-for kids, and the evenings (although they are tiring) are not particularly stressful.

A social work assistant has the last word:

> I love my part-time job and although I enjoyed the time at home with my baby I feel I now have the best of both worlds – and also my wages.

CHAPTER 13
Illness and Other Crises

All working mothers know what we mean by a crisis: when our carefully laid plans collapse in a heap, and it looks as if children, career and everything else we care about are in jeopardy. As one correspondent wryly put it, 'It's always a crisis!'

A crisis doesn't have to be a major disaster – just something completely unforeseen that throws out all your arrangements. We're not talking about general crises – what you should do if you break down on a country road and you are miles from a phone, for instance – but crises that throw your children and career into conflict. Often we find that by determination and fancy footwork we can avoid disaster – just. Everyone can sympathise with the maths teacher from Humberside who wrote about a black day when she was working part time and it looked as if everything would go wrong:

> My worst experience was when Andrea was five and Bobby three. As usual I took Bobby to the playgroup where I worked as a supervisor until 11.30, and while everything was being set up I took Andrea to school. Everything ran deceptively smoothly that morning. I left at 11.58a.m. after everything was packed up, collected Andrea from school at 12.05p.m., and took them home to lunch. That's when it all started to go wrong. In the

bathroom I found the gerbil cage open and a gerbil dead on the floor. The other one was lying decapitated in the hall: the cat had had a field day. I was desperately trying to dispose of the gerbils before the children found out when there was a knock on the door. I opened it to find a distraught lady in floods of tears. My husband is a policeman and she wanted him to sort out a problem. He wasn't in, so I had to bring the poor woman in and attempt to comfort her while I gave the kids their lunch and secretly disposed of the gerbils. I then had to use all my tact to get the lady out again so that I could rush Bobby to the childminder and Andrea back to school as well as get to work (a twenty-five-minute journey) for 1.30p.m. And I did it. It was a rest to be at work!

A crisis right at the beginning of your attempts to combine motherhood and work alerts you to the fact that you can never totally rely on the apparently cast-iron arrangements that you have made. This is what happened to Marie Burke:

The worst crisis of my life as a working mother was when my first child was baby. One week into the job the childminder announced that she could not look after my son anymore – she had a baby of the same age and had thought that she could cope with two – mistakenly. Miraculously I managed to find another childminder (through recommendation) who turned out to be worth her weight in gold.

But of course unforeseen crises can happen at any time during your children's school career. You may suddenly be faced with the fact that your children's school is closing down for the whole day because it is needed for an election, or the central heating has packed up – or it may be closed for weeks because someone has discovered asbestos dust. The teachers' strike of 1985–86 was an unforeseen crisis, and many parents found that their children were being turned out of school at lunchtime with nowhere to go and no one to look after them. While very few employers would be hard-hearted enough to mind if you had to drop everything and run because the school telephoned to say that your child had been taken ill, even the best-natured ones are going to look far less kindly on you taking time off for the reasons mentioned above.

> Minor crises have been when my son's been taken ill at school and I've had to leave work during the daytime. I've been told by my bosses that I've put people out by leaving and that my colleagues have complained, but on asking them I've found this to be untrue.

It would make this book worth twice its cover price if we could come up with a universal solution to how to cope in times of crisis, but every reader has a different set of circumstances so, as ever, we can only make suggestions. The most important points to stress are that CRISES WILL HAPPEN so you must have contingency plans, and to this end it is important to BUILD UP GOODWILL.

> When the children are ill I take leave or get in the grandparents – I have been known to ring in sick.

Developing a Support System or Network

> My biggest asset is parents-in-law, who will take the children over in emergencies and who cope with their illnesses – I would advise any working mother to try and get this sort of back-up from someone. It is *very* traumatic if there's no one to turn to in a crisis, and depending on your job, it can be very difficult to down tools at a moment's notice. I am also very fortunate in having a husband who is a vicar and who works from home – he does the afternoon shift and I do the evenings!

In a crisis there is no substitute for people you can call on at a moment's notice who will happily come to your aid. If you come from a large, close family who all live nearby then you have very little problem. But most people live more isolated lives, and working away from home makes developing friendly contacts nearby particularly hard. Paradoxically it is the mothers who don't go out to work who usually have the most people they can call on. They are the ones who have the opportunity to make friends with the neighbours – have time to chat or have a coffee in each other's houses and do the little favours that bring goodwill. They are also able to spend some time at the school gates, chatting to other mothers before and after school, getting to know them well enough so that a panic call for help is possible.

Working mothers have to try rather harder to form this kind of loose network of pleasant acquaintances, which doubles as a crucial safety net at key moments – invaluable, as so many women who wrote to us found:

> **When the children were younger, during a crisis I used neighbours or friends. And although it makes you feel guilty (I've had four different people doing things for me at the same time) co-ordinating makes you feel like an army general!**

But at least making friends is not an arduous pastime, and you will probably be wanting to do so anyway – there will undoubtedly be many that you are happy to know for themselves, rather than what they can do for you!

Cultivating other mothers

From the moment your first child is born you find that you are making friends with a whole new group of women. Other mothers, particularly with babies the same age as yours, are for a time, far more fascinating than anyone else you know. You are having common experiences – they are often the only people who seem to understand fully what you are going through – and you can freely indulge your urge to talk babies constantly. This joy in each other's company wears off after a while, but you have the basis of a series of good friendships which creates the bond between you, and which means that any of you will help when you can. Of course, sadly, if you move to another area you lose this network.

Support groups: antenatal, postnatal, working mums

You'll probably start to get to know other mothers when you go for your pregnancy check-ups at the local clinic. A good reason for attending childbirth classes near home is that you can make friends with local women who are having babies at the same time as you. NCT classes are ideal for introducing you to like-minded women. If you did not join childbirth classes you may want to join a postnatal support group through the NCT (or ask your health visitor about other local postnatal groups). While you are on maternity leave you can also make regular visits to the local mother and baby groups and begin to make friends there.

Joining or forming a working mothers group

The Working Mothers Association was started by mothers who had known each other through NCT classes and formed informal support groups for other working mothers like themselves. They soon realised that there was a need for a national organisation primarily concerned with the rights and problems of working mothers and their families. The office keeps a list of all known local groups which it gives out to members, so you can join and find if there is an existing group in your area. Otherwise they will give you help and advice to form your own.

It is obviously a very good idea to get together regularly with other working mothers who think as you do and have the same problems. A regular theme of discussions can be 'what to do in a crisis' and you can draw up a formal campaign plan, or simply agree to give each other support when necessary and pool your resources.

Neighbours

Close neighbours are often the most invaluable help of all. They are on the spot if something has prevented you getting back to let you child in, for instance. Because they live near we often feel we can ask them to help out in an emergency without putting them to too much trouble. Even if the people who live next door are ghastly, there should be others up the street or round the corner who are nice. You have the greatest chance of making friends with people who live near because it can be quite casual – calling hello when you bring in the milk, chatting as you walk down the street together, shouting over the fence, or bumping into each other at the shops. If you live in a rural area where your closest neighbour is quite far away it is obviously less natural, but your advances will probably be even more welcome.

Another good way of meeting neighbours, particularly if you have just moved into an area, is to set up or join a neighbourhood watch scheme. Your common concern about local security paves the way for a closer friendship. Others have met their neighbours by organising street parties: for fireworks night, for example, or for a royal wedding. If someone seems especially pleasant you don't need us to tell you to take the relationship further: whether it's informal suppers, morning coffee at the weekend, grand dinners, or going to the park together on Sunday with all the kids – anything that promotes the friendship and makes you relaxed in each other's company has to be good.

Getting to know women with nannies

If you have a nanny it is worth getting to know other women nearby with nannies. You'll probably be helping your nanny to make friends anyway, and at the very least you will have your nannies in common with her friends' employers! If the nannies like each other and you get on well with the other mothers, you may want to come to a more formal arrangement about crisis moments. If your nanny is ill then the other nanny may agree to help out, for instance.

Even if you don't have a nanny yourself, you may feel that you can ask a nearby nanny and her employer if she would occasionally be prepared to help out in a crisis. You could come to some financial arrangement over this.

Childminders

If your child goes to a childminder, check that she has ties with the local childminding organisation or other childminders. They often make agreements among themselves to help out in an emergency: for instance, if your childminder falls ill.

Getting to know mothers from school/nursery

Your circle of potential mother-friends enlarges if your child goes to nursery. Certainly when your child starts to go to school the opportunities to meet more women increase. Any chance to make friends informally round and about the school should be seized, though most women who work traditional hours are denied this. However, if, like this mother who worked freelance, you can spend time outside the school chatting to mothers you are likely to find it worth it:

I became part of a large noisy gang of mums who went

off to the local cafe for a cup of tea after the kids had gone in to school. We used to spend half an hour chatting and laughing before going our separate ways. For such an early hour there was an incredible intimacy – women talking about their marriage problems etc. Although I didn't see much of these women at other times we struck up quite a camaraderie, and oddly enough when I was stuck I used to feel more able to ring one of them up than one of my closer friends, or even the parents of my child's closest friends.

If you can't do something like this then attending school social functions does help, and if you join the PTA you may meet like-minded women. Another mother made friends this way:

I do a schoolrun twice a week, which means piling out of the house at whatever time it is, picking up the other children, taking them to school, and then getting myself to work. This way I introduce myself into the school social circle and prove to the other mums that I'm not just going to be asking them for favours, but that I am going to participate as well.

On the whole you'll find that it is the relationship you develop with the other mothers that is most important, and it doesn't matter if your children like theirs. You can't necessarily count on the mother of your child's best friend when you are in a jam: she's more likely to put herself out for another woman she likes than for a child she likes.

Finding a granny

If you have no family nearby, you may want to advertise for an older person who would like to be a surrogate granny for your children. Local newspapers have become quite used to carrying these adverts. Obviously it would be extremely unfair to do this just because you want emergency back-up. Find a granny if you think your children will benefit, and if you are prepared to make the practical and emotional commitment to helping the older person yourself. It may be a very occasional spin-off that you can expect some help in return, but you shouldn't rely on it.

> Thank goodness my children aren't ill very often – but I either call in the lady I used to employ in the village to come in and look after them at home, or else switch my working hours around, which, having proved myself reliable in the first twelve months, are now flexible within reason.

Building up Goodwill

Creating your network is one thing, but it won't become an effective support system unless you build up the goodwill to go with it. It may seem an odd thing to say, but this is very similar to accruing time off in lieu: if you actively help out other people whenever you can in whatever way you can, then when the time comes they are likely to be pleased to help you – and you will feel less bad about asking. That is what one woman who wrote to us found. She has two children of ten and nine and a three-month-old baby. During the 1985–86 teachers' strike she asked friends to help look after her school-age children, and as soon as she was on maternity leave she made a point of doing the same thing for them. Maternity leave doesn't come often enough for most of us to rely on it for paying back debts of honour, but there are other smaller ways that we can help out all the time.

Any mother, whether she goes out to work or not, will appreciate having her children taken off her hands for long or short periods occasionally. Don't wait till you need help from someone else before you offer to do this. From time to time, when it is no particular bother to you, you can suggest one of the following, or similar:

* Offer to take a child to school

If mornings aren't your worst time you can offer to pass by and pick up one or more children on your way to school or nursery. Most women will appreciate the extra time it gives them, even if they don't have to leave for work.

* Invite other children to stay the night

You don't need masses of space to take other children in occasionally: sleeping bags on the floor are good fun till quite a late age. You can free a friend to go out in the evening without having to pay a babysitter or rush back so that the babysitter can go home.

* Take other children on outings with you

Include a friend's child or children in a planned outing – to the zoo or the sea or a cartoon at the local cinema. Extra children are usually only a *little* extra trouble.

* Free someone for a whole day

Take all their children off their hands for a day at the weekend. You don't have to go anywhere special, they can just play with yours at home.

* Other practical favours

You may want to do something for a helpful neighbour who has no children, or whose children have left home. There are usually innumerable ways you can do this, depending on your neighbours' needs – whether it is feeding the cat and watering the plants while they are away and keeping an eye on the place, ferrying someone around if you have a car, or doing a large shop for someone while you do yours. You may be able to offer your professional skills: for instance, typing something for your neighbour, or helping her write a letter to the tax man or the DSS. Even offering a willing ear to a lonely neighbour will count in your favour.

Don't abuse the goodwill

Ration yourself when it comes to asking favours. Emergency help is different – but as soon as you can, make other arrangements. As one of our correspondents said:

> Neighbours have helped during crises in the past. We have a few friends/former 'staff' who are always willing to see what they can do. I'm usually anxious however not to use this help unless really necesary and then as sparingly as possible.

Another woman we interviewed agreed:

> I have a very good neighbour who keeps saying she would help, but I'm very reluctant to impose unless I absolutely have to – in an emergency. When we had to take our little girl to hospital and we had no one to babysit for her brother, she was over in ten minutes.

Goodwill can run out, and you can exasperate even members of your own family if you appear to take them for granted. It is particularly annoying for women who don't go out to work to be constantly used as a back-up service by you – as if you don't consider their time important. If you find yourself calling too frequently on someone for help, and you have no other alternative, then you should probably offer them some money for their services.

Paid Help

If you know no one at all who can help you out, or a crisis drags on and you have exhausted all your willing help, you may have to consider paying someone to help you out. This will usually be the case when your childcare/school arrangements are in irretrievable shambles, or your child is perhaps convalescing from an illness, and you feel you must resume normal working life. Even if you can't imagine yourself in this situation, it could happen – and it is as well to be prepared by finding out in advance about local agencies that you can call on if you ever need to (look under Nurses or Employment Agencies in your Yellow Pages). What these agencies will provide is a daily or weekly nanny or nurse to come and help out for the time being. This is going to be *very* expensive.

Your Child's Illness and Other Crises – and Your Job

> I take time off, or pretend to be ill myself. I can take my child into work if not too bad. Sometimes I take work home. On occasions I have persuaded my neighbour to look after a sick child for a bit, while essential lecture work is done.

Your children are bound to become ill at some time during your working life, particularly if you work from the time they are small. In the first few years children get all the infectious diseases going and after that even a robust child is likely to have one or two days stricken with the current flu or tummybug. Employers recognise this, even if some mothers would like to believe it will never happen.

But despite the fact that employers are so concerned about children's illnesses, the problem must be seen in perspective: unless you are very unlucky and your child is very sickly, comparatively few working days will be lost. Although it was not the prime purpose of our questionaire, a few interesting facts emerged (although they would have no statistical value). We asked how many days in the last year the mothers had taken off because their children were sick. Only a fifth had taken off any time at all; the longest time any of them had taken off was two weeks, and the average was three days!

One of our correspondents, Elizabeth Squires, is also a

personnel officer, and she put the employer's point of view:

> I have interviewed many working mothers. I am careful, I hope, not to discriminate by asking questions about how they will cope with children and work, but some women will volunteer information, such as, 'I can come to work now as my children are back at school and they are never ill.' I have asked what would happen if they were ill, and if faced by a blank look will feel they have not given the problems of work sufficent thought. One woman who said this had children who went down with chicken pox the week after she started the job! Employers will respect women who have contingency plans for emergencies. For example, one woman, who was hoping to enter work after a ten-year break, told me that all her neighbours had encouraged her and volunteered to look after her children. She got the job as she had the support she needed.

However, some women with children find that there is an automatic prejudice against them, and a feeling that they are going to be unreliable, often taking time off for children's illness. As a college lecturer wrote to us:

> Whereas male colleagues can skive off or be late in if they've had a heavy night – if you're not in your room you'll discover they're telling people you're not there because your child is ill! I've returned from committee meetings more than once to overhear that.

An operating theatre technician met a different prejudice:

> The health service seem to think that working mums should put the NHS before their children, and that it is okay for a neighbour or any other person that you can rope in to look after your child when he is ill so that you can go back to work. They don't seem to think about how it would affect the quality and safety aspects of the job I do. They honestly expected me to come in to work on the day my son had his operation. It does make me

very angry. My boss (a man with no children of his own) thinks I should put my job before my family. I have actually been told on one occasion to choose between the two. I ignored him! I have been told that I shouldn't have had a week's unpaid leave to be with my son when he was in hospital after his operation, and they hoped I wouldn't do it again. I said I would, if and when the situation arose again. I find that other women at work have encountered the same opposition.

The point is that this woman, and others who wrote to us with similar complaints, are in all respects conscientious and dedicated, proud of their careers and keen to maintain them. The only time they want and expect concessions is when their children are ill.

Julie Howell, who is a bank cashier feels strongly about this:

Allowances should be made by employers for sickness of children. At the moment I am having to hold back one week's holiday in case my son goes into hospital to have his tonsils out. I might end up holding that week for three or four years depending on how long the waiting list is, and end up taking holiday in January or February, just for the sake of using the week as it wasn't needed for the operation. I have to be scrupulous about this because it took me months to convince my old bank manager to take me on full time. He didn't believe in mothers working because of the threat of sudden days off due to illness of the children. I've found that working mums often have less time off than childless people.

Another woman who works as an assistant registrar for a family practitioner unit is as aware as Julie of having to be prepared in advance. She says, 'I always have extra time worked up in case of emergency.'

The heartening side of the story is that some enlightened employers are starting to allow extra leave for parents with sick children. And many women who wrote to us found some colleagues very understanding. Susan Lumb, who is a dental nurse receptionist, wrote:

I have found that co-workers with children are very helpful. We have usually been able to cover for each other in cases of illness or holidays. I find co-workers without children can be rather awkward. I think this is because they don't have to face the same problems as yourself. They don't seem to have the same sympathy and views as yourself.

Another woman, who is a social worker, wrote:

I have received much support from my work colleagues, all of whom are working parents. They have been very understanding and helpful when my child has suddenly become ill and I have had to take time off work unexpectedly. Unfortunately my husband's work colleagues are less understanding, consequently I must be the one to take annual leave to cover my child's sickness.

How your child's illness affects you

Illness is the crisis that makes you feel most torn: when your child is ill and needs you the desire to stay home is very powerful, unless you have other arrangements that you find satisfactory. Heather Lockett, a teacher with a three-year-old and a baby of seven months, describes feelings that are common:

My reaction at present when the children are ill is to panic. My father retires in about two years' time and is quite familiar and capable with children. Only then will I feel that I'm not living on a knife's edge. To quote my neighbour, also a working mother, a child's illness is 'a working mother's nightmare'. My eldest was ill about two months after I'd returned to work – fortunately part of the time was covered by half-term, but then I had no option other than to stay home. I felt completely torn, wrenched and an utter nervous wreck. But these are the choices we mothers have to make; there is no perfect solution, there are only ways to make the situation easier.

Those who have family to help are the luckiest. Even the best of friends has to be a saint to put up with someone else's sick child. Another teacher writes, 'Luckily my children haven't been ill in school-time, but I would stay at home if they were. My mother comes to stay with me from Ireland, November to February every year, and this covers all winter illnesses.'

> Coping with crises has been made easier by help from family. Work has been informed of the crisis a.s.a.p. We muddle through and think it can't last for ever.

To tell or not?

Many mothers seem to feel under some pressure never to let on at work when they are having problems at home for fear of being labelled 'unreliable mothers'. Anne Babb, talking about the time when she was a fashion consultant, admits:

> I made a secret pledge with myself that if my children were ever the reason for my not being able to get to work, I would never admit it. I would have made up almost any other excuse.

But Margaret Bluman advocates a different approach:

> People will always think the worst of working mothers, I'm afraid – even other mothers! It is probably better to be honest than to try to hide a problem. If you are going through a crisis – say your nanny has just quit – it is better to explain it to your employer, rather than bottling it up, feeling you have to cope without letting anyone know. The people around you will probably be aware anyway that you are not quite up to scratch at work. It seems to me that if you say it in the right way you are actually being more responsible. Explain it rationally: 'I'm sorry I was late this morning. My nanny has just quit, a friend of hers is taking over temporarily, but my child has to settle in. I'm looking for someone

else and everything should be sorted out in a week or so.' In other words what you are saying is: 'I am in control; I'm sorting this out; people have crises, but I'm handling it.' Now that should make your boss more prepared to put up with the problem: it's temporary, and you're not just being an incompetent, hopelessly out-of-control mother.

Strategies for Coping With Your Child's Illness

Sick or not sick?

The problems facing a working mother when sickness suddenly descends are: How bad is it? Does it warrant staying at home? Or (with an older child) is it genuine? As one teacher wrote, remembering when her children were younger:

> Of course, they're not ill at a set time and it was often quite difficult discovering at 7.00a.m. that they weren't well, and having to find someone by 8.00a.m. to look after them – I've dragged a few friends from their beds. Occasionally my husband took the odd day off to cope. I have rarely taken time off simply because it's really frowned on at school, as someone has to take your classes.

Faced with a child who has some vague symptoms most mothers wonder what to do. Usually you have to use your own instinct – quickly – you may have ten minutes or half an hour to decide whether to keep your child off and stay off yourself. With little ones it is usually fairly clear – they haven't got to the stage of pretending effectively. Older children, who may be going through a bad time at school, are often better at mimicking symptoms. It would be ideal if we all had a doctor next door or on the premises who could come at a second's notice to give an informed diagnosis. Failing that we have to do it ourselves.

> Luckily Lisa has been healthy, but on the few occasions she has felt unwell it has been extremely difficult to decide between staying at home with her or going into work. My husband has been able to take time off twice as he works a flexi-system and can have a day off once a month. As a teacher, someone else has to take over if I am not there. It is not as if the work will stay on my desk until I go back. Loyalties certainly conflict here.

What the doctor advises

A GP we consulted about this says that children showing obvious symptoms, such as raging fever, spots, vomiting, diarrhoea – and anything else that is clearly wrong, should of course be kept home – and it would be wise to call the doctor. You may want to check out any symptoms in your childcare book or medical encyclopaedia first.

When the symptoms are less obvious, but your child appears to feel unwell, the doctor believes strongly in using your instinct and your own knowledge of your child. Mothers (and doctors who know their patients well) usually sense when something is up, even when the symptoms are mild. A slightly higher than normal temperature is not an indication on its own that something is wrong, if your child is otherwise acting as normal: neither is a cough – if it is the only symptom. A substantial change in usual behaviour is far more reliable: lethargy and sluggishness, particularly, are often pointers to the fact that your child is coming down with something and should be kept in bed, particularly if combined with other apparently minor symptoms.

Don't let your anxiety to get to work block your instinctive knowledge of whether your child is truly off colour or not. Make time for a ten-minute cuddle, so that you give yourself a short period of calm to assess whether this is a 'real' illness or your child is trying it on. It also gives your child a chance to confess if something else is the matter. Even practised young actors tend to ham it up a bit if they are just hoping for a day off, rather different from the limp, less eager manner of the child who is genuinely sickening.

You have two main alternatives when faced with sudden sickness where the symptoms are not clear:

If in serious doubt, stay home for the day

If you strongly feel that your child is coming down with something then it is probably best if you keep your child at home and stay off work yourself. Usually a childminder or nursery won't take a child who is showing any symptoms at all.

Although suddenly calling in to say your child is sick is probably the single most irritating thing a working mother can do to her employer, you know, and your employer knows, that it is bound to happen from time to time. The fact that employers find it twice as irritating when your child is sick than when you are is what leads many working mother reluctantly to lie, giving themselves the symptoms of a twenty-four-hour something-or-other in the hope that it will all be sorted out by the next day.

Use your day wisely:

* Take your child to the doctor and find out what is wrong if possible, and how long your child may be laid up. Then make your plans.

* If you feel that you will have to stay with your child the entire time, your employer needs to know as soon as possible.

* Negotiate holiday or unpaid leave.

* If it is within your power, do what you can to make this period as painless as possible for your employer.

- Can you have work sent round to you at home?
- Is there a colleague who has previously agreed to cover for you in such an emergency?
- Can you arrange a temp or stand-in for yourself?

* If you plan to go back to work the next day you must find someone else to look after your child.
    - Can a member of your family stand in, even if it means coming from another part of the country?
    - Is there a friend or neighbour who will be prepared to help out?
    - If neither of these is possible can you quickly arrange paid help?

Continue as normal

If you have a hunch that there is nothing very much wrong with your child, or that he or she is malingering, you may want to take the chance and send the child to school/minder, or whatever, anyway. You may find yourself the most unpopular mother around if it turns out that your child has spread some violent germ; or you may feel a guilty heel if you get a phonecall in the middle of the day telling you that your child is worse and has to be collected. But the chances are that your hunch is right. If it turns out that you were wrong, then you will have to keep your child and yourself home the next day and will have to make plans as outlined above.

> I have been called away from work twice, and both times I was allowed to leave within minutes of receiving the phonecall.

Severe illness

If your child is very ill, or having an operation or otherwise hospitalised, your priorities are clearly set out for you. In these circumstances your job is going to look far less important during the critical patch, and you will almost certainly put your child first. As one woman wrote, 'When he was in hospital for a few days I slept at the hospital and stayed the whole time.'

You may be allowed, under your firm's union or staff agreement, to take off some paid or unpaid time as 'compassionate leave', which should cover the grave illness of a child.

The operating theatre technician quoted earlier wrote:

> During the period of my son's operation, I had four weeks off work (two weeks holiday, two weeks unpaid leave) after that I was visiting him during my lunch breaks and after work, This went on for the four months he was in hospital. VERY TIRING! After he came home, my husband had two weeks holiday to be with him before he went back to school.

Another woman who has a very good part time job in publishing told us:

> When my daughter started having fits we were terribly worried because they said it could be epilepsy. My husband said, 'You may have to give up your job' – and yes, I didn't even have to think about it, of course I would have done. Miraculously though, it went as quickly as it came.

Mild but lengthy illness

If your child is recuperating and getting better by the day, or is in quarantine, or has a condition that drags on and which means he or she can't go to nursery/childminder/school, you are presented with a different difficulty. You probably feel that your job will be threatened unless you return to work. One teacher who lives in Scotland wrote to us about her dilemma:

When my eldest daughter was ten she was off school for five months which was really difficult. After months of uncertainty she was diagnosed as having asthma. My parents came up from another part of Scotland and I had friends look after her. We got by, but I felt dreadfully guilty, especially when I had to take her to a friend's house when she was ill. Even more guilty when the doctor had to be given instructions to go somewhere other than home! As it lasted so long I really had a tremendous amount of pressure (or it felt like pressure) on me to give up working, but I was the main wage-earner and it would have meant selling up our house. My husband, possibly from optimism, kept thinking it would be over soon and when it boiled down to it he wasn't prepared to give up working.

The other problem is that if you have exhausted the goodwill of family and friends you may only have the option of paid help, which you may not be able to afford over a long period of time. You may want to explore the options of going part-time if possible, or rearranging your hours so that you can stagger care with a partner.

Regular illness

This could well be the hardest situation of all to cope with. A sickly child can be an almost intolerable strain, particularly when worry for your child is coupled with fear for your job – especially if your work is important to you or vital for financial security. Again, our poor operating theatre technician had this problem:

If the youngest boy is ill, which has been very regular in the past, my husband or I have taken time off work to look after him. I have, in the past, been penalised at work for asking for unpaid leave to look after him, so I have found (and so have others) that I must say that I am ill. (In fact to tell lies, which I don't like doing.) My husband now has an arrangement with his company to cope with my son's illnesses. The NHS, nevertheless, still think children don't need their mums when they are ill.

Malingering

If your child often wakes up with symptoms of illness that oblige you to take a day off but which turn out to be nothing at all, this is possibly not a medical issue. If you suspect your child is malingering it could mean problems with the childcarer/school, or perhaps your child is under stress in other ways or feels neglected by you. Clearly you must get to the bottom of this problem. Eliminate the possibilities one by one: talk seriously to the school or whoever has your child during the day, and try to find out gently from your child if there is any other cause.

A child with no real physical symptoms who still refuses to be budged, or is desperately miserable if forced, should be treated like any other sick child, and you should make arrangements for his or her care. It is important, however, to spend time sorting out the fundamental problem. Your doctor or school may be able to refer you to someone experienced in dealing with children who persistently refuse school.

Leaving your child alone

> If the children [aged eleven, thirteen and fifteen] are ill they stay on their own at home and I visit them at lunchtime.

You may decide that you have no alternative but to leave older children at home alone, particularly if there is nothing seriously wrong with them. We can't suggest the 'right' age to do this: you will know when you feel it is all right.

One mother of young teenagers told us:

> When they are really ill I nurse them. I often take care of

them in the morning and go to work in the afternoon. I'd find it difficult to take the whole day off. When you are ill the afternoon is always less bad than the morning. I leave them fed, propped up in bed, with plenty of things to do.

Some parents feel that a bedridden or otherwise subdued child is even safer left alone than a healthy, energetic one! Most of the points in *Alone in the House* (in the chapter on *School-age Children*) apply here, though there are a few things that are more important at this time:

* Make sure your child is near a phone, even if this means moving him or her to your bed, or making a bed on the sitting room sofa.

* Give your child a list of all important phone numbers, including where to contact you, as well as the doctor's surgery and a near neighbour for emergencies.

* Try to get someone to look in during the day. If you or your partner can do it that is ideal, if not, see if you can find a neighbour or friend to do it for you – this should not be particularly arduous for a non-family member, as it just requires a few minutes and a little friendly reassurance, as well as peace of mind for you.

* Phone regularly throughout the day yourself – no news is not necessarily good news in this situation. If there is no reply you will want to find out why pretty quickly.

* Make sure there is easy-to-eat food available, such as sandwiches and fruit – you don't want your child padding around barefoot in the kitchen or groggily starting to prepare a meal.

* Similarly, make sure that your child has all the entertainment necessary: books, comics or magazines – perhaps the television, radio or other music player,

even if it means lugging them away from their usual position. It might seem like spoiling, but if bedrest is the most beneficial for your child, you don't want him or her wandering round the house out of boredom.

* Make sure that there is a safe source of heat: central heating is ideal, but failing that, a fixed and well guarded electric or gas fire is safer than a portable fire that your child might position dangerously.

Accidents

Accidents don't really warrant a different approach from other illnesses, but the shock impact on the children and you is often greater, and you will almost always decide to take time off yourself to cope with the immediate crisis and the aftermath. Susan Lumb's three children have obviously had their fair share of accidents, because she is so matter-of-fact about it:

> In crisis situations which involve casualty visits I usually go, because I am not affected by blood, stitches, broken limbs, but my husband can be a bit squeamish. I can cope better with their pain, because my husband gets upset and frustrated when he cannot help them.

A local government officer wrote to us about her experience:

> The worst crisis I had was when my son, then aged twelve, trapped his hand in railings at school and was rushed up to the nearby hospital, bleeding, with his sister. School rang the office but I had taken the afternoon off to go to the hairdressers! My colleague and friend phoned the hairdressers and I ran through the town with wet hair to the hospital.

Moral: if you can, leave a message at work when you have to go out saying where you can be reached in an emergency:

I have to go out to lunch often for work, but my co-workers know I always write where I'm going in the diary on my desk.

Your Own Illness

If you are ill yourself then you have a different set of problems. It is not too bad if the illness is mild (although from our experience it seems that working mothers are far less likely than other women to take time off from work unless they feel really terrible). You may wish to keep an under-five at home with you in these circumstances. Clearly the problems facing you depend very much on the nature and seriousness of your illness, whether you are hospitalised, the age and number of your children, whether you have a partner or close family, and the kind of arrangements you had made for your child before you were ill. The possible permutations are too numerous for us to deal with sensibly here: we simply urge you to give this situation some thought while you are healthy, and to devise a general plan of action just in case. One thing is certain – this particular crisis draws most sympathy and support even from unlikely areas, people you wouldn't dream of asking for help in normal circumstances may offer themselves voluntarily.

Other Crises

During the teachers' strike a childminder has had them for lunch, or my husband has been home. There was one day when the childminder could not have them, so the children lost the day from school and went to their grandparents.

Crises that have nothing to do with illness or accidents

crop up from time to time. Most of these simply call on your organisational ability and are a test of your contingency plans. Your emotions (apart from ones of panic) are rarely engaged – unless your child has suffered an upsetting experience, as was the case with Mrs Bartley, who works as a secretary in a technical college:

> My youngest son once had an awful experience at school. While the teacher was out of the classroom some boys fooling around hung him out of the window by his legs (two floors up). He was very upset and frightened and ran out of school and home. He rang me at work and told me what had happened. I told him to stay quietly at home and I rang the school. At that time they were unaware he had left. I explained my problem at work and they let me leave early. I called the school to see the teachers and they were very upset that it had happened. The boys involved were made to apologise and the class sent him a card to say they were sorry.

The odd-day crisis

Sometimes something happens that means you have to take the odd day or half-day off work at a moment's notice – your child phones to say that the school has been closed because the central heating broke down, and the temperature has dropped below the legal minimum, for instance. Like sudden sickness, there is not much you can do about it except apologise at work and sort out whatever it is as quickly as possible. A crisis at the other end of the day – when something prevents you getting to pick up your child in time, or the arrangements go wrong in some other way is also a possibility. Rosemary Kirk has constant trouble with her car:

> I have locked my keys in the car four times and have had wheels coming off it at a critical moment – but I have always managed to contact someone to help with

the children. My neighbours are always there in a crisis, and do help.

Marie Burke describes every mother's nightmare:

> There was once a breakdown in communication between myself and the childminder resulting in my son being left at the school gates. Luckily, his teacher spotted him and looked after him – nothing can describe the horror and guilt I felt.

The crisis that persists

Sometimes the crisis looks never-ending – such as the situation mentioned earlier when schools affected by the 1985-86 teachers' strike turned children out at lunchtime, or like this unfortunate woman's experience:

> I thought that I had everything so well organised: a marvellous childminder who took my daughter early in the morning, and the mother of one of the other children who would take her home with her if I happened to be late in the evening. I couldn't imagine a situation that could arise that I wouldn't be able to cope with. But one night a gunman barricaded himself in with a woman hostage in the square where my childminder lived and the whole square was cordoned off by police and emergency services! For the length of the siege I had to make alternative plans. For the first two days my employer allowed me to bring my daughter in, but we all realised that an office was no place at all for a lively three-year-old, however well-behaved. I found a private nursery that was prepared to take her, but I don't drive and it was miles away, and closed at 3.30, so that was only possible for a few days. I kept expecting the siege to end! I then had to prevail on the goodwill of family and friends to take my daughter for an odd day each, until everyone was getting so fed up that I arranged to take some unpaid leave – but luckily the siege ended as I was about to take it – more that two weeks after it started.

Occasionally you may be able to bring your child into work with you, as this woman did. But the success of that depends very much on the age of your child and your working situation. This can never be more than a short-term solution anyway.

Another possible crisis is your childcarer – childminder or nanny – becoming ill, or suddenly giving notice. Dealing with these kinds of crises involves the same pattern as dealing with illness: use the help of willing people if you can and need to – but sparingly – then use the time you gain to make alternative plans until the crisis is past.

CHAPTER 14

Your Home and Your Partner

Housework

In our questionnaire we asked working mothers for their tips on how to cope with the house on top of everything else. One of our correspondents ticked us off: 'I find your request for 'tips for working mothers' a little irritating – why not "tips for working parents"?' Yes, quite! The sad fact is that many women do not have partners who pull their weight, and even when the man is willing and helpful it is usually the woman who oversees, delegates and takes ultimate responsibility. As this book is essentially practical rather than campaigning, we are aiming this chapter at the average working mother who has the day-to-day running of the home to think about as well as everything else. We offer all our support and good wishes to those of you who can change this in your own home, and we believe that more of us can and will do so. But meanwhile there is the ironing to be done . . .

A full-time secondary school teacher, with two children of thirteen and fifteen, who lives in Scotland, describes a feeling that many of us know well:

> It's the small things that become difficult. I always write everything down – shopping lists, things to do. I'm

pretty good at doing lots of things at once, although I sometimes stand in the middle and swear – especially when the house is really grubby. Sunday is a bad day for this. If I'm not careful I could spend all weekend just doing housework. Actually most things function fairly well unless I'm not feeling well or am especially busy (i.e. when I'm marking exam papers). Home ends up filthy and meals are haphazard.

Working mothers seem to be divided into those who need the house to look as good as if they were at home all day, and those who believe it doesn't matter. Although we don't address both types separately, we do realise that they truly feel differently about the issue.

We think it is important to get away from the pressure of the Superwoman image, which makes working mothers feel guilty if they are not doing everything perfectly. In fact, most of our working mothers did not seem to mind if their houses were less perfect than those of the women next door: all the other calls on their time are ultimately more important.

A doctor who works full time, including some Saturdays, and has two little girls aged one and four, has this to say:

> Children are important – much more than a 'spick and span' house. I am fortunate enough to have a fairly 'laid-back' attitude to housework. An untidy house, if basically clean and hygienic, doesn't bother me. We expect friends, callers, relatives, to take us as they find us and feel that people are by no means made less welcome if they have to shift a ton of Lego off a chair before they can sit down!

Betty Shepherd, who works full time as a senior industrial training advisor and has one four-year-old, speaks for many when she says:

> You can't be brilliant at your job, be a super mum and be a super housewife (no more than your husband can do a super job, be a brilliant car mechanic and

competent plumber). I am good at my job, I am a good mother – and housework comes last: I clean once a week, do the washing every evening, iron once a week. My house is clean and reasonably tidy (lived-in).

A London civil servant agrees:

Just close your eyes and ignore the mess in your place – because it's going to get in a mess. It's more important to spend time with your child and give the attention you need to your job than to have the place look spotless. You've got to sort out your priorities and stick to them.

Another civil servant, mother of two pre-schoolers, says the same:

I don't do much around the house. It gets dirty. I decided I just couldn't cope with household things as well as work and children. Something has to go, and it's the house that goes!

Every woman has her own priorities so far as housework is concerned. As another woman says, 'As long as the kitchen is clean, forget about the dust in the house.' And Jane Parkin, mother of two girls aged seven and five, points out: 'The house won't get so dirty when you're out all day!'

However it is clear from our correspondence that some women feel miserable if they sit down at the end of the day in a house that is messy or less than clean. They feel guilty and dissatisfied in this situation and don't mind the extra work involved in keeping things perfect.

Wendy Wass takes pride in the fact that although she works full time as a kitchen assistant, and has three teenage children living at home, she manages to do everything she wants. She says:

Throughout the fifteen years I have been working I have managed to keep things going as normal as well as doing all the catering for my daughter's wedding (200 guests) and my son's eighteenth birthday fancy-dress party (I also made a couple of the costumes). My house is as clean and tidy as the next person's and I also knit and bake (sometimes!). I would like more time to myself, but really don't know what people who are at home all day do with themselves.

This is echoed by Anneliese Young, a full-time social worker with two children aged four and three:

I think if I stopped work I would do no more than I do now except I would have more time to do it. I have no family locally, and I think that after about two to six months at home I would be bored stiff. I need the challenge of juggling my time, with work, interests, home and children.

Later on she sets out her cleaning routine, which is marvellously efficient:

I tend to do one room very thoroughly and just dust and hoover the rest. Then another room. So eventually you know the whole house gets done – and I include the roof space and garage in this!

Getting organised

Best tip – be as organised as possible without being inflexible. Never leave something until morning. Also, leave clearing up until child is in bed, then spend time doing all the little jobs before you sit down to relax; otherwise you won't want to get up again. Sometimes leave ironing until another day if you are tired – but don't let things pile up – it will only look worse than it is. Have at least one hour for yourself to do anything you want – or nothing if you want!

Organisation is most important when time is at a premium, whether you are houseproud or simply concerned to get the minimum of chores done. A full-time primary school teacher, with a two-year-old and a baby of fourteen months, says:

> The best way to cope with work and home, I find, is to have a fairly strict routine and never get behind, otherwise everything could crash down on top of you.

Even if the idea of everything crashing down around your ears seems rather dramatic, without a routine many women find that chores visibly building up is more stressful than the work involved in keeping them at bay.

Your priorities

How you organise yourself – and any others who help – depends very much on what essential things need to be done on a daily, weekly and monthly basis, and what extras you consider to be important. It makes sense to be brutal about non-essential chores and firmly decide that you are not going to do them rather than make a vague plan to tackle them when you have time.

* *Define the problem*

List the jobs that have to be done and see how they can slot into your timetable. Write down everything including the most obvious, such as cooking and washing up. Seeing them written down may make you realise if you are being over-ambitious, and you can decide which chores can go.

* *Cut corners*

Look at the essential items you are left with, and see if you can find ways of making things easier for yourself. For instance, everyone has to be fed each day, but you may decide to make simple meals using convenience foods, or no-cook menus when it is appropriate – or be super-organised and fill the freezer with the products of one hot day in the kitchen. The washing up has to be done, but dishes rinsed in hot water dry naturally (and more hygienically) if left to drain.

*   Using lists

Lists, as many mothers have discovered, are not only invaluable for sorting out your priorities, but also very useful on a day-to-day basis.

> I have a never-ending list on which I write jobs to be done, plus other items, such as birthday presents to be bought, items needed from shops etc, and I cross them off when done/bought.

Another woman says, 'Keep a notebook with things to do, buy, etc.

> Have a stock of all-purpose children's birthday cards and presents. People have a habit of sending birthday invitations at short notice!

Whenever you get into a state because there are too many things to do and too little time to do them, a list helps to concentrate the mind and also helps to take the edge off panic:

> Sometimes I find myself lying in bed unable to sleep because everything I have to do is running through my mind, complicated by worries about the state of the world! I find that writing a list never fails, because magically once the things are down on paper it is as if I am allowed to stop thinking about them. I write *everything* down, even if the main worry of the day is nuclear war! It may be things to do with work the next day, a book I meant to return, a dentist appointment to be made, or what I am going to cook when friends come on Friday. Once I've written them down in any old order, I may make a new list. If there are a lot of practical things to be done I schedule them for next day or later in the week. Even when there is nothing I can do about the items on my list I find that once on the paper they are off my mind.

Organising the day

Most people find that a daily routine emerges naturally. To see how some of our working mothers organise their day, turn to the Appendix for the schedules they sent us.

It certainly helps if most things happen at roughly the same time each day, as it is then easier to deal with the hiccups and minor emergencies that often crop up.

On a daily basis most of us have to:

* Offer breakfast and an evening meal.

* Make sure that the resulting washing up is done.

* Organise clean clothes for ourselves and children – and possibly partner.

* Tidy away the litter of the day.

* Make beds.

It is almost too obvious to state that these high priority duties can take as long as you let them. On a bad day a harassed and rebellious mother can probably get away with doing none of these things – and a determined woman can delegate all or some of them!

On the other hand, elaborate or difficult-to-prepare meals can take ages, and the kitchen may well need a mammoth clear-up afterwards. Similarly, if what everyone is wearing is your responsibility, and the clothes need much ironing, hand-washing, brushing down, polishing, etc, this can use up valuable evening rest time or precious early morning minutes. If everyone is 'allowed' to be messy, and you are the one who has to put things back into order, tidying round can become a daily nightmare.

Streamlining meal preparation, at least during the week, and intelligently reducing the other tasks to the minimum may need some thought, but it can be done.

Some women also feel it is essential every day to:

* Clean bathroom and kitchen.
* Vacuum carpets.
* Do some washing.
* Dust or clean other rooms.
* Prepare packed lunches.

If you can slot all or some of these chores in without feeling harassed and over-tired, that is fine. Extra cleaning during the week certainly keeps down the pile of jobs to be done.

If, however, you are working your way through extra jobs in an exhausted fashion, remember that you DON'T HAVE TO DO THEM. Many mothers don't, and neither they nor their families suffer because of it.

Your best time

> I find it's better to wash the breakfast dishes before leaving the house – nothing is more soul-destroying than cleaning up Weetabix at 5.00p.m.! I get Paul and myself dressed and washed before breakfast – I find this saves a last minute panic to get ready and we can have a more relaxed breakfast. I always prepare clothes, nappies, etc the night before – again to avoid rushing in the morning.

The less you feel you have to do every day, the more fluid you can be about when it is done. However it is worth thinking about whether morning or evening is your best time. A morning person can – as many of the women who wrote to us do – get up early and have most of the day's duties out of the way before the rush for work, school and so on. There's no reason why you shouldn't tidy up from the night before, wash up, or make preparations for the evening meal before breakfast, if that is when you are at your best.

If you have surplus energy in the evening, and don't

wind down until after the evening meal, you may prefer to cram what you have to do in the hour or so immediately after arriving home, or after the kids are in bed, if you have a second energy spurt at that time. One divorced mother with two children under five advocates, 'Lay out everyone's clothes the night before so there is not a scramble in the morning.'

Most mothers of young children find that there is *no* time when they are feeling energetic – it tends to divide into times when they are not *too* exhausted, and times when they couldn't possibly raise themselves from a chair! Working mothers inevitably become used to working through tired periods, and usually relish the moment they can flop into bed.

Discovering a routine that suits you

> I try to organise my two roles to run smoothly by preparing things the evening before. I bulk shop fortnightly and stock my freezer every six to eight weeks. I spend one day at the weekend on a good house-cleaning exercise and spend the other day doing various things with my husband and children.

If you are a new mother, perhaps fairly recently in charge of a household – and just coming to grips with combining all of this with work – it may take a while for you to find the best way of using your time. No one can tell you what that should be.

A farm secretary, with a four-year-old son wrote and told us that she needs a stricter routine on the days that she works:

> I decide the night before what I am wearing the next day and what my son is wearing, also what we will eat for tea, in case it needs taking out of the freezer. There isn't time to dither about these things in the mornings. I always do what is scheduled to be done on any

401

particular day – there's no point in procrastination. There is another quota of jobs scheduled for the morrow.

Another mother, who is pregnant, and has a two-year-old boy, says:

> I find it's better to keep on top of the housework by doing something each night, otherwise weekends are just spent cleaning up the week's mess.

Some women with large families have each day scheduled with military precision, as a glance at one of the typical working days in the Appendix shows.

Less organised women can also be quite happy with more slapdash systems that work equally well for them:

> I usually live in an untidy house. I just don't see dust, and I'm not too bothered if the carpet needs hoovering, the kitchen floor needs washing or the bathroom is overdue for a good going over. My rest, time with my daughter, generally unwinding – all these things seem much more important. But when I invite friends round for a meal I look at everything with a fresh eye and have a couple of days madly cleaning and scrubbing before they arrive. It's the only thing that gets me going on housework, and as I entertain fairly regularly it keeps the worst of it down.

Weekly or monthly chores

Some of the more organised mothers who wrote to us strongly urge fixing days and times to do the jobs that are not part of the daily routine. Weekends are the obvious time, though women whose work allows them to work extra hours and then take a day or half a day midweek every so often prefer to do outstanding chores then. Other women advocate an 'extra' chore a day on top of the regular ones.

One woman who wrote to us lives in Manchester, works full time and is divorced, with two daughters of five and two. Two evenings a week she works in a bar, and is also studying for an extra diploma. She says:

> Set housekeeping to a schedule to keep on top of work. For example, Fridays – bed-changing/washing, Saturday – upstairs thoroughly cleaned, Mondays – more washing, and so on.

A part-time midwife with a four-year-old daughter says:

> I have a big clean-up every two weeks or so when I have a day off, and do a window or venetian blind every week so things don't pile up on me.

Another woman, with two teenage children, recommends scheduling the kinds of jobs that tend to be put off, 'Try to organise one evening to do all bill paying, letter writing etc. It gets it over with.'

Certainly, anything you hate doing but that you can't ignore may need to be put into your diary or programme for the week. One woman, with a daughter of nineteen and a son of seventeen, who is divorced and works full time as a systems analyst for the civil service, reaffirms what the others say, 'Routine is important. Set days and times to do various chores, such as ironing and grass-cutting.'

Another woman wrote, 'I have a blitz whenever things look bad. It may only be once a month, on a Saturday, and then I rope in anyone I can to help.'

The magic of tidiness

> Monday to Friday when I'm working I concentrate on washing, ironing and doing a good evening meal and just flick quickly through the housework. Weekends you can clean thoroughly. There's no one in the house on weekdays anyway so things stay pretty tidy. Then I

think everyone, children included, should help a little every day. As I'm working to provide extras for everyone it's only fair.

Those of us who are least houseproud have found that when the place is tidy nothing else seems so bad. One mother who counsels doing as little housework as possible during the week emphasises that tidiness is essential – and that all members of the household should be drilled to do their bit. Even very small children can be encouraged to put their own toys away.

Another woman says, 'I try to have a place for everything (in theory at least) so that less time is spent tidying up.'

Sheila Robertson, who has a seventeen-month-old baby and is a full-time civil servant, is of the same mind. 'Tidy up often, it saves time and the house looks better (even if dusting hasn't been done).' She suggests putting out fresh flowers, which 'distract attention from dust and make the house look better'.

This philosophy is similar to that of another woman, who has brought up seven children:

Cleaning – I did as best I could but never let it be the be all and end all. People take me as they find me, we have lots of friends so they must not mind. And as my granny used to say, 'If the hearth's clean the rest doesn't look so bad' – and it's true, it doesn't.

Involving the family

We have looked at this in more detail in the chapter *School-age Children* but it is relevant to mention it again here. If you don't want to be the family slave when your children grow up it is worth training them to help when they are young, and/or giving each child a regular job or two to do. Most women who had children who helped mentioned meal-time chores, such as washing up, wiping, setting and clearing the table – but there is no reason why more of the chores shouldn't be delegated. Others said that having duvets meant that even young children could make their own beds and start to become responsible for their bedrooms.

One woman, with children of nineteen and seventeen, found that it had worked in her case to make chores such as shopping into family outings, as 'it is useful training for the children.'

Other mothers felt that it was enough for their children to look after themselves and their own clothes and rooms – anything more sometimes seemed more trouble than it was worth:

> The girls [thirteen and fifteen], over the years, have become quite independent. Perhaps they could help in the house more but it was often easier and still is to do things myself! I get it done when I want it done.

Betty Shepherd was determined to make her child responsible for things from an early age:

> My daughter [four] will tidy up before going to bed, can clean her own shoes and dress herself, though she isn't left alone to do these things.

Some women are so used to doing everything for their children that even the tiniest show of independence from them seems like a triumph. One woman proudly wrote:

> I am delighted to say my son no longer allows me to do his cornflakes as I never get the amount of milk just right. That is what I call successful training.

It turned out that her son was over fifteen!

We did hear of one woman who staged a rebellion when no one in the house would help with the washing. She strung up washing lines around the house and pegged up the dirty clothes, including cheesy socks, because she had heard this had worked for someone else. Her family were highly amused. But she wasn't, when two days went by and the things remained on the lines, while her family – seemingly oblivious – cheerfully ducked around them. Of course she ended up taking them all down and doing the washing as usual. The only drastic ploy that invariably seems to work with an untidy family is to pick up all mess and deposit it in black plastic rubbish bags which you propose to leave out for the dustmen. Mind you, the effect is only short-term: they'll sort through them and bear things off – but it rarely makes them tidier.

Machines

On the questionnaire we asked which labour-saving domestic machines our respondents would not be without. The answers showed that whatever you had been able to afford soon seemed indispensable. This was a typical comment from one of the mums who had everything:

> I have a washing machine, tumble drier and space to hang up clothes in a utility room inside. Washing can then be done any hour of the day – even overnight. My dishwasher is a real blessing. The microwave is more or less essential as meals can be dug out of the freezer and dished up with minimum of effort.

Many mothers made the point that working gave them enough extra money to be able to invest in one or more machines that made their lives easier. The washing machine was usually top of every mother's list.

Ironing

Everyone hates ironing it seems. No one had a good word to say for this chore: 'My weekly nightmare is getting clothes dried and then ironed.' Whatever can be done to get round it is seen as a bonus. Here are some tips:

I use the tumble dryer rather a lot as it saves time hanging out washing and ironing. I think I've just had to accept that my household running costs are perhaps higher because of using the tumble dryer.

Hazel Coates says:

I use drip-dry shirts for my husband – cuts down on ironing. If T-shirts and blouses are hung out carefully they can be folded without ironing. Tumble drying also helps here. I iron hankies, teatowels and jeans only!

If you don't believe in ironing hankies, teatowels or jeans either (as many don't) then perhaps your ironing problems are solved forever. Wendy Wass has some more tips:

I never do any unnecessary ironing. Everything is smoothed and folded as soon as it comes off the line. This cuts ironing by half. If you fold net curtains, duvet covers and sheets before you put them in the washer they will not need ironing. A friend told me about the folding tip. I used to be fanatical about ironing and took some convincing. Now I'm convinced! Try it!

Editorial note: this worked in Sarah's washing machine, but not in Marianne's washing machine/tumble dryer!

Cleaners

The mothers who can afford it often hire a cleaner, and everyone who did so remarked that it was an essential extra. Not all the mothers who hired a cleaner earned a lot of money, but they decided that spending money like this was not a luxury.

* Someone to clean the house is a must (especially if you have more than one child). I pay someone for five hours (spread over two mornings) and it's lovely coming home to a clean house.

* We feel it is very worthwhile paying someone to clean the house – hoover, dust, bathroom, loos and kitchen floor – two mornings per week.

* A super imaginative go-ahead lady comes two mornings a week and does basic cleaning and does it quite well. We have a not-too-big, easily maintained house. It's not weighed down with objets d'art or anything that would make maintenance more trying. Mrs R. also does basic ironing, shirts, teatowels, etc. I am only too aware that, in contrast to other mums who work, I am in a very advantageous position to be able to pay for good domestic help.

* I've made it a rule with myself not to do housework and only the minimum of cooking during the kids waking hours. Shopping is done late night once a month, meals cooked the evening before. I have a wonderful cleaner who does nearly all the chores. It's *worth* the money without a doubt. If I could find someone to do the ironing I would! My whole philosophy is to make things as smooth and organised for us all as I can, and that must mean help from machines and people like my cleaner.

The sense of relief that comes through in what these women say shows that if you can afford it, and if you can find someone to do it, hiring a cleaner may be the single most helpful thing that money can buy for you.

Labour-saving Checklist

Laundry

* Washing little and often can keep laundry from piling up

* Using a tumble dryer and folding laundry immediately when dry, or careful hanging out, saves on ironing.

Beds

* Duvets take the labour out of bed-making, especially if teamed with fitted bottom sheets; but duvet covers are an effort to change. To save washing, wash only half as often as pillowcases and bottom sheets and turn the duvet over. Or use a top sheet under the duvet.

* Use non-iron sheets.

Washing dishes

* Leave dishes to drain (get a large dishrack) – it saves on drying up. It is also more hygienic than teatowels.

* Wash up as you go along, and train your family to do the same. It will prevent mounds of washing up in the sink. Pots and pans are easier to clean when they have just been used, before fat has congealed and scraps got stuck.

* Alternatively, run water into any pots that you can't wash immediately.

Clothes

* A stitch in time saves nine! But most working mothers don't darn socks – they buy new ones. One advantage of working!

* Put out clothes for the family the night before. It will save last-minute morning panics.

* Choose clothes that don't need ironing where possible; T-shirts and jerseys, instead of shirts and blouses.

Cleaning

* Keep cleaning materials to hand where you need them, for example a sponge and cream cleanser in the bathroom, so you can give the sink and loo a quick wipe while you are in there anyway.

* Keep a bottle of inexpensive supermarket bubblebath by the bath, and get everyone to use a drop or two in their bath: this won't give bubbles, but will stop a ring from forming, and make it easier to clean.

Shopping and Food

Shopping for clothes

Shopping for clothes for yourself and your family from mail-order catalogues can take the slog and headache out of shopping, if you consider it a chore. It will also help you budget more carefully, and avoid impulse buying.

Food shopping

Food shopping and meal preparation take up a large amount of every mother's time. 'What shall I give them for dinner?' is a common cry, and for some women it is the most annoying of the daily problems. When you are working you have to decide how you are going to slot everything in.

> In order to keep Saturdays fairly free for myself and for the kids we try to shop on a Wednesday evening – I make out shopping list and husband comes home via supermarket.

The big shop

Most organised women suggest a regular shopping trip in which the bulk of the shopping, apart from perishables, is done.

If you have a car and are able to plan in advance you may want to do a large monthly/fortnightly shop. Some women with large freezers and lots of storage space even shop quarterly for certain items – bulk buying such things as toilet rolls, frozen meat and tinned tomatoes. This is not only convenient, it can also work out much cheaper.

* If you have a good co-operative relationship with other working mothers – or even stay-at-home mothers – you may want to organise a shopping rota for these kind of items. You can split a big bulk-buy with the other women involved.

However, although it might save money in the long run, some women just haven't got the money to lay out in the first place for a mammoth shopping expedition. Most women shop once a week, and get in most of the things they need – though they may have to top up during the week. Obviously the longer you buy in advance the more carefully you have to plan the menus – at least for the main ingredients.

* Go to the same supermarket every week, so that you get used to the layout and can whip round without wasting time looking for items on your list and being tempted by other things which are not on your list.

Shopping daily

Some people don't have a car or access to one, or don't like planning ahead, or find that they simply can't:

> Whenever I'm super-organised and plan and buy for all the week's meals in advance I find that I really don't fancy them when it comes to it. I prefer the lunchtime dash of getting tonight's ingredients according to what fancy takes me. I only get in weekly the things I know we'll need at some point: lots of potatoes, pasta, rice, tinned tomatoes, butter, that sort of thing – and anything we are out of like loo rolls, washing up liquid, oil.

If trying to plan ahead seems like just one more problem you can't cope with, don't be intimidated by the formidably well-organised people who bulk-buy. If it is easier for you to shop once a day (and even pop out for the odd thing at the late-closing corner shop) then that's fine. Don't waste time feeling guilty about it or totting up what you might have saved if you'd been more organised. The main rule that working mothers must live by is 'Do whatever comes easiest.'

This woman, who lives in Preston, usually manages to shop fortnightly, but then finds she has forgotten vital things. She agrees. 'Don't worry if you have to pay more by using "corner" shops between fortnightly big shops.'

A woman who lives in the north of Scotland says: 'I have my meat and vegetables/fruit delivered (perhaps more expensive but easier).'

Cooking

> I tend to be an organised person – in everything – and this certainly helps. I find I take extra things on gradually as I learn to cope more – but you have to know your own limits and say no occasionally. I love baking but tend to bake large amounts at a time and freeze.

For some women cooking is a joy and a relaxation; time spent doing it is not grudged. For others, cooking for a family has the quality of nightmare: utterly relentless, almost thankless, creating vast amounts of work and mess, yet the fruits of toil are gone in a flash.

Again, many mothers advocate careful planning. Sometimes just *knowing* what you are going to cook because you have decided a few days in advance helps. If it is one of your regular dishes you can do it on automatic.

A woman, who lives in Preston with her husband and small baby, says:

> I feel that the essence of being a working mum is to try and plan ahead and be organised. If I do this I can quite easily cope with the day-to-day events. For instance, planning weekday meals on weekends. Getting everything ready the night before so you just have to concentrate on getting up and going in the morning.

Cooking in advance is also a popular notion, especially for those with freezers. Sheila Robertson, a full-time civil servant who lives in Liverpool with her husband and seventeen-month-old baby says:

> Spend some time each week/month preparing dishes for the freezer. That way you don't always have to start work as soon as you come in every night. Monday is an especially good night to have something already prepared.

A mother of two teenagers, who lives in Sheffield and works full time in a hospital is of the same mind: 'Use the freezer to prepare meals in bulk and to store bread, veg, etc.'

But you don't have to have a freezer to cook ahead. An ordinary fridge will take some pre-prepared meals or part-meals for the week. A divorced mother of two children aged six and fourteen, who works full time writes:

> I'm always one day ahead with meals, but also keep soup or an easy meal in case they have to make it themselves if I have to work late.

413

Another divorced mother who works full time and has children aged five and two, prepares casseroles in advance:

> **We tend to eat a lot of casseroles on school days. I put food on the timer in the oven so that it is ready for when we get home.**

Some things to cook in advance

Especially good for minimum-fuss suppers are one-pot meals, dishes that need no accompaniment and still provide a hearty, healthy balanced meal – for instance, a casserole or pie containing vegetables as well as protein – you could serve these on their own, or with a salad on the side. Or a thick, home-made soup, which will provide a good meal just with some bread and cheese to go with it.

* Casseroles and stews.

* Soups.

* Pies, pizzas and savoury flans.

* Versatile sauces: bolognese (minced meat and tomato), plain tomato which can be used with rice or pasta.

* Ingredients that don't spoil when pre-cooked and stored in the fridge: rice (if slightly under-done is perfect reheated), cooked dried beans, boiled potatoes for frying up or putting into potato salad.

Here are some tips from a programmed cook:

> **On a Sunday, I often cook up a pan of thick meat sauce made from onions, garlic, minced beef, carrots, tinned tomatoes and parsley. This can form the basis of the following family meals during the week:**
>
> *** Cottage pie (by adding a potato topping: I often cheat**

414

and use Smash). Sometimes I'll add a couple of courgettes, finely chopped, to force some green vegetables down my son in disguise.

* Spaghetti (I thin the sauce by adding another tin of tomatoes).

* A kind of lasagne (layers of cooked macaroni, meat sauce and cheese sauce).

* Chilli (by adding a tin of red kidney beans and some ground cumin, coriander and chili powder).

If there is any left over, or if my family shows signs of rebellion, I can freeze it in an icecube tray so that I can heat it up in small quanitites – for a child's lunch, for example.

If cooking is just too much . . .

If you hate cooking you will benefit most from the tips above. Doing a big cook-in one afternoon over the weekend, or an evening in the week may be a drag, but it will free you for the rest of the time. Also having a small number of dishes in your repertoire that you repeat over and over again takes the mental strain out of cooking, and means that you can get preparation down to a fine art. If any member of your family objects, that is really too bad – and perhaps it will inspire that person to take over some of the cooking. But as many families quite enjoy the predictability of routine you will probably find they don't mind the 'If it's shepherd's pie it must be Wednesday.'

However you can also get away with almost no cooking at all some or all of the time. It will probably work out more expensive but if it saves your sanity you will probably decide it is worth it. You have to be responsible about this, as you want your family to be well and healthily nourished as well as full – but it is possible.

* In summer go for non-cook meals such as salads and cold meats/cheeses/eggs. Salad vegetables well-

washed and dried and put in a plastic bag keep crisp and fresh for days in the fridge, so you only really have to prepare them once, bar tearing or cutting up.

* For children's meals, keep supplies of frozen pizzas (you can get the wholemeal ones), sausages (low-fat), beefburgers, (or you can make your own economically and quickly with minced beef, breadcrumbs and perhaps an egg or some tomato ketchup to bind the mixture), fishfingers (avoid the ones with artificial colours), also tins of baked beans, sardines, tuna fish, soups.

* Buy convenience foods that just need heating through/boiling in the bag. Check for additives though. If you are cooking and eating a lot of this kind of food you must know what's in it and how it affects you – and especially young children. Happily, all the publicity about additives has encouraged a number of large supermarket chains to produce convenience foods that are clearly labelled with ingredients and which dispense with artifical additives and colourings.

* Get a take-away once in a while if there is one handy. Lucky you if there is a good one with well-cooked healthy food – then it's only the cost you have to worry about.

* Meals on toast can be very nourishing, especially if made on good wholemeal bread: baked beans, cheese, eggs, bacon, mushrooms, sardines or whatever takes your fancy.

* Make sure that there are plenty of healthy snack foods around for a hungry family: fruit, vegetables such as carrots and celery, nuts, dried fruits, cheese, yogurt, wholemeal bread, crispbread.

* Similarly, have healthy drinks in the fridge: milk, fruit juices.

If you like having people round but can't face the thought of having to prepare an elaborate meal, you can do as this woman does: she lives in Bangor with her husband and two children under three and works full time:

> I enjoy having people to visit on Saturday evenings and life became much easier when I realised I couldn't be a good mother, teacher and cook, so I gave in to Marks and Spencer's suppers – entertaining now couldn't be easier as I can spend Saturdays playing with the kids instead of cooking.

Your Partner

Your partner and housework

This is a delicate issue. The lucky few live with men who see all household chores as a shared responsibility. Those men are 'Working Fathers' in the real sense of the phrase. But a lot of men are convinced that housework is 'woman's work', and even many of the men who are admirably good about doing the housework see it as 'helping' – that is, it is the woman's responsibility rather than a joint problem. The women who have the hardest job convincing their partners that housework is something they should do together are usually those who have spent some time at home without paid work. Once their men have become used to them looking after that side of things it is very difficult to make them see that this should change now that the women are working.

Some of the women who wrote to us had willing partners who really pulled their weight:

> * A partner who is willing to share in all the household tasks and childcare is essential. John is definitely the driving force who keeps the household routine on

schedule. After all, the whole family benefits from my extra income.

* It helps if your partner agrees to wade in with the housework. The exceptions in our house is that he does DIY and I iron, the rest we share between us.

Women with helpful partners often listed their husbands, along with household gadgets, as one of the labour-saving things they could not do without!

* My husband helps by doing all the ironing, all washing up and tidies through the week.

* My husband and I 'go through' the house on Friday evenings and he cleans up at weekends.

Others had partners who were virtually useless:

I think it is *most important* that my son grows up realising that women work as well as men – with a bit of luck he will share the chores with his wife, and not expect her to wait on him, an attitude that has caused endless friction in my own marriage.

This woman had a little more success:

I insist that my husband entertains the little boy while I cook the meal, otherwise things are too chaotic. I find that I end up doing two jobs – one at work and then one at home, although my husband does wash up and help with bathing Paul.

Most partners were somewhere in between – willing to help when it suited them, but whose contribution made a very small dent in the pile of things to be done:

My husband, even after eleven years of me working, is still not well trained. He will help if I ask but I feel I shouldn't have to ask. His cooking is primitive to say the least (perhaps this is studied) and he has not yet learned to sort out washing into the correct loads. Underwear is dyed various shades! When he is sent to do the shopping the cost is astronomical. He is good, however, at taking the girls places – guides, to friends' houses etc. He also is usually able to attend school sports etc. when I can't. In my experience, although husbands are perhaps willing to help in theory – in practice they don't. They are particularly bad at coping with more than one thing at a time and tend to be a little haphazard in remembering to pick up kids on time etc. I don't think they mean to be irresponsible but it just works out that way. For example a friend's child has to walk to the swimming pool after school. While she and I would have taken the child along the route telling her when to cross etc., neither of our husbands would have considered that.

One woman, at least, believes things are improving:

If I had my time over again I would be a much more 'helpless' woman. In my experience the more you take on the more is expected of you. The young women of today having babies are much better organised in getting their husbands to help. Twenty years ago things were different. On top of everything else, my husband was newly self-employed when my first baby was born and I also had to help with his 'office' work – not a great deal as he worked from home, but still time-consuming with all the other things I had to do. In retrospect I think I deserve at least a silver medal.

Women who have helpful husbands do not understand the difficulties of those whose partners refuse to help. One woman crisply advised:

Before going back to work decide (a) if married, how jobs are to be split with partner (b) which jobs have priority – e.g. laundry and cleaning bathroom and kitchen, tidiness.

But it seems that many men have the useful ability not to 'see' undone chores, while we tend to be all too aware of them. Women determined to make their partners share the work often give up simply because the men can hold out longer not doing the required job than the women are able to put up with it being undone. Many women try their best to involve their husbands ('insist' is a word that crops up frequently), but then find it is easier to do the work themselves than to nag. However we were intrigued to talk to an advertising executive in whose household the pattern was totally reversed:

> My husband does more housework than me because he is more neurotic about it. Hoovering is his thing. I'd do it once a month, but he wants it done every day, so he does it. It's fine by me!

Most women find ways to compromise, like this part-timer:

> On the days I do not work I don't expect my husband to do anything domestic except maybe mow the lawn, but I think he should do just as much as myself if I have done a full day's work as well. After all, it is his home as well as mine and children are a joint responsibility.

And this woman has a similar solution, because her husband is sometimes at home when she is not:

> Insist that your partner does as much as you in the house. My husband works shifts. If he is at home he will have a meal ready and have been to the shops.

Some women are so relieved that their husbands feel positively about them working that they don't want to spoil things by making housework an issue:

> He is happy that I work and gives me much support. He too is heavily committed and busy. I don't mind that he doesn't do much in the way of cooking, housework, etc.

420

I'd rather he was happy and reasonably comfortable. As a result we have invested in good domestic help both human and mechanical.

Making the most of a partner who will help

It is perhaps inappropriate (or useless) for us to try to suggest ways of making your partner pull his weight if he is dead set against it. On the whole, it can be said that a working mother with a partner who is simply not prepared to pull his weight at home and who expects his wife to wait on him hand and foot even though she has an outside job is a great liability.

However, if you do have a fairly willing partner, you should bear a few things in mind:

* *Don't be over-critical*

If your partner is prepared to share the work, you should try not to moan if his standards don't reach yours. This gives an easy way out to someone who is already half-hearted about it. As this woman says:

> Most of our rows tend to be about the mechanics of the running of the house. I feel it shouldn't be all my responsibility but again I resent him trying to do 'my job' and doing it badly, or what I would consider as badly.

* *Don't take on his chores*

If you have agreed to a division of labour, don't start doing some of his jobs 'just this once'. They'll invariably end up all yours again over time.

* *Show appreciation*

This can go against the grain, particularly if *you* are rarely shown any appreciation for completing routine tasks. But if practical help is rare, you will probably *feel* grateful (or amazed). As one woman said:

> Husbands are difficult to organise. If they tidy their clothes away and do the dishes it is a great help, but they are rarely willing to do so. Let them see that even a little help is very appreciated.

But we do realise that even 'showing appreciation' when you are tired and harassed can seem more bother than doing the work yourself.

* Exploit his talents

It helps if your husband has a forte or a skill he prides himself on; encouraging him to do that (even if it is something you like yourself) often makes up for other shortcomings:

> My husband is quite a good cook, sometimes adventurous. Rather than wait for me to prepare the evening meal he gets on and does it.

* Let him choose his chores

A reluctant man is sometimes more prepared to share the work if he can pick the chores he minds doing least. This may not seem fair, but it is often better than nothing – and better than constant delegating. It will usually be the chores that require least effort and that are not dirty:

> * He is used to housework but he would rarely do the ironing, except if he needs a particular shirt! He will help with housework – except he hates doing the bathroom!

> * My husband vacuums the house weekly – usually with

our small daughter 'helping'. I cook, he washes up –
except on Fridays when he cooks.

Sharing childcare with your partner

Most of the women in our sample seemed fairly happy
with the amount of time and attention their partners gave
to their children, though almost all of them had a fairly
traditional split: the mothers were the ones most closely
concerned with their children, and organising childcare
where appropriate.

But we were very interested to hear from this woman in
York who really did share the care of her baby with her
husband for a while, and what this meant for them all:

> Our daughter was born when my husband and I were
> both full-time students. We decided from the beginning
> to share the responsibilities of parenting as far as
> possible, bearing in mind that she was breastfed.
> Consequently when I first left our daughter I knew she
> was in competent, familiar hands. However I might add
> that sharing caring with one's partner is not as
> straightforward as one imagines. It needed much
> discussion/negotiation to work out a consistent way of
> handling our daughter. I think also my husband felt
> undervalued in what he was doing. Relatives and
> neighbours assumed that he was just 'standing in' for me
> rather than being an equal partner in the caring role. He
> recalls at times he found childcare very isolating. He felt
> uneasy about dropping in on neighbours for a chat or
> attending local *mother* and toddler groups with our
> daughter. Nevertheless he is pleased that he has been
> intimately involved in caring for our daughter. Sadly, he
> is currently working in Leeds and sees very little of our
> daughter during the week because he is out of the house
> from 7.30a.m. to 6.30p.m.

And a full-time civil servant in London told us that her
partner was made redundant two months after their
daughter's birth, so through force of circumstance he has

been the main childcarer since she went back to work. They seem to have a fairly straightforward role reversal:

> He obviously spends a lot more time with our daughter, and we split the household chores about fifty-fifty. He tends to cook during the week, and I tend to cook at the weekend. We have one rule: the cook doesn't wash up. But I handle all the finances. He's useless with money, it's just idleness on his part. The only difference is that if our roles were reversed and I stayed at home while he went out to work, I wouldn't do what he does – which is shove Jenny at me when I come home in the evening, saying, 'Here! I've had enough. I've had her all day, you take over now.' I don't get time to unwind.

Anneliese Young, a full-time social worker who lives in Northern Ireland, has also managed to share care with her husband more than average:

> I have a marvellous, helpful husband. Our daily routine varies, depending on his work schedule. He works as a principal trumpet player in the Ulster Orchestra which involves evening concerts, but time during the day at home. Since the boys were babies [now aged three and four] they have been at home when he has been at home, and at the childminder when he has to work. Since my returning to work full time they have never had a complete week at the childminder. I am quite proud of that!

Another woman, who works as a programme assistant/ reporter for BBC local radio in Manchester, is able to work a full-time flexible shift rota system, because her husband is fully involved with helping with their two boys aged four and one:

> Because I work shifts and flexible hours there is no typical day. Shifts are: (1) 6.00a.m.—1.00p.m.; (2) 8.00a.m.—4.00p.m.; (3) noon—8.00p.m. – and they rotate on a two-weekly pattern.
>
> I quite often finish at 3.00p.m. on shift two as management are happy for me to work straight through

without a break – I prefer it and it often works to their advantage! Shift work is very helpful to working mums, allowing them to do some things 'normal' mums do: for example, toddler group, swimming lessons, etc. I occasionally do interviews, etc., in the evening and can take time in lieu during the day. I prefer shifts one and three as they give me maximum hours with the kids – I'm helped tremendously in this by my husband, who, willingly and competently, can get them all out in the morning when I'm on early shift and put both to bed when I'm on late. I couldn't do it without him.

Your relationship with your partner

Most relationships are put under strain with the arrival of children. Pregnancy, the postpartum period, sleepless babies – and toddlers who insist on sharing the conjugal bed – can all wreak havoc with your sexual relationship for starters. And there is no denying that children make great emotional demands on their parents, especially on their mothers, which can leave little room for your relationship with your partner. This can be very hard, especially if one or both of you is resentful of the way your children come between you. The situation may be even harder to accept if you started your family soon after getting married (or moving in together) as you may not have had enough time together on your own to build a really strong relationship.

In a partnership where both parents work there are added pressures because of the shortage of time. Making time for the children is often the working mother's priority, and this can mean that very little is left for her partner. Many will recognise the petty irritations that rise to the surface under the strain, as decribed by this teacher who lives in Scotland with her teenage children and her husband:

425

Talking most of the day means I'm happy not to speak at night – but my husband works on his own and sees few people during the day. I find he 'rabbits on' at night and I can't be bothered. If we've both had a bad day – well – neither of us is prepared to listen to the other. We end up fighting over the silliest things. I once threatened to divorce him over some really dirty washing up cloths!

A barrister expanded on this subject:

This idea that some people have of having a child to patch up a marriage seems to me a great laugh. You've got to have a rock-like marriage to make it survive with children, in my opinion. The strains include money, no time, health, the sheer worry about the kids.

Another woman, who is divorced and now living with someone else, is probably speaking with hindsight about her first marriage when she says:

Involve your partner (if you have one) in the day to day running of the family, especially where the children are concerned: remember – until the family came along, he was the centre of attention. Don't push him out.

Many women made the point that as with all your other commitments, it is necessary to work at your relationship with your partner, and not take him for granted. Many of them advocated building time alone together into your schedules, making sure you go out together at least once a week or month without the children. Here is a tip from one woman:

Try to get away on your own for at least a weekend with your husband now and then. You need to have time together on your own. Going away with young children is not a holiday – it's like being at home, only worse!

Even if they do not go out, many couples try to sit down together and pay some attention to each other in the evenings after their children have gone to bed. But with older children, who stay up later, this time alone together can be eroded more and more. And many couples seem to use their evenings to catch up on work or housework – whittling down time to chat. Making an effort to go out together regularly – for a drink, or a meal for instance – can be well worth the effort and expense, in order to have some time alone together away from the distractions of home.

Some women make the point that it can sometimes be just as important to give each other free time apart from each other and the family. One doctor from Yorkshire who wrote to us has a four-month-old baby and works full time – and full time, apparently, means seventy-four hours per week! She says: 'It is essential to arrange one night out a week with a friend, one night out a week with your husband.'

Rosemary Kirk, who has four children, and lives in Newtonabbey, Northern Ireland, says:

> I love cooking, baking, knitting, sewing and embroidery etc. But I find that ordinary routine takes over so I always make some time – either two nights a week or two or three hours at the weekend – as time for me to do what I really want to do. My husband has to take over during this time. I used to go to nightclasses two nights a week when the children were aged five, three, and one, to keep my sanity, otherwise I was a 'miserable yap' to live with.

Sheila Robertson, who has a baby of seventeen months, makes a comment typical of many that we received:

> Ensure you have a regular break – for example a night out each week or month. If you are living with a partner give each other a little time off each week while the other one looks after the child (it doesn't have to be very long).

Babysitters

Going out in the evenings means finding someone to look after the children. On our questionnaire we asked what you did about arranging babysitting help. Many of the women asked members of their family to babysit, or close friends. Younger members of the family were paid, but the others usually weren't. Almost as many combined asking members of the family with paying a babysitter from time to time, and those who did not have family close by used paid babysitters almost exclusively. Most commonly they were neighbours, or neighbours' responsible children, or children of friends. Women who had nannies paid them extra for babysitting, and some women asked their childminders, or childminders' children to babysit: in other words, the people who babysat were usually very well known to the children. Only one woman had used an agency.

Rates varied, and didn't seem to be connected to area. A common solution was a rate until midnight, when it was doubled – or a standard rate for the entire evening, often rising after midnight. If you can't give your sitter a lift home, then you will expect to have to pay for a taxi.

Babysitting agencies

An agency can be useful in an emergency, but they tend to be expensive. You often have to pay an annual membership fee and/or a booking fee to the agency, on top of an hourly rate, which is often on the high side. Agencies will also expect you to pay the sitter's fares, including a taxi after a certain time.

'Free' babysitting

If you don't have family nearby, and the cost of a

babysitter means that you can't afford to go out, there are other ways of getting babysitting help that don't cost money:

* *Find others in the same situation*

You can take it in turns to have each other's children for the night. Obviously it helps if the children are roughly the same age and like each other.

* *Overnight register*

A way to formalise this is suggested in *The Gingerbread Handbook* (for single parents, but it also works if you have a partner!). They advise each Gingerbread group to keep a register of local members who are willing to look after other members' children overnight in their own home on a reciprocal basis. They give a sample entry:

> **Mrs Anne Brown is willing to offer overnight care to two children, once a month in return for same. She has two children, both boys, aged four and six.**

The advantage of a register such as this is that you don't have to keep asking the same friends. You do need someone to administer it though, and it is more convenient to do it through a group such as Gingerbread, or a Working Mothers Group, the NCT, or National Women's Register.

The list can be sent out to participating members and updated regularly. As the Gingerbread Handbook rightly says, you don't need to have a spare room: children like being crammed together and using sleeping bags once in a while.

* *Babysitting circle*

You can start a babysitting circle with a 'token' or points

system, whereby you babysit at someone's house and are paid in tokens that you swap for someone else's babysitting help. A few of the women who wrote to us did this. The most common way was to give a token for every hour or half-hour of babysitting. Usually, you send your partner along, or go along yourself while your partner looks after your own children. This is therefore not an option for a lone parent, unless she has a portable baby.

The system works best when a large number of families join, and when all pull their weight. One woman we spoke to said that she had become so in debt to the babysitting circle that she was seriously considering leaving the area!

CHAPTER 15
Lone Mothers

Lone mothers have different problems from mothers who have partners; unfortunately we cannot cover these special problems in any detail within the scope of this book. Problems of isolation, loneliness, lack of money, perhaps legal problems or difficulty with housing or the ex-partner – these are devastating and not easily solved, and there are some excellent organisations that can give more practical help and advice than we can: we list some of these in *Further Help*.

The day-to-day problems of the single working mother are almost exactly the same as those that face other working mothers – only more severe. In traditional families there is some division of labour, even when both parents work. One partner usually carries the main financial burden, while the other assumes the main responsibility for childcare. Many two-parent families are flexible within this general arrangement: each partner covering for the other when necessary.

The lone mother does not have a partner to help share the care of the children or any of the household duties. When the children are ill there is no one to cover for her to allow her to go to work, and the problems of what to do in the school holidays and ferrying the children to and from childcarer or school all fall to her. Even popping out to bring in some extra shopping, going to a parents' meeting or out for a drink with a friend become major undertakings when there is no one else to stay in and mind the kids. The money she earns is not a pleasant extra, but the main source of income for the family, even if she has help from the father.

As one of the women who wrote to us said:

> I seem to spend most of my life having to be obligated to other people since Anna was born. In spite of the fact that I am very independent I rely heavily on my job and child-care (and my bank manager).

Our sample

The single mothers who filled in our questionnaire are not representative of single mothers in Britain. One in six families in Britain is now a one-parent family, and just under one-seventh of the replies we received were from single mothers – though as few lone mothers are able to work, this response is, in fact, higher than would be expected. But what makes our selection more unusual is that most of the women who replied were in 'good' jobs, and even when theirs was the sole income they had few money worries and a reasonable standard of living. This contrasts with the national picture: the average income of a one-parent family is 37 per cent of that of a two-parent family, and few lone mothers are able to work in well-paid jobs – 70 per cent live in or on the margins of poverty, compared to 19 per cent of two-parent families.

Therefore the replies we received tended to be from women who were coping well and felt positive and fairly happy. In *Double Struggle – Sex Discrimination and One-parent Families* (now out of print) Penny Letts says:

> Our work with one-parent families has shown that they think of themselves as a separate group, and are thought

of by others as a separate and different group, often with negative connotations.

But few of the women who wrote to us made more than a passing mention of their 'singleness'. This must partly be the fault of the questionnaire, for we asked no specific questions aimed at lone parents apart from marital status, but it was made clear that we welcomed any extra comments about anything relevant to the problems or joys of being a working mother – and many of the lone parents who replied took the opportunity to expand their thoughts on other issues.

One woman, though, was keen to mention the positive side of being a lone mother:

> I honestly can't see any disadvantages in being a lone mother. I have been very hard-up in the past – but so are lots of people. I'm a strong-minded, strong-willed person, and I think that I would have clashed with a partner in a conventional relationship. As it is, the house is fairly harmonious for me and my child. I like being able to make my own decisions about my child's welfare. Her father doesn't see eye to eye with me on everything, but he doesn't interfere – partly because he doesn't contribute any money, so I suppose he feels he has given up certain rights. There is no area of my life that I think could be improved by having a man around all the time. I have had two steady 'live-out' relationships, but that is different: I have not had a 'partner' in the true sense of the word. I'm lucky because I come from a close family who have always helped, and my child feels part of a large family, even though she has no direct siblings.

Becoming a lone parent

Some women make the choice to have a child on their own. But the majority of lone mothers become so through force of circumstances – because they split up with their partners, or their partners die. This is always a trauma, even in the cases where there is a measure of relief that an unhappy relationship is at an end. The mothers who wrote to us who had work to go to at the time found that working helped them through this period. As one woman said, 'I needed my job to pick up my confidence in myself when my husband left.'

Marie Burke, who has since remarried, wrote:

> When my first husband died my eldest child was eighteen months old. I had no family and few friends in Manchester and so work was my salvation. It was mainly colleagues who helped me through this time in my life.

Another woman, who is a part-time sales assistant with an eight-year-old daughter, also mentioned that going back to work had helped her through the break-up of her marriage. Her baby was nine months old at the time, and she had gone back to work because her husband was unemployed:

> I found it very difficult coping with both baby and work, but my marriage was breaking up, so the positive aspect of working at that time was that it kept me sane at a very difficult moment.

Of course, in some circumstances, women will find that their own understandable grief at the time makes working difficult or impossible, and other women may find that without a partner they cannot manage the children and a job.

One doctor who wrote to us had a personal philosophy that was probably directly traceable to the fact that her husband had died suddenly while her children were still young, 'I never plan far ahead – it is very easy to be bogged down by worrying about future non-existent problems.'

Long-term lone parents

None of the women who wrote to us was in the first stages of grief at the death of a relationship, and all had incorporated their lone status into their lives. Most of them were coping very well – which was perhaps another reason why few of them had much to say about being alone.

Jane Lee, who had brought up her daughter alone since the baby was six weeks old, said:

> **In a lot of ways I think it's probably easier for me not having a partner at the moment (although it would be great to have practical support if he were that sort of man). As it is, I only have to look after the pair of us. I say this because I see so many couples who are both working and the husband definitely does not pull his weight with the children and the running of the home.**

All working mothers exemplify women's capacity to work extremely hard, to adapt and to make the best of things. The lone mothers in our sample were shining examples of this. They did more than just cope – some of them had packed their lives with even more things than the average working mother – who may find that some excess energy is sapped by her partner!

One divorced mother with two small children told us that as well as working full time as a primary maths teacher she was also studying for a diploma in maths at Manchester Polytechnic, and worked in a bar two evenings a week. She admitted: 'Now I am under tremendous pressure at work – what with the reorganisation of the curriculum, studying for my diploma, trying to meet all bills and maintain the house.' But she went on to add, 'I am now doing a lot of DIY (which had previously all been done for me) as I can't afford to pay anyone to do it. This does give me a pleasant sense of achievement in doing a job well.'

Another woman wrote to us that she was bringing up her daughter alone in Darnley, Glasgow, while working as a part-time sales assistant, and was also fully involved in the Darnley after-school-care scheme, of which she was chairperson. When she wrote to us, this excellent scheme was coming up for Urban Aid evaluation, so she was spending time trying to get as much publicity for it as possible. Apart from anything, if the grant application failed and the scheme had to close, it would put her job in jeopardy – but she was cheerful, energetic and positive. Lynne Hainsworth, a full-time auxiliary nurse, bringing up her daughter alone, was also studying for an extra qualification in her spare time.

One woman perhaps does not belong in this section because she is married, but she described herself as 'effectively single' on our questionnaire, as her husband works away from home. Certainly she doesn't have the day-to-day back-up of her partner. However, she works full time and brings work home in the evenings and weekends, and is also chairperson of the PTA at her children's school.

All these women have chosen to take on extra tasks and are enjoying their lives. Although they are not representative, they are by no means unusual. Even when there is no stigma attached to being a lone parent, many women resent the accepted stereotype: that as the head of a one-parent family you are someone to be pitied.

The Working Lone Mother

The need to work

Most of the lone mothers who wrote to us said that they would work even if they didn't have to, and most of the rest said that they would work, but shorter hours (in a survey carried out by the DSS, 50 per cent of lone parents said they would work if they could find suitable childcare). Interestingly, the two who would prefer not to work had good jobs, a couple of poorer-paid women in less stimulating jobs still preferred the idea of working to staying at home.

Barbara Herbert, a part-time market-research interviewer, with two sons aged seven and ten, wrote:

> As a separated mum bringing up my children on my own I find that working gives me the interest and stimulation I need outside the home and this can only be good for the children.

Another woman, a full-time physiotherapist with three children aged between eleven and fifteen, felt that working was important all round:

> Because I have a good job my children live in a better house, we have a car, can go for holidays and weekends away – all material things but without them I'd feel a failure and wouldn't be as good a mum, even though I might have more time to be with them.

Jane Lee, whose partner left her when her baby was six weeks old, went back to work two weeks after that:

> I was quite relieved when I left her. I was going back to work and knew that I would have to work hard, but at least I would have spiritual 'space' as it were.

Jane was one of our respondents who maintained that she wouldn't work if she could afford not to. But it was only *paid* work she was referring to:

> I only work to be able to give my daughter and myself a reasonable standard of living – but having said this I do like to be independent (I am known far and wide for my

far too independent nature!) and also, perhaps more than anything I need the mental stimulation. If I was in a very good financial position and did not need to work I would have to do something useful to occupy my time and keep me active – probably some voluntary organisation working with children.

Lynne Hainsworth, who has brought up her seven-year-old daughter on her own for the last four years, wrote:

I think one important thing I must say first is that I am very proud to have a job. Some people are not as lucky as me to have a 9.00a.m.—4.15p.m. regular job with no shift work involved. (I work on the out-patients' department at the local hospital.)

My daughter has not suffered in the least from me going out to work. In fact she started full-time day nursery from the age of three and I think it has done her good to mix with other children. She fully understands that I have to work to keep us and have enough money to buy things. I have explained this to her when she asks me why! I am confident that I can cope and have done for four years. But it was tough at first. I just think to myself – we would have got nowhere living off social security – they don't give you enough to live off, not to mention little luxuries like bus fare or sweets.

Most of our sample felt that their work did not suffer because they had children – only two of them felt that it had had a bad effect on their work.

Finding work

Many mothers who have chosen to stay at home with their children find themselves in the position of having to look for work when their relationships break down or their partners die. Some of these women had never considered working while their children were young, and many are unskilled. Clearly, finding work in these circumstances is doubly difficult. If you are in this position, the chapter

Finding Work after a Break may help. But if the only work you can find is very poorly paid – watch out.

Gingerbread, the organisation for lone parents, points out that it is easy to fall into the trap of believing that any paid work will provide more money than the government benefits. They advise you to work out whether you will be better off after child-care charges and working expenses are deducted from your wages. Because of the variety of benefits, and the different rules that apply to each, in some cases you could be substantially worse off after taking a job. Sometimes it pays more to work part time and top up your earnings with benefits.

However, against that you must weigh the intangible benefits that working can give you – those mentioned above by the women who wrote to us. Having the stimulation of work, making friends, spending the day with adults, and the increase in your own self-esteem can do you an enormous amount of good. Working also provides you with essential experience, making you a more favourable candidate when you apply for other, better-paid jobs.

Letting work become too important

Perhaps this is not a problem shared by many women, but there is the danger of letting your job take over, particularly when you are worried about money and can bring extra in by working hard. One of the women who wrote to us was a freelance and she admitted to working every day of the week, an average of ten hours a day. Not surprisingly, she noted that her children (aged sixteen and twelve) hated her job. She wanted to make the point that:

> When we do go out all together or on holiday, we do let our hair down and I do not put restrictions on my time or money. Every second year we go away on holiday for one month.

Another woman, who was otherwise quite happy with her arrangements, wrote, 'Sometimes I feel we lead too fast a life, as I have so much to do and feel that life is just too timetabled.'

The lone mother and her children

As we have seen in other chapters, nearly all working mothers suffer from guilt, and worry about whether they are doing the right thing for their children. The lone mother may feel this more than most, particularly as she has the extra worry that belonging to a one-parent family could be damaging for her children. In *Double Struggle*, Penny Letts, who has looked at all the available research, says:

> **There is no evidence at all to show that a child being brought up by a lone parent is less able to grow up into a whole person than one from a two-parent family.**

There is a difference between families in which the parents split up when the children were very young, and those that did so later. A few of the women who wrote to us had children who were only babies at the time of the split, who were not consciously aware of what went on.

Older children can be drawn into the trauma of a break-up, and it can take all members of the family a long time to recover.

The mothers who completed our questionnaire clearly weren't worried about their own children. The comments they made in the sections devoted to how their children were affected by their work, and about the time they spent with their children, read much the same as those written by married or co-habiting women.

But in some cases it is clear that the mothers felt proud of a special closeness of the sort that is more difficult to develop when there is a partner around. This is particularly true where there is only one child, so that time at home is spent together, sharing activities, playing and talking.

One woman with an eight-year-old daughter wrote:

> Each day we talk about the day's happenings. I tell her what has happened at work – the funny or the terrible things. I would say we are friends as well as mother and daughter.

Another woman with a daughter of a similar age wrote:

> On weekdays we spend the evening together. After tea we play or go to the park or my daughter has some friends in the house to play with. At the weekends we are together all day. She helps with the shopping and cleaning on a voluntary basis. Activities we enjoy doing together include cycling – we each have a bike which we ride to the park or use to go visiting people a few miles away. We also go on lots of walks in the summer.

One woman with a teenage daughter felt that the benefits that she and her daughter received far outweighed any disadvantages of being a one-parent, one-child family:

> We are very close, but not unnaturally – both of us have lots of friends and busy social lives outside the home. But living alone together means that we are fairly well-tuned to each other's moods, and I would say that this means she is particularly well-adjusted, because I have been in a position to notice problems and help her solve them when they were relatively minor. I think it can be easy to fail to notice an older child who is being quietly unhappy when you are with a partner who takes up most of your time and attention in the evenings and at weekends – I've seen it with friends of hers. Some parents have little idea what is going on in their children's minds or lives, so long as they are not creating problems. We have tremendous fun together, talk about anything and everything and like and respect each other. I don't say that this kind of relationship is impossible when there are two parents, but I think you have to make more of a conscious effort in that situation.

Things are likely to be a little different when there is more than one child at home, though mothers in this situation also describe extra closeness. Barbara Herbert is cub leader of her sons' cub pack, and they all enjoy the activities this involves. When she gave us details of a typical working day, she noted that after the evening meal and homework the evening was spent, 'discussing the kind of day we've had, generally relaxing and having a bit of a laugh'.

In two-parent families the children are often encouraged to give their parents some peaceful time together in the evenings – understandably. As a lone mother, therefore, you can reassure yourself that in some ways your situation is positively beneficial to the children – who enjoy being able to share your leisure time with you.

The practical problems

The most pressing day-to-day practical problems are to do with taking your children to the childcarer or school, picking them up, and getting to and from work yourself. There are further problems when one of you is ill, and during the school/childcarer's holidays. Any plans you make to go out in the evening have to involve a babysitter. Most of the suggestions in the *Crisis* and *School-age Children* chapters apply to lone mothers as well. In particular a lone working mother has special need for a good reciprocal support system, either informally with family, friends or neighbours, or through a group, such as a Gingerbread group, or a Working Mothers Group.

In *Double Struggle* Penny Letts quotes another author on the subject of lone parents, 'Friends and neighbours are less willing to offer help in childcare to one-parent families perhaps because they see the commitment could be too imposing and irrevocable.' If you meet this attitude, it shows that it is doubly important to find ways of paying back favours.

Clearly it helps if your ex-partner is still around and able to help at times. The Manchester-based maths teacher, who also studies and works in a bar, is enabled to do this with the help of her ex-husband. Her advice to other women in a similar situation is:

> Try to be on good terms with your ex-husband. Mine might have been a poor husband but he was and is a good father. I prefer them to be with him than anyone else. He babysits on Tuesdays from 4.00p.m. to 12.00p.m. I do my shopping then, and he collects them, brings them home and does the tea. That evening I work in the bar. On Wednesday he picks them up again, as I have an evening class for my maths diploma.

Many of the divorced mothers who wrote to us were able to make arrangements for their children to spend at least part of the school holidays with their fathers, which has the bonus of allowing them a period of completely free social time, without having to worry about babysitters.

It can be particularly hard on mothers who have a number of older children to find the time to ferry them to and from evening and weekend clubs and activities. One woman who has three children said, 'It's difficult with no one to share this job at times. Fortunately they see their father on alternate weekends and he also does activities with them.'

Many of the mothers had a fairly supportive circle of family and friends. The ones who found it hardest had fewer people they could call on. Jane Lee speaks for many when she says:

> I know how desperate I have felt not having any practical source of help to turn to at times such as illness and school holidays. It's terrible when you see your annual holiday days dwindling away because you've had to stay off work because of a sick child. And when you are at your most exhausted you find you have practically no holiday left for yourself to have a rest. Within the first year of my daughter being born she

caught absolutely everything. Most mums, it would seem, get a lot of back-up from parents. Unfortunately mine have been dead for some years. I would like to see the state help mothers who are forced to work by providing some kind of support for such times as school holidays – somewhere where children can be cared for whilst mum is at work. I wouldn't expect this to be free, but subsidised.

Problems of isolation

A lone mother can feel very isolated, especially when her children are small, and offer only limited company. As going out often means finding and paying for a babysitter, some lower-paid mothers may spend most weeks in.

> Winter, I must admit, gets a little depressing: long, cold, dark evenings alone are not much fun. The most important advice I have found is to just keep busy and the mind occupied.

It's different if you have families and friends who can help out:

> I like to have one evening per week when my daughter goes to sleep at my parents house and I go out drinking with friends. This does us both good to mix with other people. The extended family is very important. They are always there when needed for help and company for us.

For babysitting solutions that don't cost anything, see suggestions at the end of the chapter *Your Home and Your Partner*.

Lone mothers who work suffer less from feelings of isolation. Being with other adults during the day means that you don't miss adult company so much in the evening.

Many lone mothers find that being single does not affect their social lives at all:

I entertain in the same way that I would if I had a man around. Granted, there is no one there to 'hold the fort' and keep the conversation going in a sticky moment while I'm in the kitchen doing something complicated – but that is rarely a problem. If I'm entertaining some people I don't know too well I might invite someone along who I can rely on for moral support, such as a very good friend or my sister, and I never worry about balancing numbers. I suppose some people are more reluctant to invite me back without a partner, particulary if they feel they have to provide a man, but I don't find myself short of invitations. Neither do I find women suspicious of me where their partners are concerned, which is supposed to be a common story. Perhaps it is because most of my friends have always known me as a single person.

Joining up with people in a similar situation

If you find managing hard, or feel isolated because most of your friends are in couples, then joining an organisation that can bring you together with people like yourself and offer help is a good idea. Gingerbread is the natural choice for lone mothers. It is open to all single parents; the local groups are independent, run by volunteers. Although they are happy to advise and be of help, the groups' emphasis is on mutual self-help – so you must be prepared to do your bit too if you are going to join.

Although they say that they can't help with providing money, housing, or finding jobs, the organisation can help with providing a meeting place; friendship; information and advice; moral and emotional support; practical help.

You can contact the national office to find out where your nearest local group is. The national office will also give you individual advice on welfare problems, or provide you with any of their excellent (award-winning) range of information leaflets on all aspects of welfare rights.

If there is no group in your area, they can give you information and help to set up a new group. They also run a penfriend scheme to put people in touch with other lone parents in other parts of the country.

A good, well-established local group is a boon. Some run Skills Swapshops for lone parents, so that you can offer to trade your particular talent (cooking, say) in return for someone else's (plumbing). They suggest keeping a register with entries such as this:

> **Mrs Bloggs wants to contact someone who will take her eleven-year-old son to football matches every Saturday afternoon. In return she will bake a cake/look after a child/put two loads of washing through her machine.**

They also suggest clothes/toys pools, where you regularly bring along items to swap or sell. You may suggest that this is done among your neighbours if there is no local group nearby.

However not all lone women relish the idea of joining a single-parent organisation. In *Double Struggle* Penny Letts quotes one mother as saying, 'Our local one-parent family group is like a cattle market, with everyone on the lookout for a new partner. Having just got out of a difficult marriage that's not the sort of thing I want.'

If those are your feelings, but you still would like back-up, a Working Mothers Group might be more appropriate – particularly as all the women members also work, not the case with a lone-parent group. Many lone working mothers feel that they have more in common with other working mothers than with heads of other one-parent families.

The Lone Parent and Money

Money problems

Money is the most common urgent worry for lone

mothers. As mentioned earlier, most of the mothers who wrote to us were lucky enough not to be in this situation. But Lynne Hainsworth, the auxiliary nurse, who wrote of her pride in having a job, also told us of the difficulties that are looming for her:

> I recently have had negotiations with the local social services. They had been financing 'before and after school care' for my daughter and also paying the childminder for me during school holidays. But now she is seven I have to start paying. Out of my low wage, a third goes on the childminder for approximately ten weeks of the year, which doesn't leave me much to manage on. I am worried that I will be forced to give up my job because I can't afford the childminder. It will be a shame, after managing all this time, to have to live off social security money and no longer support myself. It seems to me that they just don't encourage mothers like me to be self-supporting. I even wrote to the local MP, Mr Roy Galley, but he couldn't help matters either.

Mothers like Lynne, who want to go on working, should look at the available benefits with someone who knows their way around them. It could be possible to claim one of the 'top-up benefits' during the period she has to pay the childminder.

Gingerbread advisers are often more clued-up than the people in the social security office, as they are particularly used to sorting out the best financial solution for single parents.

CHAPTER 16
Finding Work after a Break

This section is for women who gave up working when they were pregnant or during maternity leave (or who have never worked before) but now want to find a job. Of course, this is a very large subject and we can only give a broad overview of the possibilities and direct you to other sources of help – but we believe that even this is useful and important because so many women feel needlessly gloomy and pessimistic about their prospects.

Some women start thinking about finding a job when their babies are young, like Jane Parkin, from York: 'By the time Heather was eighteen months I felt like working again – once they could both tell me what was happening when I wasn't there.'

Others like to wait until the children start going to playgroup, or when the children are at primary school, like Glynis Day, a teacher who had some mixed feelings about returning to work:

> I was forced to go back to work for economic reasons, although as I am doing the job I love best this is no hardship. I was determined not to work while my children were very small and although financially things were very hard (we lived on state benefits for a few years) I would not have missed a minute of the six years I spent at home – still working hard, but not earning a

penny! I went back to work four months before my younger son started school – in fact when he was still in nursery. I felt unhappy about this as if I was shirking my responsibility to Richard, doubly so because my elder son Simon had never been left with anyone.

Many mothers wait until the youngest child has started school, which may mean they have been out of the job market for ten or more years, depending on the size of their families and the age-gaps involved. That is what happened to this midwifery sister from Scotland, who was thrilled to be working again:

> I am sure I am a much more interesting and stimulating person. Before, when I was a full-time housewife for fifteen years, I was slowly turning into a cabbage, tied down with kids and not able to have many outside interests. I was often depressed when I was at home full time – but I don't have time now.

There is no useful division to be made between the different stages as far as looking for work goes, because there are so many variables: but even if you haven't worked for many years your prospects are good if you genuinely want a job, and are determined to do what is necessary to find the work.

Returning to work after a child-rearing gap has its difficulties – but the chief one is *you*. Women who have spent some time at home as housewives looking after the children commonly suffer a crisis of confidence. This is not surprising when you think how generally undervalued the work of a housewife is: an American survey of over 2,000 different occupations ranked housewives equal in skill to cloakroom attendant, parking lot attendant and poultry offal shoveller; a survey here would probably produce a similar result.

However efficent and good at your job you were previously, the endless, usually thankless, round at home can make you feel unsure of your abilities. Even women who pride themselves on the way they bring up their children and manage their household duties rarely believe that they have learned anything that is of any use to an employer.

Joan Springall, who was the spokesperson for the National Advisory Centre on Careers for Women (now Careers for Women), when we first wrote the book, said she was continually surprised at how the women who come to see her for career advice share the view that what they have been doing is of little consequence:

> Being out of the employment situation tends to deprive a woman of confidence. She doesn't understand that looking after children, managing a family, and housekeeping, require skills that she has developed very well without being paid. She says, 'I'm only a housewife', or 'I've done nothing for the last five or six years'! We have to convince her that she has not been *paid* but she has done a lot – and gained a lot of experience – and if she has managed a home then she can manage an office or a shop or an organisation.

It is time that society as a whole looked on housewives as 'home managers' and started to respect their special competence and skills. One high-powered personnel executive we talked to made this point:

> At home you need to keep two children going, with two separate activites, paying equal attention to both, and you have to be nice to the gasman at the same time, all while you are doing the washing up and remembering to switch off the washing machine. In a management job like mine, that's exactly what you have to be good at – doing lots of things at the same time, in a fragmented fashion, while keeping track of everything that's going on.

What you have to offer

The organisational skills needed to run a home are usually

450

far in advance of anything you have been required to do before, unless you were the boss: it's a twenty-four-hour responsibility for a start, which mixes having to handle daily emergencies with long- and short-term forward planning, money management and co-ordinating the people in your household – above all being sensitive to other people. These are only some of the passed-over skills that running a house forces you to develop (if you are feeling unsure of yourself, tick off your own skills on this list, and see if you can add others):

* Cooking and catering.

* Budgeting, financial planning.

* Being sensitive to the needs of others.

* Doing several things at once.

* Scheduling your time and that of others.

* Delegating and supervising the tasks of others.

* Laundering.

* Cleaning.

* Decorating (possibly interior design/making soft furnishings).

* Home repairs (possibly plumbing/electricity).

* Clothes maintenance/mending (possibly making/ designing).

* Nursing and first aid.

* Baby and child management.

* Teaching.

* Gardening (possibly garden planning and design).

* Driving.

* Any skills acquired doing voluntary work.

You also learn to keep going when you are tired, ill, or desperately under pressure; the nature of the job is unpredictable, so you become adaptable and versatile; you are where the buck stops, so you must become decisive and responsible. Even if you privately feel that you haven't been all that hot as a stay-at-home housewife and mother, the fact is that few jobs in the outside world will demand as much of you. Many working mothers who work extremely hard in their jobs say that they find the paid work almost restful compared to what they have to do at home. As Julie Howell, who works in a bank, says:

> When I got into the housewife routine after leaving work, it all seemed to be cleaning, cooking and feeding. That was when I realised that doing the most awful jobs at work was still better than what I was doing at home!

We are aware that a short pep-talk such as this will do very little to make you feel good about yourself and your prospects of finding a job if you are suffering a true crisis of confidence. Clearly if you feel diffident about what you have to offer, applying for a job may be more than you can cope with however much you might long for one, and applying when you are feeling down is probably doomed to failure. But there are ways that you can prepare yourself so that your confidence blooms, skills are learned or brought up to date, and there is help available so that you can find the job that suits you.

The kind of job you want

As a returner you are likely to fall into one of the next four categories:

You want to go back to the kind of work you did before you had children

In some ways this gives you a headstart: you have a good

idea of the work involved and you know that you can do it because you have done it before. You will know whether it is a job that takes people after a break or is only really open to new, younger people. You also have experience – that valuable qualification that many employers demand. The most important things you now have to find out are:

1. If it is possible to find such work in your area (see *Looking for work*, below).
2. Whether you can do it freelance, if that is what you wish (see *Going it alone*, below).
3. Whether you have to brush up on your skills (see *Careers advice* and *Training*, below).

You just want to make some extra money and you don't mind what the work is

This is easy in some ways because you are not confining yourself to a particular area of work. You are probably not the main wage earner and you are not specially ambitious, but you want or need the extra money and the different sort of stimulation and company that work provides. You probably want a job with easy hours that fit in with your children, in a place that is not too far away. You will want to find out:

1. What jobs are available near you (see *Looking for work*, below).
2. Which jobs have flexible or shorter hours (see *Patterns of work*, below).
3. Whether you can exploit one of your skills from home (see *Going it alone*, below).

You want a stimulating career, and you know what you would like to do, although you have not done it before

Perhaps you have always had an ambition to do this job, but marriage and family put it out of your mind. You may feel that it is now or never if you are to follow this career. If this is so, and you have a particular ambition but no previous relevant training or experience, then you must do the following things:

1. Find out whether such work exists in your area (see *Looking for work*, below).
2. Find out what training/qualifications you need in your new career (see *Careers advice*, below).
3. Find a course that enables you to meet the requirements (see *Training*, below).

You want a stimulating career but you don't have a particular career in mind

A lot of women fall into this category. Having decided that staying at home is not enough for them, they realise (sometimes for the first time) that they need work that can challenge them and that they can take pride in. You may be surprised to find yourself feeling like this, particularly if you always thought of yourself as a homebody rather than a career person. What you will have to do is:

1. Get advice to help you analyse which career would be best for you and what qualifications you would need (see *Careers advice*, below).
2. Find a course that will give you the qualifications (see *Training*, below).
3. Set about finding such work in your area (see *Looking for work*, below).

Whichever category you are in there are some important considerations that are likely to apply to all:

Restrictions

By this we mean restrictions that may make it difficult for you to work, but that have nothing to do with your own abilities or qualifications.

Joan Springall says she sometimes spends a long time talking to a woman about the kind of career that would suit her, only to have her say, 'I can only have a job between ten and three', or 'I don't have a car so I can't go far.' Quite reasonably, Joan Springall believes these should be your *first* considerations, because they will sometimes determine what work you can do, or even how committed you are to working.

It is worth making a list of your own personal restrictions before going much further. These are the kinds of things it might include:

* Having to take children to school and collect them.

* No one to look after children in the holidays.

* No one to look after young children while you train or jobhunt.

* Transport problems.

* You need training but can't afford it.

* You have a dog that needs walking in the day.

* No work near you because of high unemployment.

* You worry that your children might suffer.

* How to do all you have to *and* work.

* Husband doesn't want you to work.

Now look at your list as objectively as you can, and divide it into two: first, genuine restrictions (childcare problems) and second, excuses (your dog needs walking). How you deal with the genuine problems (and excuses) will show your determination to work or not. This book is full of the experiences of women who have overcome similar problems and restrictions, and manage to combine jobs, even careers, with their family and home responsibilities.

Take some of the restriction you may face one by one:

Your children

All the practical problems to do with children are looked at elsewhere in the book. See the chapters on *Pre-school Childcare* and *School-age Children* to find out the arrangements you can make so that your children are properly looked after while you work. And see the chapter on *Going Back to Work* for hints about leaving your child for the first time. If you are seriously worried about the effect going out to work will have on your children, look at *Why You Shouldn't Feel Guilty*. You'll see that almost every working mother has felt the same as you, but that her own experience has shown the guilt to be quite unfounded as her children thrive. Children are often pleased about their mothers working, as one woman who works in a Citizens' Advice Bureau wrote:

> The children obviously benefit financially which they appreciate. To illustrate: when I heard about getting my present job I was jumping up and down and hugged my kids (I was slightly pleased). My astute son of seven-and-a-half-years looked me straight up and down and said, 'Oh good, that means we can go on holiday now.' They benefit from a mother who no longer feels trapped, underutilised and stale. I hope when they're older they'll feel mum is a person and not just the cook and cleaner, and hopefully they will have more respect overall.

And even Glynis Day, who felt such guilt and reluctance when she first went back to work, says:

> The children are better off financially. The older one has just had a new BMX bike for his birthday. Apart from the material benefits I think our relationship is more relaxed now I am working. I do not get so ratty with the children (usually!) because I have an outside interest and come back to them tired but delighted to see them and ready to listen.

Transport problems

If travelling to work is going to be a problem because local public transport is inadequate, explore alternative options. If you have a car but can't drive, then the obvious solution is to learn. If your partner uses the car to get to work, perhaps he could drop you off, or vice versa. Perhaps a neighbour would be prepared to give you a regular lift if you offer to contribute to the petrol. Finally, if travelling is a real problem, you could explore the options of working at home. We were overawed by Jane Parkin's solution to her transport problem when she went back to work with a toddler of two-and-a-half, and a child of four:

> At first I worked sixteen hours a week, over four afternoons. I found a registered childminder within walking distance of the nursery school, and our daily travel logistics were quite amazing and, I think, worth relating:
>
> 8.15a.m. Husband to work on bike (three miles).
> 8.45a.m. I take Sally to nursery school in car (with Heather in tow), leave car at husband's office, and cycle home with Heather on bike seat.
> 12.00   Take Heather to childminder on bike (two-and-a-half miles).
> 5.00p.m. Cycle from my office to husband's office. Leave bike, collect car.
> 5.15p.m. Collect both children from childminder.
> 5.30p.m. Husband cycles home – having had the use of the car for business almost all day.

I was very determined to make a success of my job, and refused to let exhaustion take over while I was there, but is it surprising I was asleep by 9.30p.m.?

You need training but can't afford it

See if you are eligible for a grant or find out whether you can get the qualifications you need at low cost, or through evening classes, or one of the training schemes that pay you while you learn. (See *Training*, below.)

You have a dog that needs walking in the day

If you allow a problem such as this seriously to stop you working, then you probably don't have the necessary commitment. Find a neighbour who would be prepared to pop in and do it for you – and offer to pay. If it is of critical importance to you, you could consider working from home – perhaps providing a service for other people's animals?

No work near you because of high unemployment

It is unlikely that there is really no work *at all*, but your first move should be to check out whether there is any field of employment in your area in which they *do* need people. Then you could aim to get the qualifications you need for that type of work. Alternatively see if there is work you can do at home – perhaps making things that you can sell in another part of the country.

How to do all you have to and work

Look at ways you can do less: read *Your Home and Your Partner*. If you are aiming for a highly paid job, you may be able to afford someone to come in and help. However, most working mothers report that the more they have to fit into the day the more they find they can do. Work really does expand to fill the available time. Whereas while you are at home you might find that cooking a special meal takes the best part of a day, somehow when you are working you find ways to do it more speedily.

Your husband doesn't want you to work

This is potentially the most difficult problem, depending on what your husband is like, and why he is so set against you working. Try to have sensible discussions rather than rows about this, and offer good solutions to whatever his objections might be. If he is concerned that your working will affect the children, or if he has preconceived notions about working married women, arm yourself with the arguments in *Why You Shouldn't Feel Guilty*. If you suspect that his objections stem from a fear that he will be deprived of the standard of service and support he has come to expect from you, it'll be up to you to decide whether to try to reassure him – or put your foot down! Try suggesting a compromise: you go back to work for a while and if it doesn't work out you will stop. It is then up to you to see that he recognises the value of you working.

Timing your return to work

If you are newly separated, divorced or widowed, or your partner has lost his job, then you probably need to find work as quickly as possible. You will want to go straight to *Looking for work* so that you can start trying to fix up a job. However, if the only work you can find is unsatisfactory, don't give up any ambitions you might have for a better job. You can continue to look for work from the job you are in, and if you need training you can try to find an evening course or one that you can do from home. This woman, an operating theatre technician, who wrote to us from Sheffield, is a shining example of someone who found what work she could to begin with, and then managed to fulfil her ambitions:

> My first job after having my second child was for four evenings a week 7.00 to 11.00p.m. as drinks waitress in a private hotel. My husband looked after the children, but I worried (unnecessarily) about them. When the youngest boy started nursery I worked afternoons at my father's company. I had my first child at age seventeen, with no qualifications (except O-levels) to my name, so when I got to twenty-eight, with my children growing up, I decided to do something with my life. I trained for two years for my present job. I've gained a great deal of knowledge and met a lot of people and also gained qualifications in my career. Most of all, I've done something that I always wanted to do – i.e. work in a hospital in one of the caring professions. I've also proved that a woman can work full time with a growing family and make a success of it. I enjoy my work and feel that the whole family has benefited, not only financially, but through my peace of mind at having fulfilled my ambitions and having some independence.

Many returners are in the position of wanting to find work but not being in an immediate hurry to do so, usually because they have partners who are working. This is an ideal situation from many points of view: it gives you adequate time to arrange care for your children, and allows you to undertake any necessary training. It also means that you are able to hold out until the right job comes along. As Joan Springall points out:

> It can take a year to get the right job. If you are thinking about taking an education course you have to wait for the academic year to start again – which in most cases means September. Returners should have a long-term

plan. If it is not so important that they get a job immediately, especially if they can look ahead five years or so, then they can devise a strategy. They can retrain, perhaps start working part time, and plan for when their children are older when they are less committed to the home.

Choosing and Finding a Job

Careers Advice

Anyone looking for a job after a break could probably benefit from careers advice. A local advisor will have up-to-date knowledge of the employment situation in your area. If you want to return to your previous career the advisor may be able to let you know what your prospects are, and whether you need further training. If you have a career in mind, but have no experience of the work, the advisor should be able to help you to find out whether you are suitable, what the work really involves, and what qualifications you might need to do it.

Where to get free advice

* *Your library*

Looking through relevant career books is a good first move if you either have no particular career in mind or have a vague idea of what you would like to do but don't know what it involves. See the suggested reading list in *Further Help*.

* *Careers offices*

These can be found in the phone book under your local education authority. Each has a careers officer whose job is to give free advice, and who knows what qualifications you will need for each career and how you can find the appropriate training in your area. This service is usually used by school and college leavers, but not exclusively. When you make your appointment state your age and circumstances, so that if there is more than one careers officer you can be sure to see the one who has experience in advising adults or returners. Don't be put off if they are unhelpful (as some women have reported); try one of the other options.

* *Jobcentre Library*

Some Jobcentres have job libraries which provide literature on a range of jobs. Ask at your local centre.

* *Jobcentre Employment Advisor*

This person offers a similar service to the careers advisor. If after your discussion it becomes clear that you need further training you may be put on to the Employment Training Interviewing Officer if this is appropriate. Again, these people are sometimes discouraging to returners, but persist. You can find your local Jobcentre in the phone book under 'Employment Service'; look under the subheading 'Jobcentres'.

Careers advice you pay for

There are services to help you choose the right career for you, based on your personality and abilities as well as any qualifications you might have. If you are in a quandary about what career would be most suitable for you, a professional's opinion can help. Most services operate by giving you a series of tests designed to show your strengths and weaknesses. Charges vary from under £100 up to many hundreds of pounds. (Roughly, the more important the kind of work you are aiming for, the higher the fee.)

Look in the Yellow Pages under 'Careers Advice' to see organisations in your area that offer this. They will point you in the right direction, but they can rarely help you find work. See *Further Help* for suggested organisations.

Looking for work

Jobcentres

Jobcentres are set out in such a way that you can wander in and look round without committing yourself: they are usually open plan, and cards with details of jobs are put on self-service racks. You might like to look in even before you start searching for work so that you begin to get a general idea of the vacancies in your area. If you want to follow up any of the jobs that you see on display you tell the receptionist.

Employment agencies

These are private businesses. Employers inform the agencies of any vacancies and of their requirements and they attempt to match the job with the people on their books. Look up 'Employment Agencies and Consultancies' in your Yellow Pages to find the ones near you. Some agencies specialise in particular areas of work (for example, secretarial and clerical, legal, temps). They make their money by charging the employer not the job-seeker, so the service costs you nothing. Agencies will interview you, and may test your skills. As they will be recommending you to an employer, you want to make the best impression you can. You can register with as many agencies as you want, and you should keep in regular touch with them while you are looking for work so that they get to know and remember you when vacancies occur.

Local newspapers

The reference department of your library should keep all local newspapers. Find out the days that they are published so that you can apply quickly to any ads that interest you. You can also look at national papers at the same time, although the majority of vacancies advertised will be in London.

Trade journals

If you want to return to the career you had before your children were born, or have retrained for a new career, try looking for job vacancies in the appropriate trade journal in your reference library. It is a good idea to read through these regularly anyway, so that you keep up to date on matters that relate to your career. To find out about the relevant trade journals, look at the classified index of *Willings Press Guide*.

Using contacts

If you want to return to your previous career it is worth letting it be known that you are now looking for work. Call your old boss or former colleagues and ask them to put the word round, or arrange to meet if you are on friendly terms with them. Keep in touch: there may not be an opening now but you want to be in their minds if one occurs later.

Applying 'cold'

You can approach companies direct, even if they are not advertising a vacancy at the moment. Find out as much as you can about the company first so that you know which of your qualifications/experience would be of interest to them: the Jobcentre or careers office may be able to give you some background. Telephone the switchboard to find the name of the right person to address your application to: the managing director, the personnel manager, or the head of the department that interests you. Keep the letter short: you want to stimulate enough interest to be offered an interview but don't want to say too much so that whoever is dealing with it feels able to assess you purely on the strength of the letter. They may not want to see you immediately, but are likely to put your letter on file until a vacancy occurs.

Preparing and Training for Work

The interview

General confidence-building courses help you prepare yourself for interviews, and you are often given practice in being interviewer and interviewee. Some Jobcentres run seminars on a variety of subjects, which include interview technique.

Going for an interview is not very different for you as a working mother, but you must bear in mind the prejudice that many employers hold: that you are going to be less reliable because of your children. Employers have to be very careful how they bring this subject up as it is against the Equal Opportunities laws to deny you a job for these reasons. Some may not ask you anything about your children at all, which is not necessarily a good sign: it can mean that you are not really in the running as far as they are concerned. All in all, if you have made good childcare arrangements and crisis contingency plans, it is worth mentioning the subject yourself: for instance, 'I have a very good and reliable childminder, and my sister-in-law looks after my children when they are ill.'

Training

You may have a vague idea that studying is for the young: if so you will be pleasantly surprised at the welcome given to mature students. There is almost nothing that you are barred from doing: for instance, even if you left school without a single exam pass you can now decide to take a university degree – provided that you have the basic ability and determination to study for the pre-entry requirements and complete the course. Over the years you may have discovered an unsuspected talent or skill that you have been using in an amateur way; if you now want to make it pay, you can look around for training that will help you to do so. There are also courses developed to boost the confidence of returners and help you decide what work would suit you. Joan Springall believes that aiming for any qualification is good for a woman who has lost faith in her abilities: trying for a GCSE for instance:

> Passing a maths exam is useful for the woman who has always said in the past that she has a blockage with figures. Getting a qualification in maths will give her no end of a boost – whatever she eventually decides to do. It shows her she is capable of using her brain. Being at home with children you forget how to concentrate – because you have someone interrupting you every five minutes you don't get the opportunity. You have to retrain the thought processes as well.

There are so many different kinds of courses, and the provisions vary so much from area to area, that it is impossible to give more than a general guide. The librarians at your reference library can help you find your way round the various advice books and prospectuses of local colleges, or ask at your local Citizens' Advice Bureau. See *Further Help* for suggestions.

Most educational guidance services are free, or charge a

nominal fee. If you can't find such a service near you, you could phone your local college and ask if they have an advisor for older students.

Confidence building/general courses

You may find short courses such as these at your local college of further education or polytechnic. You can either go to your local reference library and look at the prospectuses for your local college, or telephone direct. (The numbers should be under 'Schools and Colleges' in your Yellow Pages). Each college is likely to have a different name for the course, so you will have to explain that you are returning to work and want a suitable general course to get you started. Most of them are part time, and you are unlikely to get a grant for a course like this, but the fees are usually very low.

Employment training

The Employment Service runs Employment Training Schemes, some specifically for women; for instance 'Women into Management' training, which can last up to a year, and 'Women in Access' training, which aims to provide training to fill realistic needs in the local labour market. To get on to an Employment Training course you have to have been unemployed for at least six months and be receiving benefit of some kind. Places are much in demand and in some areas you can wait for a year to attend. You are usually eligible to claim an allowance while attending these courses, which can include fares. Your Jobcentre should know of the courses available in your area.

Specialist training

Once you have decided on the career you wish to follow

you can find out what specialist training is required.

* The relevant professional society (if there is one) will tell you if specific professional training is called for, and where you can study.

* You can also find out if there is a relevant course at a local college by looking at the prospectuses in your local library.

* Jobcentres will advise on what courses local techs offer, and whether there is a relevant course in the Employment Training programme.

Academic qualifications

The career you have chosen may need academic qualifications, and you may have to start by taking GCSEs and A-levels (SCEs in Scotland). Some courses will waive these for the over-25s, so you should check with the college that you want to attend.

You can study for these as a mature student at colleges of further education, technical colleges or local schools – full time, part time or in the evening, depending on what is on offer.

If you want or need a university degree, find out which universities or colleges offer the course you want to study by looking at books on degree courses in the library. You can then apply to them direct to find out what the entry requirements are.

Some universities or colleges accept adults without GCSEs or A-levels who have been on an Access Course (Higher Education Preparatory Course). Contact your local college to find out if they have such programmes.

Evening classes (adult education classes)

Evening classes are worth considering if you are working

already, or haven't made care arrangements for your children but want to study. They are not generally aimed at helping you re-enter the job market, but some of them may be able to give you a grounding in the skills you seek. Evenings classes are run by the local education authority: you can contact the LEA direct, or find out about courses from your library or Citizens' Advice Bureau. The courses on offer vary from year to year depending on the demand: from GCSEs or A-levels, for example, to anything from shorthand to upholstery, pottery or computer programming.

Studying at home

Some local colleges offer independent home study schemes, backed up by meetings with the tutors at the college to discuss your progress. They have the advantage of being flexible, as they let you go at your own pace. National schemes are listed in *Further Help*.

Gaining experience

Employers often look for experience over and above formal qualifications. You can gain useful experience by doing voluntary work before you are ready to start looking for a paying job. Jobcentres have a Voluntary Projects Programme through which you can offer your help: this is unpaid, of course, though in some cases they give travelling expenses. You can also consult the *Directory of Voluntary Organisations* at your reference library, and apply direct.

Grants and other sources of money

You may be able to get a grant from your local education authority, or a State Bursary (in Scotland, a Regional Council grant) from the Department of Education and

Science. Financial help is also available from the Employment Service (which provides grants for its own Employment Training Schemes, and very occasionally for other training leading to a job).

The rules about whether you are eligible for a grant or not are quite complicated, and change regularly – so if in doubt apply anyway, and as soon as possible.

Borrowing money

In April 1986 a three-year pilot scheme, called the Career Development Loan Scheme, was started by the Department of Employment in conjunction with Barclays Bank, the Clydesdale Bank and the Co-operative Bank, with the object of lending money for job-related training lasting between one week and one year. You find the course yourself and then apply to one of the banks involved.

No loan repayments are made during the training period and for up to three months afterwards. The Employment Department pays the interest on the loan for you during this 'repayment holiday', but after that you are responsible for paying back the loan, plus any further interest, over a period agreed in advance with the bank.

Since the pilot, the scheme has become established, and 28,000 people had taken advantage of it at the time of revising this book, for training in subjects such as computer skills, driving instruction, commercial flying, sound engineering, photo-journalism, forensic science, accountancy, business management, and alternative therapies, to give just a few examples.

Patterns of Work

Sometimes the hours you work are determined by the job you choose, but sometimes the hours you can give determine the kind of job you will go after. These are the kind of patterns you can expect to find:

'Nine-to-five'

This is the traditional working day (though it may be 8.00a.m.—4.00p.m., 9.30a.m.—5.30p.m., 10.00a.m.—6.00p.m.). The point is that it is an inflexible eight-hour day. It is the most inconvenient for the working mother: particularly if she has to add on much travelling time. However, if you have young children who need full-time care, this most nearly approximates to the hours that childminders prefer to work, and that day nurseries stay open.

Flexitime

If your company offers flexitime this means you may be expected to work an eight-hour day, but within certain limits you can choose when you work the hours. The flexible hours are usually at the start and end of the working day and at lunchtime. In between there are a number of 'core' hours during which everyone is expected to be at work. Some companies allow you to work extra hours to 'save up' for the future – for unforeseen emergencies, or to take off a day or half-day when it suits you. This is obviously good for working mothers. For instance, you can arrange always to come in later so that you take your children to school, or leave earlier, so that you can pick them up. You can also legitimately leave to sort out a crisis, knowing that you have 'earned' the time off: many of the mothers who wrote to us said that they had time 'worked up' for just this reason.

Shiftwork

Some employers offer shiftwork. This means that the working day is divided into more than one working spell.

Some have round-the-clock cover, in which case there may be three shifts, one of them a night shift; others have an extra-long day, in which case there are two shifts. Sometimes shift work alternates – you have to work on each shift for a period of time, in other cases you can choose to work only on the shift of your choice. Or there is a split day: an early morning start, the afternoon off and then work again in the early evening.

If you have a partner, shiftwork can sometimes make your childcare arrangements easier: for instance if you work the early morning shift your partner can get the children to childminder/nursery/ready for school, and you may even have time to yourself at home before the children need picking up. On alternating shifts you may be able to keep young children at home at least part of the time, arranging childcare only when necessary. Childcare becomes a problem when you are on your own, or when you and your partner work similar shifts. For instance if you both work early or late it can be hard to find a childminder willing to take your children during those hours, or she may charge extra.

We have heard of a couple who both worked shifts at opposite ends of the day, so that one partner was always at home to look after the children while the other was at work. The obvious advantage of this is not having to leave the children with someone else, nor having to pay that someone; the most obvious drawback is that you would hardly see your partner during the week.

Night shifts

Some women choose to work nights so that their children are asleep and looked after by their partners while they are at work, and they can look after them during the day. This is a very hard option, as you are unlikely to get much sleep, and you will be working almost continously. A couple of the women who wrote to us had done this for a time, but you need enormous stamina:

> I worked nights when I was twenty-one and my
> daughter was under a year old. I had a friend staying
> with me who would look after her when my husband
> had gone to work in the morning. I used to get about
> seven hours sleep, but even so I was exhausted and very
> near the edge emotionally. The other women who
> worked with me seemed to cope marvellously well.
> They were mainly over forty, and had large families.
> They would get back from work in the early hours, get
> everybody up and cook breakfast, clean the house from
> top to bottom and then catch about three or four hours
> sleep before the children got back from school and they
> had to prepare the evening meal. One of them was even
> having an affair with one of the men in her breaks
> during the night shift! I was so much younger, yet I did
> almost no cleaning and the minimum of cooking at
> home, and I still couldn't handle it. It made me feel so
> guilty. One day I went to the nurse with a splitting
> headache. She told me that I was *too* young, and that it
> suited a certain kind of older woman with exceptional
> stamina best.

Part time

'Part time' is defined as working fewer than thirty hours
per week. Many working mothers choose to work part
time because it is easier to combine this with looking after
children. Part time can mean a shorter day, or a few whole
days a week. If all you want to do is earn some extra
money and have time with your children, part time can be
your best choice. A couple of women who wrote to us
found this very satisfactory:

> * I would urge any mother with school-age children to
> go to local schools and put their names down to be
> 'dinner ladies'. If they need the money it's an ideal job
> and means you are always there for school holidays –
> which are frequent. You know that every six weeks
> you'll get a week off to catch up on extra jobs. I'm not a

career person – I trained as a window dresser and I'm working with mums who have been telephonists and office workers, etc.

* I have gone out to work part time all my married life on and off, but in all that time my children were never left or ever let themselves into an empty home. I was always there, or dad was. I have had a few jobs, mainly cleaning, housekeeping and school meals, restaurant, pub work, silver service.

But if you are career-minded part-time work may not be the best choice for you. Part-time jobs tend to be unskilled. This is not *always* true: a few of the women who wrote to us worked part time and had interesting fairly well-paid jobs, like this doctor:

I feel that being part time is a great advantage. I don't get stale and give my all when I work. If I was full time I may not be able to do that all the time.

But she was well aware of the professional pitfalls:

The only problem is with male doctors who, until they know you can work as well as they can, dismiss you as only a part-time woman.

Good part-time jobs are hard to find and the promotion prospects are almost invariably poor. The better jobs are often held by women who used to do them full time and whose firms preferred to have them back part time after they have children rather than lose them. The more skilled jobs are often more pressurised too.

Anyone who wants a good job with short hours should seriously investigate job-sharing (see below) before committing herself to other part-time work.

Pluses of part-time work

* Less pressure because you are working fewer hours
* Not so hard to find part-time childcare.
* You don't have to leave your children for so long.
* It is more flexible.
* You have less conflict of commitment if the work is undemanding.
* Good as a short-term option to gain experience and show continuity of employment when you look for other jobs, or until your children can take care of themselves.

Minuses of part-time work

* If you work fewer than sixteen hours a week you have no employment rights (unless you have worked for more than eight hours a week for the same employer for five years). To qualify for many employment rights you have to have worked the sixteen hours a week for two years – so a part-timer who likes to do a variety of jobs will always be in jeopardy. You are likely to be excluded from company sick pay, maternity leave (until 1994), pension schemes and redundancy payments (unless your union agreement says different). You are also likely to have shorter paid holidays (unless you work in the education sector) which will increase your problems during school holidays.
* Many part time jobs are paid at a lower hourly rate.
* Childcare is often more expensive when paid for by the hour (a common financial arrangement when you only need the carer part time).

If you want to do part-time work and have the choice between a shorter day and a shorter week, you should consider these points:

* A short day has the drawback that you still need to travel to work every day – so your daily travel time remains the same as a full-timer's (and travel costs will be higher than if you travel on less than five days, unless you can get a season ticket that compensates for the extra cost). The advantage is that you have more time with your children every day, and may be able to arrange to pick them up from school or be there when they get home.

* A short week of less than five full days is sometimes better for the part-timer in a more high-powered job that requires her to be there for meetings; also good if you need time to get into gear at the beginning of the working day. You will probably have more free time this way as you will spend less of it travelling to and from work. You can also pay a childcarer by the day, rather than the hour. You have entire days with your children.

Job-sharing

This means that two people divide one full-time job between them, sharing the pay, holidays and benefits. They can divide the job in whatever way suits them:

> I know a couple of mums who share a job. One mum works 8.45a.m. to 12.30p.m. as a typist and the other mum minds her son. The second mum works in the same office from 1.15p.m. to 4.45p.m. whilst the first mum minds her daughter. This arrangement works very well both for the mums and the employer.

A more common way to share the hours is for each person

to work two and a half days per week; others divide the job by working alternate weeks.

The main point in its favour is that senior jobs (which are usually closed to part-timers) can be shared, though you must still work the statutory minimum hours to be protected under the Employment Protection legislation. For instance, the job of Deputy Leader of Camden Council is a job-share, and many senior jobs in other fields are also shared, most commonly doctors, librarians, housing workers and planners (these all have job-share registers). Job-sharers can be – and often are – promoted.

There are several ways to become a job-sharer:

* You can find someone with similar skills and abilities and apply together to share a job that is advertised. (This may be someone you know already: perhaps you worked together in the past; or it could be your partner: several husband/wife teams effectively share job and childcare in this way.)

* Apply to an employment agency with your job-share partner, and see if they can find you suitable work together.

* You can take a full-time job and then apply to share it at a later date. This is obviously easiest if there is a record of sharing in your company or organisation, but if you have become an invaluable employee they may consider this option if it means they keep you. If a co-worker wants to share the job with you your employer may look even more kindly on the idea. Your union may be able to help you with this.

* Apply to employers who already use job-sharers (or an employment agency) as a lone sharer: they may be willing and able to match you up.

Job-sharing is not to be confused with *job-splitting*, a government scheme to bring down unemployment, which usually involves lower-level jobs – and the criteria for selection usually mean that people who want full-time jobs are offered the work as a 'better-than-nothing' deal, and that unemployed married women are excluded.

V-time (voluntary reduced work time options)

This option is not yet available in Britain, but pilot schemes in America have flourished since 1976, and it is hoped that something similar may be introduced over here as it is potentially the most exciting flexible working option.

Employees are given the choice of reducing their working hours (and consequently pay) by anything up to 30 per cent. The way in which they take the time off is entirely up to them: they can take the whole lot off as a block (for instance, three months if they are reducing their working hours by 25 per cent in one year) or reduce each working day by a set number of hours, or work shorter weeks. They can, at any time, opt to go back to normal full-time working and do not lose any employment rights.

If you want to explore this – through your union, say – New Ways to Work (see *Further Help*) will provide you with literature and/or a speaker.

Temporary work

This is a flexible option if you have a skill to offer such as typing, word-processing, switchboard management; if you are a teacher you could become a supply teacher, or as a nurse you could join a private nursing agency. You can choose when you want to work: for instance when your children are at school but not in the school holidays – but you don't have the self-employed headache: most temporary agencies will deduct your tax and national insurance at source for you.

> I work for an employment agency [temp], which has the
> advantage that I can take a break when I need one,
> providing the particular job I am in doesn't last too
> long.

A drawback is the fact that you have no guarantee of
getting work at the time that suits you – or any work at all
for that matter. Also you may never find yourself working
in one office long enough to make friends with your
co-workers. You usually won't be eligible for holiday or
sick pay (though some agencies offer this), pension
schemes or promotion.

Working from Home

Working for yourself (particularly from home) is an
attractive idea when you have children, on the face of it:
you can arrange your working hours to fit around looking
after your children, while saving on childcare costs and the
guilt experienced by working mothers. It also allows you
to earn money when the employment prospects in your
area are poor. But in practice being self-employed can be
hard, it doesn't necessarily suit everyone. These are some
of the difficulties:

* It never stops. Because you work from home you can
  never feel that any time is your own if there is still
  outstanding work to be done. Learning when to *stop*
  can be as hard as making yourself *start*.

* It is all up to you: if you don't do the work no one else
  will. You will have to get the work in the first place,
  which may mean having to sell your skills to other
  people, or you will have to learn to sell your product.

* You have to develop the ability to shut off from all
  the other demands on your time at home: children,

housework, shopping, partner, etc. You can find yourself only able to do your work in the evenings when the children are in bed, especially if you have pre-school children – unless you earn enough to pay for childcare.

* You don't get paid when you don't work: for instance, when you are ill or on holiday. You may have to wait a long time before being paid for a job you have completed, so you may have cash-flow problems, especially if you have to pay for materials or have other expenses in advance.

* You are responsible for your own tax and all the financial and legal side of what you do. This can't be ignored if you start to earn a reasonable amount of money.

That said, if you are self-motivating and determined and enjoy a challenge, then setting up on your own could be for you – particularly if you have a special skill or have noticed that there is a local need that you believe you can fill.

What can you do?

The range of self-employed work you can do is vast. You may have a particular talent or skill that you want to exploit (cooking, teaching, typing), or want to train in a skill that could be useful (plumbing), or feel that you can offer a service (cleaning, babysitting, driving), or have space you could use in some way at home (bed and breakfast, childminding). Your best choice will incorporate your own talent with a local need – so that you know you have a market for what you are offering.

Making time to work

You may like the idea of working from home so that you can look after your children entirely yourself; but for most work you will need some uninterrupted time. The busier you become, the more essential this will be. Evenings may be enough when you are starting out (but that cuts down on time with your partner), and some work has to be done during the day: a woman who organises conferences from home says that her toddler sometimes beats her to the phone, which can make a bad impression.

One woman we know who is a very successful novelist has a nanny, even though her children are now at school. She puts in an eight-hour day and during that time does not want to be disturbed – so the nanny takes care of the school run, morning and afternoon, and gives the children tea so that she can continue to work. Another woman who runs a design partnership with her husband from home has a live-in nanny to look after their two children. She says it is very important to make it clear to the children that when you are working you are not to be disturbed, and that the room you work in is totally out of bounds. She says you have to steel yourself against rushing out of your workroom whenever you hear your child crying, and trust the nanny to deal with any problems.

Few home businesses will pay enough for you to employ a nanny, even if the idea appeals. But you may want to send your children to a nearby nursery school or playgroup some of the time when they are little. Of course, when they start school, the school hours are potentially yours. The hardest thing to do is discipline yourself to use this time for your business, particularly if there is housework to be done, but it is essential you learn to shut off everything else.

If you are at home it is also possible for you to make more casual childcare arrangements with friends and neighbours, as Jenny Clark, who makes curtains, does:

If I know I've got a very busy pressured week coming up, I arrange for them to go out after school or nursery for tea, and when I haven't got a very busy week, I reciprocate and have other children so that other mothers can have a break. As long as you don't take advantage of people you can gain yourself a lot of time like that and it doesn't cost you anything. Also you know that the children are having a nice time because they are with their friends.

Pin money and homeworking

Many people start off working for themselves by making a little extra money doing occasional bits and pieces:

> I have worked on and off for the last fifteen years doing all sorts of things to fit in with the kiddies. I've delivered fresh eggs, sold 'party plan' clothes, crocheted ponchos (when they were fashionable). I've done Avon, and even picked brambles and sold them to works' kitchens to make a few pounds. I've also had evening cleaning jobs.

Many women are content with this, particularly if they have partners who are working.

Homeworking usually means that you work for a manufacturer from home at a piece rate. This is not the same as independently turning a hobby into a sideline. This work is usually extremely badly paid and often tedious and backbreaking, and should be approached with extreme caution, as it is very easy to be exploited.

If you are thinking of taking on this kind of work, here are some points to consider:

* How much, realistically, are you going to be able to make per hour, and is it worth it? To find out the hourly rate, make an estimate of how long it is going to take you to complete each piece. Don't take the manufacturer's estimate at face value.

482

* Avoid working for any manufaturer or employer who expects you to purchase equipment or materials with your own money in advance.

* Make sure that any equipment or materials supplied are not dangerous to have lying around with children in the house.

* If what you propose to do involves any skill, could you do it on your own behalf instead?

Freelance work

You can use a skill or expertise working at home for an employer or a number of employers: typing, telephone sales, wordprocessing, proof-reading, writing, etc. You are most likely to succeed if you built up good contacts before you stopped to have your children, otherwise getting work in the first place can be hard – particularly if you are tied to the home.

Being employed to work from home

Another fairly new development is the possibility of being employed by a company as an employee, giving up your full employment rights (paid holidays and sickness and so on) but being able to do the work mainly from home. This possibility has great advantages over doing freelance or piece work, as you will have a guaranteed salary rather than having to depend on doing work as and when it turns up. If you work from home mainly for one employer, and you have a skill that is valued, it is worth suggesting getting employee status if the employer would be reluctant to lose you. F. International, a computer company, employs 90 per cent of its staff on this basis. The majority of its employees are mothers, and they can all arrange their hours to suit themselves.

Building a Business

Some women find that what starts off as a hobby or sideline when the children were little eventually turns out to have the potential of becoming a proper business.

Jenny Clark is a good example of this. She started making curtains as an occasional little earner when her two children were small. She is an experienced seamstress, having worked in the costume departments of theatres before she married. Making curtains was something she felt that she could fit round looking after her children. To start with she worked when they were asleep in the evenings, or when Emma was at nursery and Luke was asleep in the day. But she started working more seriously when Luke went to nursery school in the mornings and Emma was at school. If she was very busy she also worked when they were around: as a lot of the work is hand-sewing it was possible to sit with them and do it. When Luke started school her workload for shops and private individuals had grown so considerably that she had put herself on the waiting list for a local workshop, and was considering expanding into interior design.

Making a sideline pay

If, like Jenny, you have started making money in a small way, it is tempting to feel lucky and grateful that you can make any money at all without going out to work. When this happens you can easily fall into the 'pin money' trap, as Jenny calls it: charging too little for your services, and not being professional about it:

If you work from home and have children, people who

earn more money than you often treat you as the 'little lady round the corner' who does their sewing for them. That is one of the reasons I decided not to make clothes – people assume it will be cheaper than shop-bought clothes, which is ridiculous. When I go to measure up I look as professional as possible: I take the calculator and I *don't* take the children if it is somebody I don't know – otherwise you look like the housewife doing a little work for pin money. That doesn't do you any good at all, and you don't build up such a good reputation. You always get people who say, 'Oh I could do this myself, but I just haven't got time.' If they think like this they feel they shouldn't be paying you as much as they would a plumber or electrician, say – but you have got to make them realise that you are in the same bracket and you charge accordingly. The point is that they are *not* doing it themselves and they've got to pay somebody else the going rate to do it.

Starting up

Whether you are developing a side-line or deciding to set up on your own from scratch, it is best to wait until you have fully recovered from the birth of your babies and they have gone beyond the exhausting stage and are sleeping through the night. Starting up is usually a tiring process and involves time, worry, and may be unrewarding financially for quite a while unless you are very lucky.

If you need to borrow money (for equipment, say) you will need more than a vague idea about what you are going to do: your bank manager will want a proper business plan, and to know that you have researched the feasibility of your idea. You need to know that you can find a market for your work – which is as important as being able to do it. Someone like Jenny, with a proven track record and a number of steady clients, would be looked on more favourably than someone with a brilliant scheme but no experience. If you can, it is a good idea to work for a while for someone who does something similar, which will give you a good idea of the possibilities and the pitfalls.

Pricing your services

People who work from home often charge too little, disregarding entirely the time it takes them to do the work. If you are knitting children's jumpers, say, and charge for the wool plus a 'profit' of £10 on top, but it takes you three days to finish, then you will find it hard to make headway in your business. Obviously you have to strike a balance between what people are prepared to pay and what brings you in a reasonable amount of money. But if you feel that people won't pay what you need it is worth rethinking your business: can you use your skills in a different way that *will* pay more?

Jenny used to make her calculations according to the time it would take to make a pair of curtains:

> But then I did some work for interior design shops and saw what they charge; now I charge slightly less than that, which is more than I charged before. I have set prices for different sorts of work. If it is one window, I give them a quote on the spot, but if not I come back home and work it all out.

Alone or with others?

Some people prefer to work entirely on their own, others prefer to have a partner to share the burden. Whichever you decide to do, you should sort out the legal position.

Jenny finds it much easier having a friend who does the same kind of work. They are not in partnership, but they help each other out:

> My best bit of advice to anyone doing anything similar is to find somebody else in the same position as you. My friend has got two children nearly the same age as mine, and they get so much time together that they are like cousins. It is good because if you get terribly pressured

you've got somebody else that you can ask to help you out. We have separate clients, but if she is very busy I will have her children for the afternoon, and if I get very busy, or have to finish a job by a certain deadline and I know I'm not going to be able to do it she'll take some of it on for me, and vice versa. One weekend she had a huge amount of work to finish so we all went over there. I went to the video shop and hired films for the children and they just got on and watched their videos, played, and had their meals together while we worked. It wasn't so bad for them because they felt they were going out and doing something nice over the weekend. It was possible for us to get on with everything and made it more bearable for everybody.

Co-operatives

If you know a number of women who want to set up their own business, you could consider a co-operative. All tasks and decisions are shared co-operatively, as well as the profits, which you divide equally. A now famous example is of a group of housewives who came together to form a cleaning co-operative. They were able to borrow money for equipment, and eventually won a contract to clean an office block – making far more money than they would if they had each gone out to char separately for private customers. (See *Further Help*.)

Advice on starting a business

* The Small Firms Service will give you free advice on any queries to do with starting or running your own business, however silly the questions might seem. They can tell you about the different ways of trading, with a partner or not, and the legal considerations. They can also advise you on sources of money to help you establish yourself or expand. (See *Further Help*.)

* The Citizens' Advice Bureau can give you some legal

advice on the practical aspects of starting up a business.

* Your bank manager can give you free advice about the financial side of things, even if you don't want to borrow money – but he will take you more seriously if you already have a good idea how you are going to operate.

* An accountant is essential once your business is operating – the service costs money, but he will usually help you make savings too. He can give you advice about setting up a partnership or limited company if applicable. It is worth making a one-off appointment anyway with an accountant, who can advise you on book-keeping systems and tell you what expenses you can offset against tax – often more than you think. As Jenny says:

> I have two bank accounts – one as my personal account, one as my business account. In your business account you can put certain things down to expenses. Recently I wanted to tape interior decorating programmes on TV so I bought video tapes and put them down to expenses. One session with a local accountant may be enough to tell you what you can claim.

Training for business

Most training courses, such as Employment Training and Youth Training, are run by Training and Enterprise Councils. There are eighty-two of them nationwide. The courses they offer are different in different areas, and, confusingly, are often called by different titles even when they offer the same curriculum. In London, for example, the Enterprise Allowance Scheme is now called The New Business Support; in Southwark it is called South Thames Enterprise Programme. Individual TECs can call courses whatever they want. Persevere in working through this maze to find the right training – particularly courses for small business set-up.

Financial help

The Enterprise Allowance Scheme will supplement your earnings for a year when you are first starting up: disappointingly, they are still offering £40 a week – the same as when we first wrote the book in 1987. The main conditions are that you apply before you start operating, and that you can raise at least £1,000 of your own money to put into the business. You can get an application pack with more details from the Small Firms Centre.

The Loan Guarantee Scheme makes it easier for you to borrow money at the outset or when you are struggling, and is aimed at small businesses (your bank manager will have details). Until the end of 1992 the Business Expansion Scheme (BES) offered a similar service. You can find out if it has been replaced by a scheme with another name from the Inland Revenue or your accountant.

If you are considering applying for such a loan, you do need a proper detailed business plan, not vague ideas. For your own sake you have to be very sure that you can make your business work before you borrow money which, of course, has to be paid back.

CHAPTER 17
Your Career

The Effect of Motherhood on Your Career

Most of this book is directed towards your role as mother – the area of life that causes working mothers the greatest worry, guilt and concern. But for many of them their work is important in its own right.

Almost all the mothers in our sample took pride in their work, whether it was a conventional career, or just a job that brought in extra money. Those who felt that working gave them something (most often mentioned were self-esteem and money) wanted to repay by doing the best work they could.

In our questionnaire we asked, 'Does your job suffer because you have children?' Of those who replied to this question, 73 per cent said no, and 27 per cent said yes (although this was often qualified with an 'only sometimes'). Many women felt they were actually better at their jobs now that they had children.

As the commonly believed fiction is that women who have children perform less well at work, we want to point out the benefits that being a mother can bring to your work.

Increased efficiency

A number of mothers noted that they worked more effectively. As one woman said, 'There is a slight pressure on me to prove myself more than before the kids', and a civil servant agreed:

> Since my child was born I'm that much more organised. I have to be. I feel I've got less time, I've got to get on with it and not waste time. That spills over into my job as well. If it means taking work home, then so be it, I'll do that.

Certainly, many women found ways of wasting less time at work than their colleagues. As an airline executive reports:

> I am much more efficient than before. Not having so much time and having to get home for the children concentrates the mind. People complain that I'm not prepared to chat that much. I only allocate about half an hour to chatting with colleagues – I think that's enough.

Mothers working part time often noted that they would work through lunch hours so that they were giving maximum value during their hours.

More responsibility

Working mothers are sometimes felt to have a less responsible attitude to their work: what this boils down to is that employers fear they may take a lot of time off for their children's illnesses and other crises. (To see how unfair this is, turn to the chapter on *Illness and Other Crises*.)

For the fact is that motherhood transforms all but the very few. Having responsibility for the life and development of much-loved children tends to confer a more generally responsible attitude, even on the previously flighty. Priorities may shift: most women put the health and happiness of their children first, but this rarely has a negative impact on work. Women who appreciate how much having a job contributes to their good feelings about themselves and increases their children's standard of living are more concerned than ever to do a good job.

A single woman who wants to marry and have children may plan ahead – but she is aware that elements in her future are mysterious and may change everything. Her attitude to work may be affected by the unknown future. A woman with children is much more aware that the pattern of her life has settled. She can look further into the future, and have a rough idea of the shape of her life, and she can include work realistically in that long-term view.

New perspective

Some women find that their attitudes to their jobs change when children come along and displace work as the most important single thing in their lives. And this often has a beneficial result. As Lesley Schatzberger, a musician, found: 'Work seemed less vital – more in perspective, and consequently I perform better!'

Other women report that a more relaxed attitude means that they panic less, and are better at dealing with the problems that arise at work.

More sensitivity and maturity

Motherhood is a crash course in selflessness. Nothing and no one is so demanding as a baby, and as the principal carer you have no rights to withdraw your labour, have any time off – or even adequate sleep. The kind of love that grows, and the new experience of life that caring for children brings, can have a major impact on your personality. Most mothers find they increase in maturity and sensitivity – and in many fields this increases their worth as workers. Even some mothers who wrote to us to

492

say that children caused them to have less time for work, made the point that the positive gains from their being mothers made it worthwhile. As this infant teacher said:

> I think my job does suffer a little due to lack of time and energy in the evening for much preparation. But on the other hand my job has benefited from my being a mother as I now have a much more caring and maternal attitude towards my class.

And a psychologist from County Down says almost exactly the same:

> Work suffers because I have less time and energy for it, but it gains because my experience of having children myself makes me (I think) a better psychologist.

A GP agrees:

> I enjoy my work more now, and being a mother helps tremendously in general practice.

More enthusiasm

Many working mothers find that they are so delighted with the contrast between work and home that they bring extra energy and enthusiasm to their work. This seemed to be particularly true in the cases of the women in our sample who had taken a career break and appreciated being back at work. Many of the mothers who wrote to us showed that they had phenomenal energy reserves: the more they did, the more, it appeared they could do. A good number of our respondents managed to squeeze additional activities into their already busy lives: committees, being scouts leaders, following evening classes (writing a book . . . !).

But being a working mother has its drawbacks, and these may affect employers' attitudes.

Lack of extra time

When our correspondents mentioned the negative impact of their family responsibilities on their jobs, lack of time cropped up most frequently. You can rarely stay late to finish off something urgent because you have to rush back to the children, and it is harder to fit in overtime.

Barbara Herbert, a market-research interviewer from Paisley, complains that if she has to work on a Saturday it can be a problem finding a babysitter (she is separated), and a teacher from West Yorkshire says she is never able to attend late meetings. Several other teachers worry about not having enough time for preparation and marking in the evenings. Another market-researcher says:

> I feel I'm cutting corners. As it happens, I bring in four times as much as anyone else in the firm, but it is not up to my usual standards. With the child, I get the work done, but by the skin of my teeth. I can't work all night as I used to, to meet a deadline, then take a day's rest.

Many women try to compensate by increasing their efficiency at work. In jobs where this is possible, they work through lunch or teabreak, or take work home.

The fact that many women worry about their jobs suffering because they cannot work longer hours than they are paid for shows just how conscientious most working mothers are!

Work-related social life

Some jobs require you to socialise for work. A woman who works in an advertising agency sums up the problem:

> You want to be home by a certain time, but that's not seen to be good. It's not that you are supposed to work longer – just to be available to go to the pub for a drink. They're not being any more productive than the women

**who have to rush off, yet if you don't go along
occasionally, they feel you're not being a good sport,
and it looks like you're not putting your all into it.**

If it is important in your job to be seen to join in the social
life centred around work, you may have to prevail
occasionally on your partner (or other relative, or
neighbour) to see to your children while you go out for a
drink after work.

But as time with your children between the end of the
working day and the children's bedtime is precious, there
are other solutions. You may decline a drink but suggest
meeting after your child's bedtime, if your partner agrees
to stay in, or if you can find a babysitter. Or tell your
colleagues that you prefer to go out with them in the lunch
hour.

Lack of energy

Some women find homelife saps their energy for work,
particularly when their children are still very young and
demanding. Like this teacher from Scotland:

> **I can cope with the routine of the job but lack the time,
> energy and enthusiasm to try out new ideas.**

But if this lethargy continues when your children are older
and easier it may not be simple exhaustion. Often, lack of
energy and enthusiasm is not linked to the tiredness and
strain of doing too much, but from having too little to
stimulate your interest. If you feel you lack energy and
enthusiasm for your job, perhaps you should ask yourself
whether you are happy in your work. You may have
grown bored with it, and would feel better for a change.

Career Prospects

Your present job may not suffer from the fact that you are a mother, but there is no denying that motherhood does have a strong tendency to make your career suffer in terms of prospects, promotions and rises. The statistics bear this out: two-thirds of women who return to work following a break for childrearing do so as part-time workers, and 45 per cent of women who return to work part-time return to a job in a lower occupational category than the one they had before. Shorter hours, which are favoured by so many working mothers as a way of seeing more of their children, tend to go with low pay, low job-status, and dead-end jobs – except for the lucky few. It has been estimated that a woman's lifetime earnings are reduced by between 25 and 50 per cent if she has children.

Women with children may feel reluctant to leave a sympathetic employer. As one single mother put it:

> I am put off applying for better-paid jobs because my boss appears to be quite sympathetic to my case, and is always reasonable when I have to ring in on the mornings my daughter is ill. I really do feel, sometimes, that I would like a change, but I'm a little loth to go after something else – better the devil you know. Even in spite of these days of liberated women and equality, I still think the odds are stacked against you when applying for jobs when you have children.

Even in full-time jobs, working mothers are often passed over for promotion because they cannot extend their hours and take on more work. This teacher from Scotland explains:

> I really wouldn't like to consider promotion because it would be difficult to get the time to put in, for example, as Head of Department. In school there are no married

women with children who are in head of department jobs. That's not because they're not competent.

In the world of the high-flyer, as somebody said, promotion does not equal ability as much as flexibility and mobility – which most working mothers haven't got. They cannot, for example, move to another city, because they are tied to their husband's jobs and their childcare arrangements or children's schools. They may not even be able to move to another office in the same town because it is too far from the nursery. And they may not be prepared to do the extra travelling and socialising required, which will interfere with the time they need to preserve for their family.

This woman stayed at home when her children were small, and only went back to work when her youngest was seven:

> I think my career suffered because I stopped working when I had my kids. If I hadn't, I would have been where I am now ten years ago. And that would have opened up a lot more opportunities for me. Not that I feel I have done badly since I've been back at work. But I do think it's very hard for women to maintain their career momentum when they have children. A lot of women tend to just stay where they are. A few progress, but they're quite unusual. Most women, especially when their children are quite small, tend to just mark time, for at least five years or even longer.

We did hear from a number of women who found children no impediment, but they tended to be very highly motivated. One of the women we interviewed, who works for an airline, was actually promoted while she was at home on maternity leave. And another mother, a civil servant, reports:

> I've been promoted twice since my daughter was born almost three years ago. I had a boss who refused to send me on a training course, because he thought I ought to

be at home looking after my baby (he was a man, of course). I went on the training course anyway, and left the department. I'm now the Principal Scientific Officer in another department.

Phyl Driffield also had to overcome prejudice:

> I returned to work as a staff nurse. When I looked for promotion to deputy sister I was told I was unreliable by someone in senior management because I had a young child and would take extra time off work. I got my promotion eventually, although it took longer than usual. But in the two years I have worked since maternity leave I have proved that person wrong by taking one sickness day in the whole time. No one can say working mothers are unreliable – no more so than other people.

Many women accept that they have to sacrifice ambition and switch to a slower lane, at least temporarily, while their children are young. A good number are happy to do so because they feel having children compensates for a temporary set-back in their careers. But there are plenty of examples all around us of successful women who have not let their children slow their careers down. Superficially it seems to be easier to stay in the fast lane if you work for yourself – some of the most successful working mothers started their own businesses, often intially to get round the inflexibility of working for someone else. But if you are not highly motivated it is easier to sink than swim if you are self-employed.

Employers are often too inflexible to give working mothers the opportunities they need, but things are changing, and a number of forward-looking employers are starting to offer new ways of working that benefit the working mother.

Switching direction

Starting your own business or capitalising on a skill by working from home is an option that appeals to many women who find their job does not give them enough time with their children. Anne Babb, whom we interviewed about nannies because she runs her own nanny agency in West London, is an excellent example. She had a high-powered job in the fashion business before her two children were born, and she went back to a similar job when her youngest child was three:

> I enjoyed it because it wound me up again, because I proved I could work, that I was as good as before. But after two years the gloss went, I changed. The hours were very long, and the job involved a lot of travelling, which I enjoyed to begin with. But then I started missing the children – really missing them. My husband's concern had taken off, so we weren't relying so much on my salary any more, I decided that in ten years' time I didn't want to be working with clothes, I really wanted to do something completely different. One evening, I saw a small ad in a local newspaper for a nanny, and the penny dropped: this was something I could do from home. I was very inspired by my nanny, Liz, who had been so good: she gave me confidence to set up the agency. I made extensive enquiries first, then slowly set about getting a licence, trying to build up a stock of girls, and I set up shop about six months after I had the idea. I already had a typewriter, but my father lent me money to help with the initial expenses, like advertising. I am so pleased I made that decision. I like working for myself. I was worried that I wouldn't be self-disciplined but that hasn't been a problem – working for yourself just gets you cracking! Mainly of course, I like seeing more of the children. In the old job, when we did see each other we were all so tired that we weren't fit to speak to each other. I felt our relationship was suffering. My quality of life has improved so much. I love being part of the local community: forget about going into the

West End. If my job in the fashion industry hadn't been so draining, though, I'd probably still be there.

When work comes first

One highly successful hospital doctor explained on her questionnaire that she was putting her best energies into her career at the moment, and this included travelling for longish periods away from home. As she said:

> I feel more confident in my role of hospital doctor than that of a mum – but that's a very personal aspect. I think that might even up a bit as the children get older. I relate better to slightly older children and I find babies a wee bit frightening.

This woman is a good mother, but the urge to have children is not confined to women who make good mothers. Some mothers, working or not, don't even relate well to older children, but find their rewards when their children turn into adults. Some are at their very best with babies, and then it's downhill all the way. Others fail to make good relationships with their children at all. Good caring mothers find that they are better at some stages than others – perhaps finding a child who turns saintly after being an explosive toddler rather irritating, and coming into her own again when there are difficulties to solve in the later school years.

Career women find that there are similar peaks and troughs professionally. Sometimes, with a promotion in sight, you will want and need to work especially hard, or go away for a while, and this may make you worry that you are becoming a bad mother. But, as we point out in the chapter dealing with guilt, a happy and fulfilled mother is better than a frustrated one, and so long as you make the best arrangements you can for your children, 'going for it' in short bursts is unlikely to do harm. If you love – and like – your children, you will make it up to them when the pressure is off. Children of all ages sense how their parents feel about them: no matter what you say or do, however much 'quality time' you set aside, if you find your children boring or irritating they will feel it at a subconscious level. Conversely, children who are adored feel secure and well loved, even if their mothers are over-worked or temporarily absent.

If, frankly, you are not a 'good mother' and your relationship with your children is strained, it could be argued that your being wrapped up in your work is no worse than your being around – if you resent it. One woman we talked to, whose own mother had worked while she was a child, had this to say:

> It was unusual at the time. She worked full time, had three months off for each kid and then went back to work. I suppose I just accepted it, but I do not regard my own childhood as a happy one. She was too obsessed with her work, and not with us – very much in her own world. But I don't think she would have been much cop if she had been at home either. She's just not that sort of mother!

A mother who finds a fundamental fulfilment in her relationship with her children will usually adjust her career aims accordingly, if only for the few years that her children really need her. But usually such career adjustments need only be made for a relatively short proportion of one's total working life. For, as one mother pointed out:

> When you think how long we live nowadays, children only take up a small proportion of our lifetime. In ten years' time the children could be leaving home, and I will still only be forty-two. Why should I live my life totally for them? I've got a lot of living to do as well.

Involving Your Children in Your Work

Small children have a tendency to believe that they cause everything that happens around them – including the fact that you go out to work. It helps your children to accept the fact that you must go out to work if you explain it in easily understandable terms. A social worker with a four-year-old reports:

> My daughter has coped remarkably well with our various arrangements and she was overheard explaining to her younger friends that her parents have to go out to work to buy food and pay the bills.

As your children grow up there are extra benefits to be gained when your place of work and your co-workers become familiar. A Lancashire local government officer told us of the relaxed relationship her children have developed with her colleagues:

> They have always been able to pop into the office if they have forgotten or lost their train fare, for instance. If I am not there, my boss or one of the girls will sub them. They know that many of the 'extras' – clothes, weekend breaks, holidays etc. – are only possible because I work, as my husband's salary is eaten away by the cost of running the house, cars and housekeeping.

Also, as your children grow up they can develop a pride in what you do. For some women this is an important bonus – that their children respect them as professional individuals rather than consider them 'just' as mothers – a kind of convenient service appendage to themselves. A contracts manager who has two teenage children says:

> I think they are proud of what I do. They can boast about it to their friends, also they like the independence that it's given them, that I'm not breathing down their

necks the whole time. The nice thing about working for a publishing company is that children can understand what it means, and they see perks in what I do, like free books. They understand why their mother is away at work. They come and visit my office periodically. Sometimes they'll just turn up, or I'll invite them. It demystifies things, gives the children a sense of where you work. It also brings it home to your colleagues that you have children.

Explaining what you do

If you are a nurse, doctor, or teacher, cook or shop assistant, it will be quite easy even for a small child to understand what you do at work. Or, like this mother of four from Northern Ireland:

> My children are interested in my work and as they grow older I tell them a little more about it. I work as a psychologist in their school, so they often see me there.

But if you work at something more abstract – most office jobs, for example – it may be very difficult for a child of any age to understand exactly what it is you do there all day. Julie Howell says, 'I work in a bank and the children think all the money is mine.'

If your job is outside the grasp of your children when they are little, you should use concepts they can understand:

> My own father worked in public relations: I remember him explaining to us when we were little that this meant his job was solving other people's problems.

A simple explanation like this is better than nothing, especially when coupled with more concrete details of what it is you physically do at work, for example, you sit at a desk and talk on the telephone or write letters on a computer.

As your children grow older, you can tell them more, especially when interesting things happen in your day.

Visiting your place of work

If you can arrange it, taking your little children to visit your place of work is a good idea. This gives them a picture of where you sit, and the opportunity to meet the people you work with, so your stories about work will seem more real. Going there on the same bus or train you use every day will be a special treat and will help to make your working day familiar and imaginable in future.

Where you work may seem boring to you, but most young children will be fascinated: normal things such as filing cabinets, typewriters, VDUs, staplers, coffee vending machines and photocopiers, will be a source of interest and amusement, especially if they are allowed to bang away on an old typewriter, make a photocopy of their handprints, or even make a necklace from paperclips. Children will be fascinated to see you in a different environment: 'your' school and the children you teach, or 'your' shop, and the different way you talk and smile. Even older children are intrigued to see your professional personality and the way you relate to colleagues.

If your children are too young to behave for very long, arrange for someone else to bring them round to your place of work just before you leave, or come in together for a short while on your day off.

If there is a safety reason why children are not allowed on the premises (for example, if you work in a hospital, laboratory or factory) you can show your child your journey to work and the outside of the building. You may want to ask a colleague to take a picture of you at work, which you can give your child.

Bringing your work home to your children

When they are young your children will probably enjoy 'helping' you in your work. Susan Lumb, a dental nurse from Yorkshire, involves her children in her work like this:

> **I talk to them about diet, cleaning teeth, oral hygiene. They also help me design posters for the surgery.**

Anne Babb, who runs a nanny agency, holds a weekly open house for the local nannies she has placed, at which her children (aged eight and six) meet the girls she works with:

> **They really enjoy meeting them, and often ask me what has happened to so-and-so. They also talk about 'mummy's nannies' to their friends.**

Bringing home discarded office supplies for your children to play with will also create an imaginative link for them with your work. For example, waste paper (computer printouts are especially good) for drawing and painting on, or carbon paper, packing materials, paperclips, and rubber bands. One child we knew spent many happy hours playing with the tiny pieces of confetti collected from a tape puncher on a telex machine. Look around you: there is bound to be something about to be thrown away at work which would amuse your child.

When You Have to Travel for Work

Most mothers would prefer not to have to leave their children to travel, but in some jobs, travelling is essential – especially if you are competing for status and promotion. Here are some practical suggestions to make it easier for you and your children during enforced absences.

A number of the women we heard from took the odd business trip in their stride. Some said they had to arrange for extra paid help at home while they were away; others said their husbands took over and managed without them. In some cases, a relative came to stay. One mother we spoke to was able to combine her business trips abroad with those her husband needed to make, so they took their two-year-old along and found babysitters through the hotels they stayed in. Another mother took her baby (whom she was still breastfeeding) along to an important sales conference away from home, new nanny in tow. Unfortunately, this plan backfired as the nanny was terribly homesick and quit on the second day of the conference. Somehow, with the help of sympathetic fellow workers, she muddled through.

A London market researcher has to travel all over the country for her work, and her research often has to take place in the evenings. She is a single mother with a three-year-old, and gets round the problems by having a live-in nanny who will take over on the nights she has to be away. She also has a lodger (a friend) to call on in an emergency:

> I have a strict ruling at work that I will leave, unless I have a particular meeting, at 5.30, so that I see my son for an hour and a half every evening. I never go out socially until he has gone to bed, but I may have to stay out for work about one or two evenings a week on average. If it's an overnight trip I won't be able to see him the following morning either, but usually I'll move heaven and earth to get home by midnight, so that at least I'm there when he wakes in the morning.

If you make satisfactory alternative arrangements, your children are unlikely to suffer if you are away occasionally for short periods. But that does not mean it is not hard for both of you when they are very young:

> The first time I had to leave my baby for a business trip was the worst. As the plane took off I found myself in floods of tears, I felt so guilty at leaving him. At the same time I was terribly embarrassed because I was sitting next to my boss.

Being away from home for longer periods, or constantly having to travel, is more difficult – even when your children are older and can understand. An airline executive regularly runs week-long courses away from home and she also has to travel abroad a lot. Recently, she spent a month away in India. She confessed that her absences did create problems with her children (now aged six and four):

> Last year, I was just away too much, I was having to go to the States every other week. The children would say, 'Ooh, you're not going away *again*, mummy,' and cling to me when I left the house. There are two reasons why that's bad: because you're away such a lot, but also because you're absolutely knackered when you return, so you give your children even less attention.

But a doctor from Belfast believes that travelling should not be a problem, so long as the children are securely cared for at home:

> I've spent the occasional week away from home travelling for professional purposes and even had to work for two months in London last year. On that occasion I commuted weekly to Belfast for weekends and drafted in extra help for evenings for my husband. I am currently planning a three-month period abroad in connection with work. This is a little more difficult to arrange as help will be required at home at weekends too. However it can be done. I'm a bit apprehensive that the younger child will pine, but commonsense tells me it is most unlikely as children are in the main remarkably adaptable.

Preparing your child for your absence

When children are babies there is little you can do about preparing them for your absence. Some mothers find the fact that they *can't* explain is the most distressing part about leaving. With toddlers it is somewhat better, but they have no concept of time; there is little point trying to prepare them for the fact that you have to go away weeks in advance. The day before your departure is soon enough. Older children may need longer to get used to the idea – the older they are the more you can include them in discussions and preparations from the outset.

Young children will need reassurance that you will be coming back. Do not take it for granted that they know this. Children may develop strange fears and worries that they never voice. Try to anticipate what your children may be thinking so that you can put their minds at rest.

> I don't remember it myself, but it has become family legend about what happened when my mother went on a business trip after I had just turned three. It was very well publicised and even made the news. Everybody thought I would be thrilled to see her on the television waving and smiling. But I became inconsolable and it took them days to find out why. They kept telling me she would be coming back soon – and that made it worse. My father finally got it out of me that I thought she had been shrunk and put inside the television, and when she came back she would be a 'little mummy' – and I didn't want one of those!

Preparing your children also means letting them know when you are coming back. With a small child tomorrow may seem as remote as 'next year', so this is often difficult. One mother explained her return to her toddler in this way:

> Mummy will be back, not after tonight, when you've gone to bed and woken up in the morning, not after tomorrow when you have been to the minder's and

508

daddy has picked you up and you go to sleep, but *that* day when you've woken up again and been to the minder's. Then mummy will be back home with you.

You may be away for a lot longer than that, but it helps your children to visualise a period when you are *not there*.

Talking about feelings

Some mothers are reluctant to broach the subject of their children being upset by the parting. But you will not be putting ideas in your children's heads by talking about it. If your children don't miss you and feel sad, the fact that you talked about it won't bring the feelings on.

It is tempting for your own peace of mind to go the other way and try to elicit a positive response from your child, by saying things like, 'Now you're going to be fine when mummy's gone, aren't you? You're going to have a lovely time because you are going to Sally's party and you will be happy, won't you?'

To a young child (and even many older ones) pronouncements of this sort are like an order, and children often feel that what you say *must* be right. So sad feelings when they come (after being pushed over during musical chairs at Sally's party – *and* you are not there) are bewildering.

It is much more reassuring for children to know that their sad and gloomy feelings are legitimate and understood by their parents.

You don't have to labour it, but you can suggest coping strategies to your children for when they feel sad, such as: 'You can cuddle your teddy; or go and tell daddy and talk about it.' You can mention that you will feel sad too, 'And then I'll look at your picture and think about how I am going to see you soon.'

Even if your child has a little preliminary weep about you going away during a talk like this, it may well mean that worries not previously discussed get aired.

Involving your child in the preparations for your trip

Once your children are old enough you can explain why you are going away. If the *purpose* of your trip is too difficult to grasp, explain the practical aspects: where you are going, and how you are going to get there, so they can stay close to you in imagination. A young child will enjoy talking about planes and trains, especially if you can look at pictures of them together.

In families with older children, a business trip can be the occasion for the whole family to pore over maps and work out detailed itineraries or map out your route by sticking pins into a map. This is a good way to make your trip real and comprehensible to your children. As a fashion PR consultant said, 'I try to involve them in the excitement of where I am going.'

Other parents get their children to help them with their suitcases or count out foreign currency. The Belfast doctor reports:

> My eldest girl became quite blasé about 'Mummy's going to London'. She's quite interested in her own way and wants me to show her the places I visit sometime. Once I was packing my case and she came with her security bunny blanket thing and *insisted* it went into my suitcase. At that time luggage checks were routine at Belfast Airport and I felt I had some explaining to do when my case was opened and this grotty much-chewed pink blanket thing was displayed!

Reminders of you

* *Story tapes*

If you have a tape or cassette recorder, tape a favourite

bedtime story so that your children can listen to you talking at bedtime when you are away:

> I taped a whole cassette full of silly stories to be played to him at bedtime – with things like, 'Mummy loves you and she'll be home again soon with you.' Apparently he played it over and over again during the days I was away.

* Photographs

You can give each of your children a picture of you (preferably a happy one of you together).

* Something of yours

You may entrust a possession of yours – for example a favourite pen, calculator, bracelet or pocket mirror – to your child to look after until you return, to reinforce the idea that you are really coming back.

Keeping in touch

* Phone calls

Most of the mothers who travelled regularly said they phoned home as often as possible. If you can, arrange a pre-set time to phone home when the whole family will be around and waiting for your call. This will give your children something to look forward to (so long as you don't fail to phone – or make a mistake in calculating the time difference!).

* Postcards, letters and letter tapes

Children love receiving mail addressed to them, so do send postcards or letters even if they are too young to read:

> I wanted to send my toddler a postcard every day, but as
> I was going abroad they would only have reached him
> after I'd got back. So I wrote a card for every day I
> would be away and got my mother to post them, one a
> day, from her house. He is too little to realise that the
> stamps are wrong, and it gave him a real thrill to get
> them from the postman. They tell me he carried them
> round with him everywhere.

If you can take a small portable tape recorder away with
you then you can send back letters on tape.

One well-travelled mother counsels that if you have
several children you should put individual postcards
addressed to each child in one envelope, so that they all
arrive together.

Presents

It is common practice for travelling parents to bring back
gifts for their children when they have been away,
especially abroad. If you worry that coming back with
presents is like bribery to compensate for your absence, or
that it encourages acquisitiveness in your children,
remember that the fact that you have brought back a
present is also an indication that you were thinking of your
children while you were away.

This is one mother's attitude to presents:

> I bring them back presents, but not each time I'm away,
> to make sure they don't automatically expect me to. But
> if I go anywhere interesting, I do take them back
> something. I took a huge suitcase when I went to Cairo,
> and brought them back this camel . . .

Even if you don't bring back a 'real' present you can
probably thrill young children just as much with little
soaps and other giveaways saved from your hotel room
(pens, little sewing kits, shower caps, etc.) and little gifts
from the plane, like plastic cutlery, salt and pepper sets,

and scented towels in sachets – even empty miniature spirit bottles. If you ask, the air hostess may give you a wing badge for your child, or some of the games and colouring books often carried to amuse children on board.

CHAPTER 18
Your Rights

The Employment Protection Acts gives certain basic statutory rights to working women who become pregnant. If you fulfil the necessary conditions, these rights are:

* The right to paid time off work for keeping antenatal appointments.

* Protection against unfair dismissal during pregnancy.

* The right to maternity pay for up to eighteen weeks.

* The right to return to your old job (or its equivalent) for up to twenty-nine weeks (about seven months) after the birth of your child.

Apart from these maternity rights there are no special employment rights for working people who happen to be parents, but in this chapter we also point to the main state benefits you can obtain as a parent, as well as the extra ways in which certain employers offer help to their employees who are pregnant or parents. We also attempt to clarify your tax position.

Political background

There are no conditions attached to the right to paid time

off for antenatal check-ups, but the qualifying conditions for the three other rights listed above are so strict that they exclude about half the working women in the country. Compared to our European neighbours we are not very well off in Britain when it comes to state maternity rights and benefits. Compare, for example, Sweden, where either the mother *or the father* can take nine months' leave (or half of this time each) at 90 per cent of normal salary after the birth of their child. Or Italy, where the law entitles you to eleven months' maternity leave (five months at 80 per cent of your pay). Working parents in Britain are a very low priority, as demonstrated when Britain stood alone against all its European Community partners and vetoed a proposal to bring in a general parental-leave policy. But on the other hand, we are a great deal better off in Britain than in the United States, where pregnant workers have no legal rights to maternity leave or pay at all.

Happily, in 1992, Britain gave way to pressure from other countries in the EC and abstained in a vote on a directive that allows *all* women to take fourteen weeks of paid maternity leave, irrespective of how long they have been in their jobs. (By abstaining, Britain registered its objection but did not block the directive going through.) This still leaves Britain bottom of the European league table when it comes to taking care of pregnant women – and our representatives watered down the original proposal which called for the leave to be on full pay – but it is a move in the right direction.

At the time of revising, this is the only improvement for pregnant women and will be implemented in 1994. The revised rules for Statutory Maternity Pay (SMP) which came into force in April 1987 do represent an improvement on the old system, in that you now have some flexibility about when you take maternity leave: in order to qualify for the full eighteen weeks' maternity pay, you do not need to leave work, as before, almost three months before the baby is due if you do not want to.

But now that SMP is all paid by your employer, rather than partly as a separate maternity allowance from the DSS, as before, it means that the whole sum is now taxable.

Also, from April 1987, the £25 Maternity Grant, a single payment which used to be available to all mothers (working or not) to help with baby equipment and so on, was abolished, and the means-tested £75 (now £100, and called Maternity Payment) which replaced it is only available to women already receiving Income Support or Family Credit.

Although superficially this may seem fairer and make more sense than the old system, this Maternity Payment is only paid in full to those with savings below £500, and extra single payments for baby equipment and maternity clothes, which used to represent as much as £180 to mothers in real need, have been abolished altogether.

Your Maternity Rights

Working out your rights

Our purpose in this book is not to complain about how bad things are, but to help other working mothers make the best of the situation as it now stands. In an attempt to help you plough through the complex rules and regulations to discover which rights and benefits apply to you, we have prepared three flow-charts, on maternity pay, the right to return to work, and unfair dismissal. To help you understand the *timing* of it all, we have drawn up a pregnancy/maternity calendar. However, these charts and the calendar should only be used as a guide, not as gospel truth, as we have had to do a certain amount of simplifying. In any case, the rules are constantly changing, making it possible that our information will be out of date by the time you read this book. If you have a problem, do consult your employer or union representative, or seek advice from your Citizens' Advice Bureau and/or your social security office or Jobcentre.

1. Paid time off for keeping antenatal appointments

Every pregnant woman is entitled to this. See the *Pregnancy and Work* chapter for details.

2. Unfair dismissal

Do I qualify for protection against unfair dismissal?

See if you fulfil the conditions in the 'Unfair Dismissal' chart.

What does it mean?

The law protects you from being sacked from your job just because you are pregnant. Unfortunately, until the new EC directive becomes law, probably in 1994, if you have been working for your present employer for less than two years (or five years if you work less than sixteen hours a week) you are *not* protected. However, if you don't fulfill these conditions, and *are* dismissed, you might have redress under the Sex Discrimination Act, and you could get compensation. The Equal Opportunities Commission, or your trade union, will advise.

Does it mean I cannot be sacked at all while pregnant?

If your employer can prove to an industrial tribunal that there is an acceptable reason other than the reasons

UNFAIR DISMISSAL CHART

Note: some of these restrictions will change when the EC directive becomes law in 1994

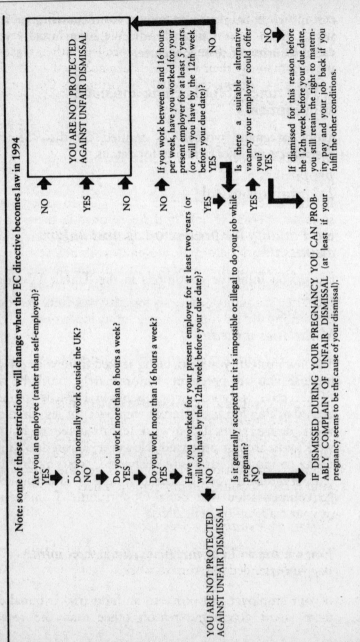

Are you an employee (rather than self-employed)?
YES → | NO → YOU ARE NOT PROTECTED AGAINST UNFAIR DISMISSAL

Do you normally work outside the UK?
NO → | YES → YOU ARE NOT PROTECTED AGAINST UNFAIR DISMISSAL

Do you work more than 8 hours a week?
YES → | NO → YOU ARE NOT PROTECTED AGAINST UNFAIR DISMISSAL

Do you work more than 16 hours a week?
YES →

NO → If you work between 8 and 16 hours per week, have you worked for your present employer for at least 5 years (or will you have by the 12th week before your due date)?
YES → | NO → YOU ARE NOT PROTECTED AGAINST UNFAIR DISMISSAL

Have you worked for your present employer for at least two years (or will you have by the 12th week before your due date)?
NO → YOU ARE NOT PROTECTED AGAINST UNFAIR DISMISSAL

Is it generally accepted that it is impossible or illegal to do your job while pregnant?
NO → IF DISMISSED DURING YOUR PREGNANCY YOU CAN PROBABLY COMPLAIN OF UNFAIR DISMISSAL (at least if your pregnancy seems to be the cause of your dismissal).

YES → Is there a suitable alternative vacancy your employer could offer you?
YES → IF DISMISSED DURING YOUR PREGNANCY YOU CAN PROBABLY COMPLAIN OF UNFAIR DISMISSAL (at least if your pregnancy seems to be the cause of your dismissal).

NO → If dismissed for this reason before the 12th week before your due date, you still retain the right to maternity pay and your job back if you fulfil the other conditions.

connected with your pregnancy for dismissing you, it won't count as unfair dismissal. We have heard several cases of women dismissed for so-called 'other reasons', when previously their work had been accepted as perfectly satisfactory. Again, the Equal Opportunities Commission will be able to advise.

What if it is dangerous or illegal to do my job while pregnant, or if it is impossible to do it properly?

In this case, your employer is obliged to offer you a suitable alternative job if there is one. If there is not another job, your dismissal will be considered 'fair'. But if you leave work before the eleventh week before your due date because of this reason, you will still be eligible for your normal maternity pay and the right to return to your job after maternity leave, so long as you fulfil the other conditions and let your employer know in writing.

How do I make a complaint about unfair dismissal?

You can complain to an industrial tribunal. Get advice from your union representative, local law centre, Citizens' Advice Bureau, regional office of ACAS (Advisory, Conciliation and Arbitration Service), or Equal Opportunities Commission. You can also get the forms from your local Jobcentre or employment office.

When do I make a complaint?

You must make your complaint within three months of the day you intended to return to work.

MATERNITY PAY CHART

Note: some of these restrictions will change when the EC directive becomes law in 1994

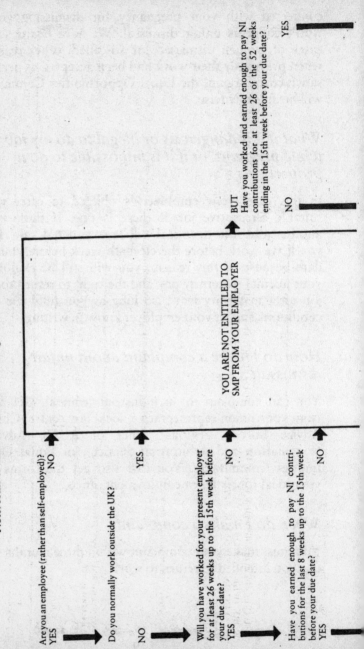

Are you an employee (rather than self-employed)?
YES   NO

Do you normally work outside the UK?
NO   YES

Will you have worked for your present employer for at least 26 weeks up to the 15th week before your due date?
YES   NO

Have you earned enough to pay NI contributions for the last 8 weeks up to the 15th week before your due date?
YES   NO

YOU ARE NOT ENTITLED TO SMP FROM YOUR EMPLOYER

BUT
Have you worked and earned enough to pay NI contributions for at least 26 of the 52 weeks ending in the 15th week before your due date?
YES   NO

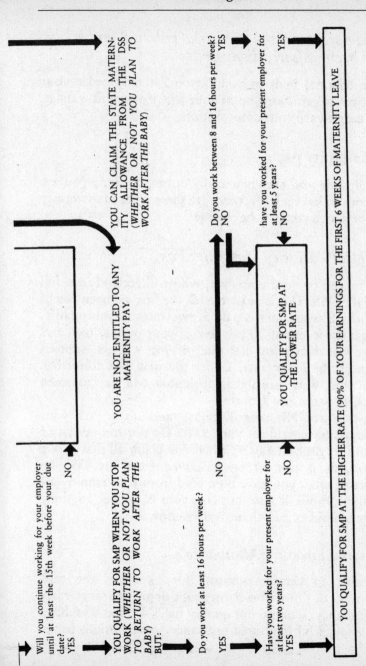

Will you continue working for your employer until at least the 15th week before your due date?
YES

NO

YOU ARE NOT ENTITLED TO ANY MATERNITY PAY

YOU CAN CLAIM THE STATE MATERNITY ALLOWANCE FROM THE DSS (WHETHER OR NOT YOU PLAN TO WORK AFTER THE BABY)

YOU QUALIFY FOR SMP WHEN YOU STOP WORK (WHETHER OR NOT YOU PLAN TO RETURN TO WORK AFTER THE BABY)
BUT:

Do you work at least 16 hours per week?
YES

Do you work between 8 and 16 hours per week?
YES

NO

NO

Have you worked for your present employer for at least two years?
YES

have you worked for your present employer for at least 5 years?
YES

NO

NO

YOU QUALIFY FOR SMP AT THE LOWER RATE

YOU QUALIFY FOR SMP AT THE HIGHER RATE (90% OF YOUR EARNINGS FOR THE FIRST 6 WEEKS OF MATERNITY LEAVE

What happens if the industrial tribunal find I have been unfairly dismissed?

If the tribunal finds in your favour, it may order your employer to reinstate you in your job, if you still want it. Or it may award you compensation.

3. Maternity pay

To help tide you over financially during the time you are off work to have a baby, there are three types of maternity pay for which you may be eligible:

A. SMP (Statutory Maternity Pay)

Paid to you by your employer, who will reclaim it in full from the DSS. This is available for the first eighteen weeks you are off work, and is paid at two rates: if you qualify, you get six weeks at 90 per cent of your normal pay, and twelve weeks at a low flat rate; or you will get eighteen weeks at the lower rate. Under the new EEC directive, those who were previously ineligible will get fourteen weeks, all at the low flat rate.

Your own NI contributions, and those of your employer, have paid for your SMP. Do not feel guilty, or grateful to your employer, when you claim all that is due to you, as *it can all be reclaimed* from the DSS by deducting what you have been paid from your employer's monthly NI bill. It does not cost your employer anything except a bit of extra administrative effort.

B. State Maternity Allowance

Available to certain women (for example, the self-employed, or those who change jobs or give up work early in pregnancy) who do not qualify for SMP, but who have paid enough NI (National Insurance) contributions in the last year. This allowance comes from the DSS for eighteen weeks and is a flat rate payment (equivalent to sickness benefit).

If you qualify for SMP or the State Maternity Allowance, you are entitled to this money whether or not you intend to return to work after the baby.

After twenty-eight weeks of pregnancy, you are entitled to the same maternity pay and leave, so long as you meet the other qualifications and conditions, even if your child dies.

C. *Additional maternity pay from your employer*

Many employers, especially large firms with union agreements, offer a special maternity agreement or policy to their employees, with additional maternity pay, which comes from the employer.

A. SMP (Statutory Maternity Pay)

Do I qualify?

See the Maternity Pay chart.

When do I start getting it, and for how long

* You do not qualify for SMP unless you work until at least the fourteenth week before your due date, but you cannot start receiving it until the eleventh week before your due date at the earliest.

* You start receiving SMP when you stop work (unless you stop work between the fourteenth and eleventh week before your due date).

* You can receive it for a maximum of eighteen weeks, and you have some choice about when to start your maternity leave. There is a 'core' period of thirteen

weeks, starting six weeks before your due date, during which you must be off work in order to qualify for the full eighteen weeks' SMP. But the remaining weeks may be taken when you like, either before or after the core period.

* If you go on working after the sixth week before your due date, you will receive less than eighteen weeks' SMP in all (but you will be receiving your full regular salary instead, so as long as you don't mind being at work, you will not actually be worse off).

What if it is impossible for me to work until the fourteenth week before my due date?

If you resign voluntarily from your job before the fourteenth week before your baby is due you forfeit your right to SMP. But if you are 'fairly dismissed', or if you are ill, you retain your right to be paid SMP as long as you make it clear to your employer that you are away from work for that reason and not because you have resigned. If you are ill, or have to stay in bed because of a threatened miscarriage, for example, you may be entitled to Statutory Sick Pay in the meantime.

How much will I get?

SMP is paid at two rates: you will have PAYE and NI contributions deducted on both.

Higher rate SMP

If you qualify for this (see the Maternity Pay chart) you will get 90 per cent of your normal, average, weekly earnings, for the first six weeks of your maternity leave.

Lower rate SMP

This is a flat rate reviewed each April, equivalent to the lowest rate of Statutory Sick Pay. Unlike SSP it is not even broadly related to your normal earnings. This lower rate is paid for the last twelve weeks of SMP if you qualify for the higher rate for the first six weeks; and for the whole eighteen-week period if you do not.

What do I have to do to get it?

To receive SMP you must:

* Give your employer *at least* twenty-one days' notice of the date you intend to stop work. It is up to your employer how formally you do this, but if you plan to exercise your right to return to work you must put it in writing.

* Give your employer medical evidence of the date the baby is due. Your doctor or midwife will provide you with a maternity certificate (form MatB1).

How will I receive it?

SMP is paid by your employer in the normal way, on your payday.

What if my employer does not pay my SMP?

If you think you are entitled to SMP but your employer does not, contact your social security office.

B. State Maternity Allowance

Do I qualify?

If you are self-employed, or if you have recently changed

MATERNITY LEAVE AND YOUR RIGHT TO RETURN TO WORK

1. BEFORE THE BIRTH

Note: some of these restrictions will change when the EC directive becomes law in 1994

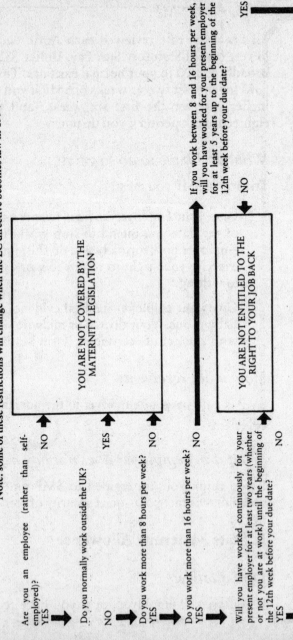

Are you an employee (rather than self-employed)?
YES →
NO ↑

Do you normally work outside the UK?
NO →
YES ↑

Do you work more than 8 hours per week?
YES →
NO ↑

YOU ARE NOT COVERED BY THE MATERNITY LEGISLATION

Do you work more than 16 hours per week?
YES →
NO ↑

If you work between 8 and 16 hours per week, will you have worked for your present employer for at least 5 years up to the beginning of the 12th week before your due date?
YES
NO ↓

Will you have worked continuously for your present employer for at least two years (whether or not you are at work) until the beginning of the 12th week before your due date?
YES →
NO ↑

YOU ARE NOT ENTITLED TO THE RIGHT TO YOUR JOB BACK

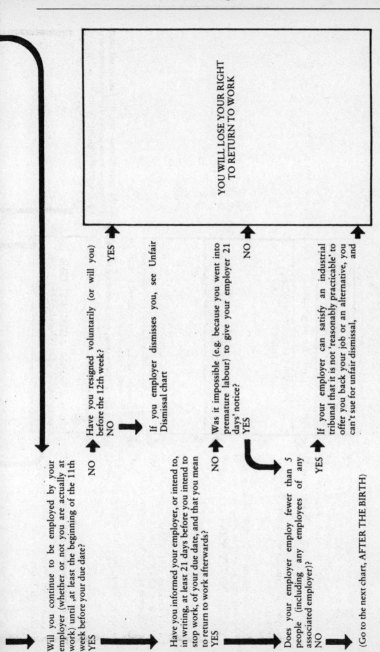

Will you continue to be employed by your employer (whether or not you are actually at work) until ,at least the beginning of the 11th week before your due date?
YES   NO

Have you resigned voluntarily (or will you) before the 12th week?
NO   YES → If you employer dismisses you, see Unfair Dismissal chart

Have you informed your employer, or intend to, in writing, at least 21 days before you intend to stop work, of your due date, and that you mean to return to work afterwards?
YES   NO

Was it impossible (e.g. because you went into premature labour) to give your employer 21 days' notice?
YES   NO

Does your employer employ fewer than 5 people (including any employees of any associated employer)?
NO   YES

If your employer can satisfy an industrial tribunal that it is not 'reasonably practicable' to offer you back your job or an alternative, you can't sue for unfair dismissal, and

YOU WILL LOSE YOUR RIGHT TO RETURN TO WORK

(Go to the next chart, AFTER THE BIRTH)

2. AFTER THE BIRTH

After the birth your employer can write not sooner than 49 days after the due date you gave to ask for a written confirmation of your intention to return to work. Will you reply within two weeks?

YES → NO →

Have you informed your employer, in writing, of the date you propose to return to work, at least 21 days before that date?

YES → NO →

YOU WILL LOSE YOUR RIGHT TO RETURN TO WORK

Is the date on which you return to work no later than 29 weeks after the birth of your child?

YES → NO →

Is the reason you have not returned to work by the 29th week that you are ill?

YES → NO →

Is the reason that you are prevented from returning to work an interruption of your work (e.g. inductrial dispute)?

YES

NO

Can you produce a doctor's certificate and return to work within four weeks?

YES

NO

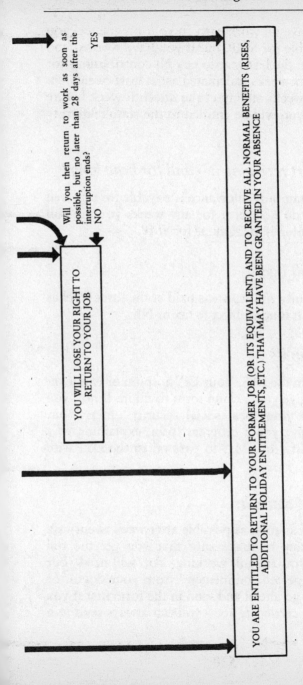

Will you then return to work as soon as possible, but no later than 28 days after the interruption ends?

YES

NO

YOU WILL LOSE YOUR RIGHT TO RETURN TO YOUR JOB

YOU ARE ENTITLED TO RETURN TO YOUR FORMER JOB (OR ITS EQUIVALENT) AND TO RECEIVE ALL NORMAL BENEFITS (RISES, ADDITIONAL HOLIDAY ENTITLEMENTS, ETC.) THAT MAY HAVE BEEN GRANTED IN YOUR ABSENCE jobs, or if you gave up work early in your pregnancy, you may not be eligible for SMP, but if you have worked and earned enough in the last year to pay NI contributions for at least twenty-six weeks (calculated as: at least twenty-six of the fifty-two weeks ending in the fifteenth week before your due date), you will be entitled to the state maternity allowance.

When do I start receiving it – and for how long?

Like SMP, the maternity allowance is payable for eighteen weeks, and you do not get it for any weeks you are still working. The timing is the same as for SMP.

How much will I get?

The State Maternity Allowance is paid at the same level as sickness benefit. It is not subject to tax or NI.

How do I claim it?

You claim it from the DSS. Your GP, hospital or employer may be able to give you a claim form to fill in. If not, you can get it from your local social security office. Your employer may give you a different form, explaining why you do not qualify for SMP, to pass on to the DSS with your claim.

When should I claim it?

Send in the form as soon as possible after week twenty-six of your pregnancy to make sure that you get the full benefit, even if you are still working. You will need your 'certificate of expected confinement' from your doctor or midwife, but do go ahead and send in the form first if you have not got the certificate yet – you can always send it in later.

How will I receive it?

You will be given a book of orders which you can cash every week at the post office.

4. Your right to return to work after maternity leave

Do I qualify for the right to return to my job after maternity leave?

See the Maternity Leave and Your Right to Return to Work chart.

How much time can I take off?

If you want to retain the right to return to your job, the *most* you can take off (unless your employer's maternity agreement offers longer than the statutory maximum) is: eleven weeks before your baby is due, and up to twenty-nine weeks after your baby is born. This works out at roughly ten months in all, depending on whether your baby is early or late.

What do I have to do?

Here are the rules you must follow in order to retain your right to your job back:

* Do not stop work before the eleventh week before your due date.

* Write to your employer at least three weeks before you leave work, stating the following:
    1. That you are leaving to have a baby.
    2. The date when your baby is due.
    3. That you intend to return to work after maternity leave.

531

* After the birth your employer may write to you no sooner than seven weeks after the due date you gave, to ask if you still plan to come back to work. If you receive such a letter you must reply to it within two weeks of receiving it (although you don't have to say at this stage exactly when you plan to return).

* At least three weeks before the date you plan to return to work, you must write to your employer and state the intended date.

What if it is impossible for me to stay at work until the eleventh week before my due date?

If you resign voluntarily from your job before the eleventh week before your baby is due, you forfeit your right to return to work. But if you are 'fairly dismissed', because your job is dangerous, illegal, or impossible to do while pregnant, you retain your right to return to work as long as you make it clear to your employer that that is your intention, by following the rules outlined above. If you are ill during your pregnancy, or have to stay in bed because of a threatened miscarriage or premature labour, you can retain your right to return to work, so long as you make it clear you are away because of illness, and that you have not resigned.

What if it is not possible to give my employer three weeks' notice of leaving work?

If it were impossible to give the necessary notice, for example because you went into labour prematurely, you should inform your employer as soon as reasonably practicable.

What if it is impossible for me to return to work by the twenty-ninth week after the birth?

If you are ill at the end of your maternity leave period and you can produce a doctor's certificate for your employer, you can put off your return for another four weeks. Also, if you are prevented from returning to work by an interruption of your work, for example an industrial dispute, you do not lose your right to return so long as you return to work as soon as possible, but no later than twenty-eight days after the interruption ends.

What if my employer employs five or fewer people?

Until the EC directive becomes law in 1994, if your employer can satisfy an industrial tribunal that he employs five people or fewer, including any employee of any associated employer, and that it is not 'reasonably practicable' to keep your job open, you will lose your right to return to work and you won't be able to sue for unfair dismissal.

What if my employer does not offer me my old job back, but a different one?

Your employer has the right to offer you 'available, suitable, alternative work' rather than your old job, if he can satisfy an industrial tribunal that it is not 'reasonably practicable' to offer you back your old job. If you refuse the alternative job you probably won't be able to sue for unfair dismissal (unless it is less favourable to you than your old job).

What if my employer makes my job redundant in my absence?

If your job is made redundant, your employer must offer

you a suitable, equivalent, alternative job, or, if one is not available, redundancy pay.

When I return to work, will I be entitled to the same pay increases, etc. as my fellow workers?

Your employer must take you back on 'terms and conditions not less favourable than those which would have been applicable' if you had not taken maternity leave. This means that any general pay increases, increases of holiday entitlement, and so on, awarded in your absence will apply to you as well.

How will my maternity leave affect my length of service?

So far as your statutory rights are concerned, the period you are away from work for maternity leave counts as a period of continuous employment towards length of service, as if you had not been away from work. So far as your rights with your employer are concerned, it depends on what it says in your letter of employment or maternity agreement, but if nothing is specified, your employer can regard your absence as a break in your length of service for the purpose of calculating your current year's holiday entitlement, pension rights, seniority, and so on.

Remember that your maternity pay, and the job you are offered back on your return from maternity leave, will be based on what you were earning and the job you were doing immediately before going off on leave. If you arrange to work part time during your pregnancy, you can only expect a part-time job to return to, and if going part time means you have not paid enough NI contributions in the period immediately before your maternity leave, you will lose your right to SMP.

Suppose I have another child within two years of my first maternity leave?

As your maternity leave counts as part of a continuous period of employment, you will be entitled to another period of maternity leave from the same employer, even if you have been back at work for less than two years.

> I stopped work seven weeks before I had Sally in June 1979 and did not return to work. I then had Heather twenty-one months later. *Important financial tip*: your State Maternity Allowance is based on your contributions in the financial year before last, so if you have your second child before the end of the financial year, having worked until after the end of the year two years previous, you can claim your allowances all over again, without having worked between having the two kids!

If you adopt a child

You have no statutory right to maternity leave and pay (although some enlightened firms are starting to offer adoptive parents the same maternity benefits as other parents).

Pregnancy and Maternity Leave Calendar

The rules for qualifying for the various benefits and the right to return to work are extremely complicated, and remembering to do the right thing by the right time will mean the difference between qualifying or not. To help you make sure you do not forget any of these important dates, we suggest you copy all the relevant points from this calendar into your diary on the appropriate dates. Then all you need to do is look at your diary regularly (even this can seem difficult when you are at home with your baby!).

BEFORE THE BIRTH

Week	
8	As soon as you know you are pregnant
9	* *Free prescription and dental treatment:* ask your GP or midwife for form FW8.
10	* *Paid time off for antenatal care:* get a note from midwife or GP confirming you are pregnant for your employer.
11	
12	* *Your firm's maternity policy:* read any special maternity agreement.
13	* *Childbirth classes:* investigate and book yourself into the one of your choice as soon as you can.
14	
15	
16	
17	
18	
19	
20	
21	
22	
23	
24	Most childbirth classes start now.
25	To qualify for SMP or the State Maternity Allowance, don't stop work until the beginning of next week, even if you do not intend to return to work after the baby.

26 * *Write to your employer* at least twenty-one days before the date you intend to stop work to qualify for SMP and maternity leave with your job back at the end of it.

* If you are entitled to the State Maternity Allowance, get the form from your social security office or maternity clinic, and apply now.

* If you qualify for the Maternity Payment, apply now at your social security office.

27

28 To qualify for maternity leave (the right to return to your job) don't give up work until the beginning of next week.

29 * Statutory Maternity Pay (SMP) and the State Maternity Allowance can both be paid from this week if you choose to give up work now.

* The Maternity Payment is also available from now.

30
31
32
33

34 Beginning of the 'core' period of SMP/State Maternity Allowance: give up work by this week if you want to get your full eighteen weeks' entitlement.

35 * Airlines will not normally accept passengers more than thirty-six weeks pregnant so don't make plans to fly after this week.

* If you work in a factory, the Factories Act makes it illegal for your employer to keep you on after the beginning of next week.

36
37

38 Make sure your case is packed – for the hospital!

39

40 BABY DUE (Good luck!)

AFTER THE BIRTH

Week

1 BABY BORN

2

3 As soon as you feel able:

* *Register the birth* (get your partner to do it) to get the birth certificate.
* *Claim child benefit.*
* *Maternity Payment/twins:* if entitled to the Maternity Payment and you have had more than one baby, claim the extra grant.
* *Childcare options* – if you haven't yet, start thinking about, and exploring the different options.
* *Playgroups/schools* – probably slightly later in the maternity leave period, start investigating local playgroups, nursery schools, and primary schools if you live in an area where these are hard to get into.

4

5

6 This is the last week for registering your baby's birth, so if you have not yet done it, hurry to the registry office, or send your partner.

7 Reply within two weeks to any letter from your employer after this date which asks you to confirm that you intend to return to work (you do not have to volunteer the date you intend to return, but if you do not write back you can lose your right to return to work).

8

9

1̣

11
12   This is the last week for claiming the Maternity Payment. Late claims will not be accepted unless you give a good reason for the delay.

13
14   Once you have decided when you will return to work, give your employer at least twenty-one days' notice in writing of your return date.

15
16
17
18
19
20
21
22
23
24
25
26   If taking the maximum maternity leave, write to your employer now to give your return date.
27
28
29   If you have taken the maximum maternity leave you should be back at work by the beginning of next week (unless your firm's maternity policy allows you more time off, or unless you are ill – in which case you may stay away for up to four more weeks).

  Have you claimed child benefit yet? If you wait until your baby is more than a year old you will lose money as it will not be backdated for more than a year from the date they receive your claim.

To work out your dates

Take your due dates (the date given by your doctor or clinic as the one on which your baby is due), then mark in your diary the Sunday before that date as the start of your 'expected week of confinement' – week forty of your pregnancy. If your baby is due on a Sunday, take that Sunday as the beginning of week forty. Next, working backwards, number the Sunday before that as thirty-nine, and so on. Then go back to your due date and label the Sunday after it as week one, representing the subsequent Sundays two, three, four, and so on. You will have to adjust the numbering of these weeks after the birth if your baby was more than a week early or late, but it is still worth copying these deadlines into your diary now in pencil, as your mind may be a bit scrambled for a while after the baby is born!

Other Universal Rights and Benefits

Apart from the maternity rights detailed above, there are several other state benefits every pregnant woman or mother is entitled to, whatever her income; make sure you claim them:

Free prescriptions and NHS dental treatment

From the time you are pregnant until one year after your baby is born. Get form FW8 from your doctor or midwife.

Child benefit

This is a weekly cash benefit for each child under sixteen (or nineteen if still at school) which is paid to any mother (or father, if the child is living separately with him) who has been living in Britain for at least six months. It can either be paid through a book of orders which you cash at the post office, or it can be paid directly into your bank account every four weeks. Payment of child benefit cannot be backdated for more than a year from the date of your claim. There is an additional *One-parent benefit*, which is paid at the same time as child benefit for single parent families.

How to claim

Claim child benefit as soon as you have registered your baby's birth, because you'll need to send the baby's birth certificate in with your claim. The forms may be sent to you, or given to you at the hospital, but if not, get them from your local social security office (CH1 for child benefit, and CH11 for one-parent benefit).

Home Responsibilities Protection (HRP)

This means that your state retirement pension rights are protected even if you are not paying NI contributions during the period of your maternity leave, or if you stay home for a period of years to look after children. You will get this protection automatically if you are receiving child benefit, without having to claim for it, if you never worked before having children, or if you paid full NI contributions before you stopped working. If you paid the married woman's reduced contribution, you must give up your right to this, or you will not get HRP. Contact your social security office for instructions on how to get this protection. If your husband is the one who stays at home to look after your children while you go out to work, *he* can get HRP: enquire at the social security office.

Means-tested Benefits

These are the additional state benefits that may be

available if you are on a low income. This is just a brief guide: if you are on a low income, do go to your local social security office or Citizens' Advice Bureau and make sure that you know about all your entitlements.

* *Maternity Payment*: a lump sum payment to help with maternity clothes and baby equipment. For many years this was £25 and available to every pregnant woman; it is now about £100, and you can only get the full amount if you are on Income Support or Family Credit, and have less than £500 savings. Contact the local Social Security office for claim form SF100. Application can be any time from eleven weeks before the week the baby is due (twenty-ninth week of pregnancy) until baby is three months old.

* *Free Milk and Vitamins* for yourself while pregnant, and for any children under five, available only if you are on Income Support or are receiving Family Credit.

* *Income Support*. This is a weekly payment if you are not in full-time work (less than thirty hours a week) and your income and savings are below a certain level.

* *Family Credit*. This is a weekly payment for working families on low pay, who have at least one child.

* *Free NHS dental treatment, vouchers towards glasses and prescriptions* for the whole family if you are receiving any of the above benefits.

* *Free school meals* if you are receiving any of these benefits.

Employers Agreements

Maternity Leave

If you work for a large organisation with active trade unions, the chances are that there will be a special house maternity agreement. Even smaller employers, especially if they employ a good proportion of women, may have a maternity policy worked out, even if they are not unionised. As soon as you are pregnant, or before if you are planning to have a baby, get hold of a copy of this agreement or policy from your personnel manager or union representative and make sure you understand what is in it. It may be much more favourable than the stautory provisions detailed earlier in this chapter; in any case, its terms cannot be any worse, as the state lays down the minimum terms.

There are probably almost as many variations of the maternity agreement as there are employers, but we think it may be useful to give some indication of the kind of thing you may find offered by your employer. Alternatively, you may get some ideas for suggesting improvements in your firm's maternity policy to your union representative or employer!

Here are some of the common ways in which employers' maternity arrangements can improve upon the statutory maternity rights:

Reduced minimum employment period

Many employers offer the improvement that you need only have worked for them for one year instead of the statutory two years to qualify for maternity leave and pay.

Increased maternity pay and leave

Many employers offer additional maternity pay and leave over and above the statutory minimum. For example, a London council pays for a full forty weeks of maternity leave, of which sixteen weeks are on full pay, and twenty-four weeks on half-pay. A publishing company allows its employees fifty-two weeks of maternity leave, twenty weeks of which are on full pay, and another ten on half pay; and a civil service department gives forty-eight weeks' maternity leave, thirteen of which are on full pay.

Most companies restrict the additional pay to those employees who will return to work after having a baby. Usually, you are required to pay back any extra maternity pay you have received on top of the SMP (which you are entitled to keep whether or not you return) if you change your mind about returning to work after your baby is born. In this case, you will be able to reclaim the tax you have paid on this money. Some companies expect you not only to return to work after paid maternity leave, but also want you to stay for a minimum period, say five or six months. If you give up work before this post-maternity period is up, you have to repay the money. And other employers only hand over the extra maternity pay *after* you have returned to work – sometimes as long as three months after your return. This makes it look more like a bribe to tempt their employees back to work than a genuine attempt to give women on maternity leave some financial support when they most need it.

Extended leave of absence while children are small

A number of forward-looking employers have introduced the opportunity to return to work after an absence of several years, for those women who want to stay at home with their small children. For example, a London council will allow an employee to return to a job in the same department for up to five years after she has left to have a child, and a high street bank guarantees you a job for up to five years after you leave, so long as you agree to return to work for two weeks in every year you are away. Other firms, while not promising a full reinstatement without loss of seniority, are prepared to give an employee who left to have a child priority consideration for any suitable job that becomes available, within a period of three to five years.

Paternity leave

An increasing number of firms are now granting new fathers some extra days' leave when their children are born, and the period immediately after it. This is usually no more than two weeks.

Extending maternity rights to foster or adoptive parents

A few employers allow a woman who adopts a baby, or fosters with a view to adoption, the same maternity rights as pregnant colleagues.

Protecting pregnant workers from infection

Many of the maternity agreements we have seen provide for making temporary alternative working arrangements to protect pregnant women and prospective fathers from a potentially dangerous infection: for example German measles, that may have been identified in the company.

Employers' aid to working parents after maternity leave

Apart from maternity benefits some progressive employers

have recently started to improve conditions for their employees who happen to be parents. These employers recognise that by helping to deal with some of the problems faced by working parents they are helping themselves to keep valuable, trained and experienced staff. We cannot pretend that many employers see it this way, but it is to be hoped that others will start to follow their example.

Increased flexibility in working conditions

What working mothers need most is more time and more flexibility within the working day. Some employers offer mothers returning from maternity leave (and also fathers concerned to spend more time with their children) the opportunity to work part time, or flexitime, or during school terms only, or to job share, which is to be commended. Also, some companies are starting to change their attitude towards part-timers, by no longer excluding them from the opportunity to be trained or promoted, and by making them eligible for company pension schemes, paid holidays, bonus schemes, and so on.

Help with childcare

Some (very few) firms have created or are contributing to work-place creches or nurseries. Since 1990, these are no longer taxed, so have become a welcome perk as well as a convenience.

However, there are other ways in which employers can help. We have heard of companies that organise the services of a local childminder for a group of their employees' children, and of a number of London companies that came together to set up a play scheme during the school holidays. And several companies we have heard of offer a childcare allowance to any employee with a child or children under the age of five.

Child sickness leave

A sick child is every working mother's nightmare. Several employers now offer their staff special leave of up to two weeks per year separate from their own sick leave and holiday entitlement, to look after a sick child. In some organisations, this leave is paid, in others it is unpaid. The most generous provision of this kind we have heard about comes yet again from the same London council. It offers working mothers up to six weeks' paid leave a year in the event of their children (or childminders) falling ill.

Tax and the Working Mother

Many working women are confused about tax – and no wonder: most of us have tax mysteriously deducted by our employers as PAYE. Since first writing this book, however, the situation has been improved and simplified – and consequently this section is shorter!

Here are the main facts about tax as they affect the working mother. (N.B. The tax allowance is the amount of money you can earn per year before you have to start paying tax.)

1. If you are married

* *There is no tax relief for children*

If you are married there is no allowance for children, whether you have one child or eight.

* *Taxation as a couple*

You and your husband are now taxed separately. As a married couple you are entitled to the Married Couple's

Allowance (usually paid to the man unless you specify otherwise), on top of a personal allowance each, before you start paying tax.

2. If you are unmarried:

* *You can get a higher tax allowance if you have a child*

If you have a child and are unmarried, separated or divorced, you can claim the additional personal allowance, which will bring you up to the level of the Married Couple's Allowance.

If you are unmarried but live with your partner, one of you can claim this personal allowance, or you can divide it between you. If you have two children, you can each claim the additional personal allowance, bringing you up above the Married Couple's Allowance – the allowance is not payable per child, but per person claiming it, so a married couple can't claim for two children. This is one of the unfairnesses of the present tax system, and is one reason (for some) for not getting married! The allowance is for dependent children only and ceases when the child is sixteen or nineteen, if still in education.

3. There is no tax relief for childcare

Unlike many other countries, Britain offers no tax relief for childcare for the under-fives when both parents work, or even for single parents. Contrast this with provisions in certain other EC countries: in the Netherlands, for example, families with two working parents get a flat rate allowance for children up to twelve years old, and single parents can deduct the total cost of their childcare from their tax bills.

Many of the women we interviewed and who filled in

the questionnaire thought it was wrong that there was no tax relief for childcare, which for many women with small children accounted for one-quarter to one-half of their take-home pay (a few confessed to paying two-thirds, nine-tenths, even *all* their own wages to the carer to enable them not to make a career-damaging break at a crucial time).

A nursery officer from Preston writes:

> I feel very strongly that as an essential priority childcare should be tax deductible. I feel women are penalised financially when having a child. But please don't be misled into thinking that I feel you can ever put a price on my beautiful daughter's head.

And a farm secretary from Lincolnshire writes:

> I don't mind providing another woman with income for minding my child but I don't see why I can't claim a tax allowance against that expense. It is after all essential to my being able to work. If men had to fork out for childminders so that they could work, they would jolly soon find a way to claim it back.

Housekeeper Allowance

The only tax relief approximating to the idea of childcare is the Housekeeper Allowance, which you can claim if you are widowed. But you can't claim this allowance *and* the additional personal allowance, so if you are a widow with a dependent child, you should claim the additional personal allowance, which is very much the higher of the two. So this tax benefit is apparently not directed at widowed people with children at all.

4. Not only is childcare not tax deductible, in certain circumstances it represents an additional tax burden to parents

* *Nannies*

If you employ a nanny or mother's help in your own home, you are responsible for paying your employee's tax (and NI contributions) by PAYE as if you were a big company. Although technically the tax comes out of your nanny's salary, in reality nannies and mother's helps, who are paid weekly, negotiate their salary on the basis of their take-home, cash-in-hand, pay – and it is usually the employer who has to find the additional money on top of that to pay her tax. (The Simplified Domestic Scheme is explained in greater detail in the chapter on *Nannies, Mother's Helps and Other Help in Your Home*).

Not only does this involve you in the work of dealing with the tax office, but if you are a salaried employee on PAYE yourself you are actually being taxed twice, as you are paying the mother's help or nanny's tax out of your own net take-home pay. This must make working mothers (or single fathers) the only class of employers who have to pay an employee's tax and wages out of their own net profits!

* It has been suggested by some of the women who talked to us that if you are an employee a sympathetic employer may be prepared to put your nanny on the payroll. Her wages, tax and NI would still come out of your wages, but before tax. Although this could work in theory, a tax inspector who knew the situation might decide that you should be taxed on the entire amount.

The self-employed employer

If you are self-employed and employ a nanny, you'll still find her wages and tax are not tax deductible. However, if she also performs some secretarial function you will be able to deduct a proportion of her wages as an allowable expense.

APPENDIX

Examples of a Day in the Lives of Working Mothers

To show you how other mothers combine housework, time with their children, going out to work, and so on, here is a selection of typical working-day schedules from some of the women who completed our questionnaire.

Full-time head of teacher's centre from Sheffield; married with one child aged three:

6.45 a.m.	Get up – bemoaning the fact that if life is to be streamlined, organised and pleasant I should really get up at 6.30!
6.45 – 7.25	Washing, blowdrying hair, attending to make-up, dressing for work, preparing briefcase, getting child up.
7.25 – 7.55	The briefest of breakfasts, washing pots, selecting toys/books to take to childminder. Partner dresses child, makes beds, attends to both cars.
8.00 ish	Both of us leave home with the child, amidst shouting, last-minute dashes back to the house to retrieve teddy, keys, cash card

	for the supermarket or important papers for work! (I have honestly very nearly gone to work in my slippers on numerous occasions!).
8.15	Drop child off at minder's.
8.20 – 8.30	Begin a day's work attempting to appear lively and fresh, well prepared and with a free mind!
8.30 – 5.00p.m.	In service education work for Local Education Authority and general administration of a teacher's centre.
5.00	Frantically dash off to collect my child – I sometimes use side doorways to avoid colleagues who arrive unexpectedly, so that I don't have to say 'I can't stop now!'
5.45	Arrive home (both of us and child).
6.00 – 6.30	A rushed meal (salad a speciality!).
6.30 – 9.00	At least one of us playing with, talking specifically to, reading stories with child – the other very likely to be attending a meeting from 7.30p.m.
9.00 – 10.30	Do a domestic job (cleaning a drawer, sewing repairs, or do some homework/preparation for work).
10.30 – 11.15	Have a quiet drink/talk with partner.
11.30	A bath – a nightly must – I'd rather miss tea.
12.00	Collapse into bed vowing to read my library book and get up early tomorrow.

Part-time consumer adviser from North Bedfordshire; married with two children aged seven and five:

6.15a.m.	Wake. Think about getting up for a while before succeeding.
6.45	Wash and dress whilst making cup of tea and being assaulted with latest Lego models, works of art, need for button on shirt, new shoelaces, seven-course dinner plans etc . . . until . . . Breakfast and then getting children ready for school, feed cat.
8.50	Leave house – take children to school, travel to work.
9.10	Arrive at work with a chance to do some things before phone starts and constant knocks on the door for advice.
3.10p.m.	Where's the day gone to? Punch drunk from all the questions with no immediate answers. Good satisfied feeling.
3.30	Arrive at school to collect children: demands for friends to come and play, drinks, biscuits, 'Can I change when I get home?' Star for tables, new reading book. Talk to and attempt to organise play for children, often give up and just potter around outside with them, or if too tired will sit down in front of TV for one hour of children's TV. The TV off for tea and rest of evening.
6.00	Bathtime. Water play. Lots of shouting at boy not to drown girl.
6.45	Calming down time. Half-hour reading to them, then listening to them read latest school book.
7.30	Tucking in time for them both and cuddles for me. Now the work starts, clearing up the bombsite, hoovering, washing, ironing, cooking etc.

9.00	(or 10.00pm – depends how organised I've been) Sit down for news.
11.00	Bed – brain can't stop churning so chat in bed with husband for half an hour if we don't nod off before.

Full-time nursery officer from Preston, married with one baby aged eight months:

6.00a.m.	Wake up baby and breastfeed.
8.00	Leave for half-hour journey to take baby to minder, and then on to work.
8.30	Start work. I am a nursery officer in a child development centre. It is a very demanding job, dealing with children with special needs (various handicaps). Twice a day we have various groups of children who attend the centre for therapy (occupational, physio, speech, play) with which I am involved. The parents attending the centre expect (and receive) your full attention, cheerfulness, alertness and co-operation.
12.30p.m.	Lunch till 1.30.
4.30	Finish work. Pick up baby from childminder.
5.00	Home. Sit down with baby and cup of tea. Breastfeed.
5.30	Teatime.
6.30 – 7.00	Playtime. Family time.
7.00	Bathtime, breastfeed and baby's bedtime.
8.00 – 10.30	or 11.00 Various household activities and time together. We each have a different night out during the week, and go out together on weekends.

Part-time social work assistant from Newtonabbey, Northern Ireland; married, with four children aged two, eight, ten and twelve:

7.45a.m.	Get up and washed and dressed. Husband gets baby's breakfast. Others get their own breakfast although I have set table night before.
8.00	I eat my own breakfast and make four packed lunches. I hate making packed lunches but used to pack them the night before – that was even worse. So I now do them in the morning with the children around, and ask them what they want.
8.15	Stack dishwasher and brush kitchen floor. Stack washing machine.
8.25	Get baby washed and dressed.
8.35	Start shouting to eight-year-old and check he is clean and tidy.
8.40	Leave house with two-, eight- and ten-year-olds and drive them to school and baby to gran's.
9.10	Arrive at work.
9.15	Have coffee and start on phonecalls.
10.30	Out on calls or meetings.
1.00p.m.	Lunchtime – but as I am employed twenty-five hours a week I always eat and write up files and feel I cannot be seen to be wasting working hours. If I am out on calls I go to the supermarket at lunchtime.
2.00	Travel home, picking up baby on the way.

2.30	Arrive home. Play with baby till around 4.30. Other children arrive home and get snacks, etc.
4.30 – 5.30	Get meal ready. Organise washing and get children to tidy their rooms. If I get a chance house gets a quick hoover if necessary and bathroom a quick clean.
5.30 – 6.00	Eat meal. Stack dishwasher. Clean kitchen.
6.00 – 7.00	Sit down for coffee. Listen to homeworks.
7.30	Baby ready for bed. Watch TV.
8.00 – 9.30	Play and read to baby and try to get him to settle down.
9.30	TV.
10.30	Bed.

Part-time midwife from Newtonabbey, Northern Ireland, married with one daughter aged four:

Rise at *6.45a.m.*, waken my daughter, get myself washed, go downstairs, get her bag (with her needs for the day) and things together, put everything in the car, take it out of garage and reverse in proper direction. Upstairs again, child awake but still in bed, put on her snowsuit and hat if cold. Call my husband. By *7.20* he's usually dressed. I put child into car and he takes her up to my mother-in-law. Meanwhile I finish getting ready, no time for breakfast. He brings car back again and I go on in it to work. I start at *8.00*. My mother-in-law takes the child to nursery and collects her at *1.00p.m.*. I collect Anne again at *1.30* and spend the afternoon with her, usually doing household tasks, shopping or visiting my elderly parents. I return to work at *4.30* and leave Anne with her granny again and am back on duty at *5.00* – usually exhausted!!! I work until hopefully *8.30* and am home around *9.00*. Meanwhile my husband has picked Anne up and brought her home and she is in bed. I then tidy up, put her clothes away and sort things out for the morning. I wash all the breakfast and tea dishes, then ironing, washing or sewing if any time left, going to bed around *midnight*. I usually work three splits a week which I find is quite enough.

Full-time district nursing sister from Lincolnshire, married (but husband works abroad), daughter aged seventeen months:

6.30a.m.	Get up and dressed. Take dog for ten-minute walk. Feed two lambs – bottle fed at the moment. Feed cat.
7.00	Prepare breakfast.
7.15	Dress Elizabeth. Wash etc.
7.30	Breakfast.
8.00	Take messages off Ansaphone and distribute to nurses concerned.
8.10	Get ready to leave house – with Elizabeth.
8.15	Take Elizabeth in car to childminder one mile away – next village – on way to work. Drive to Lincoln.
8.30	Commence nursing duties.
1.00p.m.	To health centre to collect any new patients via Ansaphone then carry on with nursing duties.
3.30	Collect Elizabeth from child minder.
3.45	Home.
4.00	Feed lambs again. Take dog out again – Elizabeth in push chair.
4.30	Listen to Ansaphone messages.
4.45	Elizabeth's tea.
5.00	Play with Elizabeth.
6.00	Bathtime.
6.15	Elizabeth to bed.
6.20	Prepare evening meal.
6.45	Work out tomorrow's work list, make phone calls etc.
7.00	Supper.

7.30	Washing, ironing, tidying up etc.
8.30	Try to relax.
10.30	Bed.

Full-time teacher from Merseyside; married with two children aged seven months and three years, and a stepson of twenty-three who lives at home:

6.00a.m.	Get up, washed and dressed. Husband puts kettle on and warms baby's bottle, starts to feed baby.
6.20	Wash and dress baby. Husband washes. Finish feeding. Baby goes back to bed to sleep.
6.45	Pack baby's dinner (home-made from freezer); make own lunch; husband puts baby-walker and bag in car, gets car out of garage.
7.00	Get up older child; wash and dress her (husband makes own toast and eats it meantime!).
7.15	Breakfast for myself and older daughter.
7.25	Husband leaves for work.
7.40	Wash up; leave dishes to drain.
7.45	Clean older daughter up; clean teeth.
7.50	Get baby up, put on coats etc, leave house.
8.00	Drive off, feeling relaxed at last.
8.25	Arrive at 'Auntie Carol's'.
8.30	Arrive at work. Do some preparation.
9.00	Children arrive. Teaching.
10.30	Five minutes' break, if I'm lucky (officially 15).
12.00 – 1.00p.m.	Lunch break, usually twenty minutes at most, rest is preparation time.
2.15	Break – again about five minutes.
3.00	School closes.

3.10	Pick up children, drive home.
3.45	Arrive home, drinks for everyone.
4.00	Bath and playtime for children.
5.00	Prepare meal (quickly). Baby sleeps; Older daughter plays.
5.45	Dish up and have meal.
6.00	Get baby up and feed her. Husband washes dishes, stepson dries them.
6.30 – 7.30	Playtime with children, supper for both.
8.00	Children's bedtime.
8.00 – 9.00	Washing/ironing/sterilising bottles/preparation of work for school/children's clothes ready for morning.
9.00 – 9.30	Fall into chair exhausted. Watch TV or read.
10.00 – 10.30	Get ready for, and fall into, bed.

Part-time sales assistant from Glasgow, divorced with one daughter aged eight:

We get up at about *7.45a.m.* I give Caroline her breakfast and I have a shower while she eats it. Then she gets herself ready while I get myself ready. As I work in a fashion store I have to put on my make-up and make myself presentable so we usually end up running at the last minute. The school is on the way to the bus stop so I drop her in and make it for the *9.00* bus and get to work for *9.45* to start at *10.00.* I quite enjoy my work and the girls I work with are all very nice. I don't know what I would be like if I did not have my job as it keeps me going. If I am finishing at *2.00*p.m. I stay on and have a chat and a cup of tea in the staff room. Then depending on what day it is I either collect Caroline from school or leave her to go to the after-school care. If I am working later they collect her anyway. I usually collect her from the centre about *5.00* after she has had her snack. If the weather is good she likes to go out to play before her dinner. If not she stays in and we talk about the day while we are getting dinner ready. She then does her homework and we watch TV until she goes to bed about *8.30*. I then catch up on any housework and watch TV or read until I go to bed about *11.30*. Pretty boring, eh?

Part-time dental receptionist from West Yorkshire; married with three children aged nine, fourteen and eleven.

7.15a.m.	Get up, use bathroom, start on breakfast, take tea out of freezer.
7.30	Drag the two youngest boys out of bed.
8.00	Start rushing round like someone mental, finding parts of missing uniforms, books, games kits etc.
8.15	If time, wash breakfast pots. Hate coming home to a sink full of pots. Leave instructions for preparing tea on message pad.
8.30	Change into uniform, make-up on, kids in car, set off for work (hopefully). Check the children have door keys.
8.30 – 9.00	Drop children at schools, get to work on time if no more traffic jams.
9.00 – 12.30p.m.	Working in surgery.
12.30 – 2.00	Have lunch. Get any shopping needed. Catch up on any gossip.
2.00 – 5.30	Work in surgery.
5.45 – 6.00	Arrive home, boys having made tea from instructions. They have eaten theirs, my husband's and mine is in oven. Kitchen usually looks like bomb site. I check their bedrooms to make sure they have made their beds. No beds made, no playing out.
6.30 – 7.00	Wash up tea things with husband. Chat about our days at work.
7.00 – 7.30	Vac if necessary, dust if company is expected.

7.30 – 8.00	Sit and relax with evening paper. Husband feeds his racing pigeons.
8.00 – 10.00	Boys in from playing out. Suppers made, showers and teeth cleaned. Chat to boys about school, homework, friends, etc.
10.00 – 10.30	Peace at last, all in bed, watch news in peace.
10.30 – 11.00	Collapse into bed. Goodnight.

Full-time doctor from Belfast; married with two children aged four and sixteen months:

7.45a.m.	Get up (sometimes with difficulty). Breakfast: I don't have any, husband makes his own – a long-established custom. Children usually up and running around. They get a drink and breakfast if they want.
8.30	Nanny arrives – takes over care of children – breakfast, dressing, takes older child to playgroup, etc.
8.40	I leave for work by car. Husband (a GP) leaves soon after. About one day a week manage to shop one hour at lunchtime. Also shop on way home one day a week, therefore arrive later.
5.15p.m.	approx. Arrive home from work. Nanny leaves approx. 5.30. Evening activities depend on what time my husband comes home. Children have had tea/early evening meal about 4.30. *Either* husband and I have early meal – hastily prepared (usually out of freezer) at about 6 p.m. Children often join in for a sort of second supper! My husband plays with

562

	the children when I prepare meal. *Or* if my husband is not in till later I have quiet cup of tea and spend next hour or so playing with children. Odd moments snatched to get meal prepared in kitchen for later on. I do regard this time as the children's time and enjoy them even if they're under my feet in the kitchen!
6.45	approx. I take younger child up to bath. As I need to stay with her, older girl either plays alone downstairs or watches video (prerecorded children's programmes, not whatever is on TV). Bathtime for both children usually lengthy and we see it as an important play and recreation time for them. I usually sit on bathroom floor with knitting kept specifically in bathroom for the purpose.
7.15	approx. Younger child usually in bed. Either start putting older child to bed or negotiate a possible bedtime around evening meal if appropriate!
8.30	Older child usually settled by now. Time for: evening meal (some evenings); tidy up and cup of tea.
9.00	BBC NEWS!!! an important evening landmark this!
9.30 – 11.30	Work (house or professional); reading; cooking – I may spend an hour or so preparing meals for future use.
11.30	Collapse into bed.

Full-time social worker from Bangor, Northern Ireland; married to a musician with two children aged three and four:

One thing that hardly varies is that I get up first! Usually *8.00-8.15a.m.* weekdays. Children are already up, either playing or watching cartoons on the video. I empty the dishwasher, heat milk for cereal and give boys breakfast. Get them washed, nappy off, get them and myself dressed, or dry hair if washed. Bring husband cup of tea.

I go to work at *9.00-9.15*.

If he doesn't have to work in the morning he will often dress them and take them to playgroup for *9.30*. Otherwise I take them and get into work late. (This time can be made up by not claiming time off in lieu of overtime.)

At *1.00p.m.* I collect boys from playgroup and either take them home for lunch if my husband is in or to the childminder if he is at work. I eat lunch at home and return to work at *2.00*. Lunchtimes involve a blitz on the house or getting washing in, or putting a casserole in for tea. If my husband is home at lunchtime but not teatime, we have our meal midday – he makes it.

I collect the boys at *5.10* after work and take them home for tea/dinner. They play until bathtime or bedtime between *7.30 – 8.00*.

Evening activities for me depend on whether my husband is home. When out, I bake, sew, knit, clean, iron, garden, watch a selected programme on TV – it's my time to do whatever needs to be done. When he is home I may go out to play squash for one and a half hours. Wednesday evening *6.30 – 8.00* I conduct a junior choir practice. Or else when he is at home I sometimes just watch TV with him. I'm afraid if I do nothing but watch TV (even if exhausted) I think the time wasted! I go to bed anytime between *11.00* and *1.00a.m.*

Full-time kitchen assistant in a school in Lincoln; married, with three children still at home aged nineteen, fourteen and thirteen:

6.30a.m.	Get up, washed and dressed. Make bed. Put away aired clothes out of airing cupboard. (I put

clothes for each person on the top landing bannister and as they get up they have to put away and hang up their own clothes).

6.55 Quickly tidy bathroom. Put clean towels out, wipe handbasin, take second load of washing out (see below about first load).

7.05 Do husband's and eldest son's packed lunch. Peg out or put in tumble drier first load of washing. Put second load of washing in washer. I drink tea as I am doing this.

7.30 Get two youngest children up. Everybody makes own bed.

7.40 I make a hot drink and children get whatever they want for breakfast – usually cereals and toast.

7.50 I leave for work – children wash their own dishes.

8.00 – 3.00p.m. I'm doing kitchen work. I have half an hour for lunch which is provided and I've got to have it there.

3.30 I pop to see my disabled mum for an hour and pick up any shopping on the way back. Sit, talk and unwind for an hour. Or . . .

3.40 Back at home I prepare evening meal, do veg, put meat on.

4.20 Take out load of washing which has been in the washer since morning – either peg out or tumble dry depending on weather.

4.35 I now usually have a coffee while I'm doing a bit of ironing and talk to the children as they come in about their day. I never have a great deal of ironing as I never

	iron anything that's not necessary, so I'm done within half an hour.
5.00	Sit and talk to kids about homework, etc.
5.30	Children set table. Husband and eldest son arrive home. We have evening meal.
6.15	I *never* sit long after a meal as I know that as soon as the dishes are done the evening is *mine*! The two youngest take alternate nights helping with the dishes.
6.30	I empty bins, flick hoover and duster around quickly and rub mop over floor.
7.00	Till 10.30. Relax.
10.30	Fill washer for husband to turn on at 6.00a.m. when he gets up.

Full-time local government officer from Lancashire; married with two children aged seventeen and fifteen:

My husband is a journalist and leaves at 6.00a.m. to catch the train.

6.15a.m.	Call children. Son into shower. Daughter takes breakfast back to bed. Sometimes I cook breakfast – perhaps three times a week. I tidy up, iron odd bits of uniform if necessary and clear the kitchen.
7.30	Into bath or shower, do hair, dress, make-up. We leave for work and school at 8.10.
8.20 – 12.30p.m.	Office. I take half an hour for lunch to shop, go to bank, post office, etc. I eat at the office – sandwiches from home or bought in town – and read the paper.
1.00 – 5.00	Office. I work till 5.00 normally to accrue flexitime. I leave at 4.00 sometimes if I need to or if I

am tired. Flexitime is great because we can take a day off or two half-days every four weeks. I enjoy an afternoon at home in the week when it is empty. It is essential I feel to have time on your own to catch up on housework without kids underfoot or just to potter with plants or in the garden.

5.10

I am home in ten minutes unless I call at the supermarket for shopping I can't carry at lunchtime. My husband has already started the meal as he is home at 2.30 – preparing the vegetables, for instance. We all tend to prepare the meal together and catch up on each other's day. With teenagers it is essential to be around at teatime to chat, advise, nag or sympathise with them. When the meal is over they have homework to do. My daughter is doing A-levels so she has loads. Rob is more interested in doing his quickly so he can watch TV, or go to play football at the park in summer.

6.00 – 7.00

The children have had a snack so we eat between 6 and 7 usually. I have one or two glasses of homemade wine while we cook and eat, which helps me relax. After the meal I try not to do the clearing up – dishes go in the washer and the children do pans and bowls used in the microwave.

Weekends

Working mums' weekends tend to be a joke – I spend mine washing, shopping, cooking and cleaning. I try to relax on Sundays now as I feel you need one day to do what you want – I go to church in the morning and garden or bake if we do not go out before cooking dinner.

Further Help

CHAPTER 1: WORK AND PRE-MOTHERHOOD
The Working Mothers Association, 77 Holloway Road, London N7 8JZ; tel. 071 700 5771. If you join, they will give you a list of their corporate members (employers committed to policies that help working parents), and can also tell you which employers belong to Opportunity 2000.

Books
Equal Opportunities: a Careers Guide by Ruth Miller and Anna Alston (Penguin)

CHAPTER 2: PREGNANCY AND WORK
The Working Mothers Association (details under Chapter 1, above). As a member, you will be told the contact for your local group.

The National Childbirth Trust (NCT), Alexandra House, Oldham Terrace, London W3 6NH; tel. 081 992 8637. They will give you details of your nearest branch.

The Active Birth Centre (the main office for the Active Birth Movement), 55 Dartmouth Park, London NW5 1SL; tel. 071 267 3006.

Association of Radical Midwives, Ishbel Kargar, 62 Greetby Hill, Ormskirk, Lancs L39 2DT; tel. 0695 572776. They will give you information on groups all over the country.

Society to Support Home Confinements, Lidgate Lane, Wolsingham, Bishop Auckland, DL13 3HA; tel. 0388 528044.

Specialist shops for maternity wear

Great Expectations, 78 Fulham Road, London SW3 6HH; tel. 071 584 2451.

Bumpsadaisy, Head office: 52 Chiltern St, London W1M 1PP; tel. 071 486 3065. A maternity-hire franchise which has branches around the country.

Books
Maternity Rights Handbook by Ruth Evans and Lyn Durward, (Penguin). For a fuller examination of health hazards at work relating to pregnancy.

Suggested reading on pregnancy and childbirth and childcare
We asked the women we interviewed which books they had read, and which ones had been most useful. Here are the ones they particularly recommended:

Pregnancy by Gordon Bourne (Pan). This was the book that was mentioned most frequently. It is a comprehensive guide to all the physical aspects of pregnancy and labour, if from a rather patronising GP's point of view (he does not believe that a pregnant woman should work beyond the twenty-ninth week, and there is no mention of returning to work):

   * Very bossy, but I loved it. It was my bible. I read it till the covers fell off.

   * It was quite helpful in that it gave you details of what was actually happening to your body, but on the other hand it could also worry you about all the things that can go wrong.

The New Pregnancy and Birth Book by Miriam Stoppard (Dorling Kindersley). Well-designed, packed with easy to absorb information, charts, and so on. Dr Stoppard is of course a working mother herself.

Your Body, Your Baby, Your Life by Angela Phillips (Pandora and Sphere).

*   It goes through all the stages of pregnancy, giving you the medical details, but it's also humorous and sympathetic.

Pregnancy Book (the Health Education Council). This is handed out free by hospital or GPs and is an excellent, though simplistic overview.

Book of Childcare by Hugh Jolly (Unwin Paperbacks). A classic, updated to include 'new developments' in families today (for example, single parents). Now out of print, but your library might have it.

The New Baby Care Book by Miriam Stoppard (Dorling Kindersley). Like her pregnancy book, this is a practical, easy to follow book, neutral about working mothers.

Baby & Child by Penelope Leach (Penguin). Interesting, well-designed childcare and child development book. Only about babies and children – nothing about their parents!

*   She helps you get inside the skin of babies and children and makes incomprehensible behaviour logical and understandable.

*   It's transparent she disapproves of working mothers!

The Parents' A-Z by Penelope Leach (Penguin) Useful child health book in alphabetical order (sometimes hard to follow: if your child has a tummy ache, you have to guess to find it under 'Abdominal Pain'). A ten-page section on Working Mothers – before 'Worms'!

Toddler Taming by Christopher Green (Century). Reassuring, joky book about toddlers.

I just love his approach – he thinks mothers have an awful lot to cope with. He injects humour into it as well as giving practical advice.

CHAPTER 3: MATERNITY LEAVE BLUES

Cry-sis, BM Cry-sis, London WC1N 3XX; tel. 071 404 5011. Contact them if your baby cries a lot and it is driving you mad.

The Association for Post-Natal Illness, 25 Jordan Place, London SW6 1BE; tel. 071 386 0868. They offer a one-to-one support scheme where mothers who have suffered postnatal depression but are now cured counsel mothers who are currently suffering. This is done by telephone, letter and sometimes personal visits. They also publish leaflets.

MAMA (Meet-a-Mum Association), 58 Malden Ave, South Norwood, London SE25 4HS; tel. 081 656 7318. They provide a support network for women suffering from postnatal depression or who just feel tired and isolated after birth – both in social get-togethers and in one-to-one meetings with other mothers who have been through the same thing themselves. Send SAE for your local group.

Books
The New Mother Syndrome by Carol Dix (Allen & Unwin).

Post-Natal Depression by Vivienne Welburn (Fontana).

Depression after Childbirth by Katharina Dalton (OUP).

Towards Happy Motherhood: Understanding postnatal depression by Maggie Comport (Corgi).

CHAPTER 4: GOING BACK TO WORK
The Equal Opportunities Commission, Overseas House, Quay Street, Manchester M3 3HN. Contact them if you have to pay back maternity pay, and want to fight it.

CHAPTER 5: BREASTFEEDING AND WORKING
The National Childbirth Trust, (details under Chapter 2, above). They have a nationwide electric breastpump hire distribution network and breastfeeding counsellors throughout the country and will give you a contact number in your area.

La Leche League of Great Britain, BM 3424, London WCIN 3XX; tel. 071 404 5011. You will be given the name of a breastfeeding counsellor in your area. They can also help with advice about the buying or hire of electic breastpumps, organise breastfeeding support groups, and have a number of relevant leaflets.

Association of Breastfeeding Mothers, 347 Central Markets, Smithfields, London EC1A 9NH; tel. 081 778 4769. They have a 24-hour telephone advice service about breastfeeding. They also run local breastfeeding support groups. They have a few counsellors who specialise in the problems of working and breastfeeding.

Branches of Mothercare, John Lewis and Selfridges stock a range of breast pumps.

Books
The Experience of Breastfeeding by Sheila Kitzinger (Penguin).

Breast is Best by Drs Penny and Andrew Stanway (Pan). Both these books are very useful on breastfeeding and expressing techniques, but not very encouraging to working mothers, so be warned.

The Breastfeeding Guide for the Working Women by Anne Price and Nancy Bamford (Century). A breastfeeding book written specifically for the working mother – very helpful, (but written from an American point of view). This is now out of print, but might be in your library. The American edition is still available.

CHAPTER 7: CHILDCARE FOR THE UNDER-FIVES
The following organisations are all doing their best to campaign for better state provision of childcare and nursery education for the under-fives. Contact them if you are interested in finding out more about their activities.

The Maternity Alliance, 15 Britannia Street, London WC1X 9JP; tel. 071 837 1265.

National Childcare Campaign, Kingsway Hall, Wild Court, London WC2B 6ST; tel. 071 405 5617.

National Childminding Association, 8 Mason's Hill, Bromley, Kent BR2 9EY; tel. 081 464 6164.

National Council for One Parent Families, 255 Kentish Town Road, London NW5 2LX; tel: 071 267 1361.

Working for Childcare, 77 Holloway Road, London N7 8JZ; tel. 071 700 0281.

The Working Mothers Association (details under Chapter 1, above)

CHAPTER 8: CHILDMINDERS
The National Childminding Association (details under Chapter 7, above).

CHAPTER 9: NURSERIES AND OTHER FORMS OF GROUP CARE
Working for Childcare (details under Chapter 7, above).

Pre-School Playgroups Association, 61/63 King's Cross Road, London WC1X 9LL; tel. 071 837 0991.

CHAPTER 10: NANNIES, MOTHER'S HELPS AND OTHER HELP IN YOUR HOME
The Lady, Classified Department, 39-40 Bedford Street, London WC2E 9ER; tel. 071 836 8705. They do not take ads over the phone. An ad received by first post Wednesday will normally appear in the following week's issue (it comes out officially on Thursdays, but some newsagents have it on Wednesdays). Buy a copy of the magazine to read their instructions. You must send payment with your ad (they will reimburse you or invoice you for the difference if you get it slightly wrong).

Nursery World, Child-Care Classified Department, 51 Calthorpe Street, London WC1X 0HH; tel. 071 837 7224. An ad received by Friday will appear in the issue that comes out the following Thursday.

Nanny agencies
Swansons Nanny Agency, 12 Thornton Avenue, Chiswick, London W4 1QG; tel. 081 994 5275.

The Nanny Service, 9 Paddington Street, London W1M 3LA; tel. 071 935 6976.

Knightsbridge Nannies Ltd, 5 Beauchamp Place, London SW3; tel. 071 584 9323.

Nannies Incorporated, 18b Princes Place, London W11 4QA; tel. 071 229 1214.

Norland Nursery Training College, Denford Park, Hungerford, Berks, RG17 OPQ; tel 0488 682252.

Occasional and Permanent Nannies, 2 Cromwell Place, London SW7 2JE; tel. 071 225 1555.

Mar's Au Pair Agency, 16 Spencer Road, Chiswick, London W4; tel. 081 995 0246.

Working Mothers Association (details under Chapter 1, above) offer a nanny contract, and members are put in touch with local groups that have nanny-share registers.

CHAPTER 11: SCHOOL-AGE CHILDREN
Kid's Clubs Network, 279 Whitechapel Road, London E1; tel. 071 247 3009. You can join as an individual or group. They produce literature to help you get started.

National Playbus Association, Unit G, Arno's Castle Trading Estate, Brislington, Bristol, BS4 5AJ.

The Child Accident Prevention Trust, 28 Portland Place, London W1N 4DE. For advice on child-proofing your home.

CHAPTER 13: ILLNESS AND OTHER CRISES
National Childbirth Trust (details under Chapter 2, above). For information on postnatal support groups.

Working Mothers Association (details under Chapter 1, above). Become a member and you will be given advice on starting a group or joining an existing one in your area.

Neighbourhood Watch Scheme: your local police will give you advice on how to start one.

CHAPTER 14: YOUR HOME AND YOUR PARTNER

Books
The Relate Guide to Better Relationships and *The Relate Guide to Sex in Loving Relationships* by Sarah Litvinoff (Vermilion). Both practical guides to your relationship with your partner, with sections on the emotional and sexual changes that occur when you become a parent.

CHAPTER 15: LONE MOTHERS

National Council for One Parent Families, 255 Kentish Town Road, London NW5 2LX; tel. 071 267 1361. A campaigning organisation 'pressing central and local government and other bodies for the policies and services which one-parent families need'. They don't give advice to individuals, but run return-to-work courses, and have an extensive list of publications covering every aspect of lone-parenting. They also produces a regular newssheet *One Parent Times* covering the latest issues affecting one-parent families.

Scottish Council for Single Parents, 13 Gayfield Square, Edinburgh EH1 3NX; tel: 031 556 3899.

Gingerbread (national office), 5 Wellington Street, London WC2E 7BN; tel. 071 240 0953. You will get a full list of Gingerbread leaflets and publications on application to the national office, or from any one of their local self-help groups. Most of their publications concern rights and welfare entitlements. They also publish *Just Me and the Kids – a manual for lone parents*, and a bi-monthly paper. Some local groups run daycare facilities for under-fives. A few have after-school and holiday schemes.

Gingerbread (head office for Scotland), 39 Hope Street, Glasgow EG2; tel. 041 248 6840.

Gingerbread (head office for Northern Ireland), 169 University Street, Belfast BT7 1HR; tel. 0232 231417.

Gingerbread (head office for Wales), 16 Albion Chambers, Cambrian Place, Swansea, West Glam SA1 1RN; tel. 0792 648728.

Books
The Relate Guide to Starting Again by Sarah Litvinoff (Vermilion) A guide to the emotional aspects of dealing with a separation, and how to help your children.

CHAPTER 16: FINDING WORK AFTER A BREAK

Careers for Women, 2 Valentine Place, London SE1 8Q11; tel. 071 401 2280. A non-profit-making organisation, offering a counselling service, which is cheaper than most. They will also answer postal queries for a small fee if you can't get to London for an interview.

Vocational Guidance Association, 7 Harley House, Upper Harley Street, London NW1 4RP; tel. 071 935 2600. You are given a four-hour test for aptitude, personality and ability, followed by a consultation. You are then given a typed report with job recommendations. During the next two years you can have further consultations at no extra charge.

The National Extension College, 18 Brooklands Avenue, Cambridge, CB2 2HN; tel. 0223 316644, offer excellent correspondence courses in a wide range of subjects up to degree level. The college is concerned to guide prospective students to the right course, and it has a learning support department for any problems (including financial).

Open University, Walton Hall, Milton Keynes, Buckinghamshire MK7 6AA; tel. 0908 274066. This is open to anyone – you don't need any qualifications to be accepted, though you do need to be very self-disciplined to complete the course. Many more people apply then there are places, so send your application in early. Most of the work is by correspondence, with radio and TV lecture programmes for you to follow, but there are regular meetings with tutors and other students. Each year there is a residential summer school, (though no childcare facilities). You may be eligible for a grant from your local education authority or from the Open University itself.

National Association of Adult Education and Guidance Services, The Open University, Eldon House, Regent Centre, Gosforth, Newcastle Upon Tyne NE3; tel. 091 284 1611, gives guidance on courses to follow.

Open Tech Programme. These courses are for improving technical, managerial or supervisory skills while working at your own pace at home, usually backed up by tutorial help at your nearest college. You should be able to get a leaflet called *Open Learning: the role of the Open Tech Programme* from your Jobcentre. *The Open Tech Directory*, which you should find at your reference library or Jobcentre, lists all Open Tech projects and training materials available, as well as details of the Open Tech Centres. These centres are usually based in Local Education Authority Offices and local colleges. During office hours (and sometimes longer) they display the open learning materials and may provide access to computers where appropriate.

Educational Guidance for Adults, PO Box 109, Hatfield Polytechnic, Hatfield, Herts; tel. 07072 79499. This is a free service. You are given a one-hour interview, after which advice is given on which educational courses would suit you, and where you can find them.

Further Education Unit, Unit 3 Citadel Place, Tinworth Street, London SE11 5EH; tel. 071 962 1280. Will send you leaflets on further and higher education around the country.

Career Development Loans, call 0800 585505 free of charge, between 9.00a.m.-9.00p.m. Monday to Friday.

New Ways to Work (The Job Sharing Project), 309 Upper Street, London N1 2TY; tel 071 226 4026. They offer a list of regional job-sharing groups or contacts and addresses of job-share registers for doctors, librarians, housing workers and planners; literature for you as a potential job sharer; literature for employers considering taking on job-sharers (you may want to give this to your personnel department if you are currently trying to change your existing job into a job-share – it explains all the benefits to the employer).

The Low Pay Unit, 9 Upper Berkeley Street, London W1H 7PE; tel. 071 262 7278, will give guidelines on minimum wage rates.

Co-operative Development Agency, Broadmead House, 21 Panton Street, London SW1Y 4DR. For details on forming a co-operative.

The Small Firms Service: Dial 100 and ask for Freefone Enterprise.

The Women's Enterprise Development Agency (WEDA), Aston Science Park, Love Lane, Aston Triangle, Birmingham B7 4BJ; tel. 021 359 0178, gives specialist advice and support to new or existing businesses.

Women in Enterprise, 26 Bond Street, Wakefield, WF1 2QP; tel. 0924 361789, offers information and help to women who are hoping to run their own businesses, or who are already doing so.

Books
Equal Opportunities – A Careers Guide by Ruth Miller and Anna Alston (Penguin). An alphabetical list of every job that you can imagine, which is particularly useful because it looks at each career from the woman's point of view, and tells whether it is feasible to take a career break, or enter it at a later stage. It also tells you what qualifications you will need and organisations to contact in each case.

Getting There – Job Hunting for Women by M Wallis (Kogan Page).

Second Chances by A Pates and M Good (COIC).

It's Never Too Late by Joan Perkin (Impact Books).

Getting the Job You Want by H Dowding and S Boyce (Ward Lock).

Coping with Job Hunting by C Phillips (Newpoint).

Women Working it Out by J Chapman (COIC).

Hours to Suit By Anna Alston and Ruth Miller (Rosters) Looks at how to obtain work with hours to suit for women with domestic responsibilities.

The Returners Pack (Working Mothers Association) includes sample CVs and job application forms. Obtainable by post from the Working Mothers Association (details under Chapter 1, above).

Returning to Training: Education and Training Opportunities for Women, (Women Returners Network). Up-dated annually, it gives information about childcare linked to the courses, as well as up-to-date details on education and training for women.

Directory of Degree Courses (CNAA).

Which Degree? (Haymarket).

Floodlight, a directory of all adult education classes in London which appears before the beginning of each academic year.

Student Grants and Loans: A brief guide (Department of Education and Science).

Student Grants in Scotland (Scottish Education Department).

Earning Money at Home, with ideas of work you can do, plus general tips and information (cutting down on housework, insurance, planning permission, how to sell your work); and *Starting Your Own Business*, covering practical aspects, such as choosing between being a sole trader, partnership or limited company, keeping books, and finding staff (both published by the Consumers' Association/Hodder and Stoughton).

CHAPTER 18: YOUR RIGHTS

DSS/Social Security: To find your local social security office, look in the phone book under 'Social Security, Department of'.

Freefone DSS: for free telephone advice on social security and benefits. Dial 100 and ask for Freefone DSS (although in our experience this number is perpetually engaged).

Citizens' Advice Bureau: look in the phone book under C.

The Equal Opportunities Commission (details under Chapter 4, above).

Where to find your tax office (for enquiries about tax if you are self-employed or planning to employ someone): look in the phone book under I – 'Inland Revenue, Taxes, H.M. Inspectors of'. For enquiries if you fall under the PAYE scheme, ask your wages office for the address of the tax office they deal with.

Books
The Employers Guide (Working Mothers Association) A guide to initiatives by family-friendly employers – could give you ideas on what you can ask your employer to offer *you*. Available by post from the Working Mothers Association (details under Chapter 1, above).

INDEX